Multination States in Asia

As countries in Asia try to create unified polities, many face challenges within their own borders from minority groups seeking independence. This book brings together international experts on countries in all regions of Asia to debate how differently they have responded to this problem. Why have some Asian countries, for example, clamped down on their national minorities in favor of homogeneity, whereas others have been willing to accommodate statehood or at least some form of political autonomy? Together these experts point out broad patterns and explanatory factors that are rooted in the domestic arena, including state structure and regime type, as well as historical trajectories. In particular, they find that both the paths to independence and the cultural elements that have been used to define post-colonial identities have decisively influenced state strategies. This is a global phenomenon – and this book explains the broader theoretical and political implications – but violence and ethnic unrest have been particularly prevalent in Asia. This is as true of China in its relationship to Tibet as it is of Burma and Sri Lanka in relation to their national minorities. As the first book to analyze this phenomenon across Asia, *Multination States in Asia* will attract a readership of students and scholars across a broad range of disciplines.

Jacques Bertrand is Associate Professor of Political Science at the University of Toronto. He is the author of *Nationalism and Ethnic Conflict in Indonesia* (2004).

André Laliberté is Associate Professor in the School of Political Studies at the University of Ottawa. He is the author of *The Politics of Buddhist Organizations in Taiwan, 1989–2003* (2004) and has edited, with Marc Lanteigne, *The Chinese Party-State at the Turn of the Millennium: Legitimacy and Adaptation* (2008).

Multination States in Asia

Accommodation or Resistance

Edited by

JACQUES BERTRAND
University of Toronto

ANDRÉ LALIBERTÉ
University of Ottawa

CAMBRIDGE
UNIVERSITY PRESS

CAMBRIDGE UNIVERSITY PRESS
Cambridge, New York, Melbourne, Madrid, Cape Town, Singapore,
São Paulo, Delhi, Dubai, Tokyo

Cambridge University Press
32 Avenue of the Americas, New York, NY 10013-2473, USA

www.cambridge.org
Information on this title: www.cambridge.org/9780521143639

© Cambridge University Press 2010

First published 2010

Printed in the United States of America

A catalog record for this publication is available from the British Library.

Library of Congress Cataloging in Publication data
    Multination states in Asia : accommodation or resistance / [edited by]
    Jacques Bertrand, André Laliberté.
       p.   cm.
    Includes bibliographical references and index.
    ISBN 978-0-521-19434-1 (hardback)
    1. Multinational states – Asia.   2. Asia – Politics and government – 1945– I.
    Bertrand, Jacques, 1965– II. Laliberté, André, 1959– III. Title.
    JQ24.M85 2010
    320.95–dc22   2010005653

ISBN 978-0-521-19434-1 Hardback
ISBN 978-0-521-14363-9 Paperback

Contents

List of Tables and Figures

List of Maps

Contributors

Jacques Bertrand is Associate Professor of Political Science, University of Toronto. He is the author of *Nationalism and Ethnic Conflict in Indonesia* (Cambridge University Press, 2004).

Rajeev Bhargava is Senior Fellow and Director of the Programme of Social and Political Theory, Centre for the Study of Developing Societies, Delhi. His publications include *Individualism in Social Science* (Clarendon Press, 1992), *Secularism and Its Critics* (Oxford University Press, 1998), *Multiculturalism, Liberalism and Democracy* (ed. with A. Bagchi and R. Sudarshan, Oxford University Press, 1999) and *Transforming India* (ed. with Francine Frankel et al., Oxford University Press, 2000).

Sujit Choudhry holds the Scholl Chair at the Faculty of Law, University of Toronto. He is the editor of *Constitutional Design for Divided Societies: Integration or Accommodation* (Oxford University Press, 2009) and of the *Migration of Constitutional Ideas* (Cambridge University Press, 2007). Professor Choudhry is currently working on a book, *Rethinking Comparative Constitutional Law: Multinational Democracies, Constitutional Amendment and Secession*.

Sumit Ganguly is Rabindranath Tagore Chair in Indian Cultures and Civilizations, University of Indiana at Bloomington. He is the author and editor of several books, including *Fearful Symmetry: India and Pakistan Under the Shadow of Nuclear Weapons* (co-authored with Devin Hagerty), jointly published by Oxford University Press and the University of Washington Press; *The Crisis in Kashmir: Portents of War, Hopes of Peace* (Cambridge University Press and the Woodrow Wilson

Center Press, 1997); and *Government Policies and Ethnic Relations in Asia and the Pacific* (ed. with Michael E. Brown, MIT Press, 1997).

André Laliberté is Associate Professor in the School of Political Studies at the University of Ottawa. He is the author of *The Politics of Buddhist Organizations in Taiwan, 1989–2003* (RoutledgeCurzon, 2004) and has edited, with Marc Lanteigne, *The Chinese Party-State at the Turn of the Millennium: Legitimacy and Adaptation* (RoutledgeCurzon, 2008).

Anthony Reid is Professor Emeritus in the College of Asia and the Pacific, Australian National University. He is the author of *The Blood of the People: Revolution and the End of Traditional Rule in Northern Sumatra* (Oxford University Press, 1979); the magisterial *Southeast Asia in the Age of Commerce, 1450–1680*, Vol I: *The Lands below the Winds* (1988) and Vol II: *Expansion and Crisis* (1993), published by Yale University Press; *Indonesian Frontier: Acehnese and Other Histories of Sumatra* (Singapore University Press, 2004); and *Imperial Alchemy: Nationalism and Political Identity in Southeast Asia* (Cambridge University Press, 2009).

Edward Schatz is Assistant Professor of Political Science, University of Toronto. He is the author of *Modern Clan Politics: The Power of "Blood" in Kazakhstan and Beyond* (University of Washington Press, 2004).

Ardeth Maung Thawnghmung is Associate Professor of Political Science, University of Massachussetts at Lowell. She is the author of *The Karen Revolution in Burma: Diverse Voices, Uncertain Ends* (East-West Center, 2008) and of *Behind the Teak Curtain: Authoritarianism, Agricultural Policies and Political Legitimacy in Rural Burma* (Kegan Paul, 2004)

Gray Tuttle is Leila Hadley Luce Assistant Professor of Modern Tibetan Studies, Department of East Asian Languages and Cultures, Department of History, Columbia University. He is the author of *Tibetan Buddhists in the Making of Modern China* (Columbia University Press, 2005).

Acknowledgments

This book has its origins in a workshop held at the University of Toronto in September 2007 on "Multination States: East and West." It first posed as an empirical puzzle a contrast between European and North American experiences in the recognition and accommodation of sub-state nations, and Asian ones, which are deemed far less responsive to these groups. It soon became clear that such a contrast was exaggerated, if not altogether wrong. Variance within Asia seemed just as large as between some of its counterparts in Europe and North America. If fact, this variance became the new question that our book addresses. Rich discussions at this workshop provided the stimulus for this volume, and we are very grateful for the inspiring quality of those exchanges. We would like to thank those who provided formal comments on those initial papers, including Tutku Aydin, Bruce Berman, Joe Carens, Marijo Demers, Susan Henders, Rafael Iacovino, Sanjay Jeram, Elisabeth King, Marie-Eve Reny, Richard Simeon, Arjun Tremblay, Phil Triadafilopoulos, and Luc Turgeon. Of course, this book relies on the contributions from our authors, who have been exemplary in their dedication to this project. Ardeth Thawnghmung and Gray Tuttle deserve our particular gratitude for having stepped in late, long after the workshop, and enriched our comparative analysis by adding further cases.

The Social Sciences and Humanities Research Council of Canada, through the Ethnicity and Democratic Governance (EDG) project, provided generous funding for the workshop from which this book originated. The EDG is a major collaborative research initiative, an international project studying one of the most complex and challenging issues of the world today – governing ethnic diversity. The foundational query of the EDG project is to explore the ways in which societies respond to the opportunities and challenges raised by ethnic, linguistic, religious, and cultural differences, and to do so in ways that promote democracy, social justice, peace, and stability. The EDG team strives to produce a "toolbox of conceptual and practical options" reflected both in innovative academic analysis and in an array of strategies available to citizens and governments working through their own ethno-cultural conflicts, tensions, and opportunities. It is our hope that readers will discover embedded within this book – and in other EDG outputs – new understandings of previously neglected or understudied aspects of the nature of ethnic-identity formation, the causes of ethnic conflict, and the relationship between ethnic conflict and democratic governance.

Several individuals deserve our special gratitude for making this book possible. We owe many thanks to Isabelle Côté, Sanjay Jeram, and Jing Feng for helping to prepare the manuscript for publication. Jennifer Clark and Anne Linscott, from the EDG project office, provided invaluable support leading up to and following the workshop. We are very grateful to Marigold Acland, from Cambridge University Press, for supporting and guiding this project toward publication. We would also like to thank our two anonymous reviewers for their constructive criticism of an earlier draft of the book. Finally, we thank our families for their unwavering support of our scholarship.

Jacques Bertrand and André Laliberté

Maps

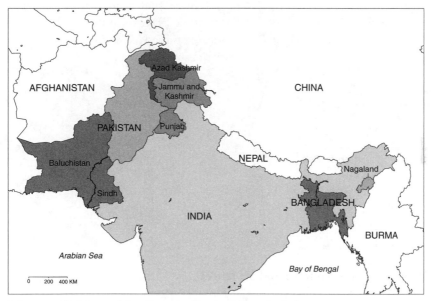

Map 1.   Pakistan, Northern India, and Bangladesh.

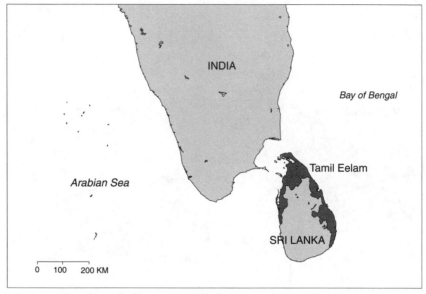

Map 2. Southern India and Sri Lanka.

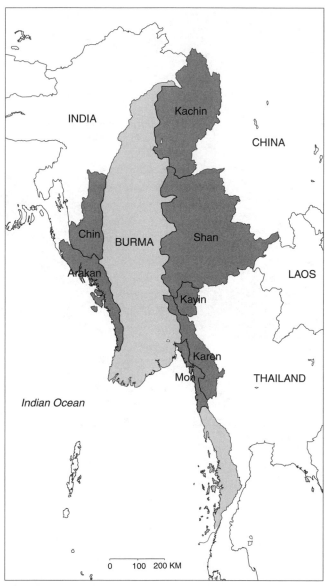

Map 3. Burma (Myanmar).

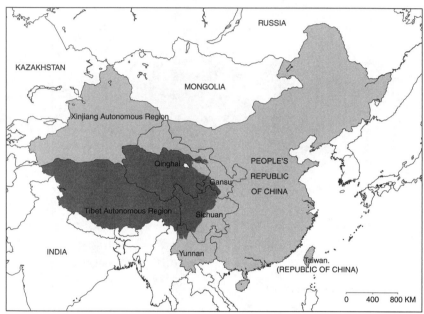

Map 4.   China.

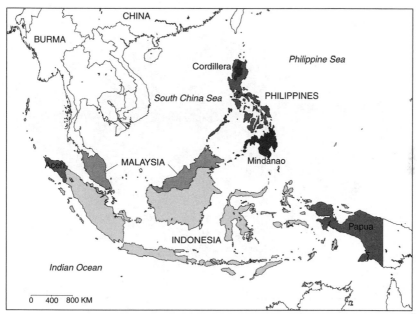

Map 5.   Indonesia, Malaysia, and the Philippines.

Map 6.   Central Asia.

I

Introduction

Jacques Bertrand and André Laliberté

Multination states have been unstable. The presence of more than one group seeking status as a "nation" within the boundaries of a single state has given rise to strong tensions that have generally been difficult to overcome.[1] The means by which these tensions are addressed and the instruments available for seeking compromises between states and such groups largely determine the extent to which violence can be avoided.

In the worst cases, the world has witnessed long periods of violent conflict. The breakup of the former Yugoslavia and the subsequent war, as well as the long-standing conflict in Sri Lanka are two of the most glaring examples. More often than not, one group gains control of the state and imposes its own view of an overarching national identity. This is rejected by the other group, which sees itself as a distinct nation. The conflict often takes the form of a sub-state nationalist movement against the state, but in reality it reflects intense disagreements based on competing nationalist visions. While one group may make strong claims that the state represents a single nation that can be defined inclusively, it may clash with a group within the state that refuses to be encapsulated within

---

[1] We use the following criteria to identify nations: (i) groups that have some sort of awareness as belonging to a sovereign people, and aspire to (or have) a form of self-determination; we do not include groups that simply do not see themselves as a people and who display no evidence of seeking self-determination; (ii) most often the latter implies that there is a political organization for this purpose, and that there is some good level of support for this conception of the group, at least at the elite level. This being said, in many cases, popular support or awareness is not necessarily very widespread. As a result, we are thinking of it as a political process as well (nationalism), by which the group or the state is seeking to promote the idea of a nation (coincidental with existing boundaries of the state, or with a smaller political unit).

that vision. As happened in Sri Lanka, such a single nation might even exclude a group entirely by defining itself in cultural, exclusivist terms. The particular structure of competing claims and the forms they take may vary, but they result when at least two groups seek recognition and status as nations.

Multination states are thus states in which more than one group seeks equal status and recognition as a constitutive member, usually making claims to self-determination. The constitutive members are nations in that they seek a state, or representation within a state, that gives them powers of self-determination either in the form of autonomy or federalism or through power-sharing arrangements based on equality with the other constitutive nations. Although the term multination state sometimes carries a normative dimension, it is used here strictly as a descriptive category denoting the presence of more than one group seeing themselves as nations within a single state.

Aside from violence, conflict between nations has often been addressed by compromise, negotiation, and accommodation. Federations have often been built on the notion of two or more nations creating common institutions while retaining large jurisdictional areas under each nation's control, in the form of self-government for each of the constitutive members. Certainly, at its origins, the Canadian federation had some of these features. More recent forms, such as that of Belgium, have evolved into such an understanding. Federalism, however, is only one form of compromise and accommodation. A more common form is territorial autonomy, which leads to devolution to one special region without equal decentralization across the board. In this case, nations seek equal status but may be up against a state controlled by a much larger group, making territorial autonomy the best available compromise. Other institutional forms of accommodation can also be achieved, such as power sharing in relatively centralized states or the creation of specific jurisdictional areas of exclusive control.

Regardless of the form that accommodation may take or the violent outcomes that may arise, multination states face similar structures of conflict. Their existence poses a fundamental challenge to the idea of the homogenous nation-state, or to its emulation. After World War I, the Westphalian nation-state system created a standard upholding the notion that each state represented a single, relatively cohesive nation. Where this was absent, such a nation needed to be built either on the basis of a common cultural heritage or on the basis of shared political principles. Compounded by the League of Nations' adoption of the right to self-determination of nations, the movement toward making the boundaries of states and of nations coincide became increasingly strong. In the European context, this meant the redrawing of boundaries after the demise of the Ottoman and Austro-Hungarian empires to create states representing single nations. Later, during the decades of decolonization, leaders of the new states promoted "official nationalist" projects (Anderson 1991), by which they sought to unify culturally and ethnically diverse populations around the notion of a single, unified nation.

Attempts at nation-building were accompanied by endeavours to build strong, centralized states. Although these are parallel processes, they were mostly distinct efforts. Building strong states entailed the establishment of executive capacity, including cohesive and responsive bureaucracies, militaries, and police forces to secure the state's borders, establish internal order, and create the capacity to formulate and implement policies. In many states, centralization was deemed to be the best means of achieving these objectives, and state leaders sought to create unified, homogenous nations on which state foundations could lie. The accommodation of ethnic minorities or groups contesting single-nation status was considered to be a potential source of state disintegration or weakness at best.

It is against this backdrop that more recent trends need to be considered. Whereas past emphases on nation-building were accompanied by policies designed to integrate and assimilate various groups into a common core, in recent decades the array of policies has changed quite dramatically. Although sometimes retained as primary policies, integration and assimilation have become much less common. Instead, accommodation of minorities and the establishment of alternative means of representation have become relatively widespread in such varied places as the United Kingdom, Spain, Canada, India, and even several Latin-American countries. Some states have accommodated diversity by adopting a set of policies known as "multiculturalism," denoting a specific approach to accommodation of ethnic minorities arising primarily from immigration (Kymlicka 1995). Indigenous peoples have been increasingly recognized and given special status in Latin America and elsewhere. Failures to create stable, strongly centralized states also led to widespread use of decentralization as a strategy, mainly for more effective governance but with some important consequences in terms of group representation and accommodation.

Sub-state nationalist groups,[2] however, have not been as easily accommodated. The exceptions include the United Kingdom, where the Scots and Welsh were given new representative institutions and powers of autonomy; Canada, where the Québécois exercise considerable group power through provincial institutions; and Belgium, where the central state gave way to a highly decentralized federation between the Flemish and the Walloon nations. The Czech Republic and Slovakia, of course, decided to peacefully secede in order to create an independent state for each nation. In other places, sub-state nationalist groups have been denied accommodation. Corsicans have no special status within France, nor do the Kurds in Turkey. The Tamils have violently resisted the Sri Lankan state over its refusal to accommodate them. Although there has been a movement away from integration, assimilation, and state centralization, this trend has by no means been across the board and, where it has occurred, has certainly not led to great leaps in accommodating sub-state nationalist groups.

Similarly, many Asian states retain structures that assert the primacy of the unitary nation-state despite the fact that many groups claim or ask for recognition as nations within the state or seek secession. This premise is puzzling in this context. There clearly has been a trend elsewhere to move away from assimilationist and centralizing policies that were seen as perpetuating unstable outcomes. Yet the resistance to accommodation in Asia continues to be very strong. There have been some significant exceptions, such as in India, and some significant departures, such as in Indonesia, as well as some official forms of recognizing nations even if the recognition is not followed by substantive accommodation, such as in China. The result is a varied pattern of accommodating the idea of several nations within one state, with a generally weak tendency to do so. We collectively explore Asian states

---

[2] We distinguish a nation that is coincidental with the boundaries of the state from sub-state national groups (or sub-state nations) that do not have their own state. The latter usually seek, implicitly or explicitly, recognition as a "nation." Seeking autonomy, federalism, or any special status, we think, demonstrates evidence of seeking recognition as a "nation," usually alongside others with the same state, or even as a nation within the broader nation that encompasses the whole state (although more rarely the latter case). We have chosen to use sub-state nationalist rather than "ethnonationalist" groups as the latter assumes that nationalist mobilization below the state level is necessarily based on ethnic ties, in opposition to a more civic and inclusive form of nationalism that coincides with existing boundaries of the state. Analytically, we prefer a more neutral term to characterize nationalisms (or nations) below the state level, leaving for the analysis of each case, where relevant, a characterization of these nationalisms.

to explain the circumstances under which some have accommodated sub-state national groups (usually implicitly) and the broader trend of resisting such accommodation. Asian cases provide a broad comparative pool that has been relatively neglected in comparative studies of these issues.

A bird's eye view of the region suggests that there is variance among countries on three counts. First, as mentioned previously, states differ in the extent to which they formally recognize nations within their boundaries. China, as well as other formally socialist states, institutionalizes this recognition in its constitution, declaring itself a "unitary *multinational* state." Other states recognize groups in ethnic terms but do not distinguish nations from other ethnic groups. For instance the Indian federation is organized around linguistic groups, but makes no distinction between groups that see themselves as nations, and those that don't. Some states give recognition implicitly in the form of autonomy while not recognizing nations explicitly (Indonesia, Philippines). Second, states vary in the ways they have responded to the claims made by groups asking for recognition as nations. Some states have accommodated such groups by granting them territorial autonomy and/or by adopting policies that allow the pursuit of their interests. These same states have sometimes reversed these policies and repressed these groups. The sequence of responses, or the contradictions in some of these responses, has created varied patterns of resistance. Third, even among states that have appeared to accommodate sub-state nationalist groups, not all have followed through on their commitments.

We analyze collectively this varied pattern of recognition and accommodation. We have been guided by the following set of questions: Why have some states departed from the homogeneous nation-state concept, and why have most not done so? Have different historical trajectories or differences in the construction and origins of nationalist movements had a strong impact on today's differences among Asian states in their accommodation of sub-state national groups? Why? Have changes to accommodate national minorities led to *actual* empowerment of nations within the state? For states that give with one hand, while taking away with the other, what are the consequences of adopting discourses or giving symbolic recognition to nations while denying them real power? Although we do not claim to answer these questions exhaustively, our comparative analysis of Asian cases has yielded some general patterns and trends that we outline in our conclusion.

NATIONS, STATES, AND MULTINATIONALITY

Multination states have often been unstable because state boundaries or self-definitions of inclusiveness have been contested by sub-state national groups advancing their own claims to nationhood. Multination states defy our common understanding of the classic nation-state, which embodies the principle of congruence between a state and a nation. A "nation" consists of a group of people that collectively see themselves as belonging to the same entity, whether or not this entity is defined by ethnic markers of identity such as language, religion, custom, or any other common cultural trait or by a shared sense of belonging shaped by historical experience. In other words, this definition of the single nation-state can include the kind of states that "ethnic" or "civic" nationalists seek to create (Greenfeld 1992). In this ideal type, the overwhelming majority of the population believes that it belongs to the same nation. Such a congruence between nation and state is achieved either through nation-building from the top, via assimilation into a dominant national core, or through the gradual integration of different peoples into a common national core. It can also be achieved through the secession of a national minority seeking to create its own state, or one that joins with a neighboring state that it perceives to be its homeland.

Clashes between groups with different conceptions of the nation and concomitant state boundaries have often had violent consequences. After the Cold War, such violence was evident in many countries of the former Soviet Union, Eastern Europe, and the Balkans. Several studies have rightly deplored this situation as a source of international instability, but they have tended to paint with the same brush both extreme nationalists who promoted "ethnic cleansing" and the nationalist movements that accepted moderate forms of accommodation on the part of existing states (see Snyder 2000).

In many countries, particularly democratic ones, the recognition and/or accommodation of several nations within the boundaries of a single state has not led to such conflict and disintegration. The diverse policies of recognition for nations within states, power-sharing mechanisms, devolution schemes, and proportional representation that have been adopted by European and North American states have accommodated differences, if not celebrated them, in the name of preserving the integrity of the existing political structure.

For newly democratic countries, accommodation may offer a path toward compromise that avoids violence, yet several states refuse to adopt such a path. This conundrum can be very significant for the future of democracy and can have disastrous consequences for stability. As Linz and Stepan (1996) have observed, democratic consolidation requires that questions of "stateness" be resolved in that all groups must recognize the legitimacy of the state's boundaries. Where a group sees itself as a state-less nation, such a condition can lead to secessionist mobilization, particularly if it does not have the possibility of negotiating recognition and equal status. The question becomes how far can states move away from rigid conceptions of a "nation-state" – the idea that the nation should coincide with the existing boundaries of the state – without facing the disintegrative tendencies of excessive devolution toward extreme forms of multinationalism – in which several nations would be recognized and accommodated but without a strong loyalty or bond to the common state (Linz, Stepan, & Yadav 2007).

In spite of recent trends, including the possibility of more peaceful outcomes through the accommodation of sub-state national groups, the nation-state paradigm is resilient because it is rooted in strong historical tendencies. As scholars of the origins of nationalism, such as Anderson, have argued, the idea of a single nation coinciding with the boundaries of the state has been a very strong source of legitimacy in the modern state system. Originating in the Americas, nationalism spread to Europe and destroyed the old monarchies' basis of rule. Epitomized by the French Revolution, nationalism created a new set of legitimating principles based on the principle of the modern state as being representative of a "nation." Such nations were constructed out of shared experiences, languages, and sometimes, cultural traits. Acknowledging the power of this idea, monarchs even reinvented themselves as nationalists and used state power to construct nations from above, often through a state-induced process of vernacularization and reinvention of historical origins (Anderson 1991; Hobsbawm & Ranger 1983).

Against the backdrop of the nationalist models inspired by the French Revolution and by the experience of the Americas, two significant factors led to a trend toward the model of a unitary nation-state. First, national-ism spread from Europe to other parts of the world in the late nineteenth century, thanks to the transmission of ideas to the colonial elites, many of whom were influenced by the European view that the ideal modern political community was the nation-state. For nationalist leaders such as Sun Yat-sen, M. K. Gandhi, Sukarno, and Jommo Kenyatta, seeking national self-determination under colonial rule seemed the logical next step. Many of these leaders, however, understanding the heterogeneity of their societies within the colonial boundaries, tried to think of ways to develop a sense of shared national identity that would transcend the differences. Sun, lamenting that the "Chinese were like a loose heap of sand," sought to encourage a Chinese patriotism that transcended regional identities (Sun 1924), whereas Nehru advocated a secular India that would overcome communal and linguistic cleavages. Once they achieved the goal of independence from imperial rulers or colonial powers, these leaders developed different forms of "official nationalisms," in which they promoted "nation-building" strategies that nurtured a sense of shared destiny for every citizen within the existing boundaries defined by their former rulers. The "nations" created this way were mere facts of territorial demarcation and historical accident, but some of them were successfully grafted onto relatively strong nationalist movements that fought for independence and managed in that struggle to create a more or less cohesive sense of belonging to the same imagined community (Anderson 1991).

Second, after World War I, the emergence of the principle of self-determination gave the idea of convergence between nations and states a new sense of urgency. The breakup of the Central European empires encouraged movements that sought to recognize the right of European nations to obtain their own states in accordance with the norms of the Westphalian state system. This evolution, which led to the emergence of states such as Czechoslovakia and Yugoslavia, set a precedent that made the demands for self-determination in the colonies of Asia and Africa all the more pressing. The principle of self-determination proved a powerful source of inspiration for anti-colonial nationalist movements that Western colonial powers found increasingly difficult to resist. These movements sought independence from colonial powers on the basis of existing boundaries demarcated by foreign powers. The boundaries of the nation were defined by the state, not the other way around. These states were far from homogeneous culturally, and the challenge that most anti-colonial leaders faced was to manufacture overarching identities that could be shared by all citizens within the new political entities.

One significant exception to that trend was the Soviet Union. The new state had emerged before the end of World War I and Wilson's promotion for the idea of self-determination of nations. The Communist Party of the Soviet Union created an unprecedented system of political-administrative units that were defined in national-territorial terms. It is unclear historically why this choice was made; nevertheless, it created a logic by which federal units replicated layers of party and state officials along ethnic lines, eventually laying the foundation for the emergence of new nationalist movements. Ironically, the Soviet Union, as well as Yugoslavia and Czechoslovakia, strengthened, and sometimes even created, national identities by recognizing and extending official languages, promoting national educational curricula and culture, and constructing "native" elites. They also provided resources to build the administrative, economic, and political structures of states, thereby giving these national elites the levers of state power, albeit under a centralized umbrella state (Brubaker 1996; Bunce 1999, pp. 47–52; Roeder 1991).

In China, a similar logic prevailed. After the 1911 Revolution, Republican leaders wanted to preserve the territorial integrity of the empire they had inherited and therefore came up with the idea that the Republic of China was an association of peoples (Schiffrin 1970). Similarly, to ensure during the Long March the neutrality of the non-Chinese people of the Western periphery while it fought the Republican regime, the armed guerrilla of the Communist Party promised that it would grant some form of recognition to the minorities after its eventual victory. Both the Republican regime and the Communist Party, then, either provided or promised an early form of multination state at the symbolic level. The substance of that policy, however, could not be implemented because of the prevailing circumstances of political division, foreign invasion, and civil war during the Republican era (1911–1949) and because, once in power, the Communist Party was reluctant to encourage any policy that might threaten the country's newfound national unity (Ghai 2000a, pp. 78–81; Mackerras 1994).

In sum, except for some European socialist states, the general thrust toward building and strengthening unitary nation-states was a powerful force throughout most of the twentieth century. Both European states and the decolonizing states of Asia, Africa, and Latin America espoused this model and engaged in homogenizing policies of nation-building to reach this goal.

SUB-STATE NATIONALISM IN HISTORICAL PERSPECTIVE

The strong centrifugal forces that created nation-states from below or above have met with significant resistance. Sub-state nationalist movements have emerged among groups that see themselves as distinct nations seeking their own state institutions. In multination states, where at least one group claims nationhood alongside, or separate from, the dominant nation espoused by state elites, homogenizing tendencies have often led to violent resistance and conflict. Because they are territorially

TABLE 1.1. *Proportion of Sub-state National Groups Per Region*

Region	Western Democracies and Japan	Asia	Sub-Saharan Africa	Eastern Europe	North Africa and Middle East	Latin America and the Caribbean
Number of countries	21	23	43	26	19	23
Number of ethnic groups	79	126	362	120	74	90
Number of ethnonational groups (MAR) per region	5	15	4	6	4	0
% of countries per region that have ethnonational groups	19%	39%	9%	12%	21%	0%

Notes: Based on Minorities at Risk (MAR) data. We recoded some groups after consultation with regional specialists and avoided double counting, where groups were present across borders. We recognize the limitations of classifying sub-state nations, according to our definition. We treat this data as rough estimates for broad illustrative purposes.

concentrated, these groups have often been able to organize strong resistance to the central state. Many groups have been particularly threatening, demanding secession or some form of self-determination within the existing state boundaries. For the most part, such groups have been perceived as threatening the integrity of the state, challenging its legitimacy, and rejecting its attempts to forge a single nation. In many instances, these groups have sought secession, but, in several other cases, they have accepted autonomy or federalism.

In Asia, we see a particularly high number of countries with sub-state national groups relative to other regions of the developing world, as can be seen in Tables 1.1 and 1.2 and Figure 1.1. By our definition, out of thirty-four such groups, almost half are in Asia. Thirty-nine percent of Asian countries contain sub-state national groups, relative to 21, 19, and 12 percent, respectively, for North Africa and the Middle East; Western Europe, North America, and Japan; and Eastern Europe. Latin America and the Caribbean have no such groups at all.

This particularly high concentration of sub-state nationalist groups can be explained, in part, by different historical experiences of nationalism.

TABLE 1.2. *Sub-state National Groups by Region*

Western Democracy and Japan	Asia	Sub-Saharan Africa	Eastern Europe	North Africa and Middle East	Latin America and the Caribbean
1. Québécois	1. Karens	1. Basters	1. Bosnian	1. Kurds	
2. Basques (Spain)	2. Shans	2. Diolas in Casamance	2. Muslims	2. Turkish Cypriots	
3. Corsicans	3. Tibetans	3. Baganda	3. Abkhazians	3. Palestinians	
4. Catholics in Northern Ireland	4. Kashmiris	4. Afars	4. Adzhars	4. Saharawis	
5. Scots	5. Sikhs		5. South Ossetians (Georgia)		
	6. Acehnese		6. Tatars (Russia)		
	7. Moros				
	8. Sri Lankan Tamils				
	9. Nagas				
	10. Papuans				
	11. Malays				
	12. Taiwanese				
	13. Uygur				
	14. Baluchis				
	15. Bougainvilleans				

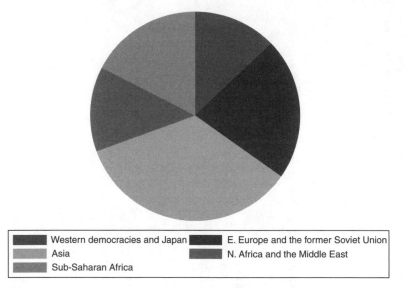

FIGURE 1.1. Proportion of sub-state national groups per region.

In Latin America, for instance, nationalism emerged from Creole communities that were denied equal status with their Spanish counterparts.
In response, they developed an anti-colonial consciousness that laid the
groundwork for the nationalist movements that ensued. The homogenizing processes of state formation created a distinction with indigenous
communities that were less subjected to the assimilationist tendencies of
the colonial period, but these groups did not have the kind of strong
political and social organization that characterized some Asian groups.
In addition, although a few of the indigenous groups have organized
politically, and many of them articulate demands for recognition that
include a territorial dimension, they do not advocate secession. Similarly,
Sub-Saharan African states were superimposed over a large number of
small, culturally distinct groups whose identities were much more flexible
because their political representation was localized and only occasionally
amalgamated into larger, relatively ephemeral kingdoms. Although this
situation might resemble that of pre-colonial archipelagic Southeast Asia,
it certainly differs from the more established kingdoms and empires in
many other parts of Asia that created strong and stable political, social,
and cultural institutions that solidified group identities. Throughout Sub-
Saharan Africa, the principle of maintaining existing boundaries was
quickly endorsed by all new states: their leaders feared the prospect of

endless revisionist claims if ethnic groups were to follow the example of Europeans and begin to think of themselves as nations deserving recognition. They saw this as a first step in a trajectory that could ultimately lead to the redrawing of boundaries to achieve congruence between these nations and states. The Nigerian-Biafran War (1967–1970) represented the embodiment of that fear, and African leaders have consistently tried to prevent a similar recurrence. Most post-colonial leaders in Africa have thus sought to prevent the transformation of ethnic consciousness into a national identity that could compete with that of the new states.

Accordingly, most Sub-Saharan African leaders have sought to develop national identities that avoid a reference to ethnicity; they have attempted to devise their own versions of civic nationalism through the discourses of socialism, anti-colonialism, and pan-African solidarity, adopting secular institutions and often replicating European political institutions at the symbolic level. These leaders have advocated the development of hybrid national identities that supersede other ones, which are dismissed as "tribal," "parochial," or "ethnic." To avoid appearing to favor one ethnic group at the expense of others, most African states adopted the former colonial powers' languages as the national language. With the notable exception of Ethiopia, which promotes Amharic; Somalia, which uses Somali; and Tanzania, where Swahili is the de facto national language, colonial powers' languages remain in use as official languages all over Sub-Saharan Africa.[3] This contrasts with the Asian situation, where local languages – old and new ones – are being used as official languages.

The issue of the recognition and accommodation of multinationality in Asia also differs from that of the post-colonial states of north Africa and the Middle East in one important respect. Post-colonial states' leaders have often advocated ideologies of pan-Arabism, thereby pursuing an agenda similar in its content to that of pan-Turkism or pan-Islamism, which advocated the unification of sovereign states within broader entities. The ideology of pan-Arabism promoted by Nasserite Egypt or Baathist Iraq, which looked back with nostalgia at the Arab caliphates of the previous centuries, could not be reconciled with the demands for recognition by sub-state national groups, whether the Kabyles in Algeria or the Kurds in Iraq. Even Turkey and Iran, which during the colonial era were regional and multinational empires, until their demise in the early

---

[3] This is the case for French in twenty-one states, English in nineteen, Portuguese in five, and Spanish in two. Arabic is also used along French in twelve states.

twentieth century, could not recognize such groups out of fear that this would launch a process of further boundary revisionism .

The Cold War created a context in which few states changed their boundaries. Sub-state nationalist movements were often linked to proxy wars between the Soviet Union and the United States. The Soviet Union maintained strong repression over the countries in its sphere of influence, while extending institutional recognition to the groups it considered national minorities. Outside the Soviet bloc, however, it supported insurgency movements that, at least on the surface, espoused communist ideology. For sub-state nationalist movements, the need for resources and weapons provided strong motivation to seek a relationship with the Soviet Union. Americans often found themselves on the side of those defending state integrity against insurgents, giving support to repressive policies as part of their containment policy.

EXPLAINING SUB-STATE NATIONALIST MOBILIZATION

Besides the specific historical circumstances described above, different sets of theories have been advanced to explain the rise of sub-state nationalist mobilization. Although many of these groups emerged and have been shaped by historical circumstances, they nevertheless maintain very strong identities once they become politically mobilized. Grievance-based theories provide explanations based on discrimination by the state or resentment of dominant groups. They do not differentiate, however, other forms of ethnic conflict by attributing such mobilization to cultural, socioeconomic, or political discrimination (Gurr 2000). Structural theories influenced by political economy have noted that, in advanced industrialized societies, differentiated patterns of economic development may have increased group awareness and triggered nationalist responses (Hechter 1999). Institutionalist theories, particularly in the case of postcommunist states, have made a strong case that giving administrative autonomy to particular groups (whether they are defined by the state or respond to group mobilization) can create a new set of resources that can enhance the group's mobilization and claims, thereby leading to sub-state nationalist mobilization, instability, and secessionist tendencies in some cases (Brubaker 1996; Cornell 2002). Yet, there are other strands of this debate that have seen various forms of recognition and accommodation of sub-state nationalist groups as the best means of preventing secession and instability. The reasons states have tended to resist such options are clear when they are faced with these potential threats but less obvious if accommodation and recognition provide the basis for reducing sub-state nationalist mobilization through compromise and negotiation.

Grievance-based theories started with the observation that in many countries of the developing world, violent ethnic conflict emerged as groups that had been previously favored by colonial rulers often dominated the state's institutions and played a major role in defining the nation's character. Minority groups (and occasionally majority ethnic groups) sometimes felt aggrieved by state policies that seemed to exclude them. As Horowitz (1985) described at length, many groups mobilized on the basis of a politics of "entitlement," by which they sought to gain access to state power by virtue of being "sons of the soil," for instance, or of having been treated as "backward" groups that deserved at least equality of status. The structure of these conflicts tended to consist of struggles over state power, resources, or allocation of representative positions rather than over the nature of the nation itself, or apportionment of the territory. By treating all types of conflicts, regardless of the nature of the groups that were making the claims, Horowitz does not account for some specific sources of conflict or for state responses to specific types of ethnic groups that define themselves as nations.

A second set of theories inspired by political economy has emerged to explain the presence of sub-state nationalist movements even in advanced democracies, such as in western Europe and North America. Where groups already had a strong group consciousness and a shared sense of a separate history, it was difficult to assimilate them. The French resisted assimilation and integration after New France was conquered by the British. Eventually, by the 1970s, this resistance would develop into a full sub-state nationalist movement of the Québécois for their own state. Catalans and the Basques in Spain, having controlled their own territory and developed fairly strong political communities, resisted attempts at assimilation, particularly from the Franco regime, and developed strong sub-state nationalist responses. Although these sub-state nationalist groups originate in core ethnic groups, they have often cast their nationalist aspirations in more inclusive terms to account for minorities living within the territories they claim as their homelands.

In the context of globalization, the state's capacity for accommodation in advanced democracies has diminished in recent decades while nations within states have increased their demands (Keating 2001, p. 46). Under the European Union and the North American Free Trade Agreement, for instance, the state's capacity to manage its economic affairs autonomously has been eroded. Not only has the emergence of global markets increased state interdependence, but also the presence of these regional organizations or deeper market integrative processes have constrained states even more. As a result, states are no longer able to use economic allocations to create loyalty and support, which was part of the system that had sustained sector-based, class-based, and corporatist politics in Europe and North America (Keating 2001, pp. 55–56). In these conditions of weakened state capacity, citizens often shun the legitimacy of established nation-states that seem too distant, and throw their support behind sub-state entities that seem more responsive and closer to their interests. When these sub-state entities have distinctive cultural characteristics, the emergence of sub-state nationalist identities is more likely. These theories provide many important insights, but they do not carry well to the Asian context.

Third, institutionalist theories emerged after a large number of sub-state nationalist movements mobilized much more strongly, and sometimes violently, as a result of the demise of communist regimes in the Soviet Union and eastern Europe. Several scholars have warned of the dangers of institutionalizing sub-state national identities. Brubaker (1996) has perhaps most strongly shown the effects of institutionalizing these identities in the former Soviet Union and Eastern Europe. As mentioned above, they contributed to the instability and breakup of states after the demise of communism. Autonomy since then has also increased volatility in the Caucasus (Cornell 2002). In addition, we should not underestimate the institutional dynamics of the Soviet bloc itself to explain the rise in sub-state nationalist mobilization in Eastern Europe and the former Soviet Union after 1989. As Bunce has argued, the institutional ties were very strong between party structures and the whole apparatus of socialist states between the Soviet Union at the core and dependent eastern European states at the periphery. These ties were so close that they were all vulnerable to systematic changes occurring in one or more of the parts. Once institutions began to falter in some parts of the Soviet bloc, the whole structure of institutional ties began to unravel, thereby creating the reverberating effects that led to the sequential collapse of socialist regimes across the region (Bunce 1999, pp. 40–44).

The case of the Soviet collapse and the emergence of the ex-Soviet Republics also raised new theoretical challenges about the effects of democratic transition on the political mobilization of sub-state nationalist movements and the state's response to this mobilization. On the one hand, many have seen in the processes of democratic transition an opportunity for rehabilitation of ethnic nationalism and the idea that states' boundaries should coincide with ethnic groups. On the other hand, many have seen in these developments the kind of threat to national coherence that rapid democratization entails (Snyder 2000).

Yet, these debates that were more specific to the former Soviet Union and eastern Europe occurred against long-standing debates about the institutional conditions of stability of mulitiethnic societies, with some relevance to multinational states. Consociationalists, following Lijphart's conception, advocated power-sharing arrangements between major groups, veto rights, proportional representation in central institutions, as well as autonomy over the territory they control (Lijphart 1977; O'Leary 2005). Others primarily emphasized autonomy or federalism as the best way to accommodate such demands, especially when they are territorially concentrated (Horowitz 1985, pp. 601–628). Some states were more likely to be responsive because they were created early on as federal states. Although rare, some states even changed the fundamental nature of their constitutional order. Belgium perhaps best exemplifies the shift away from a unitary state to a full federal one (Hooghe 2004). Other cases include Canada, Spain, the United Kingdom, Indonesia, and India.

Although there are good reasons to also be skeptical of some instances of accommodation, the record appears fairly successful in many cases. If so, then the question becomes why sub-state nationalist groups are not accommodated more often? Why are demands for autonomy viewed mostly suspiciously and compromises difficult to reach? If ethnic groups have been able to obtain United Nations (UN) recognition of their rights as minorities, and indigenous peoples have also gained such recognition and rights, the record is relatively dismal for sub-state nationalist groups, despite some successful cases and a very dubious record indicating that accommodating these groups leads to instability (Kymlicka 2007). The reluctance might originate from a particularly skewed perspective based on the specific experience of the former Soviet Union and eastern Europe. It might also originate from the discomfort of the strong historical tendency to view the nation-state as a unitary and homogenous entity, as argued above.

Against the backdrop of this general tendency, there has still been some variance among states in their willingness to accommodate sub-state nationalist demands. A few propositions have emerged to explain this variance, but they remain undeveloped and certainly unexplored in the Asian context.

A democratic framework has been more strongly amenable to various forms of accommodation such as autonomy, but as noted above, the pattern has also varied within entrenched democracies (Gurr 2000, pp. 151–177). States that began as federal states were obviously more likely to accommodate sub-state nationalist demands. These states have been much more likely to accept changes to their federation that increasingly give recognition or more powers to sub-state national groups (Stepan 2004). Other states have been persistently resistant, including federations such as the United States, which have been based on territorial rather than multinational principles.

The diffusion of norms might also explain some slight tendency toward more accommodation in some regions, but it is very limited. Certainly multiculturalism was developed and spread in countries, such as Canada, where groups continued to feel aggrieved as they were denied rights, thereby leading to discriminatory responses that could not be redressed by policies that strictly emphasized regimes of individual rights (Kymlicka 1995, 2007). The latter argument was mainly applied to all types of ethnic minority groups, however, without specifying differences that might arise among different categories of groups. The spread of the norm of multiculturalism in most cases did not extend to sub-state nationalist groups.

Some states have gone so far as to recognize groups as nations, yet this form of recognition has been an exception rather than a trend. There have been historical moments when two or more nations appeared to reach an agreement for a union. Some have argued that this was the case at the foundational moment of the United Kingdom of Great Britain and Northern Ireland, established with the Union of England and Scotland's Crowns. In other instances, the state has recognized its multinational nature through some form of constitutional amendment as a result of mobilization by political parties and actors claiming allegiance to the nation hitherto deprived of recognition, such as when the Spanish government, after decades of political pressures from Catalans, recognized Catalonia as a distinct nation. Nevertheless, in most democracies the politics of recognition remain constantly in flux, and the status of nations continues to be renegotiated (Gagnon & Tully 2001). These cases have often been debated in terms of the normative principles for recognition and accommodation, but such debates have focused less on explaining the variance in accommodation of sub-state national groups.

In sum, existing theories provide few insights on the variance in state accommodation of sub-state nationalist groups and have been too regionally specific. They are even limited in terms of explaining why these groups have mobilized in the first place. Many theories are too closely related to the experiences of specific regions. Recent institutionalist theories, for example, have been overly influenced by the experiences of the former Soviet Union and eastern Europe. Others have too closely debated the same cases of accommodation in North America and western Europe. Few, if any, of these theories have explored Asian cases where, ironically, there is a high number of cases of sub-state nationalist mobilization relative to other regions.

One exception is a recent study edited by Will Kymlicka and Baogang He. Various authors present a set of case studies of very different types of groups, ranging from sub-state nationalist groups to domestic workers (Kymlicka & He 2006).[4] They attempt to assess the degree to which some general forms of accommodation for all types of ethnic groups could be implemented in Asian states alongside liberal democratic forms. Several of the chapters appear more hopeful than their empirical assessments indicate, however, and there are no strong comparative explanations of state policies toward sub-state nationalist groups. More analysis is required to understand varied patterns of accommodation of sub-state nationalist groups.

This book addresses this lacuna by discussing comparatively the large number of cases of sub-state nationalist mobilization in Asia. Because of the type of group involved, the form of mobilization, and rationale for group claims, the analysis of state responses requires that we treat these groups separately from ethnic groups and mobilization in the broader sense since they have made different kinds of claims. Furthermore, states have responded sometimes in quite contradictory ways and departed significantly from their general policies toward ethnic groups that do not have national claims.

MULTINATION STATES IN ASIA

Very few states in the world can claim to have achieved congruence between a nation and a state, and this has certainly been the case in Asia. Of the six states that might be said to have achieved this end, three represent very approximate cases of congruence. Bangladesh, which was

---

[4] Similarly Brown and Ganguly (1997) were focused on policies toward ethnic groups more broadly, and were mainly concerned with issues of minority rights rather than accommodation of sub-state nationalist groups more specifically.

until the breakup of the Soviet Union the only successful case of secession from a post-colonial state, had a distinctive identity in the nineteenth
century as the homeland of a thriving literary tradition within a territory
that was much larger before the partition of 1947. After this date, the
State of Bengal was split into two entities, Western and Eastern Bengal,
which were then incorporated into two new states, the Indian Union
and Pakistan.⁵ South and North Korea represent another case of a larger
nation split between two states. Although there are enormous differences
in social and economic conditions between the north and the south, their
people consider themselves as part of a single nation, and their respective
governments encourage that belief (Kim 2006). Thus, only Japan and,
to a lesser degree, Cambodia and Mongolia can qualify as states whose
boundaries are more or less coextensive with those of the nations they
claim to represent.

A number of Asian states can be considered polyethnic but are not
multinational (Brown & Ganguly 1997). Although many ethnic groups
have distinctive identity markers that distinguish them from the majority of the people in the polity where they live, they are not identified
with a territory as a homeland. For example, while Chinese and Indian
minorities in Malaysia practice religions and speak languages that differ from those of the Malay majority, they have no claim to a territory
within the state of Malaysia. States such as Vietnam and Thailand could
be described as entities that are ruled by a nation that represents the
overwhelming majority of the population. The Chinese minorities or
hill tribes in these states do not represent communities identified with a
specific territory either.⁶

The overwhelming majority of Asian people, however, live in multinational states. Of the 3.8 billion people who live in the area stretching from
Pakistan in the southwest to Hokkaido in the northeast and Indonesia in
the southeast, close to 2.9 billion people live in states that accommodate
within their boundaries more than one nation. China represents a class in
itself. Although "only" 8 percent of its population are considered "minority nationalities" – to borrow from the official Chinese jargon – this is a
group of 100 million people (Mullaney 2004), more than the total number of inhabitants of some Asian countries, spread out over a territory

---

⁵ The shared language and pre-colonial history, however, are not enough to inspire a sense
of shared Greater Bengali identity. See Jones (2008).
⁶ For a discussion of the deceptive suggestion that Thailand lacks cultural diversity and is a
hegemonic nation-state, see Keyes (1997).

that covers more than half of China. Furthermore, as we will discuss, the official denomination of minority nationalities conceals more than it reveals about the multinational reality of China. To start with, most of the fifty-five nationalities that have been identified along with the Han majority would not qualify as nations. Some, such as the Manchus, have lost their languages. Others, such as the Hui, the Miao, or the Yao, are scattered across the country and share little culturally. On the other hand, linguistic groups among the Han majority are not considered nationalities, even though some of them, such as the Fukienese, the Cantonese and the Hunanese, can claim identification with a territory, a literature, and in previous centuries, even statehood. Finally, the case of Taiwan raises the issue of the multinational state in a way that has yet to be fully appreciated in East Asia: the principle of national self-determination, whereby nations are defined not by cultural traits, and even less by race, but by their adherence to shared political values.

India represents the culmination of this type of multinational state. One of its unifying principles makes reference to the value of secularism, which proclaims state neutrality towards religion, and the refusal to identify the nation with one set of beliefs.[7] The importance of Islam and other religions in the country makes it clear why it is necessary to put in place this constitutionally enshrined refusal to let the values of Hinduism, the dominant tradition of the country, determine Indian politics. Yet, this approach has also brought its own form of intolerance: demands for recognition based on religious identity are anathema to India. The collective trauma of Partition has been evoked by most Indian governments to justify their refusal to accede to any demand combining nationhood claims with religious identity. The strife in Punjab has to be read in light of that fear: acceding to demands of Sikh extremists for a Khalistan, Indian leaders believe, could not be tolerated lest it encourage demands for a Hindu India and aggravate the dispute with Pakistan over Kashmir. On the other hand, India has been far more successful at adapting to demands made by ethno-linguistic groups: the redrawing of state boundaries, the carving up of new entities within the Union, and many other mechanisms have been tried with various degrees of success (Brass 1994). As the continued insurrections in Assam and other northeastern states shows, however, achieving a stable multination state remains difficult.

Another category of states bears mentioning. In some multinational states or states with one dominant nationality, even accommodation

---

[7] For a classical reference, see Smith (1963). For a rebuttal, see Madan (1987).

and recognition may not suffice to meet the aspirations of an aggrieved nationality. Such nations may not seek independence but reunification with a neighboring state or group across its borders. For example, while the Punjabi majority and the Sindhi struggle among themselves and with the Mohajirs for the control of Pakistan, some Pashtuns seek instead to follow in the footsteps of their former compatriots in Eastern Bengal-cum-East Pakistan, who created Bangladesh in 1971. Pakistani Pashtuns believe that they have more in common with fellow Pashto speakers in Afghanistan (Ahmed 1998). The Malay Muslims of Thailand represent a similar case in that they have sometimes mobilized in favor of reunification with neighboring Malaysia (Pitsuwan 1985). The tacit agreement in Southeast Asia on the inviolability of borders, however, has made this prospect highly unlikely.

Despite the reality that there are multiple nations within states in Asia, the idea of granting recognition to these nations generates controversies. In many cases, there are concerns that recognizing the multinational nature of many Asian states runs the risk of creating political division and fragmentation reminiscent of earlier eras. These considerations bear heavily on the minds of state leaders in India, Indonesia, or Pakistan, for instance. Conflict continues to characterize relationships between substate nationalist groups and the state.

The origins of sub-state nationalist mobilization in Asia coincide at times with legacies of past attempts at state centralization and assimilation, even prior to the age of nationalism. Large and populous states such as China and India have historical legacies that include a complex and diversified heritage upon which it has always been difficult to impose a homogeneous identity. China's successive dynasties have acculturated over centuries a large number of populations with varying degrees of success. Populations in eastern China, for instance, were completely assimilated but the populations of inner Asia (Mongolia, Xinjiang – also known as East Turkestan – and Tibet), which were incorporated later during the Qing Dynasty, maintained their own cultural characteristics. Since then, their distinctiveness has been recognized, even in the People's Republic of China, which granted some form of autonomy to Mongols, Turkic-speaking Uighurs, and Tibetans (Dreyer 1997).

At the end of the nineteenth century, most colonies in Asia were faced with demands for self-determination from local elites, who were largely inspired by nationalist and Marxist intellectual currents. Nationalist movements selectively retrieved from local histories and folklore the myths that would serve as the building blocks of a new nation, as they tried to foster unified identities from widely diverse populations. Populations living at the periphery of colonies, in remote locations away from the centers of economic and political power, did not always recognize themselves in the images of the new nations these elites wanted to create.

Nation-state structures were reconfigured, often by majority groups with past histories of large empires or kingdoms, with homogenizing effects that have often denied representation to minority groups, particularly those seeing themselves as nations in their own right. For example, the People's Republic of China, which claims to be the successor to imperial states, imposed Mandarin as the official language at the expense of the linguistic diversity among Han Chinese, who speak countless dialects, and to non-Han citizens alike, even those whose culture has more in common with that of Islamic central Asia or Southeast Asia. In Asian countries without a history of long-lasting pre-colonial imperial unity such as Indonesia and Pakistan, hybrid and minority literary languages, such as *Bahasa Indonesia* or Urdu, were imposed over other languages, such as Javanese and Punjabi, which had far more speakers, to avoid giving the impression that the linguistic majority was imposing its culture (Brown & Ganguly 2003; Hayes 1984). In those states where new nations were engineered by mass education in those languages, the affirmation of national differences within the new states were bound to be sensitive and to be seen as a rejection of the attempts at state-building.

Demands for self-determination by aggrieved majority populations in the colonies were generated soon after similar demands from sub-state national groups. Yet, leaders of Asian states remained reluctant to respond to these demands, despite long histories in which diverse populations were only loosely amalgamated in many of the larger imperial states. Some of these groups even had their own histories of statehood. For example, Indonesia's province of Aceh was a major regional power in the sixteenth and seventeenth centuries; Sikhs had a state in the seventeenth century; Tibet became incorporated into the Qing Empire after a centuries-old history of independent statehood; and Tamils of south India and Sri Lanka claimed continuity with the kingdoms of Pallava and Pandya in the third century AD. The integrative history of colonialism and nation-state formation in Asia incorporated strongly established social and political groups with their own cultural or social institutions that were often strengthened, rather than weakened, by these integrative pressures. After independence, they were confined to nation-state structures that clashed with their own aspirations.

Beyond these historically grounded empirical differences with countries in other regions of the developing world, there remains a fairly large variance within Asia that requires explanation. The chapters in this volume collectively provide a set of propositions to explain this variance, while also exploring various facets of the recognition and accommodation of sub-state national groups in the region.

THE ORGANIZATION OF THE BOOK

The case studies in this book present a wide variety of sub-state national groups in Asia. Chapters are grouped together on the basis of geographical coherence, which reflects to some extent shared historical experiences that have had significant consequences on the origins and accommodation of these groups. We first consider states in South Asia and continental Southeast Asia, where the presence of multiple nations is more common than in East Asia. India, Pakistan, Sri Lanka, and Burma share a common institutional legacy of British colonial rule, some partially shared memories of pre-colonial statehood, and cultural traits. The chapters on the archipelagic Southeast Asian states of Indonesia, the Philippines, and Malaysia follow logically, as these states have also emerged as a result of anti-colonial struggle. China, in its dealing with Taiwan and Tibet, may appear to represent a class in itself because it has not been colonized by European powers. Yet, the nature of the People's Republic of China as a revolutionary state during the first decades following its inception invites parallels with Indonesia and Burma, and, arguably, the Philippines. The concluding chapter, on the former Soviet Central Asian Republics, completes the circle. These states represent the legacy of a former empire, and point to a future that China would like to avoid for the inner Asian region that still remains under its control.

Rajeev Bhargava addresses the case of India, a state usually celebrated for the extraordinary achievement of bringing together in a relatively peaceful manner different populations holding different religious beliefs and political views, as well as speaking a wide range of different languages. Yet, as Bhargava demonstrates, the framers of the Indian state have had difficulty in conceiving of India as a multination state despite its diversity. While they have gone so far as to accommodate linguistic diversity along a federal principle of equality among states, they have been unwilling to conceive of asymmetrical forms to accommodate a wider range and depth of ethnic differences. This conceptual failure, he argues, explains the tragic inability of the central government to accommodate demands for recognition from groups of people who do not see themselves as members of the Indian nation.

Sumit Ganguly discusses the case of Pakistan, a state that was created out of limits to India's ability to accommodate religious diversity. Ganguly offers a grim assessment of Pakistan's failed effort to manage its much more limited multinationality. The hegemony of one shared religious belief in that country could not prevent continuing insurrections in its western part and the secession of its former eastern part, which became Bangladesh. Ganguly argues that the dissatisfaction expressed in these sub-state nationalist movements stems from the failure to develop representative institutions and a deep crisis of identity that has moved various governments, even democratic ones, to deny any accommodation of sub-state nations or ethnic minorities, whether based on religious, linguistic or other differences. With these problems compounded by repression, military dominance, and the primordial notions of identity held by the Pakistani national movement, state elites were unable to appreciate the culturally diverse nature of Muslim communities in South Asia, and therefore, could not devise institutions representing adequately the diverse populations of the new state, thereby fuelling subsequent sub-state nationalist mobilization and crisis.

Sujit Choudhry's examination of Sri Lanka's predicament offers some sobering thoughts on the possibility for multinational democracies to achieve national unity while substantially recognizing their diversity. In contrast to Pakistan, and even more to India, Sri Lanka has a very simple configuration of ethnic relations, being a society in which two distinct national groups of unequal weight are striving for two different, irreconcilable national projects. Yet, even in what appears to be a radically simple situation, some fundamental disagreements can make accommodation to the demands of sub-state nationalist groups extraordinarily difficult. Hence, Choudhry argues that differences over the procedures of constitutional change itself present an even greater obstacle to reconciliation between antagonists than their disagreement over the substance of constitutional change, which is about the preference of the Sinhalese majority for a unitary state and the wish of most Tamils for a federal state.

If the above case studies show that democracies and semi-democracies have difficulty in properly addressing the demands from sub-state nationalist movements, Ardeth Thawnghmung's contribution on Burma

suggests that authoritarian governments, which show scant concern
for criticism from within their own societies, are not necessarily more
successful than democracies at preventing the emergence of demands
for accommodation from sub-state nations. But she also departs from
other contributors to this book when she cautions that federalism does
not always help achieve stability and may in fact exacerbate demands
from various sub-state nationalist groups. She argues that the various
strategies employed to dampen the demands from various groups may
entrench further their sense of grievance rather than lead them to com-
ply with the wishes of the ruling junta for a unified state. She adds that
the sub-state nationalities of Burma are too fragmented and that this
makes it impossible for the government to provide stable arrangements
that meet every group's expectation. She believes therefore that Burma
should return to the ideal of the historic leader U Nu for the creation of
a liberal yet unitary state, respectful of different cultures but sharing a
common Burmese identity.

Anthony Reid, by comparing Indonesia and Malaysia within the
broader Southeast Asian context, argues that the preference for unitary nation-states in Asia is related closely to the legacy of revolutionary
struggle to achieve independence from colonial rule. His argument can be
broadly cast to understand historical trends in Vietnam and Burma, and
also in other revolutionary states, such as the People's Republic of China,
that were not subjected directly to colonial rule. By contrast Reid argues
that states that have chosen an evolutionary path to independence, such
as Malaysia, have developed institutions that were more accommodating
of diversity.

Several of the chapters, nevertheless, cast doubt that democracies
have had a better record of accommodating sub-state national groups.
Chapters on India, the Philippines, and other Asian countries show evidence of democratic regimes repressing demands of groups for recognition, or even accommodation, of sub-state nationalist claims. Jacques
Bertrand goes even further by arguing that accommodation might lead
to reduced mobilization of these groups and provide a symbolic form of
recognition in the short term, yet remain devoid of substance. By analyzing various instances of autonomy granted to Papuans, Acehnese, and
East Timorese in Indonesia, as well as to the Moros in the Philippines,
he shows that constitutional or legal provisions for autonomy under
authoritarian and democratic regimes have most often been devoid
of substantial power of self-government in their implementation. As
a result, these groups became disenchanted, increasingly suspicious of

offers of autonomy, and often remobilized more forcefully in spite of a democratic context.

The Chinese state, which was built from a quintessential revolutionary path in the first decades of the post-colonial era and the Cold War, stands out as an example of a multinational state that offers generous promises of recognition and autonomy, but refuses to grant sub-state national movements the instruments to achieve the substance of that autonomy. Andre Laliberté discusses how this policy clashes, ironically, with its stance on the Republic of China, known as Taiwan. The latter represents a unique but significant case of a nation that has achieved the substance of independence without receiving so far recognition from the state that claims authority over it. While previous chapters have shown that symbolic recognition without substance does not mean much, this chapter illustrates that de facto independence without symbolic recognition does not go very far either.

Gray Tuttle stresses a different point about China's approach to sub-state nationalist movements, but this time with respect to Tibet, at the other end of the multinational Chinese state, both geographically and institutionally. In contrast to Taiwan, Tibet does not have the substance of autonomy, but it does receive symbolic recognition. Tuttle argues that Tibetans accepted their incorporation within the Chinese state when the latter recognized effectively the distinctive nature of their government, with a religious figurehead. His case study suggests that, as is the case for India's management of its multinational character, an asymmetrical form of governance for a multinational China could maintain unity of the state at lesser cost for all parties concerned.

Edward Schatz explores the outcome of more proactive approaches to the multinational character of a state. He argues that, when states give real substance to autonomy to prevent the emergence of radical sub-state nationalist movements that would seek secession rather than integration, the process can trigger unforeseen consequences. Starting from the premise that national identities are social constructs, he argues that the paternalistic approach of Leninist states to the recognition of nationalities ultimately failed to achieve its intended goals to hold a vast state together. Furthermore, it created new problems in states where a disembodied nationalist elite seeks to build ethnically based forms of national identity that fit uneasily with the multifaceted aspects of diversity in these societies. These arguments find particular resonance in other countries where similar proactive policies have been followed. The move from autonomy to independence for these Republics represents a possible future of

China's Inner Asian regions of Xinjiang, Tibet, and Inner Mongolia that leaders in Beijing would like to avoid at all costs.

In the concluding chapter Bertrand and Laliberté draw together the theoretical insights provided by previous contributors. After reexamining the Asian cases in relation to a wider historical and international context, they provide two broad sets of propositions explaining the variance in state accommodation of sub-state national claims in Asia. In general, they find that democracy does not predict more accommodation of these groups. Specific historical trajectories, rooted in state conceptions of the nation and elite interests for centralized power, explain much of the variance in state responses. Among comparatively strong factors a few stand out: elite perceptions of threats to the state; paths to independence; revolutionary past; types of "official nationalist" constructions; and the presence or absence of cultural cores.

2

Revolutionary State Formation and the Unitary Republic of Indonesia

Anthony Reid

Recent trends in Europe whereby established states have surrendered some powers toward a supranational Europe, on the one hand, and subnational regions on the other, make it possible to speak of a relaxation of the "sovereign equality" model that dominated the post-war world in which nation-states were presumed to be the sole and equal possessors of sovereignty. We should, however, be very careful about generalizing this globally. In particular, the new states of Asia have been in an intense period of nation-building since 1945. The type of nationalism which Tønnesson and Antlov (1996) label "official," I prefer to call "state nationalism" to avoid Anderson's (1991) negative use of the term, since it is the universal currency of states in seeking to create loyalty and homogeneity (Reid 2009). This type is still extremely vigorous in Asia, where the task of turning "peasants into Chinese" (or Indians, Indonesians, etc.) is by no means complete. The acceptance by China in 1997 and Indonesia in 2005 of a certain degree of asymmetry in the position of Hong Kong and Aceh, respectively, may look like pragmatic retreats from the nationalist project, but there is still profound resistance in both these states toward recognizing the validity of self-governing "nations" within established states.[1]

It would be wrong to see this difference, however, as a consequence of either Asian cultural norms or long-term patterns of Asian statecraft.

[1] On June 6, 2007, for example, the Chairman of China's National People's Congress, Wu Bangguo, seemed to undercut Asia's most impressive achievement of asymmetric pluralism in recent times, by telling the representatives of Hong Kong that "Hong Kong's administrative autonomy is not intrinsic…it is granted by the Central Government," *Straits Times,* June 7, 2007.

Asia in general, and Southeast Asia in particular, has remained plural
in its social organization, in contrast to the states of western Europe or
the New World. Highland and small-island peoples remained unincor-
porated into states at all until the early twentieth century, and in many
parts of Southeast Asia they are only becoming fully integrated in the
current era of TV, mass education, and mobile phones. Before the twentieth century most Asian polities remained relatively resistant both to
"Westphalian" norms of formal equality between sovereign nation-states
and to the internal cultural homogeneity that accompanied this model.
Many states continued to render tribute, or acknowledge asymmetry, in
dealing with several international parties in different levels of deference
(Reid & Zheng 2009). Brantley Womack has made the point that "international relations theory, which remains rooted in the modern European
experience of competitive nationalism," has much to gain from considering the older history of Asian ways of managing relations between polities (Womack 2006, p. 23).

This chapter will argue that the strong commitment of Indonesia after
1945 (and by implication, of China and Vietnam) to a single homogeneous
nation within former imperial borders is not an Asian but a post-revolutionary phenomenon. The states most uncompromisingly committed
to radical political uniformity were those that entered the contemporary
world through a political revolution that was committed to an ideal of
a single, equal, and unqualified citizenship for all, without recognizing
the legitimacy of older political legacies. The chapter will show with reference to the Indonesian case how the embracing of the revolutionary
idea by the political elite in the middle decades of the century produced
an uncompromisingly unitary model of state. The absence of historical
roots for such a model, other than that of the reviled Dutch imperial
system itself, served paradoxically to strengthen the persuasiveness of the
uniform Indonesian identity – imagined but neutral. As pointed out in
the introduction above, other (communist) revolutions emerging from
lengthy guerrilla movements were more indebted to minorities that had
supported them in opposition, and hence made concessions to "nationalities" as first adumbrated in the Soviet model. Nepal is an intriguing
contemporary example. Yet in all such post-revolutionary regimes, political legitimacy is held to derive from the revolution itself, so that concessions to minorities are but means to a uniform end. Only to the extent
that revolutionary legitimacy is eroded in the longer term and replaced
by state nationalist rhetoric drawing again on history (the trend of post-
Mao China), can other historic claims to identity make their comeback.

This chapter aims to establish the post-revolutionary model as an essential tool in the typology of twentieth-century state formation, in contrast to other options.

DIFFERENT PATHS TO INDEPENDENT STATEHOOD

The crucial watershed of the 1940s and early 1950s saw the birth or rebirth of most of Asia's states, which endured surprisingly effectively over the subsequent half century. Several of them achieved this state form through a revolutionary declaration in or around 1945, which the world powers accepted reluctantly only after considerable bloodshed, from both external and internal challenges. I will take the Indonesian case as my prototype of this path, though China, Vietnam, Pol Pot's Cambodia (the extreme), and to some extent Burma, might be equally instructive.

By contrast, those new states born through an evolutionary path (particularly under British decolonizing auspices) accepted, in the interests of pragmatism, a diverse inheritance of asymmetric political forms. In particular, the extraordinary complexity of the Indian federal system, with its multiple political and language rights, is an understudied model for such formations, which this book helps to address. In Southeast Asia, post-war Malaysia provides a marked contrast with its fellow-Austronesian- and Malay-speaking neighbor Indonesia, as is explained further below. Like Malaysia, the Philippines, the third major state with a diverse Austronesian population, achieved its post-war independence by peaceful evolution and negotiation. It had, however, also defined itself through revolution, like Indonesia, but a half century earlier in the uprising against Spain (1896) and the subsequent Malolos Republic. The commitment to a centralized state with equal sovereignty defined in this revolution began to fade only eighty years later, when the government made its first autonomy agreement with representatives of the Moro nation (*Bangsa Moro*) in 1976. This marks the beginning of the reconceptualizing of the Filipino state as multinational, with increasing discussion of a switch to federalism, balanced by continuing pressures to uphold the unitary ideal of the Malolos Republic. The vital question hanging over Indonesia's 2005 Memorandum of Understanding with the Aceh independence movement is how far Indonesia, too, can relax its definition of Indonesian national unity as the revolution that took place sixty years earlier loses its monopoly of legitimation.

In the centuries preceding the watershed of the 1940s, the "Malay World" appeared extremely unlikely to be on a path leading toward strong, unitary states. It never developed bureaucratic, law-giving states of its own, and interior populations remained wary of the externally supported states on the coasts. Even the highly complex polities of pre-colonial Java and Bali seemed to have "an alternative conception of what politics was about" (Geertz 1980, p. 135). A marked trend of modern scholarship on early modern Indonesia has been the quest to define the social and cultural glue that enabled these societies to develop great complexity in the absence of Weberian bureaucracy (Day 2002; Drakard 1999).

The modern legal/bureaucratic state was introduced to the region by Dutch and British colonial regimes, which built their power, not by taking over pre-colonial states so much as by gradually building their own port-based regimes, first alongside, but eventually above more personal indigenous hierarchies. When in the twentieth century these colonial polities became effective states, they still maintained a facade of very diverse rajas, sultans, *adathoofden, bupati,* and chiefs, who served as sources of both legitimacy and mediation with the diverse populations for which they became responsible. Immigrant Chinese, Europeans, Indians, and Arabs provided the middle class for these colonial states but were not discouraged from continuing to think of their citizenship and "nationhood" as being elsewhere. Hence, the prevailing wisdom in both the Indies and British Malaya in the 1930s was that independence was scarcely viable. B. C. de Jonge began his term as Governor-General in 1931 with the statement that Holland had been in the Indies for 300 years and would be there for another 300. Toynbee famously declared "When I touched at the Straits Settlements on my way out East I realized that British Malaya was destined, by 'peaceful penetration,' to become a new Chinese province" (Toynbee 1931, p. 259).

Insofar as there were attempts to evade the nationalist pressure by devolving authority to more manageable units, feebly in the 1920s and 1930s but almost frenetically after 1945, complex structures of diversity seemed the only viable option. The map of Federal Indonesia constructed by the Dutch in 1946–1949 as they sought an alternative to the Indonesian Republic was extraordinarily complex in its attempts to accommodate ethnic, linguistic, and political diversities (Reid 1974, pp. 106–19; Schiller 1955).

The diverse local aristocracies being tutored in modernity by the Dutch may have found these federal structures appropriate, or even too radical. However, there were by the 1930s plenty of radical nationalists with little stake in traditional structures of any kind and a very low regard for them. In the early 1920s, Indonesia had the strongest communist party in Asia, riding a popular messianism about a golden future without oppression or inequality. The Dutch authorities arrested 13,000 alleged communists in 1926–1927 and effectively eliminated the party from political participation for the rest of the colonial era. Revolutionary dreams, however, remained strong, especially outside Java where the colonial presence itself was new and relatively fragile.

What was the focus of longing for such radical nationalists? Lacking a name for their collective selves other than *Indier* (Indian), students from the Archipelago in Holland picked up the musty academic neologism "Indonesia" used in the title of a book by a German ethnographer (Bastian 1884). Ki Hadjar Dewantoro first used it for his Indonesian Press Bureau in 1913, but from 1917 on the influential organization for the students from the Archipelago in the Netherlands called itself (in Dutch) the "Indonesian Union of Students." The idea spread quickly, borne by the aspiration that Indonesia's unity lay in its future, not in any particular past formation. It was a name entirely free of associations. When it acquired such associations in the 1920s by frequent reiteration, they were again those of the future. In 1924, the Indonesian communists founded the first political party to adopt this new term, calling their organization the Partai Komunis Indonesia, or PKI. The nationalist students in Holland called their journal "*Indonesia Merdeka*" (Free Indonesia) in 1925; in the same year, the international communist activist Tan Malaka published in exile his *Toward the "Republic of Indonesia."* In 1927, Sukarno established the Indonesian National Association (later Party – Partai Nasional Indonesia, or PNI), to fight for unity and independence, and popularized the slogan "Indonesia Merdeka," These associations tended to stick with the new term Indonesia – "free," "national," "republic" (Elson 2008).

In October 1928, a meeting of regional youth movements, mainly supported by those studying in Dutch-medium high schools and universities in Java, decided to embrace the new idea in preference to established ethno-linguistic identities. In the subsequently famous Youth Oath (*Sumpah Pemuda*) they declared, "We the youth of Indonesia acknowledge only one fatherland, Indonesia. We acknowledge only one nation [*bangsa*], Bangsa Indonesia. We uphold only one language, the Indonesian language." With this, the generation that would later drive the Indonesian revolution had already laid the basis for portraying an emphasis on their particular ethno-linguistic identities as anti-national. Although they largely spoke in Dutch, they were aided by the possibility of elevating the commercial and Islamic lingua franca of the Indies, Malay, to be the national "Indonesian language" of their aspiration. Only 2 percent of the

Indonesian population was listed as Malay in the 1930 census, and this language threatened nobody, as Javanese (46 percent of the 1930 population) would have done.

Idealistic, educated Indonesian youth, therefore, already had a dream of independent modernity that was singular because it was detached from the divided present. The political nationalists among them, moreover, were inclined to dismiss the traditional aristocracy through whom the Dutch ruled, with all their culturally specific hierarchies, as an anachronistic and "feudal" facade, perpetuated by the colonial power to divide and rule. From their Dutch education, they absorbed an admiration for the modernity of democratic nation-states, and a distinct lack of respect for the decorative but largely impotent monarchs through whom the Dutch ruled. Despite the appearance of great political diversity in Netherlands India, they perceived the underlying reality of centralized colonial bureaucracy.

Sukarno was an ideal mouthpiece for the unitary "Indonesia" idea. From his emergence as a leader of nationalist forces after the suppression of the PKI in 1926, he consistently championed the unity of all the *sini* (here) against the *sana* (there), in effect a racial unity that epitomized anti-imperial nationalism. He had phases of greater drawing on Marxist and Islamic sources, but he never wavered in proclaiming that the key to the "golden bridge" to a glittering independence lay through subordinating differences to the single great goal. In perhaps his most characteristic expression, the speech and pamphlet, "Achieving Independent Indonesia" (*Mentjapai Indonesia Merdeka*, 1933), Sukarno drew on Marxist literature very selectively to demonize the West as a capitalist hell for the poor. Thereby, parliamentary democracy and individualism became the great evils to combat. Collective action under the guidance of a single vanguard party should galvanize the masses to uphold "socio-democracy" and "socio-nationalism" against the evils of individualism and capitalism (Sukarno 1933, pp. 66–7). Moreover, the party itself should have just enough Leninist theory (if not organization) to leave no intermediaries between the leadership and the masses, and give total control to its leader. "The democracy of the vanguard party is the democracy which foreigners call 'democratic centralism,' a democracy which gives the top leadership the authority to punish every deviation, to oppose[2] any member or section of the party that endangers the struggle strategy of the masses" (Sukarno 1933, p. 50). These ideas were only one strain among many in

---

[2] The translation of Dahm (1969, p. 155) based on an earlier text, renders this as "expel," which may indicate some sanitizing in the 1970s version I used.

the Dutch period, but they became very central after 1942 and triumphed through a revolutionary process.

As a control counterexample, the British had established in Malaysia an admittedly less centralized colonial unit. Their domain in the "Malay World" was a patchwork of constitutional diversity. It included the Crown Colony of the Straits Settlements (Singapore, Melaka, and Penang), in which Chinese were a majority; the first four Malay monarchies on the Peninsula to be "protected" in the 1870s, which would later be welded into a common federal government in 1896; and five other "unfederated" sultanates jealous of their sovereignty as protectorates. It also comprised the "white raj" of Sarawak, which reluctantly surrendered sovereignty to the British in 1946; an autocratic sultan in Brunei; and a chartered company in North Borneo (Sabah). The conflict in the Peninsula between a robust Chinese nationalism (which was taking an increasingly communist path with Mao's rise), and a Malay ethno-nationalism seeking to retain sovereignty or at least dominance in Malay hands, dwarfed any dream of a unifying anti-British nationalism. Finally, Britain was in a position to reoccupy its territories quickly after the Japanese surrender, which the Netherlands was not, providing a much more promising revolutionary opportunity in the Indonesian case.

THE MYTH OF UNITY IN THE REVOLUTIONARY 1940S

The Japanese military administration (1942–1945) gave Sukarno the direct access to the masses that the Dutch had gone to great lengths to deny him – for which he remained very grateful to Japan (Sukarno 1966, pp. 161–3, 173). Though never wavering in his aim of Indonesian independence, Sukarno endorsed the Japanese wartime ideal of a do-or-die struggle against the West, with its corrupting evils of liberalism and individualism. Far more than others who cooperated for tactical, opportunist, or survival reasons, Sukarno passionately advocated the slogan of "Live or Die with Dai Nippon." To his increasingly skeptical fellow nationalists in the wake of Japanese defeats, he pleaded in October 1944: "Do all the comrades understand...that independence can be realized only by way of cooperation with Japan. I ask this here because I know that there are still many among our people...who are still intoxicated by liberalism, who make individualism an ideal, and do not want to participate in the war with its burden and bitterness" (cited in Dahm 1969, pp. 281–2).

The Japanese occupation resulted in other remarkable contributions to the revolutionary ideal of unity, despite Japan's own intentions to divide the Archipelago into different spheres of permanent Japanese rule. Firstly, they had absolutely no use for Dutch as lingua franca (in contrast to the preference of anglophone and francophone Japanese administrators in other colonies) and brutally forbade its public use, resolving the language question by promoting the use of Malay. Secondly, they further downgraded the status and autonomy of self-governing rulers and created a plethora of unitary organizations for all Muslims, all Christians, all women, and so forth. The greatest contribution to the unitary idea, however, was paradoxically, in their very different treatment of three regions. Java under the 16th Army was the only region for which Japan envisaged a token independence and where the military encouraged Java-wide political movements and leadership. The Japanese 25th Army initially saw oil-rich Sumatra as too valuable ever to let go, and only in March 1945 did it permit token Sumatra-wide representative bodies. In the Navy-ruled Borneo and the East, Japanese authorities did not allow any political activity because they envisaged these scattered and under-populated islands as a permanent part of the empire.

Only Java-based delegates attended the principal opportunity to debate the shape of the future independent Indonesia, the Body for the Investigation of Indonesian Independence (*Badan Penyelidik Kemerdekaan Indonesia*, or BPKI) at the end of May 1945. Although a tenth of its sixty-two members had been born outside Java, none lived there, and there was no voice for protecting the interests of distinct ethnic and regional interests. The only challenge to the nationalist dream came from Muslim delegates demanding some form of an Islamic state. Nationalists offered them a compromise in May but withdrew it in August after consideration of the non-Muslim regions' support. The BPKI, unsurprisingly, voted overwhelmingly for a unitary republic. A Christian Ambonese who was active in nationalist politics in Java, Johannes Latuharhary, found in the nineteen-man constitutional subcommittee only one supporter for his plea for a federal state. Only six delegates in the full body favored monarchy over a republic. Only Hatta and Mohammad Yamin, both Mingkabaus born in Sumatra, made vain pleas for building individual and regional rights into the constitution (Yamin 1959, pp. 230–9, 259, 299–300, 330–6). In the hothouse atmosphere of the late Japanese occupation, quasi-fascist ideals of unity, articulated in integralist form in a draft constitution by law professor Supomo, appeared untroubled by any practical diversity on the ground. Most of these same delegates believed their future unitary Indonesian state should extend to include Malaya, British Borneo, and Portuguese Timor (Reid 1974, pp. 19–25).

Facing the growing certainty of an Allied return to eastern Indonesia, Borneo, and Sumatra, Tokyo subsequently overruled the desire of the local military authorities in these areas to keep them separate from the rapid independence preparations in Java. On the very day of the Japanese surrender, August 14, 1945, three ill-prepared delegates from Sumatra and five from Borneo and the East arrived in Jakarta for what was expected to be the next step towards a Japanese-managed "independence" for Indonesia. Suddenly the theatre became reality. After independence was hastily proclaimed in a manner the Japanese could accept on August 17, the Japanese-sponsored Committee for the Preparation of Indonesian Independence (PPKI) was called upon to authorize the constitution, which had been prepared earlier in Java, and laid the basis for a new state in a hurried three-day meeting.

The delegates from outside Java were uniformly concerned about the Java-centered state that was likely to result, but they had little effect on a format that had already been determined without them. The most articulate of these delegates, Dr. Mohamad Amir from Medan, pleaded "that the maximum decentralization be allowed for the islands outside Java, that governments be set up there, and that the people there be given the right to manage their domestic affairs to the widest extent" (Yamin 1959, pp. 410, 419). Far from allowing natural ethno-cultural units their own expression, however, the PPKI decided to establish only eight large provinces for the whole country – one each for Sumatra, Borneo, and Sulawesi and two for the smaller eastern islands. Except for the three in Java, each of the other five provinces was a mosaic of pluralism, with no dominant ethnicity or even religion (Reid 1974, pp. 19–29). The governors appointed to these provinces had negligible power on the ground. Youth movements, some Japanese-trained, some Islamic, some communist, provided the real dynamic of revolution at the local level, and all were impatient with the compromises made by the established local elites. For these newly mobilized youth, Java and centralism represented the distant dream of a purer republic, not a threat to local autonomies in which they had little stake.

If the Japanese administration set the stage for the unitary charter of the Republic's beginnings, it was the revolutionary assertion of independence that provided real legitimacy and charismatic power. The established elites, with their local interests to protect, were on the defensive against the unitary dream throughout the revolution. They could not prevent the violent "social revolutions" of 1945–1946 that swept away the kind of self-governing rulers the Malayan constitutions were designed to protect. Despite its ambivalence about these violent actions, the Republican leadership accepted their consequences as signaling the end of monarchy in Sumatra (Kahin 1985; Omar 1993; Reid 1979). In the 1950s, a uniform pattern of administrators (called *bupati* and *camat* on the Javanese model) appointed by the Interior Ministry in Jakarta eased out dozens of other monarchies in Borneo and eastern Indonesia through less violent means.

Aceh was the most critical test of the Republic's intentions for regional autonomy. Having fought determinedly against the Dutch conquest and endured its brief "colonial peace" only reluctantly, the Acehnese were known to be least likely to accept the restoration of pre-war conditions. Hundreds of recalcitrant Japanese soldiers and intelligence agents chose this place to continue their fight after August 1945. The question whether its resistance would be in the name of Aceh or Indonesia was quickly resolved in the six months following the Japanese surrender. This period saw the culmination of a struggle between provincial aristocrats (*ulèëbal- ang*) on whom the Dutch had relied to lead 102 little "self-governments," and a popular Islamic movement (led by religious teachers, *ulama*), which had already sought the overthrow of the former at Japanese hands. After the Japanese surrender, the most aggressive of the *ulèëbalang* provoca- tively sought Dutch help to reestablish their pre-war position, whereas the youth wing of the *ulama*-led movement persuaded its leaders to embrace the revolutionary Indonesian Republic. On October 15, 1945, four prominent *ulama*, including Teungku Daud Beureu'eh, issued a declaration stating that "Every segment of the population has united in obedience, to stand behind the great leader Ir. Sukarno" because the anti- Dutch struggle of the Republic was a "holy war" like that which their ancestors had fought against Dutch conquest forty years earlier (Reid 2005, p. 346).

The *ulama*-led group prevailed in a brief civil war of December 1945, and its leader Daud Beureu'eh became the dominant figure in the subse- quent Republican government (Reid 1979, pp. 185–217). Aceh remained the vital bastion of Republican strength after successive Dutch military actions retook all the key urban areas and economic assets elsewhere. Up until the victory of the Republic through the transfer of sovereignty at the end of 1949, the local population accepted this *ulama* leadership as the local government with complete autonomy in practice. The conflict that emerged after 1950 was between the de facto autonomy of Aceh and many other localities that had made their own revolutions, and the unitary ideal proclaimed in 1945. Because they had fought for the revolutionary ideal, the provincial leaders could not readily transform themselves into federalists or separatists once they experienced the realities of central control after 1950. They claimed instead that the ideals of the revolution had been betrayed, and fought their battles with Jakarta on the basis of a different vision of the Republic as a whole.

In much of the rest of Indonesia, federal structures and a constitutionalism of checks and balances was developed from 1946 to 1949, but these were fatally compromised because of their Dutch authorship as well as their internal weaknesses and pluralities. The revolution had disenfranchised the upholders of this system as traitors to the revolutionary idea, rather than as endangered minorities needing constitutional protection. The compromise under which the Netherlands and the world accepted Indonesian independence in 1949 was in fact a federal Indonesia, uncomfortably merging the unitary Republic that held authority over most of Java and Sumatra with the elaborate federal structure the Dutch had built everywhere else. In Borneo they had patched together five weak federal states – two federations of rajas in the east, one "special region" in the west, and two "neo-lands" still too inchoate to have much sense of identity. In East Indonesia, the Dutch succeeded better in building an overarching federal state, the Negara Indonesia Timur (NIT), at a conference in Bali in December 1946. In the capital of this new state, Makassar, they constructed a fragile new edifice made up of a cabinet, parliament, and civil service. Internally, this structure rested on an extraordinary mosaic of local bodies. Some, representing pro-Dutch Christian areas like South Maluku (Ambon) and Minahasa, had indirectly elected representative councils; others were little more than confederations of traditional rulers, as in Bali and South Sulawesi. In Java and Sumatra too, the Dutch erected federal structures after they had reconquered, in July 1947, the most productive plantation areas in East Sumatra and West Java and the oil-rich Palembang area of South Sumatra (Chauvel 1990, pp. 233–57; Reid 1974, pp. 106–120).

Even though it was endorsed by the international community as an appropriate Dutch–Indonesian compromise, however, the federal constitutional structure collapsed completely within eight months of the transfer of sovereignty. Those who had feared the populist unitary thrust of the Republic found constitutional legality no protection against the "revolutionary political reality" on the ground (Feith 1962, p. 71). The Republican army, one of the forces most hostile to the Dutch-created structures, did not have to assert itself very strongly to bring about the dissolution of those states which had any military capacity of their own.

The only serious armed resistance to the process came from Ambonese soldiers of the former colonial army who were now serving in the East Indonesian federal state. They provided the muscle behind the independence declaration of the Republic of the South Moluccas (RMS) in April 1950, after the Republic of Indonesia had sealed the fate of the federal NIT. For five months, they defended their capital in Ambon against a much larger Indonesian force and continued a guerrilla resistance in adjacent Ceram until 1962 (Chauvel 1990, pp. 347–92).

At an ideological level, the symbolic power of the revolutionary ideal of unity contrasted strikingly with the factionalism of every local structure in the islands outside Java. The Dutch withdrawal magnified the problems they had faced in building any intermediate focus of loyalty between the local community or ethno-linguistic group and the *bangsa Indonesia* of revolutionary aspiration. The East Sumatran NST was built on three squabbling "indigenous" (*asli*) ethnic groups – Malay, Karo, and Simelungun – but could not ignore the even larger groups of Javanese and Toba Batak within it. Its attempts to raise another intermediate focus of loyalty to balance Java, notably through a *Muktamar Sumatera* (Sumatra Conference) bringing together sixteen regions in 1949, served only to demonstrate how diverse and leaderless such a grouping would be (Omar 1993, pp. 152–4). In contrast, when Sukarno made his appeal for a single Indonesian focus in the multiethnic capital of the NST, Medan, it resonated precisely because it seemed to be in the realm of future aspiration, above politics: "We are one nation (*natie*), not three or four, but one *bangsa* Indonesia. There is no *bangsa* Kalimantan, there is no *bangsa* Minangkabau, there is no *bangsa* Java, Bali, Lombok, Sulawesi or any such. We are all *bangsa* Indonesia. There is no *bangsa* Sumatera Timur. We are part of a single *bangsa* with a single fate."[3]

"RETURNING TO THE RAILS OF THE REVOLUTION" UNDER SUKARNO

So marginalized and demoralized were Indonesia's ex-federalists in the 1950s that the regional challenges of that period all came from the ranks of the revolutionary winners, who suppressed their ethno-nationalism under the cloak of rival visions of a unified republic. In 1949, a Republican guerrilla movement in West Java refused to disarm and declared its cause to be the Islamic State of Indonesia (Negara Islam

---

[3] *Propinsi Sumatera Utara*, speech of January 23, 1950, pp. 386–7.

Indonesia –NII) under S. M. Kartosuwirjo. In January 1952, another disgruntled group of Makasar-Bugis guerrillas in South Sulawesi, under Kahar Muzakar, declared its support for this organization, even though its spirit was anything but national.

In 1951, feeling strong enough to return to a uniform system of administration throughout the Archipelago, Jakarta revoked the de facto self-government that Aceh had established during the revolution. Sumatra had proved impossible to govern through the original single province, and Jakarta broke it into the three provinces that had already been decreed in 1948, before the Dutch occupation of most of them. Aceh was amalgamated with a North Sumatra province with its capital in multiethnic Medan, and few Acehnese in its official leadership. There was no place in the new scheme for Daud Beureu'eh and many of his Islam-educated colleagues. In September 1953, he led a rebellion, initially taking most of the Aceh war veterans with him. His grievances were regional, but he expressed them in theological terms, insisting that violence against the Dutch had only been justified by pursuit of an Islamic state. Hence, rebel Aceh, too, declared itself part of NII (Feith 1962, pp. 54–55, 212–14; Sjamsuddin 1985; Sulaiman 2000, 2006).

Aceh's disaffection with centralism was deeper than most, and it continued to fester despite the appearance of a return to central control by 1957. Jakarta restored Aceh's provincial status on January 1, 1957, but more importantly, the Indonesian military heightened its vigilance and its internal centralization. The army in the 1950s was still largely territorial, and a mixture of bribe and coercion became necessary to integrate local veterans of revolutionary action under a unified command structure. The difficulties of this process stimulated the greatest of Indonesia's military challenges, the "colonel's revolt" of 1957–1958. This began in December 1956, when the military commanders of both north Sumatra and central Sumatra declared martial law, suppressed communists and militant unionists in their regions, and broke their ties with the Jakarta government, insisting on the rights of their relatively wealthy regions to trade directly overseas. It was anti-communist disaffection among politicians in Jakarta, not any regional or federalist theory in itself, that provided the political leadership for this movement and a related one in North Sulawesi. The first national-level politician to join the colonels was leading economist Professor Sumitro, in May 1957. The leading politicians of the largest Islamic party, Masjumi, joined the movement in February 1958, and when their demands for a more moderate government were rejected, they declared an alternative one – the PRRI

(Pemerintah Revolusioner Republik Indonesia) – led by former Prime Minister Sjafruddin Prawiranegara.

The overall effect of this polarization was to speed the demise of democracy and the ascendancy of the center over the provinces outside Java. The military and Sukarno, supported by communist and nationalist parties, acted swiftly to suppress the rebel forces militarily. They dispatched troops from Java and succeeded in taking major towns by July 1958, resulting in the loss of several thousand lives. The troops from Java became a kind of occupation army for many years, while the representation of non-Javanese in the army officer corps dropped to below 40 percent. As in the defeat of federalism in 1950, these events disqualified another generation of regional leaders from the political contest.

A drift toward authoritarianism, supported by both the military and the communist party but eloquently articulated by Sukarno, accompanied this suppression of regional revolts. Martial law had been in force since March 1957, justifying the military's taking-over plantations and factories confiscated from their former Dutch owners and acting firmly against striking workers. Claiming a political stalemate on crucial issues such as the status of Islam in the state, Sukarno in 1959 abolished by decree the Constitutional Assembly, which was planning revisions to the federal constitution of 1950. The country would "return" to the 1945 Constitution that placed very few constraints on a powerful president. A little-noticed supplementary decree allowed the right to operate only to the political parties that proved their national credentials by having branches throughout the country. Sukarno justified these steps in a notable Independence Day speech of 1959, which he called, "Returning to the Rails of the Revolution":

Liberal democracy, which was born of the foam of the waves of that evil compromise [of 1950] and which dammed up and caused confusion in the Indonesian revolution, has now been blown clear away by the patriotic spirit and the fighting spirit of the People of Indonesia…the course of the Indonesian Revolution…lost its way for a while, [but] finally found its way back to its own true rails. (Sukarno 1959, cited in Feith & Castles 1970, p. 109)

The shift to what Sukarno dubbed "Guided Democracy" in 1959–1965 was a partial victory for one vision of what the revolutionary turmoil of the 1940s had been about. It marked "the victory of those who had wanted a more fundamental restructuring of society on 'national' and 'revolutionary' lines, involving the destruction of virtually all centers of power outside the government itself" (Feith 1967, p. 56). Yet the elements that supported this solution remained fundamentally divided, between the army, communists, and traditionalist Muslims. The establishment of Guided Democracy raised the rhetoric against the "enemies of the revolution" to a fevered pitch, only heightening the stakes between the contestants on the ground. The upshot of this period was, at the end of 1965, a dramatic turn to the authoritarian right amidst an appalling trauma of violence, which inaugurated a new period of centralized authoritarianism.

In this radicalizing context the supporters of a more federal or plural construction of the state had to lie very low or flee. Chief among them was Mohammad Hatta – Sumatran, pragmatic, technically competent – who as vice president had been considered the necessary balance to the flamboyant and Javanese Sukarno. Hatta was also on record for favoring both federalism in principle (Sukarno 1966, p. 195) and ending the obsession with revolution (Hatta 1954, IV, p. 171). He resigned his position in 1956 and had no further influence. At the other political extreme, the rebels who had originally expressed their opposition in Indonesian terms now moved to federalism or independence. In September 1955, the Acehnese rebels declared Aceh to be a federal state (*negara bagian*) of Indonesia, with Daud Beureu'eh as its head of state (*wali negara*). Hasan Tiro, who in 1945–1946 had been a passionate young advocate of Aceh's struggle being one with Indonesia's, developed from his exile in New York a preferred format for a federal Indonesia (Tiro 1958, pp. 98, 103–4, 150–3). When he returned to Aceh during a period of ceasefire and negotiations in 1959, he could claim that the idea of a federal state was gaining ground among the other elements that had joined the PRRI uprising in 1958 (Feith & Castles 1970, pp. 330–5; Sulaiman 2000, pp. 400–19). Only during Suharto's New Order did Tiro move to the idea of independence.

SUHARTO'S AUTHORITARIAN CENTRALISM, 1966–1998

The triumph of Suharto and the Army amidst a reign of anti-communist terror in 1966 marked a dramatic turn away from Sukarno's leftist international stance and his catastrophic neglect of the economy. In terms of internal political control, however, the Suharto regime was able to implement the kind of authoritarian centralism about which Sukarno could only dream. Far from returning to the tentative pluralism of the 1950s, which had provided for both a vigorous multiparty system supported by a free press and (in legal theory, at least) for Province and Kabupaten (district) executives chosen by their local elected assemblies, Suharto emphatically endorsed Sukarno's condemnation of this "Liberal" period.

The Army, itself newly unified by the traumas of the 1960s, provided the muscle for him to impose what his political theorists called "mono-loyalty," whereby all government officials were required to support the state party, Golkar, and many other centralized organizations established to deliver developmental goals. Mergers into two other parties and a prohibition from having any other basis than the state ideology *Pancasila* emasculated all political parties.

Law number 5 of 1974 revoked formally the autonomy legislation of the liberal 1950s. In the new system, the center effectively chose governors, and decided on their budgets and guidelines. In 1979, this centralizing trend was carried down to the village level, replacing what had been extremely effective local institutions in places such as Bali and West Sumatra by a uniform system based on a simplification of practice in Java. Stiffened by a military element down to village level, the new village councils and the village-level women's and security bodies were chosen by "consensus," with the central bureaucracy having a large say (Malley 1999).

The terror that inaugurated the New Order, the control of the media on issues such as national unity, and the militarization of the national myth as the basis for historical education at every level (McGregor 2007), made critical discussion of the ideology of "the unitary state of Indonesia" very difficult under Suharto. Instead, the most alienated elements began frankly planning for independence.

In New York, Hasan Tiro intensified his reading of Aceh history in the early 1970s. He grew increasingly excited by the independent role among the nations that Aceh had played up until 1873, in striking contrast to his youthful insistence during the revolution that "Aceh is an indivisible part of the Negara Republic Indonesia, so also its history too is one undivided part of Indonesian history" (Tiro 1948). In 1973, he claims to have "celebrated for the first time in many generations, in New York" the anniversary of the "glorious day" when Aceh defeated the first Dutch expedition sent to conquer it, in April 1873 (Tiro 1982, p. 62). At this stage, his mentor Daud Beureu'eh may have endorsed Tiro's call to pursue a path of independence.

The Indonesian invasion of East Timor in 1975 and the resistance to this new addition to the unitary Republic, both by sections of the international community and by the Timorese guerrilla movement, may have stiffened Tiro in this direction. In October 1976 he returned surreptitiously to Aceh, and on December 4 he raised a "thousand-year-old flag" in a jungle clearing, where he read a lengthy declaration of Aceh independence based, essentially, on history. "Our fatherland, Acheh, Sumatra, had always been a free and sovereign state since the world begun [sic]. Holland was the first foreign power to attempt to colonize us when it declared war against the Sovereign State of Acheh on March 26, 1873....If Dutch colonialism was wrong, then Javanese colonialism which was squarely based on it cannot be right" (Reid 2004, pp. 305–8; Tiro 1982, pp. 15–17).

REFORMASI AND THE NEW PLURALISM

The fall of Suharto in May 1998 inaugurated a remarkable period of democratic reform (*reformasi*), including the freedom of a vigorous and plural press, the gradual removal of the military from the political process, and free and fair elections at the national and, eventually, regional levels. Aeronautical engineer B. J. Habibie, chosen to be vice president by Suharto in part because of his implausibility as a challenger for the presidency, nevertheless ascended to that office on Suharto's resignation. His most dramatic step was to resolve the East Timor running sore by allowing a referendum on independence, thereby offering new hope to separatists in Aceh and elsewhere. In a heady reaction against Suharto's heavy-handed bureaucratic centralism, the Parliament passed radical new autonomy laws in 1999, which provided for elected local officials a generous sharing of revenues. The government permitted the first serious debate on federalism since 1950 (Bourchier & Hadiz 2003, pp. 269–72; Mangunwijaya 1998).

In the liberal atmosphere of 1998–2001, Jakarta's response to the clamor in Aceh for a referendum on independence was to attempt even more extensive autonomies than were being offered to other provinces and districts. An Aceh autonomy Law of July 1999 was stillborn because it looked to Acehnese like nothing more than the discredited and ineffective "special region" (*Daerah Istimewa*) deal that ended the 1959 rebellion. A more consensual drafting effort under the Abdurrahman Wahid presidency led to the NAD Law of July 2001, so called because it renamed the Province *Nanggroe Aceh Darussalam* (NAD), using the ambiguous Acehnese term *nanggroe* rather than Indonesian *negara,* long used for sovereign and federal states. Its concessions to Aceh – 70 percent of the oil and gas revenues for eight years and 50 percent thereafter – gained the support of Acehnese politicians working within the Indonesian structures, but did little to attract either the guerrillas of the independence movement (GAM) or the youth-based movement for a referendum (Miller 2006, pp. 301–10).

As had happened with the 1959 peace agreement, military intervention in the name of suppressing armed rebellion totally vitiated these autonomies. On May 19, 2003, President Megawati reestablished military rule in Aceh, bringing the level of military and police presence to between 45,000 and 60,000 strong, the highest it had been in Aceh's 130 years of intermittent military occupation (Schulze 2006, pp. 247–58, 262–4).

In light of this renewed quest for a military solution, the Helsinki agreement of August 15, 2005, which ended the war with a radical new proposal for Aceh self-government, was a striking turnaround for Jakarta. Two factors had made it possible. First, the election of the Indonesian President, Susilo Bambang Yudhoyono (SBY) and second, the massive earthquake and tsunami that devastated coastal Aceh, including its capital, on December 26, 2004. Suddenly, international attention was focused on Indonesia's response to the crisis, and the continuation of violence no longer seemed acceptable to anyone. The Helsinki-based Crisis Management Initiative brokered a Memorandum of Understanding between GAM and the Indonesian Government. It proposed the deployment of an international Aceh Monitoring Mission led by appointees of the European Union but also comprising delegates of the Association of Southeast Asian Nations (ASEAN).

If we exclude the decision to let go East Timor, this peace agreement is the most significant sign so far that the unitary dynamic of post-revolutionary nationalism is weakening. It granted to Aceh "authority within all sectors of public affairs," excluding "foreign affairs, external defense, national security, monetary and fiscal matters, justice and freedom of religion." National laws and international agreements "of special interest to Aceh" would only be agreed after consultation with the Aceh legislature. Aceh would have its own flag, crest, and hymn, and a ceremonial head of state called a *wali nanggroe*, the term that GAM had applied to Hasan Tiro. Aceh could raise its own external loans and international investments, administer its ports and airports, and enjoy 70 percent of the revenues from oil and gas "and other natural resources," in perpetuity. In return for GAM's acceptance of Aceh's place within Indonesia, the center would permit its fighters to play their part in the regional election of officials that was agreed for April 2006, though eventually held only the following December. This agreement waived Sukarno's rule that only nationally organized political parties could contest elections in Indonesia and gave GAM activists the opportunity to campaign as independents and to create or support an Aceh-specific party.[4]

[4] The full text is available at http://www.cmi.fi/files/Aceh_MoU.pdf [Accessed March 3, 2009.].

A greater test as to whether the post-revolutionary period had passed was the need to get through the Indonesian Parliament a "Law on Governing Aceh" that would embody these concessions in Indonesian law, replacing the 2001 NAD law. Just as in the former Soviet Union, the favorable window of opportunity making it possible for democratization to translate into self-determination for disgruntled minorities had lasted only for about three years after 1998. Nationalist rhetoric quickly reestablished itself among elected members of Parliament, making many of them more resistant to asymmetric concessions than the government itself. Centralist sentiments were equally strong in the Ministry of Home Affairs, which produced a draft for Parliament sharply different from both the Helsinki agreement and the draft proposed by legislators and officials in Aceh itself. When Parliament did enact the much-debated law four months behind schedule, in July 2006, it provoked a one-day strike in Aceh and much criticism from international stakeholders in the peace process. It was even harsher in spirit than in practice, reasserting Jakarta's overarching sovereignty by inserting central government oversight into virtually all areas.[5]

The changes on the ground, nevertheless, are already a significant departure from Indonesia's unitarist traditions. These changes brought GAM into mainstream politics, allowing one of its intellectuals, Irwandi Yusuf, to take office as an elected Governor in February 2007 through an electoral process that was unique to Aceh. The Aceh concessions have inaugurated a first step toward asymmetric government after sixty years in which the momentum was entirely in the other direction, toward imposing legal and bureaucratic uniformity on an exceptionally diverse society. The concessions support Michael Keating's argument that accepting differential claims on the state can be the strategy that is most compatible with justice and democracy when communities have very different histories and memories (Keating 2001, pp. viii, 102–33). A distinctive memory by Acehnese of both Aceh's own pre-colonial sultanate and its unusual relationship to the state nationalism of Jakarta requires some acknowledgment of Aceh's difference. If it turns out that an anomalous or asymmetric status is the only way to keep Aceh within Indonesia peacefully, Indonesia will have discovered through a bitter and painful route a formula that Malaysia had had thrust upon it at birth.

---

[5] See Taufiqurrahman (2006) "Aceh Bill Passed Despite Opposition," *Jakarta Post*, July 18, 2006, and International Crisis Group (2006) "Aceh: Now for the Hard Part", *Asia Briefing* [Online] 48(29), March. Available at: http://www.crisisgroup.org/home/index. cfm?id=4049 [Accessed April 6, 2009].

MALAYSIA'S ASYMMETRY AS CONTRASTING CASE

In complete contrast with Indonesia's path to independence, in Malaysia the communists, the only group with the arms and ideology to move, did not seize the revolutionary opportunity presented by the Japanese surrender. The British Commonwealth forces, in alliance with the conservative Malay establishment, subsequently defeated and marginalized the Malayan Communist Party. While its cadres in principle shared with Indonesian revolutionaries a view of undivided and equal sovereignty, leaving no place for historic or ethnic particularities, they were too culturally Chinese and oriented to the PRC leadership to appeal effectively to other ethnic groups. What prevailed was therefore a pragmatic British style of compromise and constitutional complexity, stitching together radically dissimilar constitutional entities as well as ethnically very diverse populations.

The defining moment of Malay nationalism occurred in the same frenzied period when Indonesians were overthrowing their traditional rulers, but led in the opposite direction. The party that channeled Malay nationalism for the subsequent sixty years, UMNO, emerged from the struggle to reject Britain's moves to transfer sovereignty from the nine sultans to a nation-state-like Malayan Union in 1946. While young Indonesians were motivated by "the sovereignty of the people" (*kedaulatan rakyat*), young Malayan Malays campaigned for "sovereignty for His Majesty" (*daulat Tuanku*) (Omar 1993). The British were compelled in effect to erect even more complicated federal arrangements than they had anticipated, making allowance for the maximum continuity between nine separate Malay sovereignties and the new state. Recent studies have confirmed the dominant hand of Britain in designing the architecture of independence (1957) as well as the formation of a broader Malaysia that included Singapore, Sarawak, and Sabah (1963) (Fernando 2002; Harper 1999; Tan 2008). For all this, one can argue that the elaborate series of deals and compromises that made Malaysia possible reflected political reality rather better than the heroic ideal of national unity and solidarity did in Indonesia.

Without a revolution, federalism was the only possibility to emerge from this situation. By detaching Chinese-majority Singapore and suppressing a Chinese-dominated communist insurgency, the British had stitched together a Federation of Malaya in 1948 that became independent in 1957. It linked the nine Malay monarchies, each jealous of its sovereignty, with the two cosmopolitan settlements of Melaka and Penang under appointed governors. The headship of state, rotating among the nine sultans, retained British-era rights over religious affairs and land, while elected state and federal governments took over from the British the business of running the booming economies and multination societies. The federation became still more asymmetric with the formation of Malaysia in 1963. The problem of pro-China sentiment in Singapore was resolved by bundling it into the federation with fewer elected representatives than its population warranted. By giving more seats than their populations merited to the new Borneo states of Sarawak and Sabah, the government also intended to balance the Chinese majority. Brunei's autocratic Sultan Omar Ali Saifuddin proved unwilling to accept a position equivalent to one of the Malayan sultans and eventually went his own way to independence. Singapore enjoyed autonomies in financial and legal arrangements, and Sarawak and Sabah in internal migration into their states. There were reassuring guarantees (overridden in time) about maintaining the place of English and resisting the hegemony of Islam in the newly joining states.

These makeshift arrangements are not universally accepted as a success (Case 2007). Singapore's departure after only two years in the federation demonstrated its internal tensions and left Kuala Lumpur and the Malay-dominated federal government more dominant over the states than had been envisaged. Yet, in contrast to East Timor's entry and exit from Indonesia, Singapore's story seems a triumph of pragmatism and peacefulness. In addition to different states having different rights, Malaysia's asymmetry extends to a multiethnic form, whereby "Malays, Chinese, and Indians" (often forgetting the numerous minorities, especially in Sarawak and Sabah) are accepted as separate ethnic groups with different claims on the state. In East Malaysia, diverse indigenous peoples have better claims to indigeneity than most Malays but lack the political leverage to draw similar benefits for themselves. They nevertheless succeeded, in 1995, in having two of their languages, Iban in Sarawak and Kadazandusun in Sabah, accepted into the state curriculum in their respective states (Reid 1997), succeeding where far stronger ethnic groups in Indonesia failed.

In marked contrast to post-revolutionary Indonesia, which heroically asserted the sovereignty and equality of all its people, Malaya/Malaysia emerged as a typically British muddle of inconsistencies and compromises. The Malaysian state appears permanently flawed by its inability to treat its citizens equally, even in law, and still less in political rhetoric. These inconsistencies came about through the pragmatic compromises, often British-inspired, deemed necessary to bring different groups into the state (if not altogether the nation). By comparison with the revolutionary assertions of principle in Indonesia, they look messy and morally indefensible, yet they have on the whole kept the peace and made possible both an economic growth and a stable democracy that are the envy of Malaysia's neighbors.

CONCLUSION

Indonesia's post-revolutionary unitarism, like that of France and China, has achieved remarkable success in turning "peasants into Indonesians," and liberating its people from entrenched differences of class, race, and descent. In the very long term, this should prove to be a source of great strength for the nation-state. This spectacular achievement, however, has come at a very high cost over the first sixty years. The issues that can be readily measured, such as the toll of violence (horrendous in Indonesia, especially in 1965–1966 and 1996–2005 – Anderson 2001; Coppel 2004) and economic performance, suggest that Malaysian asymmetry has been far more successful than Indonesia's unitary state (Reid 2007, pp. 157–62). The overriding of legality involved in the revolutionary path also had incalculable costs for Indonesia's legal system, while the need for affluent minorities to buy protection rather than rely on legal and constitutional guarantees has helped corrode the military and bureaucracy with corruption.

Given the extreme heterogeneity of the Archipelago and its historic resistance to bureaucratic states of any kind, it may be that the quasi-mystical space that a unitary Indonesian Republic sought to fill in its people's imagining was the only way it could perform the miracle of nation building. Yet there were also clear dangers in this path, indicated by the steadily greater role the military came to play in state affairs between 1945 and 1980 and its frequent resort to force to suppress dissent. While Indonesia's course looked more promising than Malaysia's in the 1950s, the reverse has been the case at most periods since. However, the remarkably democratic outcome of the 1998 *reformasi*, including the readiness to attempt new solutions in East Timor and Aceh and the legislation for regional autonomy in general, may mean that the balance sheet is about to turn again, and Indonesia may prove able to experiment more effectively from its unitary foundation than can Malaysia from its entrenched asymmetries.

3

The Crisis of Border States in India

Rajeev Bhargava

There are many reasons for the crisis of several so-called border states in India. My objective in this chapter is not to summarize the causal narrative of these crises. Rather, I wish to draw the attention of the reader to one factor to which enough attention has not been paid. My very tentative claim appears to be in line with the main contention of the editors of this book: the governing elite in India, perhaps even the larger political elite, has always had a conceptual block about recognizing multiple nationalities in India. But this way of putting it may, in the Indian case, be too crude. I am not suggesting that India should have been named and understood as a multination state from its very inception. My point, I believe, is more subtle: given India's size and complexity, it should have recognized and worked with what might be called a deeply asymmetrical federalism that recognized some societies within it as nations but not others. Over time, the governing elite in India did imagine an inclusive-enough state in India, one that granted recognition to different cultural communities, but it just fell short of grasping the precise form of recognition for which some societies increasingly yearned. This was a political as much as a conceptual failure. Moreover, the hold of some conceptions was so strong that the elites could not imagine an even more inclusive variety of federalism. Instead of responding even more democratically to multilayered difference, the Indian state, which had recognized difference fairly early, responded to it with force. Furthermore, it could not imagine that the organizational principle of different states could itself be very different,

Acknowledgments are due to Ritupan Goswami for assisting me with research on this chapter.

that some regional units could be formed on the basis of language, others on the basis of religion, and still others on the basis of traditional ways of living. Only then could groups with multilayered differences – in religion, language, and an entire way of life – be accommodated within a single state. The crisis of border states in India must be accounted *also* in terms of this deeper conceptual failure.

The chapter is divided into three parts. In the first section, I briefly outline the four different conceptions of nation-states that have been prevalent in India since the late nineteenth century. In the second, I provide a brief history of how the country slowly gravitated from one to the other of these conceptions and how institutional arrangements in India came to embody a conception that helped establish India as a linguistically federal nation-state. In the third section, I argue that neither this conception of the nation-state nor the linguistically federal state that flows from it satisfactorily captures or fits the ever-deepening multilayered diversity of India. So, this move from one to the other conception of nation-state does not take India far enough. Since the governing elites of India were not willing to take the important further step, they contributed to the crisis of Indian federalism and nationalism. To demonstrate this, I use the example of the way the Indian state dealt with the aspirations of the Nagas.

FOUR CONCEPTIONS

Roughly a century before India achieved independence from British colonial rule, two basic models of nationalism developed in the subcontinent, yielding four different conceptions. The first model, as succinctly articulated much later by Gellner, manifested the idea that a community bounded by a single culture must have its own state. This model generated two conceptions. One defined culture in ethno-religious terms and was embraced and advocated by the Hindu Mahasabha and the Muslim League – *ethno-religious nationalism*. In this view, both Hindus and Muslims, defined respectively by their common religious allegiances, were separate nations. For the Hindu Mahasabha, Indian nationalism simply had to be Hindu nationalism. The entire territory of the subcontinent was the home of Hindus, and other communities whose religion was born outside the subcontinent could live in India only at the sufferance of Hindus, at best as second-class citizens. This primacy of Hindu identity had consequences not only for Muslims and Christians but also for those Hindus who considered other identity-constituting features equally, if not more important. For Hindu nationalists, to be a Hindu was of overriding importance, much more so than, say, being a Tamil, Telugu, or Punjabi. Hindu nationalists define their culture as possessing a thick unity of purpose and as a friction-free whole.

The second manifestation of this conception of nationalism was articulated by vulgar Nehruvians, including occasionally by Nehru himself.[1] This view accepted the premise that a nation is defined by a common culture and that a people whose identity is constituted by that common culture must have a state of their own, but their idea of common culture was not ethno-religious. The common Indian culture, in this view, was defined by shared historical experience and a joint struggle against British colonial rule. It was also constituted by cultural elements generated out of the interpenetration of beliefs, values, and practices that, when they first encountered one another, were separate. For want of a better term, let us call this *composite-culture nationalism*. The substance of this composite-culture nationalism is very different from Hindu or Muslim nationalism. Here, because cultural identity is not defined in ethno-religious terms, the ensuing nationalism is far more inclusive. However, the basic form of composite-culture nationalism is not very different from Hindu nationalism, and as a result it has equally negative consequences for those who take particularist identities seriously. Because it is also defined as having a thick unity of purpose, it has a tendency to become exclusionary. Other regional or sub-national identities are thrown to the margins, reduced to near insignificance.

The second model of nationalism does not require that a culture be defined in terms of a thick unity of purpose. It insists on a common culture but not that the particular cultures of different regions or communities be seen by their adherents to be of less overall significance. It seeks only contextual priority of common culture and generally attempts to create mechanisms and policies by which possible conflicts and hard choices in favor of one or the other are prevented.

This model also comes in two versions. The first, which I call *coalescent nationalism*, is willing to recognize that each of the separate cultures within India is more or less self-sufficient, approximating what Kymlicka calls the "societal culture," one that is territorially concentrated and has the potential to organize from within its own resources a large number

---

[1] By vulgar Nehruvian, I mean a position that read and understood Nehru's writings crudely, entirely removing their complexity, nuance, and subtlety and converting his ideas into a simplistic perspective capable of generating only blunt policy instruments. This view was formulated by some of Nehru's more radical followers and later, in a certain phase of her political career, by Indira Gandhi.

of important educational, legal, economic, political, and media-related public and private institutions (Kymlicka 1995, p. 75). In short, each federal unit is more or less a distinct society. And yet, these distinct societies see themselves as part of a larger, equally significant common culture. If the commitment of every subunit within this larger polity to the common culture is strong, then a state linked to this common culture cannot be called a multinational state. It is a fairly strong coalescent nation-state of multiple but distinct societies, each with some form of limited but largely acceptable self-government rights. This is an ethnically demarcated federal state. One might even say that this is a multinational state without labels, one that does not call itself such.

The second of these two versions is not shy about calling itself a multinational state. In short, it accepts that a single state can work even with dual or multiple nationalities and with different conceptions of what constitutes a nation. Here each group defines its culture and identity as it sees fit and organizes its state in terms of a self-endorsed organizational principle. This results in a robust, deeply federal state, parts of which are multinational. This is a *loosely coalescing nationalism* in which a single nation-state is seen to be always in the process of being achieved rather than presumed to be already accomplished. The difference between the two versions is minor but important because one model sees a unified nation-state as an achieved *condition* while the other views it as a never-ending *process*, a permanent possibility that is internally riven with unavoidable but manageable tension.

Which of these conceptions have been realized in India? In the 1930s, each of the first three conceptions, ethno-religious, composite-culture, and coalescent nationalism, were at play among political elites in India. By the 1940s, however, coalescent nationalism had been submerged by the other two, which emerged as the only two serious contenders in the game. The impending success of Muslim League nationalism plunged composite-culture nationalism into crisis. Yet, when the Constitution was adopted in 1950, India rejected ethno-religious Hindu nationalism. Instead, it adopted composite-culture nationalism, installing it as the official ideology of the Indian state. It was not long, however, before this official conception faced yet another serious crisis. Coalescent nationalism, which had been put on the backburner, came right back into the game as India shifted its allegiance slowly toward it. This coalescent nationalism has served India well for several but not all groups. It has been severely inadequate for the border states of India. An important reason for this is that, having come so close to inclusion, finding ways to bring these groups into the Indian polity, the political elite in India has failed to take the important next step: timely recognition of their distinct national identities.

To amplify this point, India's complexity is such that it can only be run by a *deeply asymmetrical federalism*. A form of federalism that is merely asymmetrical does not question that there is just one basis, say language, on which the constituent units of the federation are formed. The boundaries of states are determined roughly in accordance with the location of speakers of the dominant language in different parts of the country. Thus, Indian federalism is symmetrical in the sense that all its constituent units are grounded in a single, uniform principle. But equally, it is asymmetrical, as a result of the varying needs of different linguistic units. But another possible form of asymmetry may arise from variation in the grounding principle itself. Here, the bases on which the subunits of the federation are formed are different. Some boundaries are drawn, for example, on the basis of language, others on the basis of religion, and still others by a distinct culture formed by layers of deep differences in language, religion, and a way of life. This is what I call *deeply asymmetrical federalism*, one that accepts plural foundations for state organization because in these societies multiple pluralities go very deep; yet people may be able to live together if political recognition is given to different grounding principles of the constituent units of a federation. This means, as I mentioned, that some subunits may call themselves linguistic regions within the Indian nation-state, and some may call themselves distinct nations within a multinational state. Thus, deeply asymmetrical federalism allows for different peoples of India to see it either as a coalescent-national or as a multinational state. It gives each people the cultural autonomy of collective self-definition and the choice of owning up or not owning up to a label that is commonly regarded as significant. For some, it is significant and therefore owned up. For others, it is also significant and for that very reason given up. While asymmetrical federalism is tied to a strong coalescent nationalism, deeply asymmetrical federalism is linked to a loosely coalescing nationalism.

A failure to recognize the above distinction and therefore deeply asymmetrical federalism has led to rigidities within the political system and among policy makers. It has resulted in unwarranted violence from the state and led to a vicious and pathological syndrome. Later in the chapter, I shall try to explain this point in some detail. But before doing so, it is important to give a historical narrative of how we came to be where we are.

EVOLUTION OF LINGUISTIC FEDERALISM AND COALESCENT NATIONALISM IN INDIA

Although it is true that the federal idea had some resonance in non-modern traditions, the current federal arrangement in India has its origins in colonial modernity. Under British colonialism, provinces were the result of an ad hoc and completely arbitrary process of annexation, accomplished by outright conquest, by treaties that lapsed from a combination of maneuvering and neglect, or that had been negotiated under conditions of unequal bargaining strength. All these large provinces were multilingual and multiethnic. They were not the result of a policy of divide and rule, a key instrument of colonial power but, once formed, they were certainly sustained by such a policy. In many cases, people speaking the same language were broken up to form parts of different provinces. This happened, for example, to the Oriyas, the Kannadigan, and the Marathas. The vastness of the empire – the sheer size of its territory – compelled the British to devolve power to these provinces. Yet no matter how substantive the devolution of authority to the provinces under the 1919 Government of India Act, nor how apparently federal the provisions of the 1935 Act, power was centralized and always in British hands.[2] This was to shape the political structure of independent India in the initial period of its formation.

Early resistance to colonialism did little to unsettle the multilinguistic and multiethnic character of provinces. Later, the necessity of broadening the base of resistance, turning it into a mass anti-colonial struggle, made it very tempting for political movements to mobilize on the basis of linguistic, or even religious, identities. The Indian National Congress,[3]

---

[2] The British government attempted a series of reforms to address the problems of their empire in India. The first of these reforms resulted in the Government of India Act of 1919. This Act introduced substantial changes in provincial administration such as the transference of subjects such as local self-government, education, and law and order becoming the preserve of provinces. Legislative and executive power in the provinces increased on an unprecedented scale, though a small franchise and limited availability of finances continued to present serious limitations. Similarly, in the early 1930s, the imperial government invited prominent Indians to three Round Table Conferences in London in which along with British politicians they discussed the making of a new constitution with which to govern India. These discussions finally took shape in the 1935 Government of India Act. The Act was a recognition by the government that the continuation of the empire in India posed a massive political problem for which an immediate political solution had to be found. Its main aim was to "buttress the empire not to liquidate it." However, for all its limitations it was a major experiment in the devolution of power in a non-white part of the British Empire. For details, see Brown (1994, pp. 205–9; pp. 251–316).

[3] The Indian National Congress was formed in 1885 by Indians educated in Britain. It was inspired by Dadabhai Nauroji who lived in the imperial capital and attempted not only

the main protagonist of the freedom struggle, recognized the potential of having relatively stable ethno-linguistic territorial identities. To channel this potential and ensure that it was tapped exclusively for an anti-colonial struggle that would be aimed at building an inclusive civic nationalism, it evolved an organizational framework for the integration of such linguistic identities into a newly imagined political community. The *pradesh*, a democratic, ethnically sensitive alternative to the colonial province, was projected as the basic territorial unit of a new federation. Language was to be the organizational basis of each pradesh. Thus, sub-national linguistic identities were recognized and given their legitimate due, but in a manner that contributed to the larger civic national identity. By 1920, the Congress decided to reorganize all its units along linguistic lines. From then on, national politics began systematically to draw deeper sustenance from various aspects of these language-based regional cultures. The Congress recognized, not only that the struggle for Indian nationalism had to be pursued along federal lines, but also that a responsible, representative government of the future needed a linguistically organized federal state. At the Karachi Session of the Congress (1929), a policy of giving substantial powers to the provinces was adopted. Gandhi, in particular, realized the significance of ethnic identities and sought to forge a unity without glossing over the country's diversities. The Cabinet Mission Plan,[4] in 1946, envisaged a very weak center in a confederation-like arrangement. The jurisdiction of the union was to be limited to foreign affairs, defense, communications, and the power to raise money in order to finance these functions. All other subjects were to be within the jurisdiction of provinces. They were also to be vested with residuary powers. Thus, until as late as the 1940s, there was little disagreement about the need for a federal constitution.

to foster a sense of Indian identity but to pressure British rulers to make public policies more sensitive to Indian needs. Until the First World War, it remained a pressure group, composed of elites who wanted more recognition from the British Empire and greater participation in its activities. Later, largely due to efforts of Gandhi, it became a mass organization and demanded, at first a greater degree of autonomy and, later, complete independence from the British Empire.

[4] The Cabinet Mission put forward a plan for a three-tiered constitution of a federation, groups of provinces which chose to act together for agreed topics, and provinces at the base. This plan was at the center of a fierce controversy between the Indian National Congress and the Muslim League. The Congress President, Nehru made it clear that once an Indian Constituent Assembly came into being it would not be bound by the Cabinet Mission Plan, particularly on the issue of voluntary grouping by provinces. The League then rejected this plan on the ground that the new Constituent Assembly might not safeguard the interests of Muslim majority areas (see Brown 1994, p. 334).

Along with the idea of language-based federal units, however, came the notion of religion-based segments and constituencies. Just as the partition of Bengal in 1905 had propelled movements of linguistic solidarity everywhere, its annulment[5] consolidated a trend toward the possible organization of political units based on religion. The idea of separate electorates for Muslims had always found favor with Muslim elites. Had Muslims been dispersed more evenly in the territory of the subcontinent, and had they not been a majority in some provinces, both religion and language could have been given political recognition without practical contradiction. Self-governing units could have been drawn along linguistic lines and special representation rights could have been given to religious minorities. But a large concentration of Muslims in North-West India and in East Bengal ensured that either religion or language could become the basis of self-governing political units, and therefore both religion and language began to compete for the same political space. This conflict between two competing forms of ethnicity suited the designs of the imperial power. To contain the growing popularity of the national movement, the British exploited the religious division and proposed a power-sharing arrangement that included representation along ethno-religious lines. A parallel mobilization process was then set in motion on the basis of religious differences. From then on, the Muslim elite felt that provinces grounded purely on language reflected a Hindu bias. Now, one ethnic principle of self-government was to be in continuous conflict with another ethnic principle of self-government.

As is well known, the independence of India was accompanied by its partition along religious lines. This had a traumatic impact on the psyche of members of the Congress party. Most of them began to be obsessively concerned with the dangers of further fragmentation and disintegration and began to view with suspicion the political expression of even linguistic identities. No one was more uneasy with these identities than Nehru himself. During the course of his work on the Committee that inquired into the demand for the linguistic organization of states, Nehru wrote:

---

[5] Partition came about because Bengalis, with a strong linguistic identity felt that the imperial government had sought illegitimately to divide them. This led to a burst of solidarity. Once Bengal was divided, however, it also created a Muslim majority in East Bengal and a Hindu majority in West Bengal. This helped foster the politicization of religious identities and the birth of the idea that a religious community can be the sole bearer of all economic, social, and political interests. The annulment of partition destroyed the "communal" hopes of Muslim elites in East Bengal.

[This inquiry] has been in some ways an eye-opener for us. The work of 60 years of the Indian National Congress was standing before us, face to face with centuries-old India of narrow loyalties, petty jealousies and ignorant prejudices engaged in mortal conflict and we were simply horrified to see how thin was the ice upon which we were skating. Some of the ablest men in the country came before us and confidently and emphatically stated that language in this country stood for and represented culture, race, history, individuality, and finally a sub-nation. (quoted in Banerjee 1992, p. 56)

Both ethno-religious and coalescent nationalisms were rejected. The unitary mindset that had been shaped by the experience of a centralized colonial state was now resurrected, and for a while, it appeared that the idea of a multicultural Indian federation was lost forever. Although it was committed to the maintenance of pluralism and to granting of powers to provinces, the Congress reversed its stand after independence, giving the security and unity of India as its primary reasons. It is true that Nehru believed that "some kind of re-organization" was "inevitable," but he was convinced that language must be supplemented by cultural, geographic, and economic factors. The question of linguistic provinces was examined by a special committee appointed by the Constituent Assembly. After an exhaustive inquiry, this committee, known as the Dar Commission, concluded that "the formation of provinces on exclusively or even mainly linguistic considerations is not in the larger interests of the Indian nation and should not be taken in hand." Another three-member committee that included Nehru was appointed by the Congress to examine the report of the Dar Commission and make final recommendations. This committee also felt that "the present is not an opportune moment for the formation of new provinces." Yet, they conceded that "if public sentiment is insistent and overwhelming, we, as democrats, have to submit to it, but subject to certain limitations in regard to the good of India as a whole..." They all agreed that the assembly must not attempt to solve the problem "when passions are roused," but "at a suitable moment when the time is ripe for it."

Given the vast size and diversity of the country, however, federalism in India was less a matter of choice than of necessity. India has eight major religious systems, at least fifteen major language groups and about sixty sociocultural subregions with distinct sub-national identities. India also has one of the largest tribal populations in the world. This, along with its huge population, made it impossible for India to be anything but "a continental federal polity constituted into a single territory" (Khan 1992, p.2). (See Tables 3.1, 3.2, and 3.3 below on the multicultural base of India.)

TABLE 3.1 *Population by religion (India)*

Religions	1971 Number (Million)	1971 % to Total	1981 Number (Million)	1981 % to Total	1991 Number (Million)	1991 % to Total	2001 Number (Million)	2001 % to Total
Hindus	453.3	82.7	549.7	82.6	672.6	82.41	828.0	80.5
Muslims	61.4	11.2	75.6	11.4	95.2	11.67	138.0	13.4
Christians	14.2	2.6	16.2	2.4	18.9	2.32	24.0	2.3
Sikhs	10.4	1.9	13.1	2.0	16.3	1.99	19.0	1.9
Buddhists	3.8	0.7	4.7	0.7	6.3	0.77	8.0	0.8
Jains	2.6	0.5	3.2	0.5	3.4	0.41	4.0	0.4
Others[1]	2.2	0.4	2.8	0.4	3.5	0.43	7.0	0.7
Total	548.2	100.0	665.3	100.0	816.2[2]	100.0	1028.0	100.0

Including unclassified persons.
Excludes Assam and J&K.

Note: 1981 data do not include Assam.

Source: 1) *Census of India,1981, Series I, Paper 1 of 1995 (Religion), Paper 1 of 1991 (Religion)*.
2) *Census of India, 2001, The First Report on Religion Data.*

TABLE 3.2 *Population by major language group (India)*

	Number (in Million)		Percentage	
Languages	1971	1981	1971	1981
Hindi	208.5	264.5	38.0	42.9
Bengali	44.8	51.3	8.2	8.3
Telugu	44.8	50.6	8.2	8.2
Marathi	41.8	49.5	7.6	8.0
Tamil	37.7	3.8	6.9	0.6
Urdu	28.6	34.9	5.2	5.7
Gujarati	25.9	33.1	4.7	5.4
Malayalam	21.9	25.7	4.0	4.2
Kannada	21.7	25.7	4.0	4.2
Oriya	19.9	23.0	3.6	3.7
Punjabi	14.1	19.16	2.6	3.2
Assamese	9.0	0.1	1.6	0.01
Sindhi	1.7	2.0	0.3	0.3
Kashmiri	2.5	3.2	0.5	0.5

Notes: This statement excludes Assam as no census was taken there due to disturbed conditions at the time of the 1981 Census.
This statement excludes language figures of Tamil Nadu as the entire record of Tamil Nadu state under "P" sample have been lost due to floods at the time of the 1981 Census.
Source: *Census of India, Part IV-B(ii) Series-I India-1981.*

But although its federal character had the air of inevitability, the form it assumed and the justifications for it, did not. India was formed as a federation, but the second tier of government was justified primarily in functional terms. Thus, despite a strong social base for federalism, its institutional expression, at least in the initial period, was weak. Arguably, this was due to the anxieties of a newly empowered political elite, which showed a lack of faith in the power of the democratic process to appropriately articulate and channel ethno-regional aspirations in such a way that they led neither to violent conflicts nor toward separation. Nehru's reasons for being reluctant to endorse a linguistic organization of states, however, had some merit. First, he believed that a federation structured along ethno-linguistic lines would give some politicians an opportunity to mobilize permanently on the basis of language and give rise to regional chauvinism. This, he feared, might divert attention from issues of welfare and material well-being. Second, such

TABLE 3.3 *States and union territories by population size (India)*

Rank in 1991	State/Union Territory	Population 1991	Population 2001
1	Uttar Pradesh	39,112,287	166,197,921
2	Bihar	86,374,465	82,998,509
3	Maharashtra	78,937,187	96,878,627
4	West Bengal	68,077,965	80,176,197
5	Andhra Pradesh	66,508,008	76,210,007
6	Madhya Pradesh	66,181,170	60,348,023
7	Tamil Nadu	55,858,946	62,405,679
8	Karnataka	44,977,201	52,850,562
9	Rajasthan	44,005,990	56,507,188
10	Gujarat	41,309,582	50,671,017
11	Orissa	31,659,736	36,804,660
12	Kerala	29,098,518	31,841,374
13	Assam	22,414,322	26,655,528
14	Punjab	20,281,969	24,358,999
15	Haryana	16,463,648	21,144,564
16	Delhi	9,420,644	13,850,507
17	Jammu and Kashmir	7,718,700	10,143,700
18	Himachal Pradesh	5,170,877	6,077,900
19	Tripura	2,757,205	3,199,203
20	Manipur	1,837,149	2,293,896
21	Meghalaya	1,774,778	2,318,822
22	Nagaland	1,209,546	1,990,036
23	Goa	1,169,793	1,347,668
24	Arunachal Pradesh	864,558	1,097,968
25	Pondicherry	807,785	974,345
26	Mizoram	689,756	888,573
27	Chandigarh	642,015	900,635
28	Sikkim	406,457	540,851
29	Andaman & Nicobar	280,661	356,152
30	Dadra & Nagar Haveli	138,477	220,490
31	Daman & Diu	101,586	158,204
32	Lakshadweep	51,707	60,650

Rank in 1991	State/Union / Territory	Population 1991	2001
33	Chhattisgarh		20,833,803
34	Jharkhand		26,945,829
35	Uttarakhand		8,489,349

Notes: 1) The 1991 Census was not held in Jammu and Kashmir. The population projections of Jammu and Kashmir as on March 1, 1991 made by the Standing Committee of Experts on Population Projections (October 1989) is given.
Source: Census of India 1991 final population totals (1) PCA Part-II-B(i), 1991 (2) PCA-Part-IIB(i), 1981 (PPXX).

2) The total population and rural population include estimated population of 127,108 for Mao Maram, Paomata, and Purul subdivisions of Senapati district of Manipur. India's population without the estimated population of these areas is 1,028,610,328 (532,156,772 males and 496,453,556 females).
Source: Census of India 2001.

a federation would "freeze" ethno-linguistic identities, or certain forms thereof. The fluidity, flexibility, and multiplicity of identities would then give way to a valorization of one single identity. It would also prevent the formation of other more inclusive collective identities. But most of all, he feared that these frozen collective identities would increase the likelihood of intra-ethnic violence, encourage separatism, and eventually lead to the balkanization of the country.

This third reason was decisive and gave Indian federalism a strong centralizing and unitary bias. Article 1 of the Constitution speaks of a dual polity.[6] But, because of the provision of single citizenship; a single, integrated judiciary; uniform criminal law for all the states; and a unified all-India Civil Service (see Articles 5, 11, 14, 15, 44, 131–141, 312 of the Constitution), India remains a unified polity. The Constitution gives general supremacy to the Union Parliament and Executive in all matters vis-à-vis the states (Article 365), especially in the making of laws on items that are included in the State List, in the appointment and dismissal

---

[6] The reference to dual polity clearly suggests a commitment to a form of federalism. However, several other features of the Constitution suggest that this federalism was hugely attenuated. The reference to dual polity was made initially by B. R. Ambedkar, the main architect of the Constitution. Introducing the draft Constitution, he said, "The proposed Indian Constitution is a dual polity with a single citizenship. There is only one citizenship for the whole of India... There is no State citizenship." (*Constituent Assembly Debates* VII, I, p.34).

of Governors, in the dismissal of State Ministry officials, and in the appointment of Judges to the States' High Courts. It not only gives the residual powers to the Union (Articles 245–46, 249–54, 356) – a clear index of centralization – but also envisages easy and flexible procedures of constitutional amendment (Article 368) and assigns a larger share of the revenue and a greater fiscal authority to the center (Part XII). But more even than this, it has provided a legitimate means, in the form of emergency powers (Articles 352–360) to enable the center to transform the federal system into a virtually unitary system under three conditions: external aggression or internal disturbance; breakdown of the machinery of law and order; and threat of financial breakdown. There is no right of secession for the states, on the principle that, in Ambedkar's words, "the union is indestructible." The Union also has the authority to create new states, adjust boundaries between states, and generally restructure the Indian Union (Articles 2–3). The President's rule in the states, which was declared ninety-five times between 1951 and 1995 (that is, on average, more than twice a year for the last forty years) and the dramatic imposition of a state of national emergency between June 1975 and March 1977 underlined the capacity of the center to dominate the federal polity.[7]

When the Constitution was inaugurated in 1950, the country was divided into four kinds of states. There were the Part A states – former provinces of British India, such as Assam, Bihar, Bombay, Madras, Orissa, Punjab, Uttar Pradesh, and West Bengal. There were Part B states, which resulted from the integration of the princely states. These included Hyderabad, Jammu and Kashmir, Mysore, Rajasthan, Saurashtra, Madhya Bharat, and Travancore Cochin. Part C states were either the former Chief Commissioner's provinces or units formed by the integration of princely states. These included Ajmer, Bhopal, Delhi, Himachal Pradesh, Kutch, Manipur, and Tripura. Finally, there was one Part D

---

[7] On June 26, 1975, the President of India, at the request of the Indian Prime Minister Mrs. Indira Gandhi, imposed a national Emergency on the ground that there was a grave internal threat to the security of the country. In fact, the move was propelled by a massive opposition to her continuation in office. In 1973–1974, food shortages and rising prices had produced violent demonstrations in several Congress-ruled states. In 1974, Jayaprakash Narayan, one-time Congress member, a socialist and a friend of Nehru, took the leadership of the agitation in the Indian state of Bihar and offered a direct personal challenge to the authoritarian rule of Mrs. Gandhi. In June, 1975, the Allahabad High Court invalidated the election of Mrs. Gandhi on grounds of corrupt practices. A mass mobilization campaign was launched against Mrs. Gandhi who responded by arresting all her principal opponents and unleashing a short period of terror.

state – the Andaman and Nicobar Islands. As is evident, this structure was the result of historical accident rather than the realization of a coherent principle for the organization of territories.

This system of states, based on the absorption of ethnic identities into a larger civic identity and therefore on the rejection of every trace of ethnonationalism, proved inadequate. As Rajni Kothari (1988, p. 225), pointed out, it began to fall apart when, thanks to its democratic nature, it was forced to encounter mass politics. Demands were immediately made by regional and ethnic leaders for autonomy and for political power sharing. The issue of linguistic states became the focus of popular agitation. After a massive agitation in 1953, the state of Andhra Pradesh, where a large number of Telugu-speaking people live, was created. This once again foregrounded the question of whether the entire structure of states in India should be reorganized on a linguistic basis. In 1954, the States Reorganisation Commission was set up. In the committee, the advocates of linguistic reorganization gave the following reasons in its favor. First, the creation of such states would remove the frustration and anxieties of minorities within the existing heterogeneous regions. Second, the alleviation of tensions and internal harmony within regions that would result would foster national unity. Third, a unilingual region would involve less administrative complexity, thereby enhancing administrative efficiency. Fourth, political units with a greater degree of homogeneity would encourage internal cohesiveness within regions and facilitate more democratic governments locally and at the central level (see Narang 2003, pp. 74–5).

Based on the Commission's recommendations, Indian states were reorganized in 1956. Instead of the four-tier structure, there were now only states and union territories. Even so, the linguistic principle was only partially recognized. It took another mass agitation to divide the province of Bombay into Maharashtra and Gujarat. In 1966, Punjab was reorganized into three units: the core Punjabi Suba, the new state of Haryana, and Himachal Pradesh. Several new states have since been carved out in response to popular agitation. These include not only the states of the North-East but, more recently, the states of Jharkhand, Chattisgarh, and Uttaranchal. Although the Constitution did not originally envisage it, India is now a multilingual federation. Each major linguistic group is politically recognized and all are treated as equals.

It is of course true that this political recognition does not cover every large linguistic community. Only the languages that had received official recognition under British rule, undergone some grammatical standardization and literary development, and become entrenched in the government schools in a particular region could claim to be dominant. Such a claim itself required immense political mobilization. Only linguistic groups that were capable of this mobilization could be granted equal political recognition. The current form of linguistic federalism in India depends, as Paul Brass demonstrates (1990, pp. 172–4), on four formal and informal rules.

The first rule is that no secessionist demand shall be recognized. The Indian Constitution does not give any state the right to secede and can therefore suppress such an effort using force. The Indian army has ruthlessly suppressed secessionist demands of tribal groups in the North-East and of groups in Assam and Punjab, and it continues to be militarily engaged in Kashmir. Whenever a linguistic group has dropped its secessionist demands, however, as the Dravida Munnetra Kazhagam (DMK) did in Tamil Nadu in 1960s, the Government of India (GOI) has made concessions and even granted statehood to placate leaders of groups that were previously dubbed secessionist. The second rule is that the state shall not accommodate the religious principle of state organization. It took a long time for the Indian state to reorganize Punjab along linguistic lines because it was widely believed that the creation of a Punjabi-speaking state would merely be a cover for a Sikh-majority state. A separate Punjabi-speaking state became acceptable only when the sincerity and loyalty of the leader of the Punjabi Suba movement was believed to be entirely trustworthy. The third rule is that the mere existence of a distinct language group shall not be sufficient to justify the formation of a separate political subunit of the federation. Such language groups had to find political articulation. Even political articulation was not enough, however, if it was limited to the cultural or literary elite; it had to have popular backing. Without democratic legitimacy, no language could be the basis of a new state. Finally, the fourth rule: the reorganization of a province was unacceptable if the demand for it was made by only one of the important language groups in the area. Thus, Madras was reorganized because it had the backing of both Tamil-speaking and Telugu-speaking peoples, but Bombay had to wait until 1960 because reorganization had the support only of the Marathi-speaking people and was not backed by the Gujaratis.

The reorganization of states on the basis of language gave equal recognition and dignity to all dominant language groups.[8] Throughout much of India, democratic and linguistic federalism has managed to combine

---

[8] I do not address here the question of how these states have fared in the treatment of their own internal linguistic minorities. Generally speaking, the picture is very mixed. Several state governments have pursued a discriminatory policy toward their minorities.

claims to unity with claims to cultural recognition. India's transition from composite culture-nationalism to coalescent nationalism has been reasonably successful and has resulted in a federalism with some noteworthy features. First, despite the initial unitary bias of the Indian constitution, there are important constitutionally embedded differences between the legal status and prerogatives of different subunits within the same federation. Unlike the constitutional symmetry of American federalism, Indian federalism has been constitutionally asymmetric. In a sense then, just as India in some respects is less federal than the United States, in other respects it is more federal. To meet the specific needs and requirements of some subunits, it was always part of the original design of the constitution farmers to have a unique relationship with them or to give them special status. For example, the accession of Jammu and Kashmir to the Indian union was based on a commitment by the constituent assembly of India to safeguard its autonomy under Article 370 of the Constitution. Kashmir is meant to be governed by its own constitution.

Second, the proper functioning of asymmetrical federalism in India requires contextual reasoning. This reasoning does exist. To a remarkable degree, flexibility and pragmatism are built into several institutional designs in the Indian polity. Politics in India have rarely been a field for the implementation of single principles, and this is how it should be. In politics, one should not try to apply a *single* principle to any given situation. Rather, one should act in every context while keeping several principles in mind. Very occasionally, our actions may realize our principles fully. Sometimes, they may partially embody them. But one must recognize that at other times our actions are unable to realize any of our principles at all. This way of conceiving the relationship between political thinking and political practice differs from a dichotomous way of thinking, according to which one either implements principles perfectly or completely disregards them. It also recognizes that occasionally, in the process of taking action, our principles are modified or even transformed.

This context-sensitive conception of federalism embodies a certain model of contextual moral reasoning. This it must do, because it is a multivalue doctrine that accepts the inevitability of value conflicts and admits that no general, a priori procedure can antecedently arbitrate between competing value claims. Rather, whether one value will outweigh or override others will be decided entirely by the context. Frequently, such situations necessitate a trade-off or compromise, albeit one that is morally defensible. A contextual model of federalism, then, encourages accommodation – not the giving up of one value for the sake of another but rather their reconciliation and possible harmonization. This accommodation may be accomplished in at least two ways (Austin 1966, pp. 308–25): by placing values at different levels and by seeing them, not as belonging to water-tight compartments, but as being sufficiently separate so that an attempt can be made to recognize a value within its own sphere, without being in open conflict with a value operating in a different sphere.

Such an attempt to make concepts, view-points, and values work simultaneously does not amount to a morally objectionable compromise. Nothing of importance is given up for the sake of something less significant – something without value or with negative value. Rather, what is pursued is a mutually agreed middle way that combines elements from two or more equally valuable entities. The roots of such attempts at reconciliation and accommodation lie in a lack of dogmatism, a willingness to experiment and to think at different levels and in separate spheres, and a readiness to make decisions on a provisional basis. It captures a way of thinking that is characterized by the following dictum: why look at things in terms of this or that, why not try to have both this and that? This way of thinking recognizes that, although we may currently be unable to secure the best of both values and are therefore forced to settle for a watered-down version of each, we must continue to have an abiding commitment to search for a way to transcend this second-best condition.

Such contextual reasoning was not atypical of the deliberations of the Constituent Assembly[9] in which great value was placed on arriving at decisions by consensus. Yet the procedure of majority voting was not given up altogether. On issues that everyone judged to be less significant, a majoritarian procedure was adopted. It is by virtue of this kind of reasoning that the Indian constitution appears at once federal and unitary, and why it favors both individual and group-specific rights. If federalism embodies contextual reasoning, it must be understood that this is not private, moral reasoning applied to politics, but rather public, political reasoning infused with a moral character. Third, Indian federalism today is not just of the "holding together" variety but rather has come to possess features of the "coming together" form of federalism, what I have called coalescent nationalism. Regional parties are becoming stronger not only in the regions but also at the center.

[9] The Constituent Assembly was set up in December 1946 to draft the Constitution of independent India. It completed its work in December 1949 and the new Constitution was implemented when India was declared a Republic on January 26, 1950. Between August 15, 1947 and January 26, 1950, the Constituent Assembly became a provisional Parliament.

THE BORDER STATES OF INDIA: PUNJAB, KASHMIR, AND THE NORTH-EAST

I have claimed that there is a fairly robust political arena in India that allows for the play of multiple identities that complement one another. But is this true everywhere? Alas, the linguistic reorganization of states has not been an unqualified success. The greatest problem exists in the border states, such as Punjab, Kashmir, and the North-Eastern states, which have been wracked by secessionist movements.[10] Here, the crisis of federalism is acute and has resulted in bitter, sustained, and violent confrontations between self-determination or secession movements, the Indian army, and national paramilitary forces.

Some argue that secessionist movements grow up only in border states. This happens, they claim, because linguistic or cultural differences, which are accommodated in the rest of India, are exploited by neighboring states in furtherance of their own ends. However, although interference by Pakistan and China cannot be entirely denied, the roots of separatism lie within because Punjab, Kashmir, and the states of the North-East are all marked by deeply layered, superimposed differences.

Punjab, which has been the least problematic from the point of view of the Indian nation-state, at least since the late nineteenth century, has been marked by linguistic or cultural difference that is overlaid by religious difference. Indeed, sections of the Sikh elite had demanded a separate Punjabi Suba before the partition of the subcontinent. Neither composite-culture nationalism nor coalescent nationalism permitted the fulfillment of this demand in the first decade and a half after Indian independence. However, in 1966 a separate Sikh-majority State of Punjab was finally created. This was an admission by the State that India could be stable only under a deeply asymmetrical federal structure. Why, one might then ask, did a Punjab secessionist movement nevertheless emerge in the late 1970s? This requires a deeper socioeconomic explanation that is beyond the scope of this chapter. Suffice it to say that the formation of Punjab as a virtual Sikh-majority state preempted any possibility of a *successful* secessionist movement. Indeed, a new, soured form of Sikh nationalism would not have taken shape had the leadership at the center been wiser. A weakened Congress party had by then begun to use all kinds of unfair methods to stall the growth of regional parties. (Brass 1990, pp. 193–201). The secessionist movement had arisen predominantly for

---

[10] On the crises of linguistic federalism, see Brass (1990, pp. 192–227).

political causes/reasons, and although it turned bloody and lasted a long time, it eventually failed because something akin to a deeply asymmetrical federal system had been reluctantly established well before it had begun.

The Kashmir problem is especially intractable.[11] By 1950 the political elite in India had recognized that only a special status – as was enshrined in Article 370 of the Constitution of India – could prevent a secessionist movement in Kashmir. Unlike Punjab, the Kashmiris have always believed that they are a distinct society or nation. Religion is partly responsible for this distinctiveness as long as we remember that Kashmiri Islam is different from forms of Islam found elsewhere, even on the subcontinent. The recognition of Kashmir, of the need to grant Kashmir special status as a distinct society, supports the view that a loosely coalescing nationalism had already taken shape in 1950.

Why, then, has Kashmir been so deeply troublesome for the Indian nation-state? This, too, has a political explanation. Had the Indian state been true to the letter and spirit of Article 370 of its Constitution, I would have unhesitatingly concluded that federalism in India was deeply asymmetrical at its inception and has continued to be so and that the model of a loosely coalescing nationalism had already begun to sideline both composite culture and strongly coalescent nationalism. However, Indian political elites could not fully reconcile with what they had reluctantly accepted in the Constitution. Even Nehru, who had conceded both coalescent and loosely coalescing nationalisms in practice, could not come to accept the legitimacy of at least the latter. He never explicitly endorsed loosely coalescing nationalism and virtually always denounced it as a destabilizing force. In his world view, although the composite-culture nationalism he favored could give way in the Indian context to a tolerable, linguistically grounded coalescent nationalism, it could never fall in line with religiously grounded, sub-state nationalism. This made Nehru and people like him suspicious even of those who did not explicitly ground their politics in religion. Nehru was suspicious, not only of Sikh politics, within which religion and language overlapped, but also of the politics of Kashmiris like Sheikh Abdullah. When Abdullah imagined a politics of genuine regional autonomy, different from that envisaged by those who wanted Kashmir incorporated into either Pakistan or India, he was never entirely able to convince Nehru of his sincerity.

It was this anxiety and insecurity that made even Nehru adopt a manipulative and overly interventionist real politik in Kashmir. Sadly, the

[11] On Kashmir, see Behera (2000); Ganguly (1999); and Puri (1993).

more he pursued this approach, the more alienated the Kashmiri people became. After Nehru, the government at the center treated the successive state governments of Kashmir as a fiefdom of the central government. Over time, such governments were thoroughly discredited in the eyes of the Kashmiri people, particularly Kashmiri youth, who responded to the demands of militants and turned to insurgency. Once an insurgency started, an attempt was made to suppress it violently and with this, the alienation of Kashmiris from India was nearly complete.

The North-Eastern states are even more intractable.[12] Many of their problems result from the intersection of different kinds of ethnic confrontations. These involve Hindus and Muslims, Assamese and Bengalis, plains people and tribal hill people, plains tribals and non-tribals and the indigenous population, and a large migrant population. However, the most intransigent of these concern the tribal people who fiercely reject an Indian identity. Secessionist movements in the North-Eastern tribal areas are based, not only on linguistic and religious differences, but also on their cultural distinctiveness, which has often centered around their traditional way of life. Allow me to illustrate this point by examining the relation between Nagas and the Indian state.

THE NAGA STRUGGLE FOR A SEPARATE HOMELAND

For most periods, the struggle for a Naga homeland has aimed for complete secession from the Indian state. One of the least-known, bloodiest, and most protracted militant movements in post-independence India, it has raised fundamental questions about the nature of Indian nationalism and federalism as well as the functioning of the Federal Indian nation-state.

Who are the Nagas? According to Naga oral history, they migrated to their present homeland in two waves, passing through the Yunnan province of western China. The first wave crossed upper Myanmar and settled in present-day Arunachal Pradesh. The second wave settled in Myanmar, with a section migrating westward into present-day Nagaland, Manipur, and North Cachar Hills of Assam. Over time, the Nagas have developed a distinct social life – a set of unique laws, customs, and a system of administration that centers around the village. Every village is an independent unit in the "tribe" and is managed by a council of elders elected by the village.

Part of the Naga territory was annexed by the British in the first half of the nineteenth century. Between 1835 and 1851, they conducted at least seven

---

[12] See Baruah (2003); Gohain (1989, p.1377) and Hussain (1992, pp. 1047–50).

major military expeditions in an attempt to subjugate the Nagas. In 1878, the British occupied Kohima and by 1881, the Naga Hills District had been established, covering the southeastern part of the Naga-inhabited areas within the province of Assam. But the northern and eastern parts, which constituted two-thirds of the Naga territory, were not annexed. The conquest was not assimilationist, and the distinctness of Nagas was implicitly recognized in the Government of India Act 1919. The Naga Hills District, another name for the Naga territory, was declared a "backward tract" by the Indian Statutory Commission of 1930, which meant either that the Naga were so far behind the threshold of civilization that the people living there needed special protection or provisions, or that they were deemed unfit to be ruled by normal constitutional provisions. This was put by the British but accepted by independent India who used it in the second sense of "being unfit" to be ruled by normal constitutional provisions. This unfortunate term of "backward" clearly signaled that laws passed by the Indian legislature would not be applicable in the Naga Hill District. Peaceful resistance to the British conquest began early in the twentieth century, with the formation of the Naga Club by the various Naga tribes in 1918, the first-ever Naga organization. The Naga club made a demand for self-governance as early as 1929 during a visit to Kohima by the Simon Commission (the Indian Statutory Commission), under the chairmanship of John Simon and committee member Clement Attlee. The committee wanted the Nagas to accept the scheme of governance that would later be formulated as the Government of India Act, 1935. In response, The Naga Club submitted a memorandum to the Commission demanding that the Nagas be "left alone" when the British departed from India.

Formed in March 1945, the Naga National Council (NNC) represented the aspirations of the Naga people. Its representatives met with the Cabinet Mission in April 1946 and were given the option of deciding within ten years to either join or be independent of the Indian union. In a move that is widely considered a landmark in Naga history, the NNC launched a process of a voluntary plebiscite in 1951 to further its demand for self-governance, aimed at determining whether or not the Nagas wanted to remain in India. According to Naga historians – 99 percent of the Nagas voted in favor of a free Naga homeland (Brass Rule-3). In the next year, they boycotted the first Indian parliamentary elections and opted to continue the freedom struggle. "These two events are the building blocks of a modern Naga national project and are reiterated to emphasize the legal continuities of the struggle of oppressed peoples and the process of decolonization" (Kikon 2005, p. 2833). Yet it was not entirely clear whether this was a vote for a separate nation-state or for a separate homeland within the Indian union, a move toward coalescing nationalism and deeply asymmetrical federalism. Moreover, this ambiguity may have been deliberate, given that inflated demands are established norms of negotiations in a hard bargain.

Unfortunately, the GOI preferred to see things in a more clear-cut manner. They chose to see these aspirations of the Nagas as secessionist and used brute force uninhibitedly to suppress the movement (Rule-1). This hardly encouraged any hope of a negotiated settlement. On March 22, 1956, the Nagas declared the formation of a "Naga Federal Republic," a federated unit including the "free Nagaland" and all the areas inhabited by the Nagas across state and international boundary. An armed unit known as "Naga Home Guards" was formed that later became the Naga Army. Henceforth, the Indian Army and the Nagas were on the war-path, till a ceasefire agreement was signed in September 1964 between the Indian government and the Nagas.

Effected exactly nine months after the formation of the state of Nagaland in December 1963, the ceasefire was a result of the efforts of the Peace Mission consisting of Jayprakash Narayan, Reverend Michael Scott, and B. P. Chaliha. Offering a new perspective and approach to the problems of Nagas, the Peace Mission's proposals marked a sharp departure from the accepted position of the center and the leadership of the Congress on the Naga struggle. It was acknowledged that the Naga struggle was not a mere law and order problem egged on by the pro-verbial "foreign hand," but an expression of Naga national sentiment. The Peace Mission clearly stated that it "appreciates and understands the desire of the Nagas for self-determination and their urge to preserve their integrity" (Misra 2003, p. 594).

The Peace Mission became the first attempt by civil society to bring about normality in Nagaland without expounding on what self-determination means: political autonomy or independence. Confusion surrounding this term – the GOI and the Naga underground gave oppos-ing interpretations – has remained the major obstruction to the success of future negotiations.

After the ceasefire agreement, the Government of Nagaland and NNC signed a peace accord – the Shillong Accord – with the GOI in 1975. The former NNC unconditionally agreed to lay down arms and to accept the Constitution of India. But soon thereafter, the national Assembly of the Nagas, held in August 1976, condemned the

"Shillong Accord" which it regarded as a shameful capitulation to the enemy. Soon, the NNC gave way to the new National Socialist Council of Nagaland (NSCN) that waged an armed struggle against the Indian army. In 1996, the NSCN and the Naga Federal Government entered into another ceasefire agreement with the GOI, hoping for a political solution through dialogue. In response, the Indian government recognized the unique history of the Naga people.

I have provided the bare bones of this fraught history. Where has it brought us today? Fifty years of insurgent politics have made all sides of the conflict wiser. The Indian state seems to have realized that it is suicidal to steamroll the wishes and aspirations of even the smallest nationalities that make up this deeply diverse country. Those struggling to achieve an independent Nagalim (or Greater Nagaland, a territory that includes, according to those who demand it, some territories of Assam and Burma too) seem to have accepted the need for a negotiated settlement. Prior to the arrival of the British, the idea of a well-defined territory for the Naga or the other tribes was virtually nonexistent. It has been a long journey from the Naga "village republic" to the concept of a unified Nagalim, covering approximately 120,000 square kilometers of land, that includes all those who consider themselves Naga, regardless of whether they are domiciled in the states of Assam, Manipur, Arunachal, or outside India, in Myanmar.

"Why does a multicultural democracy like India lack a stable framework to tackle some of the more radical and enduring demands of ethnic groups and nationalist movements, other than by coercion?" (Kikon 2005, p. 2836). Initially, there was little effort on the part of the GOI to understand the Naga mindset. According to Udayon Misra, prejudiced assumptions about Nagas obfuscated the center's ability to properly see a viewpoint articulated outside the framework of "mainstream" of Indian politics and culture (Misra 2003, p. 593). This is an ambiguous but interesting claim, and captures a point that I have suggested from the start in this chapter. The differences between Nagas and the rest of India lie not just in language but in religion, local customs, and even race. Instead of a ham-handed, panicked, xenophobic response, these deeply layered differences require nuanced responses from the state. The composite-culture mindset of the democratic state, interpreted to mean a historically evolving syncretism, a harmonious amalgam of what once were distinct strands with different origins, was barely accustomed to the political articulation of deep cultural difference. This mindset was always ill equipped to handle the distinctiveness of the Nagas. The Nagas are a truly separate people who, in other contexts and circumstances, should have had a separate nation-state – they were part of the Indian union solely because of British conquest and the way boundaries were drawn by them – but given the nuanced constitution that India developed, they could equally be accommodated as a distinct part of the Indian union. The demand for recognition by a group with such complex layers of difference threw the Indian state off balance, when all that was required was the long overdue, much needed finessing of the simplistic notion of composite culture. Thus, the NNC's demand for the protection of the Naga way of life within an autonomous framework (the NNC was never clear on what it actually meant by self-determination) was viewed by the center as a demand for secession from India. Once the issue was put in a national-security frame, the Indian government left itself little option but to apply force (Brass's rule 1).

Second, the impact of the army's brutality transformed the demand for recognition of deep difference into an even more solid demand for separation and the desire for autonomy became a legitimate demand for secession. But physical force alone could not have brought about this transformation – the hidden message in the use of force was far more critical.

Allow me to elaborate.[13] Many Nagas believe that the struggle against the Indian state might not have erupted in the early 1950s had the Indian army not killed three village elders and paraded their bodies in the marketplace. The Nagas had always had a sense of collective individuality along with the claims of authenticity that spring from it, but, at best, this would have led to a demand for greater autonomy within the Indian union. What turned many Nagas into secessionists is the killing of the elders, which was an affront to their collective dignity. This killing was not just a murderous assault on individuals but much more. The undiluted message of the Indian state to the Naga people was that their collective self-worth did not really amount to much and that their self-respect and spirit could be damaged and broken with ease. The governing elites of India not only misunderstood the original demand of the Nagas – secession when they sought self-determination – but also failed to see that recognition and self-respect are intertwined. Recognition is an affirmative notion. To recognize a cultural community may not entail endorsing

---

[13] What follows is an "ethnographic" account drawn from my own visit to Imphal, the capital of Manipur in the North-East before I wrote this chapter. Here I met some scholars at a conference, both Meiteis who live in the plains and who are Vaishnavs (Hindus) as well as Nagas who inhabit the hills which surround these plains. This account is gathered from my conversation with them.

every aspect of its overall practice and belief but it does entail a positive attitude, more than mere toleration. A failure to recognize and a deliberate denial of self-respect is a double blow. Killing village elders constituted not just a physical assault but was a fundamental misrecognition of what the Naga people deeply value and therefore inflicted a humiliating mental wound. Their need for recognition and to reassert their dignity spurred the Naga's movement for secession.

I have spoken of a mental wound, but perhaps the term "ethical injury" is equally apt. The relationship between Nagas and the murdered village elders was no ordinary one. Four features characterize it. Village elders are not just older, more experienced folk, but figures of reverence. Because they are key performers of many sacred rites, they are virtually imbued with a quasi-religious character.[14] They are not just people from whom advice is sought but moral exemplars worthy of emulation, whose virtues must be integrated into one's own personalities. It is a lived ethical relationship.[15] The deep resentment caused by the use of force against elders flowed from a feeling among the Nagas that their relationship to the elders had been violated in a deep ethical and spiritual sense. Second, it is a deeply intimate relation. The army's use of force was not just an invasion of their territorial autonomy but also an intrusion on this intimate relationship. Third, because it is an affective relationship, the Naga's anger at seeing the mutilated bodies had to emanate from the gut; it was at once psychological, physiological, and emotive. Finally, the injury inflicted was felt not just individually but also as an affront to their sense of collective self-esteem and self-respect. Each of these is an ingredient in what might be called a collective ethical sensibility. The reason I use the term ethical injury is because the murders were a deep affront to this sensibility. The modern state and its governing elites lack resources to understand this sensibility and fail to *see* or understand the injury it causes.

Let me sum up. When Nagas spoke of maintaining their distinct way of life, it included, among other things, the protection of this ethical sensibility. The killing of village elders was not only a rebuff to their demand but a violation of this sensibility, and it led to the emergence of a narrow ethno-nationalist sentiment, a belief that one's way of life can be protected only by one's own army and state.

[14] On the Naga tribes and their village elders, see Godden (1897) and Von Furer-Haimendorf (1938).
[15] This point was clarified during my conversation with Saba Mahmood who spoke of something similar in an entirely different setting.

It is no doubt true that eventually Indian civil society organizations and ultimately even the state recognized this sentiment. The Peace Mission proposals I referred to above were preceded by the 16-Point Agreement between the GOI and the Naga People's Convention paving the way for the formation of the Naga Hills-Tuensang area as a separate state within the Indian Union. This agreement provided the Nagas with a large degree of autonomy. Clause 7 of the agreement reiterated terms of the 1919 Act by which no act or law passed by the Union parliament that affected the religious and social practices of the Nagas, their customary laws and procedure, and any criminal justice system contingent on their customary law was to have any force in the new state "unless specifically applied to it by a majority vote of the Nagaland Legislative Assembly." Clause 8 of the agreement stated that every tribe must retain powers of rule making and administration of its own affairs through local bodies like the Village Council, the Range Council, and the Tribal Council. These bodies would also retain their power to deal with disputes involving breaches of customary laws and usages. Thus, despite their limitations, the 16-Point Agreement and the subsequent formation of the state of Nagaland were a major step toward satisfying the aspirations of the Naga people.

In the light of all this it may be said that the Thirteenth Amendment of the Constitution of India (1962) by which the state of Nagaland was formed, not only proved the flexibility and accommodative power of the Indian constitution, but also indicated that the Indian state, its repressive face notwithstanding, was also slowly learning to adjust itself to the autonomy demands of its small nationalities. By inserting clause 371A (and thereby incorporating all the demands mentioned above) along the lines of Article 370), this amendment reasserted the deeply asymmetrical character of Indian federalism and underscored the presence of a loosely coalescing nationalism. Thus the Indian parliament cannot on its own change (i) religious and social practices of the Nagas, (ii) Naga customary law and procedure, (iii) administration of civil and criminal justice involving decisions according to the Naga customary law, and (iv) ownership and transfer of land and its resources shall apply to the state of Nagaland. These special provisions go a long way in protecting the Naga "way of life."

So, what does this mean for my assertion that multinationality has not been properly recognized by the Indian state? Here, I make two points. The first is the pivotal role of timing in politics. This decision to grant Naga autonomy came after an underground extremist movement for secession had already been strengthened. This is too late. Second, it is one thing for a peace mission to recognize the national sentiment; it is quite another for the state to do it. Even if the state does recognize it, it is one thing for it to legally recognize a group and another to inscribe it substantially into practice. The fact is that the Indian governing elite and the army act contrary to the relevant law of the Constitution. They act differently with "normal" and "deviant" states, with a coalescent conception of nationalism with the former but with a unitary conception with Border States. Faced with difference, it responds with contextual reasoning and negotiation. When faced with deeply layered, superimposed cultural difference (linguistic, religious, traditional rather than modern, even racial), it abandons reason and reacts with force.

A linguistic reorganization of states can only work if it follows certain rules. The most important of these is that nonviolent regional demands of autonomy are to be treated with sympathy, compassion, and subtlety. A non-manipulative negotiation and deliberation is the most appropriate response to the legitimate demands of regions with a distinct culture and language. With this model of contextual moral reasoning, wise politicians sought to accommodate the needs of one region, also keeping in mind the aspirations of neighboring regions and the good of the entire country. Linguistic federalism succeeded only when and for as long as this principle was followed. Problems occurred when an insecure government at the center dealt with regional aspirations in a ham-fisted, manipulative, and self-seeking manner. Moreover, the policy of "the carrot and stick" simply does not work for self-respecting people. The assumption that the carrot would be effective with an elite that can be hoodwinked into co-option and that the stick would eventually instill fear in masses who are prone to violence is entirely wrong. For a start, regional elites can be equally manipulative: Take the carrots and give nothing in return. Second, people can be fearless and ethical. As Dolly Kikon puts it, "The Indian state's paternalistic carrot-and-stick policy of using military force intermixed with liberal doles of 'development' money has not gone well with the people in the region" (Kikon 2005, p. 2835). Moreover, the continual military presence only reinforces the idea that the Indian state is inured to democratic demands and aspirations of its citizens and immune to their rights and the desire to have an autonomous way of life. In the North-East, low-intensity conflict between militants and the army is inevitable and a system of dual loyalty has yet to develop.

Two further points emerge from the problems of linguistic federalism in India. To the first, I have already drawn the reader's attention. Whenever a hitherto dominant political party begins to lose its grip, it abandons the very principles that brought it success in the past. Failure to abide by basic principles of constitutional democracy, in my view, remains one of the principal causes of the crisis of Indian federalism. Second, this crisis is also due to the intransigent nature of any religiously grounded politics in the subcontinent. The roots of this intransigence go back to the formation of extremist Muslim and Hindu political parties that eventually led to the partition of the country. Suspicion about religiously grounded nationalism and sub-nationalism made it impossible for framers of the Constitution to even consider the possibility of a deeper asymmetry in constitutional arrangements. Could the country have evolved a constitution with a secular state in a multireligious society, one that organized some states on the basis of language and others on the basis of religion? A federal state with *all* its subunits organized wholly along religious lines was legitimately unacceptable to the leaders of the national movement. In their political imagination, the furthest one could go was to give political recognition to linguistic communities. But what if *some* religion-based subunits were permitted? It is hard to tell. But what is certain is that even the presence of a differently religious ingredient in the overall culture of a group raises the hackles of the governing elite. The problem gets worse when the state is confronted with deeply layered and superimposed differences such as in Nagaland. Here differences exist over language, religion, social customs, and race, all of which are intertwined. Alas, the conceptual failure to imagine and design a set of institutions to accommodate such deep difference is a major obstacle to a peaceful, democratic resolution to the problem.

Overall, then, it is the failure to realize that only a deeply asymmetrical federal system could work in a country with India's size and diversity that constitutes the source of the problem. As I said, this is a form of asymmetry that is not just about different legal provisions but the organizing principle of the federation itself. Unless India recognizes that the grounding principles themselves can vary from state to state (at least in the case of some states), the problem of secession will persist with legitimate complaints that "the Indian state often contradicts the Constitution that promises the protection of deep cultural diversity and guarantees a pluralist political system" (Kikon 2005, p. 2835). Neither the electoral system, nor the "solutions" such as the carving out of Nagaland as a state from Assam in 1963 has addressed the core of Naga aspirations.

To conclude, a deeply asymmetrical, open, and democratic framework, based on the recognition of emerging discourses of human rights, minority rights, and indigenous rights, will only serve to strengthen the Indian polity and pave the way for successful negotiation of the Indo-Naga conflict. At the same time, respecting rights is never enough. Public acknowledgment and apology for wrongs committed by the state will now have to be part of the solution.

4

Pakistan: Neither State Nor Nation

Sumit Ganguly

Pakistan, one of two states that emerged from the breakup of the British Indian Empire, had been created as the putative homeland for the Muslims of South Asia. From its very genesis, the precise social and political dimensions of the state have been contested.[1] If it is the "homeland" of the Muslims of South Asia then what status should it accord to its religious minorities, as well as to sub-state nations?[2] How should it accommodate the demands of linguistic, sectarian, and regional minorities? Beyond the shared Islamic faith, what other attributes could serve as the constituent elements of nation building? And even if Islam constituted the unifying basis of the state, what role would it play in the everyday life and practices of its citizenry? These are questions to

I wish to thank Scott Nissen, a doctoral candidate in Political Science at Indiana University, Bloomington for able research assistance and Aqil Shah, a doctoral candidate at Columbia University for trenchant comments on an earlier draft of this paper. All remaining errors of fact and interpretation are necessarily mine.

[1] For an early treatment of this subject see Binder (1963). Also see the discussion in Jaffrelot (2002).

[2] After pursuing an inexorable campaign on the basis of religious nationalism and separatism, Mohammed Ali Jinnah, the founder of Pakistan, in his inaugural speech to the Constituent Assembly, on August 11, 1947 stated that: "You are free; you are free to go to your temples, your are free to go to your mosques or to any other place or worship in this State of Pakistan. You may belong to any religion or caste or creed that has nothing to do with the business of the State." Available at: http://www.pakistani.org/pakistan/legislation/constituent_address_11aug1947.html [accessed April 12, 2009].

which the founders of the Pakistani state had paid scant attention.[3] Yet they came to the fore almost immediately in the wake of Independence and Partition. They have also dogged the existence of the country ever since, and they have been the subject of vigorous and violent contestation (Ahmed, 1997). Sixty years after its creation, Pakistan is no closer to addressing these vital concerns. Instead they pose a continuing challenge to national identity and integration.[4] Specifically, Pakistan still faces important sub-state national movements in Baluchistan, in the North-West Frontier Province (NWFP), and Sindh.

In this chapter, I argue that these failures of the Pakistani polity to encourage and foster ideas of cultural, religious, and linguistic pluralism, and to craft the requisite political institutions in an extremely diverse polity, have been of no minor consequence for the country and substantial portions of its citizenry. The chapter will initially deal with colonial and nationalist legacies and their impact on the post-independence Pakistani state. It will then turn to questions of sectarian violence, sub-state nationalism in the province of Sindh, the secession of East Pakistan, the bilateral conflict with India over Jammu and Kashmir, and sub-state nationalism and terror in Baluchistan and the NWFP.

It is pertinent, at the very outset, to underscore that regime type in Pakistan has not been closely linked with greater regard for minority rights, decentralization, or cultural and regional autonomy. Pakistan's political regimes, whether civilian or military, have evinced scant regard recognizing sub-state national demands, or even minority rights, more broadly. Nor have they been especially sensitive in addressing demands for local autonomy or federalism. Instead all regimes, to varying degrees, have remained comfortable with a highly centralized administration.[5] Such a centralized structure has ill-served the needs of a highly diverse and plural society.[6] Instead it has contributed to a range of regional tensions, which in turn has led the regime in Islamabad to resort to repressive measures to curb such demands. The problem of the Pakistani state is prior and deeper, located in a crisis of identity that prevents not

---

[3] For a particularly idiosyncratic account which argues that Mohammed Ali Jinnah, the founder of the Pakistani state, had not genuinely sought to create a separate state but ultimately became a prisoner of his own rhetoric and choices, see Jalal (1985).

[4] For a broader discussion of these questions see Cohen (2004); also see the detailed historical discussion in Samad (1995).

[5] For a particularly thoughtful discussion that traces the origins of the propensity toward centralization see Waseem (1992).

[6] For a sophisticated Marxist analysis of this propensity toward centralization see Alavi (1972).

only recognition and accommodation of sub-state nations but of ethnic minorities more broadly. It is also important to bear in mind that not a single civilian regime has been allowed to complete a full term in office. Invariably, the military has truncated the natural life cycles of every civilian government. Consequently, liberal democratic norms have never had the opportunity to take root in the Pakistani soil.

The abject failure to adopt these policies contributed to the rise of Bengali nationalism and the breakup of Pakistan in 1971, when the eastern wing of the country seceded after a sanguinary civil war (Zaheer 1994). India, Pakistan's long-standing adversary, felt compelled to intervene on behalf of the beleaguered Bengali population of the province in the aftermath of the flight of some ten million refugees into eastern India (Jackson 1975). I will show that Pakistan's fundamental inability to accommodate the legitimate demands of other sub-state national groups (or nascent ones) has also resulted in much fratricidal and internecine violence in the provinces of Baluchistan, the NWFP, and Sindh. Finally, sectarian violence continues to stalk the land as Shia-Sunni differences have acquired greater salience as a consequence of both domestic and international politics. In turn, myopic regional and national governments have encouraged these cleavages and differences in order to pursue other political and diplomatic ends (Nasr 2000).

What explains the failure of the Pakistani state to develop an inclusive vision of nationalism while addressing the needs of its ethnic, linguistic, and cultural minorities within an institutional context? The answers to this question are complex. In large part, Pakistan's failure to mediate and negotiate these demands stems from the chronic institutional debility of the Pakistani state.[7] This explanation, in turn, begs another question. Why did Pakistan, which emerged from the same British colonial tutelage, fail to develop, nurture, and sustain viable representative political institutions, while its neighbor India, despite its problems of size and greater ethnic, religious, and linguistic diversity, succeed (Ganguly, Diamond, & Plattner 2007)? The answer, I argue, is twofold. First, it can be traced to the failure of the Pakistani nationalist movement to promote internal democracy and the norms of debate and argument, and thereby to provide a foundation for the growth of representative institutions. Second, the movement was self-consciously based upon a vision of primordial ethnic nationalism. Unfortunately, this conception

---

[7] The classic statement on institutional debility and its dangers remains Huntington (1968).

of nationalism completely overlooked fundamental differences amongst the Muslim community within British India. Muslims, as thoughtful historical scholarship has shown, were hardly a monolithic community who had little or nothing in common with their Hindu counterparts (Hasan 1997). On the contrary, regional, sectarian, linguistic, and class differences characterized this diverse community.

Yet the exigencies of mobilizing significant segments of the Muslim population to oppose the secular, civic vision of the Indian National Congress prompted the leader of the Muslim League, Mohammed Ali Jinnah, to emphasize the distinctiveness of the Muslim community, its putative cohesiveness, and the ostensible inability of the Indian nationalist movement to grant equal treatment to this vast minority. This strategy of ethnic political mobilization obviously met with a level of success: Jinnah did carve out a separate state. However, since neither he nor his cohort had devoted any effort toward the creation and sustenance of representative institutions, the new state, hastily cobbled together on the eve of British colonial withdrawal, found itself singularly unprepared for the tasks of governance and national integration.[8] In the absence of robust institutions, the nascent state proved utterly incapable of coping with growing ethnic, regional, and class differences and tensions in the wake of independence. Not surprisingly, the two institutions that had a degree of autonomy and coherence, the Pakistani military and the highly elitist civil service, quickly formed an iron-clad nexus in their quest for the maintenance of public order. As the Pakistani political elite struggled with the task of constitution making, these two entities, which were hardly imbued with democratic values, evinced little regard for fostering representative institutions. When the makers of the constitution finally generated a constitutional order, it proved fragile and incapable of coping with growing public disorder. The military and the civil service elites worked in concert to quickly stultify the growth of institutions. As early as 1958, barely a decade after its independence, Pakistan saw its first military coup (McGrath 1996).[9] The military regime, which lasted until 1969, did little to address the question of building viable, working, representative institutions nor, for that matter, did it seek to address the fundamental question of Pakistan's national identity. Its principal preoccupation, beyond sustaining itself in power, was to promote anti-Indian propaganda and focus attention on the unresolved question of the dispute of the state of

[8] Some of the difficulties of state formation are discussed at length in Jalal (1990).
[9] For a more recent treatment of the subject see Siddiqa (2007).

Jammu and Kashmir.[10] This idée fixe about Kashmir, however, was not universally shared across Pakistan. In East Pakistan, the political leadership was far more concerned with regional disparities between the two wings than with any form of unremitting hostility toward India on the Kashmir question.

COLONIAL AND NATIONALIST LEGACIES

To understand the failure of representative and federal institutions in Pakistan it is necessary to briefly discuss the ideology, structure, and organization of the Pakistani nationalist movement. The Pakistani nationalist movement can be traced to the late nineteenth century and the writings and political activism of a prominent Muslim intellectual, Sir Sayyid Ahmed Khan. When confronted with the development of a form of incipient nationalist political consciousness on the part of the Hindu population of British India, Sir Sayyid quite persuasively argued that the Muslims of the subcontinent constituted a distinct, primordial nation. More to the point, he contended that, with the advent of Westminster-style representative institutions, Muslims, who had long ruled the subcontinent prior to the advent of the British, would be placed in a position of permanent political inferiority and at the mercy of the majority Hindu population.

As he wrote at the time:

Let us suppose first of all that we have universal suffrage as in America and everybody, *chamars* (i.e. persons of low caste) and all, have votes. And first suppose that all Mahomedan electors vote for a Mahomedan member and all Hindu electors for a Hindu member ... It is certain that the Hindu member will have four times as many (votes) because their population will have four times as many ...(A)nd how can the Mahomedan guard his interests? It would be like a game of dice in which one man had four dice and the other only one. (Sir Sayyid Ahmed Khan as quoted in Hardy 1972, p.130)

Accordingly, he strenuously argued that the British should grant the Muslims of the region a special dispensation which would guarantee their rights.[11]

Sensing an opportunity to cast discord within the nascent nationalist movement, in 1909 the colonial government enacted the terms of the

[10] On the question of Kashmir see Dasgupta (1968); for a Pakistani nationalist perspective see Khan (1970).
[11] For a discussion of Sir Sayyid's views see Robinson (1974).

Minto-Morley Reforms. These reforms, among other matters, created limited representative institutions in India, with Muslims being granted separate electorates. This institutional arrangement helped to artificially solidify the Muslim community within India because it showed scant regard for divisions of social class, regional ties, and sectarian differences within the community.

As Mushirul Hasan, an important historian of nationalist politics has written:

The Act of 1909, introduced to defuse the Congress demand for a greater share in administration and decision-making, was a calculated master-stroke. Separate electorates, along with reservations and weightages, gave birth to a sense of Muslims being a religio-political entity in the colonial image – of being unified, cohesive and segregated from the Hindus. (Hasan 1997, p. 35)

In turn, the creation of this system of electorates on the basis of religious orientation greatly facilitated the mobilization of the Muslim community around the sole issue of potential religious discrimination following the end of British colonial rule. Indeed, this became the principal rallying cry of the Muslim League under the leadership of the tenacious, British-trained lawyer, Mohammed Ali Jinnah.[12] Jinnah carefully adumbrated upon the views of Sir Sayyid and insisted that Muslims and Hindus as religious communities shared little or nothing. Indeed he contended that the two groups constituted distinct, anti-thetical, and mutually exclusive groups, thereby amounting to two discrete nations.[13] As he wrote:

Islam and Hinduism are not religions in the strict sense of the word, but are, in fact, two different and distinct social orders...The Hindus and the Muslims belong to two different religious philosophies, social customs, and literatures... To yoke together two such nations under a single State, one as a numerical minority and the other as a majority, must lead to growing discontent and the final destruction of any fabric that may be built up for the government of such a State. (Mohammed Ali Jinnah as quoted in Jaffrelot 2002, p. 12)

This so-called two-nation theory emerged as the cornerstone of Pakistani nationalism. It faced vigorous opposition from the principal vehicle for Indian nationalism, the Indian National Congress, which was

---

[12] For a discussion of Jinnah's tactics and strategies of political mobilization see Jalal (1985).

[13] Of course the historical evidence suggests otherwise. There is considerable evidence of syncretic movements through much of Indian history. Perhaps one of the best statements of this can be found in Eaton (1993).

committed to an explicitly secular ideology and espoused a vision of civic nationalism.[14] Despite its formal, stated commitment to these principles, the INC's efforts to realize its vision at the grass roots sometimes flagged. Consequently, it was unable to fully address Jinnah's misgivings and those of a significant portion of the Muslim community.[15] Jinnah forcefully, relentlessly, and ultimately successfully argued that the rights of the Muslim minority would be at risk in a notionally secular but Hindu-dominated post-independence India.

Despite his success in promoting his separatist agenda, Jinnah and the Muslim League paid little heed to the critical task of promoting internal democracy within the party, building a nationwide network of grass roots support and fashioning a distinct political ideology beyond the appeal to notions of primordial religious sentiment. Not surprisingly, in the aftermath of Independence and Partition, the Muslim League proved to be utterly incapable of coping with the daunting task of governance.[16]

NATIONALISM AND SECTARIAN VIOLENCE

Pakistan has justified its preoccupation with and involvement in the Kashmir question on behalf of the putatively oppressed Muslim population. Nevertheless, it is important to underscore that important sectarian faults have long characterized Pakistan's own polity and society. The strength of these sectarian identities have waxed and waned over time. However, their political mobilization has frequently raised questions about the cohesiveness and coherence of Pakistan's national identity. The periodic rise of violent sectarian movements in Pakistan reflects the failure of the Pakistani state to recognize and accept the presence of cultural and religious pluralism.

Some of these movements originated in the early days of the Pakistani state. However, they continue to pose a challenge to the stability and well-being of the state in the contemporary period. The initial as well as

---

[14] One of the clearest statements of this vision of secular, civic nationalism can be found in Nehru (1941).

[15] The failure of Congress to reassure Jinnah and large segments of the Muslim community about their rights and privileges in a post-independence India is the subject of a major historical debate. For a popular but thoughtful discussion see Guha (2007); for a critical account of Congress' failure to assuage Muslims' concerns at a critical juncture see Azad (1960); also see the debates in Phillips and Wainwright (1970).

[16] Even though he fails to trace the structural roots of the problems of governance and the maintenance of public order, an admirable discussion of the problems that Pakistan faced in the aftermath of independence can be found in Bin Sayeed (1960).

present-day problems with sectarian identities and their politicization bear discussion. Shortly after the creation of Pakistan, a small Muslim sect, the Ahmadiyyas, fell afoul of the conservative Muslim clergy. The Ahmadiyya community consists of the followers of Mirza Ghulam Ahmad (1835–1908), a religious leader who had declared himself to be the second messiah of Islam. Orthodox Muslims, whether belonging to the Sunni or Shia sects, consider his declaration to be blasphemous. Accordingly, they accused the community of apostasy. As early as 1949, with the connivance of the Pakistani state, the Ahmadiyya community became the object of persecution. In 1953 the Pakistani religious party, the Jamaat-I-Islami, precipitated a riot against the Ahmadiyyas in the Punjab. The government of Pakistan instituted an inquiry into the origins of the riots, but the effort was mostly perfunctory. Discrimination against the community continued but the next major set of riots was to take place about two decades later, in 1974. Instead of coming to the aid of the besieged community, the civilian regime under Zulfikar Ali Bhutto chose to declare the Ahmadiyyas a non-Muslim community through a constitutional amendment. The condition of the Ahmadiyyas worsened under General Zia, who in 1984 again amended the constitution to place Islamic law over national jurisprudence. He also created a legal basis for the prosecution of anyone who professed the Ahmadiyya faith. Both Bhutto and Zia pursued these policies solely for the purpose of bolstering the sagging legitimacy of their respective regimes and to curry favor with the conservative Muslim clergy.[17] The conditions of this small, beleaguered community are no better today.

Sectarian violence in Pakistan has hardly been confined to the hapless Ahmadiyya community. Since the 1980s Pakistan has also witnessed a steady rise in sectarian violence, especially between Sunnis and Shias. Such sectarian violence once again underscores that the common bond of Islam is an anemic basis for the construction of a robust and common national identity. The origins of such violence could be located in both domestic and external sources.[18] Domestically, the rise of Sunni extremism can be traced to the policies of General Zia-ul-Haq (1977–1988). In 1979 he undertook a program of Islamization to shore up his military regime. Despite professions of Islamic universalism it had a distinctly pro-Sunni tinge. Consequently, the Shia community saw it as an assault on its

---

[17] Much of the material cited here has been drawn from Ganguly (2007).
[18] On the international sources of domestic developments see Gourevitch (1978).

interests.[19] Simultaneously, the Iranian revolution had also contributed to the growth of radicalism within the Shia community.

External forces, in turn, came to quickly reinforce this shift toward religious orthodoxy and political assertion on the part of the Shia community. The new revolutionary regime in Iran was hostile toward the Zia-ul-Haq regime owing to its attempts to shore up the Shah's government in its waning days. Consequently, they moved with dispatch to both morally and materially assist the Shia within Pakistan. Such external involvement and the concomitant rise of Shia assertiveness contributed to increasing Shia-Sunni tensions and ultimately culminated in a series of violent clashes. This schism, which openly manifested itself in the early 1980s, continues to periodically erupt. The civilian regimes of Benazir Bhutto and Nawaz Sharif did little to contain their growing differences. Unfortunately, external meddling in Pakistan's domestic schisms did not come to a close with the end of military rule. Saudi Arabia, which had developed close ties to Pakistan during the Afghan war years, continued to play an important role in the country's internal politics. Specifically, it provided financial assistance to Pakistani *madrassas* in an attempt to influence the religious orientation of Pakistani Islam. It is hardly surprising that Nawaz Sharif, a relatively conservative politician, sought refuge in Saudi Arabia after General Pervez Musharraf deposed him in a military coup in October 1999.

The subsequent military regime of General Musharraf, though notionally committed to limiting the sectarian and religious tensions failed miserably in that endeavor. In the absence of enlightened state policies that seek to actively ameliorate this breach, the country will inevitably countenance recrudescent Shia-Sunni violence. Clearly, Islam failed to provide the glue that can hold together Pakistan. Besides the sectarian divisions just discussed, it could not mend the ethno-linguistic divisions within the country.[20]

INCIPIENT TENSIONS AND FRUSTRATED SUB-STATE NATIONALISM IN SINDH

One of the first fissures that emerged within Pakistan after independence was that between the so-called *muhajirs*, Muslims who migrated from India at the time of partition, and the inhabitants of the region of Sindh,

---

[19] For a particularly thoughtful treatment of this subject see Nasr (2000).
[20] For a recent discussion of sectarianism in Pakistan see Ollapally (2008).

in the southern part of Pakistan. Local Sindhis came to deeply resent the sudden influx of significant numbers of immigrants. Their reaction was not based solely on some form of intrinsic xenophobia. Instead, it could be traced to their straightforward anxieties about competition for scarce employment, housing, and access to various public goods (Khan 2002).

These tensions that emerged in the aftermath of partition have continued to periodically wrack the province, resulting in much internecine and fratricidal violence. Parties have coalesced around ethnic identities and have organized militias that have frequently resorted to strong-arm tactics to intimidate opponents, threaten voters, and rally supporters. To compound matters, instead of acting as neutral arbiter and enforcing social order, various military regimes at particular junctures have aligned themselves with specific political parties and organizations involved in this long-running feud, and have thereby fueled further tensions and violence.[21]

At the same time, the Sindhis had developed their own sense of nationhood long before the idea of Pakistan itself emerged. A provincial autonomy movement had emerged in 1917 in response to British colonial rulers' plans to merge the Sindh province with the Bombay presidency. The movement for a Sindhu Desh, however, quickly yielded to the growing mobilization for Pakistan, and many Sindhis supported the new state. However, after independence, the massive migration of Muhajirs discussed above disrupted the demographic make-up of the province. In addition, the overwhelming presence of Punjabis in the military and the civil service convinced many Sindhis of the necessity to push for provincial autonomy. These tensions led into early protest movements against the central government in 1968–1969.

After the independence of Bangladesh and the resignation of General Yahya Khan, Zulfikar Ali Bhutto became president of a truncated Pakistan. Bhutto, a prominent landlord from Sindh, successfully mobilized, thanks to his Pakistan People's Party, the population of Sindh. As the head of that powerful political organization, he promoted the interests of the Sindhis at the provincial level and defended the interests of the oppressed at a national level. His populist agenda, for a time, undercut the idea of Sindhi sub-state nationalism. However, after General Zia-ul-Haq arrested him in 1977, and after a sham trial had him executed, unrest arose again in Sindh. The population protested the domination

---

[21] For a nuanced discussion of the military's partisan involvement in the conflict in Sindh see Ahmed (1996).

by the military, but General Zia had successfully conspired to use the Mutthahida Qaumi Movement (The United National Movement, hereafter MQM), and encouraged the rise of Islamist militancy, to increase insecurity in Karachi, the multiethnic capital of Sindh and Pakistan's largest city. The ethnic strife in the major port became emblematic of the country's inability to achieve national unity.

THE BREAKUP OF PAKISTAN

The most striking failure of the Pakistani state, however, lay in its inability to pursue a viable language policy that would accommodate the legitimate demands of more than 50 percent of its population, the Bengalis of East Pakistan. As early as 1948, Jinnah, in an attempt to forge a common national identity, chose to adopt Urdu as the national language of Pakistan (Oldenburg 1985). The choice of Urdu as the national language met immediate resistance from the Bengali-speaking population of East Pakistan.[22] Despite protests, which were violently suppressed, the decision to make Urdu the national language of Pakistan was not rescinded (Ayres 2002). Worse still, thanks to the location of the bulk of political power and privilege in West Pakistan, the Bengalis of East Pakistan faced systematic discrimination in every conceivable arena of government employment. To compound matters, most foreign investment was directed into West Pakistan, and the largest share of international assistance was disbursed there (Jahan 1972). Some statistical evidence on the prevailing socioeconomic disparities will bolster this argument. For example, at a macroeconomic level in 1969–1970, per capita income in West Pakistan was 61 percent higher than in East Pakistan (Jackson 1975). Other contrasts were equally vivid. East Pakistan, with a population of 75 million had 7,600 physicians, while West Pakistan with a population of 55 million had 12,400. Similar disparities were mirrored in the educational sector. Between 1947 and 1969, the number of colleges in West Pakistan grew from 40 to 271 while their number in East Pakistan went from 42 to 162. In the military realm, East Pakistani representation was equally lopsided. Even though East Pakistan had 54 percent of the total population of Pakistan, only 5 percent of the officer corps of the army, 15 percent of the air force, and 20 percent of the navy were drawn from the province. Matters were no better in the elite Civil Service of Pakistan

---

[22] For a detailed discussion of the evolution of Pakistan's language policy see Rahman (1996).

(CSP). In 1970, only 16 percent of the CSP were composed of Bengali officers (Sisson & Rose 1990).

In large part these highly discriminatory policies stemmed from deep-seated cultural prejudices and beliefs about the Bengali-speaking population of East Pakistan. Significant portions of the West Pakistani elite were contemptuous of their Bengali-speaking Muslim brethren. This contempt, in turn, was deep-rooted and could be traced to the British colonial notions of the "martial races" of the subcontinent.[23] A quote from the autobiography of the self-styled Field Marshall Mohammed Ayub Khan, exemplifies the beliefs of the Pakistani political establishment:

East Bengalis who constitute the bulk of the population, probably belong to the very original Indian races. It would be no exaggeration to say that up to the creation of Pakistan, they had not known any real freedom or sovereignty. They have been ruled either by caste Hindus, Moghuls, Pathans, or the British. In addition, they have been and are under considerable Hindu cultural and linguistic influence. As such they have all the inhibitions of downtrodden races and have not yet found it possible to adjust psychologically to the requirements of new-born freedom. (Ayub Khan 1967, p. 63)

These prejudices, which were widely shared among the West Pakistani elite and the Punjabi-dominated military, played a vital role in shaping the brutal response to the rise of the demands for regional autonomy in East Pakistan in the aftermath of the country's first free and fair election in November 1970. In the wake of these elections, the East Pakistan–based Awami League (AL), won 160 out of a possible 162 seats. The West Pakistan–based Pakistan's People's Party (PPP) had chosen not to contest any seats in East Pakistan. On the other hand, the AL, which had contested seven seats in four west Pakistani provinces, won none. In the West, the PPP was the clear-cut winner, obtaining eighty-one seats (Sisson & Rose 1990). Instead of moving with dispatch toward a viable, representative, power-sharing arrangement, the politico-military elites of West Pakistan resorted to every possible ploy to stymie the results of an election that would have granted East Pakistan its legitimate share of political authority. When all these stratagems to forestall power-sharing arrangements failed, the Pakistani military embarked upon a virtually genocidal campaign against their hapless Bengali citizenry.[24]

[23] On the subject of "martial races" see Robb (1995). The British, for purposes of colonial administrative convenience, had developed an elaborate pseudo-anthropological classification of "races" and had declared some to be "martial" and others "non-martial." The Bengalis of the subcontinent were deemed to be both "non-martial" and effeminate.

[24] The term "genocidal" is used advisedly. The American Consul-General in Dacca (now Dhaka), Archer Blood, was the first person to use that term in a telegram that he sent to

This military crackdown led to the flight of millions of refugees into India. The Indian political leadership under Prime Minister Indira Gandhi was thereby faced with both a crisis and an opportunity. The crisis was primarily humanitarian. India, a poor country, could ill-afford to absorb close to 10 million refugees into its already overcrowded territory. However, the refugees' presence in India and the ongoing civil war within East Pakistan also presented India with an important opportunity: the possibility of breaking up Pakistan. To that end, after May 1971, India's political elite carefully embarked upon a politico-diplomatic strategy designed to alert the major powers to India's dilemma. Meanwhile, it steadily drew up war plans for an invasion of East Pakistan should these diplomatic efforts to resolve the crisis and ensure a safe return of the refugees fail. When the major powers did little or nothing to exert significant pressure on the military regime in West Pakistan to end the ongoing crisis in East Pakistan, Indian forces managed to deftly provoke Pakistan to launch an attack on India in December 1971. Once the Pakistanis attacked, Indian forces, which had been carefully arrayed to carry out an effective military campaign in East Pakistan, put their plans into action. The war lasted for a mere twenty-two days, resulted in an overwhelming Indian victory, and culminated in the creation of Bangladesh.[25]

The Pakistani political elite has yet to fully come to terms with the role of their military and political leadership in precipitating the crisis in East Pakistan that culminated in the genesis of Bangladesh. This was evident when General Pervez Musharraf, the Pakistani military dictator, visited Bangladesh in 2002. Instead of forthrightly accepting responsibility for the atrocities of the civil war of 1971 he merely expressed his "regrets" about them (Habib 2002).

JAMMU AND KASHMIR: THE ENDLESS WAR

Despite the breakup of Pakistan in 1971, all Pakistani regimes, regardless of political orientation or composition, have maintained an irredentist claim to the former princely state of Jammu and Kashmir (Dasgupta 2000; Hodson 1969). Such a claim is ironic because the collapse of the Pakistani state, albeit with Indian assistance, demonstrated the clear limits of Jinnah's "two-nation theory." Obviously, religion alone, as noted

the U.S. Department of State using the so called dissent channel, which allows American diplomats to disassociate themselves from a policy that they feel that they cannot support. On the question of genocide in Bangladesh see Rummel (1998).

[25] For a detailed account of the process of Indian involvement and the breakup of Pakistan see Ganguly (2001); also see Lieutenant-General Jacob (1997).

previously in this chapter, failed to cement the two wings of the state. Nevertheless, for the Pakistani political and military establishments, the status of the disputed state of Jammu and Kashmir represents the "unfinished business of partition."[26] The origins of this dispute are complex. They are rooted in the British policies of colonial withdrawal from the subcontinent in 1947. At the time of Independence and Partition, there were two classes of states in the British Indian Empire. In the first, the states of British India were under the direct rule of the British Crown. The second, so-called princely states were nominally independent but recognized the "paramountcy" of the British Crown. With the end of British rule, the doctrine of paramountcy drew to a close. Accordingly, Lord Mountbatten, the last Viceroy, informed the rulers of the princely states that they had the choice of joining either India or Pakistan, depending upon their demographic composition and geographic location (Ramusack 1977). Muslim-majority states would join Pakistan, while those states that were predominantly non-Muslim would go to India. The option of independence was effectively ruled out to prevent the balkanization of the subcontinent. For the vast majority of the princely states the issue was quickly settled because of their location or demographic composition. The state of Kashmir posed a unique problem. It had a Muslim-majority population, a Hindu monarch, and shared borders with the two emergent states. The ruler of Kashmir, Maharaja Hari Singh, had little interest in joining either India or Pakistan. He was loath to join India because he feared that the Indian National Congress under the leadership of Prime Minister Jawaharlal Nehru, who had definite socialist proclivities, would dismantle his vast land holdings. Simultaneously, as a Hindu monarch who had done little to improve the lot of his Muslim subjects, he was equally leery of casting his lot with Pakistan. Even after Independence and Partition he had refused to accede to either state.

Ultimately, a decision was forced upon him when a tribal rebellion broke out in early October 1947 in the western reaches of his state. Sensing an opportunity to wrest the state from Indian control, the Pakistani political establishment promptly moved to support the rebels. Faced with the imminent fall of his capital, Srinagar, to the Pakistan Army–assisted rebels, Maharaja Hari Singh appealed to New Delhi for assistance. Prime Minister Nehru agreed to provide military assistance if the ruler met two conditions: he would have to formally accede to

---

[26] For a discussion of Pakistan's involvement in and support for separatist *jihadi* movements in Kashmir see Swami (2006).

India, and Sheikh Mohammed Abdullah, the leader of the largest popular and secular organization in the state, the Jammu and Kashmir National Conference, would have to grant his imprimatur to the accession (Sisson & Rose 1990). Once these two conditions were met, Indian troops were flown into Kashmir where they successfully stopped the rebel onslaught but not before they had succeeded in capturing about one-third of the state.[27] On the advice of Lord Mountbatten, India referred the case to the United Nations Security Council as a breach of international peace and security. With UN intervention, the first Kashmir war came to a close in January 1, 1948.

The Pakistani claim to Kashmir has two components. The first is *moral*, and the second *legal*. At a *moral* level, even though their co-religionists in East Pakistan chose not to remain within the domain of the Pakistani state, the Pakistani leadership still insists that Kashmir, owing to its predominantly Muslim population, needs to be incorporated into Pakistan. The origins of the claim, of course, must be traced back to the very rationale for the creation of Pakistan, namely, that it was a homeland for the Muslims of South Asia. The moral claim is best illustrated with a quotation from a work by Pakistan's erstwhile leader Prime Minister, Zulfikar Ali Bhutto, who wrote:

If a Muslim majority can remain a part of India, then the raison d'être of Pakistan collapses. ...Pakistan is incomplete without Jammu and Kashmir both territorially and ideologically. It would be fatal if in sheer exhaustion or out of intimidation, Pakistan were to abandon the struggle, and a bad compromise would be tantamount to abandonment; which, in turn might lead to the collapse of Pakistan. (Bhutto 1969)

Their *legal* claim to the entire state of Kashmir is based upon a highly contested corpus of evidence about how the partition line was drawn at the time of independence. Pakistani apologists claim that Lord Mountbatten showed partiality toward the nascent Indian state, while Indian partisans claim otherwise. The evidentiary basis for either claim is convoluted and murky (Lamb 1991).[28]

Leaving aside the strength and veracity of the competing moral and legal claims, it is a fact that a range of Pakistani regimes from 1947 onward have waged three separate wars (1947–1948, 1965, and 1999)

---

[27] The best description of the Indian military response can be found in Sen (1969).
[28] For a challenge to Lamb's claims see Jha (1996); for a mostly dispassionate account see Whitehead (2007).

with India in attempts to wrest control over the original territory of the disputed state. Despite the expenditure of considerable amounts of blood and treasure they have not met with any success in this endeavor. India has tenaciously and steadfastly refused to concede any ground on the Kashmir question.[29]

Since 1989, Pakistan has been deeply involved in directing, supporting, and steering an ethno-religious insurgency in the Indian-controlled portion of the state.[30] The origins of the insurgency were mostly indigenous and could be traced to the political malfeasances of a series of national governments in New Delhi that had sought to manipulate the internal politics of this state. Despite this support for the insurgency, which Pakistanis refer to as a "war of a thousand cuts,"[31] the country is no closer to undermining India's continuing grip over the state (Ganguly 2006). Even though thoughtful Pakistani commentators have deemed this quest to be futile, the Pakistani military, and a permanent civilian establishment, have evinced no interest in abandoning this quest.[32] In part, the continuing preoccupation with Kashmir enables the Pakistani military to justify its substantial budgetary allocations and thereby helps maintain its preeminent position within Pakistan's polity and society (Racine 2002).

Pakistan's own relationship with the portion of Kashmir that it came to control as a consequence of seizing the territory in the 1947–1948 war is quite complex. Notionally, "Azad Kashmir" ("free Kashmir") has a considerable degree of autonomy and its own prime minister. However, for all practical purposes it is under the firm control of the regime in Islamabad. The inhabitants of Azad Kashmir were granted the right of adult franchise only in 1970, and those of the adjacent Northern Areas as late as 1994. Under the aegis of the 1974 constitution of Pakistan, two executive bodies were created for Azad Kashmir. They were the Azad

[29] India's intransigence on the Kashmir question can be traced to two concerns. At one level, India, as a constitutionally secular state, believes that a Muslim-majority state should be able to thrive under the aegis of a civic polity. At another, Indian elites are convinced that the secession of Kashmir could generate a powerful demonstration effect and bolster other incipient movements for secession. For a more extensive discussion of this problem see Ganguly (2001).

[30] For evidence of Pakistani involvement in and support to the Kashmiri insurgents see Byman (2005).

[31] Available at: http://www.time.com/time/magazine/article/0,9171,257107-2,00.html [accessed April 12, 2009].

[32] On the futility of Pakistan's quest see Gauhar (1999) "Four Wars and One Assumption." *The Nation*, September 5.

Kashmir government located in the provincial capital of Muzaffarabad and the Azad Kashmir Council located in Islamabad. The constitution called for the prime minister of Pakistan to preside over the council and would include six federal ministers, the prime minister of Azad Kashmir, six Azad Kashmir members elected by its assembly, and the Minister of Kashmir Affairs. Practically all subjects of any significance affecting the population of Azad Kashmir fell within the purview of this council.

The situation in the Northern Areas of Kashmir was not much better. In October 1994, the first party-based elections were allowed in Northern Areas, and this culminated in the creation of a 26-member elected body known as the Northern Areas Executive Council. This entity, however, was only granted advisory powers. For all practical purposes, political power remained vested in the hands of the Ministry of Kashmir and the Northern Areas Executive Affairs Council in Islamabad. In the aftermath of a Pakistan Supreme Court judgment in March 1999, the first Northern Areas Legislative Council was elected in 2000. It was granted the rights to legislate on local matters and to impose and collect local taxes. However, the overall structure of administration remained unchanged.[33]

Pakistan's professed commitment to the self-determination of all Kashmiris notwithstanding, it has abjectly failed to address the legitimate political aspirations of those Kashmiris within its formal jurisdiction. The denial of political representation, systematic repression, and the fear of Indian domination have enabled the Pakistani state to contain any substantial attempt on the part of the Kashmiris to assert themselves politically.[34]

SUB-STATE NATIONALISM REDUX: BALUCHISTAN

Despite the emergence of Bangladesh and the ongoing problem of Kashmir, Pakistani elites seemed incapable of fashioning an institutional strategy to cope with the demands of sub-state nationalism. The demands for autonomy in Pakistan have been simultaneously regional and ethnic. Particular ethnic groups are concentrated in specific regions, and they have often felt that the national government has neglected their interests and needs. These sentiments have periodically come to the fore and have

[33] Behera (2000) "Looking within the other Kashmir," *Asia Times [Online].* Available at: http://www.atimes.com/atimes/South Asia/EB2oDfo7.html [accessed April 12, 2009].

[34] On political repression in Azad Kashmir see Human Rights Watch (2006) *With Friends Like These...* New York: Human Rights Watch, September 21.

manifested in attempts to secure regional rights in the western province of Baluchistan. This region, which accounts for almost 40 percent of Pakistan's total land area, is rich in coal and natural gas deposits. It is also the poorest region of the country and is bereft of agricultural resources. The aridity of much of the region renders it unsuitable for sustained, settled agriculture. During the period of unified Pakistan, both civilian and military regimes did little to promote economic development or provide representation to the native Baluchis in either governmental services or the military. In addition, the government exploited the rich resource base of the region (Jetly 2004). Ironically, it was after the emergence of the first democratic regime in Pakistan, that of Prime Minister Zulfikar Ali Bhutto, that one saw the emergence of a violent Baluch nationalism. The Baluch resorted to violence against the Bhutto regime primarily because of the dismissal of an elected local government on tenuous grounds.

The regime's response was nothing short of harsh. In the wake of East Pakistan's secession, neither the Pakistani political elite nor the Pakistani military were inclined to permit the growth of yet another separatist movement. Consequently, they resorted to rather brutal military tactics to suppress the Baluch insurgency. In the East Pakistan case, the military establishment in Islamabad had faced two important handicaps. They could not fly over Indian territory, and they also had to deal with the military involvement of a far more powerful neighbor. In the Baluch case, there were no serious external supporters, and the geographic contiguity facilitated military logistics. Ironically, the military regime of General Zia-ul-Haq, while unwilling to countenance the emergence of any representative institutions in Baluchistan, nevertheless adopted a policy of co-optation and conciliation. To this end he released large numbers of Baluch insurgents and political leaders who had been incarcerated under Bhutto.

In the aftermath of General Zia's regime the Baluch movement started to wane. However, in recent years it has shown signs of recrudescence. The regime of General Pervez Musharraf opted to pursue the same coercive strategy that had characterized the Bhutto regime. In its attempt to quell an incipient insurgency in the region, Pakistani forces killed Nawab Akbar Khan Bugti, a former chief minister of Baluchistan. In the wake of his killing a spate of violence ensued to which the Musharraf regime responded with further repression.[35]

---

[35] See Shahid (2006) "Bugti killed in operation: Six officers among 21 security personnel dead." *Dawn*, August 27.

THE PROBLEM OF PAKHTOONISTAN

Another region of Pakistan has an equally tortured history of rebellion and resistance. This is the NWFP, Pakistan's North-West Frontier Province. In the aftermath of the tragic events of September 11 and concomitant American-led efforts to eviscerate the Al Qaeda and the remnants of the Taliban regime, this region has received much journalistic attention.[36] However, quite apart from its proximity to Afghanistan, and thereby its significance as a possible redoubt for neo-Taliban forces and elements of Al Qaeda, the region has a long history of resistance to Pakistani rule. Indeed, the sentiments for regional autonomy and separation run deep and can be traced to colonial times.[37]

In the NWFP, Jinnah's Muslim League had a difficult time establishing a significant foothold because of the towering influence of Khan Abdul Ghaffar Khan, who was known as the "Frontier Gandhi." Khan, who had organized a powerful non-violent, non-cooperation movement in this region, has some affinity for the Indian nationalist movement and the principles of Mohandas Gandhi in particular.[38] Accordingly, when a referendum was held just prior to independence, Khan's followers boycotted it. Nevertheless, about 51 percent of the eligible electorate voted to join Pakistan, and the province became part of the new state. The Pashtun movement, however, continued to smolder as significant segments of the population acutely resented the Punjabi domination of the Pakistani polity.

In subsequent years, thanks to significant military recruitment from the province and increased economic integration into the larger polity, some of the regional grievances subsided. However, demands for regional autonomy persisted because of the failure of the national government to promote significant economic development. One of the ongoing issues remains the issue of the proper share of royalties from hydroelectric power resources (Kukreja 2003). A related issue remains the opposition to the construction of the Kalabagh Dam on the Indus River. According to local activists opposed to the construction of the dam, the principal beneficiaries of this project would not be the inhabitants of the province but those of the Punjab.[39]

[36] Two excellent journalistic accounts of the American efforts tackle the Al Qaeda as well as America's ambivalent relationship with the Taliban? Coll (2004) and Wright (2006).

[37] For some historical background see Erland (1981).

[38] For an extraordinary ethnographic account of Khan and his *Khudai Khidmatgar* movement, see Banerjee (2000).

[39] I am grateful to Aqil Shah of the Department of Political Science, Columbia University, for bringing the contentious issue of the Kalabagh Dam to my attention.

In the February 2008 elections, the Awami National Party managed to successfully rout its opponents and won thirty-one out of a possible ninety-six seats in the provincial assembly. As the party with a plurality of seats it managed to stake a successful claim to the chief ministership of the province, a goal that had eluded it for the past sixty years. With a regional party now at the helm and with the restoration of democracy at the national level, the NWFP had hoped to secure a more equitable distribution of resources.

Unfortunately, two factors have vitiated such prospects for the foreseeable future. The country's crude, inept, and harsh counterinsurgency strategy that is directed against an infestation of the Taliban forces in parts of the NWFP, most notably the Swat Valley, has alienated significant segments of the local population. Worse still, the Taliban have managed to gain ground in the Swat Valley through an amalgam of vicious tactics and the exploitation of the limitations of the flawed counterinsurgency efforts.[40]

A FISSURED NATION AND STATE

There is little question that after sixty years of its independent existence, an identification among the elites with the Pakistani state has emerged. In part, this elite nationalism relies upon a common hostility toward India to promote a sense of national solidarity. Yet beyond this perception of difference it is unclear what else the vast majority of Pakistanis can turn to as sources of national identification. Obviously, for a certain segment of the population, a return to some pristine variant of Islam as the basis of nation building remains the preferred alternative. However, as discussed earlier in this chapter, key doctrinal differences remain among the Sunnis, Shia, and of course, the small and beleaguered Ahmadiyya community. These differences, in and of themselves, are not the sources of conflict. However, the tenuous legitimacy of various regimes, whether civilian or military, has often provided an important temptation to exploit these differences for short-term political ends thereby resulting in periodic outbursts of violence, and, in turn widening and sharpening the existing fault lines.

The return of viable representative institutions in Pakistan might provide an arena for the airing of divergent views about the country's national identity and questions of the status of sectarian minorities, substate nations, and regional rights. Whether or not Pakistan will make

---

[40] See Oppel and Shah (2009) "A Radio-Controlled Reign of Terror for Pakistanis Under Taliban." *The New York Times*, January 25.

such a transition to democracy remains a fraught question. More to the point, even such a transition would not guarantee a prompt focus on these long-standing and vexing questions because they have become so deeply embedded in Pakistan's political culture.

The military, thanks to its long history of interventions and rule, has now managed to entrench itself as a central component of the Pakistani political order. With each successive involvement, its role has expanded, perhaps most dramatically under the rule of General Pervez Musharraf. Accordingly, even if the military nominally returns to the barracks, it will still remain an organization that is primus inter pares. As a corporate entity, it will not permit other institutions to assert themselves beyond limits that it deems tolerable. It is able to exercise such control over other competing institutions within the polity for two compelling reasons. First, despite the recent assertiveness of the Pakistani Supreme Court, virtually all institutions within the country have been either rendered anemic or are subservient to the military. Second, as an able Pakistani political scientist, Ayesha Siddiqa, has painstakingly documented, the military has managed to expand its reach across every sector of Pakistan's state and society (Siddiqa 2007).[41] Any nascent civilian regime will face a sisyphean task as it seeks to roll back the spread of military influence in Pakistan.

Consequently, for the foreseeable future Pakistan's nationalist enterprise will remain subject to intense sub-state nationalist, regional, sectarian, and ethnic contestation. Such contestation will not be confined to institutional arenas. Given the weakness of formal institutions, individuals and groups repose little faith in them, and so they resort to social movements, which are fraught with the potential for conflict and frequently lurch toward violence. Whether the fragile institutions of the Pakistani polity can still manage to contain these differences and prevent them from erupting into large-scale violence is a question that both analysts and policymakers will have to ponder.

In the wake of the February 18, 2008 elections and the emergence of a legitimately elected civilian regime, the Pakistan polity may yet have another opportunity to resuscitate a number of its nearly moribund civilian institutions.[42] Simultaneously, if the civilian government does not quickly succumb to internal political bickering and also avoid the temptations to raid the exchequer, it may be able over time to assert

---

[41] For the decline of political institutions and the growth of the military's influence into civilian sectors see Kukreja (2003).

[42] See Ganguly (2008) "Musharraf's End." *The San Francisco Chronicle*, February 21.

some semblance of authority over the military. The past performance of a range of civilian regimes does not offer substantial hope that they will be able to set aside petty partisan differences, avoid fiscal malfeasance, and insist upon the supremacy of elected civilian authority. However, after the rampant abuse of political power under General Musharraf's military dictatorship after the coup of October 1999, it is possible that previously feckless politicians may finally evince some interest in restoring the autonomy, probity, and efficacy of Pakistan's civilian institutions. Only through the reconstruction and eventual expansion of viable representative institutions can Pakistani polity begin to address the deep ethnic and regional fissures that have threatened its viability.

5

Constitutional Politics and Crisis in Sri Lanka

Sujit Choudhry

In *Multicultural Odysseys,* Will Kymlicka observes sharp differences in the way North America and western Europe, on the one hand, and eastern and central Europe and Africa and Asia, on the other, have responded to the claims of minority nations (Kymlicka 2007). Some multinational polities such as Canada, Belgium, the United Kingdom, and Spain have come to see themselves not as nation-states, but as multination states and have, accordingly, given symbolic recognition to minority nations and reconfigured themselves constitutionally to reflect their multinational character. Other states have rejected and even suppressed – often violently – the political claims of minority nations. This appears to be particularly true in Asia. Kymlicka suggests that, with the notable exception of India, Asian states have been extremely resistant to the claims of minority nations, for a variety of reasons – the legacy of colonial divide-and-rule strategies which empowered minority ethnic groups, concerns over geopolitical security, fear of petty tyrannies, and the belief that ethnic mobilization would disappear as a result of modernization and development.

Sri Lanka is one of the many examples Kymlicka cites. It is not hard to understand why. Demographically, Sri Lanka fits his model of a multinational polity. It contains a large, Sinhala-speaking majority (74 percent of the population), as well as a large, Tamil-speaking minority (13 percent) who traditionally hail from the northeast of the island, where they

Thanks to George Anderson, Jacques Bertrand, David Cameron, André Laliberté, Bob Rae, Asanga Welikala, the participants at the Multination States: East and West workshop, and two anonymous reviewers for Cambridge University Press for helpful comments and suggestions, and to Nathan Hume, Rohit Jha, and Tiffany Tsun for helpful research assistance. The views expressed herein are strictly my own.

constitute a majority.[1] Both the Sinhalese majority and the Tamil minority are engaged in competing projects of nation-building. The centerpiece of Sinhalese nation building has consisted of the designation of Sinhala as the official language, especially the internal working language of government. It has also entailed the maintenance of the unitary state inherited from the British, and the refusal thus far to recast Sri Lanka along federal lines. The sources of Sinhalese linguistic nationalism are diverse, ranging from resentment to the disproportionate professional success enjoyed by Tamils under colonial rule, to the use of official language policies to expand educational and employment opportunities for an increasingly literate and demanding Sinhalese population, to the pressure arising from the growth and consolidation of the state in the post-independence period to interact with the population in indigenous languages. Tamil nationalism arose as a defensive response to Sinhalese nation-building and has consisted of a series of demands that have escalated from linguistic parity to federalism and, eventually, to secession and independence for Tamil Eelam in the northeast of the country. At first, Tamil nationalists advanced their claims through the political process and civil disobedience. The Sri Lankan state was resistant to these claims, and responded to Tamil civil disobedience with increasing levels of violence. Frustrated with their lack of success, Tamil nationalists then turned to violence. The result has been a civil war since 1983, now between the Government of Sri Lanka (GOSL) and the Liberation Tigers of Tamil Eelam (LTTE), albeit punctuated with several truces and rounds of peace negotiations.

The Sri Lankan case demonstrates the importance of the distinction between questions of constitutional *substance* and constitutional *process*. In a multinational polity, questions of constitutional substance go to the issue of whether multiple nations share a common state, and if so, on what terms – in other words, federalism, multiple official languages, power sharing at the center, symbolic recognition, and so on. Questions of constitutional process concern the procedures created by the constitution within which debates over constitutional substance occur and pursuant to which substantive changes are made. This distinction helps to illuminate both the causes of, and potential solutions for, the Sri Lankan conflict. The descent into civil war in Sri Lanka ultimately arose from a breakdown of the Sri Lankan constitutional order. One dimension of

---

[1] According to the 1981 census, which was the last census completed in every district across the island. As a consequence of the civil war, it has been impossible to conduct a census across the island since then.

this breakdown concerned a fundamental difference over the substance of the constitutional arrangements to frame the relationship between the Sinhalese majority and the Tamil minority. This is a familiar story that has been extensively canvassed in the literature (DeSilva 1998; De Votta 2004a; Wilson 1988).

But what has received far less attention is an equally fundamental disagreement over the constitutional procedures that should govern the debate over substance. This is potentially much more serious because constitutional procedures allow the constitutional politics of substance to occur. In the absence of agreement over process, future agreement on substance may be impossible. The reason there is a lack of agreement over the procedures that regulate constitutional change – the rules governing constitutional amendment – is that those rules are not perceived as indifferent among the competing substantive positions on the constitutional agenda. Tamil nationalists deplore that those rules pre-suppose an understanding of the Sri Lankan polity as a single nation in which the constituent actor is the Sri Lankan people as a whole. Tamils are merely a linguistic minority, and that status does not give them any special standing in the process of constitutional amendment. In opposition to this vision, Tamil nationalists have conceived of Sri Lanka as a multinational polity, where the ultimate power of constitutional change vests with its constituent nations – the Tamils and the Sinhalese. Since the choice between these two versions of the Sri Lankan polity was at the very heart of the civil war, rules governing constitutional amendment that are based on one of these conceptions of Sri Lanka has been viewed as partial and cannot serve as a neutral framework for constitutional change. Indeed, the Sri Lankan case vividly demonstrates how rules governing constitutional amendment are not neutral in their effect on constitutional reform. At several different points, these rules have provided the institutional and legal resources to thwart the accommodation of the Tamil national minority.

In exploring the Sri Lankan case, I am pursuing a broader intellectual agenda on method in the literature on multinational polities. One of the most striking features of the literature is its focus on the political sociology of competing nationalisms within the same state. Will Kymlicka (2007) and Michael Keating (2001), for example, devote most of their attention to questions of political identity. In contrast, far less attention has been devoted to institutions and to the constitutions and statutes that create and regulate those institutions. This is surprising, because the conflict between competing nationalisms within multinational polities often plays out in terms of competing sets of proposals for institutional design that are advanced by majority and minority nations. Seemingly technical debates over constitutional design are an arena of conflict between under-lying and competing conceptions of the fundamental character of the polity. So, by closely examining debates over institutions, we can unearth these competing nationalist narratives and sharpen our understanding of the political sociology of multinational polities. Indeed, constitutional arguments are an important part of Sri Lankan political discourse, so they merit close attention.

A related issue is how to pursue this institutional agenda. Neil De Votta (2004a) and A. Jeyaratnam Wilson (1988) have produced impor-tant, institutionally focused accounts of the constitutional politics of Sri Lanka. However, these institutionalist approaches to the study of minor-ity nationalism could benefit from a closer engagement with constitu-tional theory. For example, De Votta offers an institutionalist explanation of the causes of the Sri Lankan conflict in which legal policy instruments occupy center stage, and argues that the constitutional restructuring of Sri Lanka is necessary for the attainment of a stable and enduring settle-ment to the conflict. In this respect, he builds upon the discourse of Tamil nationalists, who attribute the breakdown of Sri Lanka to the design of its constitution, which empowers its Sinhalese minority and does not pro-tect Tamils from the consequence of being outvoted in the political pro-cess. However, his account is ambiguous over what dimension of existing constitutional structure is at fault and what aspects must be changed. For example, he attributes the Sri Lankan conflict to a situation where "the state's most important institutions egregiously favor one particu-lar group and concurrently enable the subjugation of other groups" and states that "a lasting peace is unlikely until Sri Lanka's leaders can craft the requisite institutions that would treat all citizens dispassionately" (De Votta 2005, pp. 141, 146–56). The distinction between substance and process raises the additional question of whether the breakdown of the Sri Lankan constitutional order is attributable to the perceived unfairness of the substance of existing constitutional arrangements, the procedures for the adoption of new ones, or both.

CONSTITUTIONAL POLITICS IN SRI LANKA: SUBSTANCE

It is clear that Sri Lanka is – and has been for some time – in an extended round of constitutional politics, even as it was mired in a civil war for over a quarter century. To a large extent, these rounds of constitutional politics have been debates over substance. Political discussion over the constitutional arrangements to govern the relationship between the Sinhalese and the Tamils extend back to the pre-independence period. Facing the prospect of universal suffrage and the political empowerment of the Sinhalese majority in 1931, Tamil politicians unsuccessfully argued against the extension of the right to vote and for communal representation in the colonial legislature, and later, for parity of representation between the Sinhalese and minority communities ("fifty-fifty") in the post-independence constitution (the Soulbury Constitution), which came into force in 1946 (Wilson 1988, chapter 1). In the post-independence period, the principal issues have been language, regional autonomy, and independence. The historical record reveals that all of these questions have been on the constitutional agenda since independence. Nonetheless, one can delineate distinct periods.

Language: Between independence in 1948 and 1956, the principal issue was language. Tamils initially demanded institutional bilingualism at the national level. The post-independence constitution was silent on the issue of language. In the immediate post-independence period, Sinhalese politicians affirmed their commitment to official bilingualism. However, in 1956, Parliament enacted the Official Language Act, which declared Sinhala to be the sole official language. The GOSL began to implement the policy in the 1960s. Sinhala became the official internal working language of government, of written communication between the government and the public, and of the all-important civil service examination, which had the effect of restricting access to state employment to Sinhala speakers. Later, the Language of the Courts Act expanded the official language policy to make Sinhala the sole working language of the courts in 1961. Perhaps the most fateful decision taken under the rubric of the Sinhala-only policy was with respect to university admissions, which at first consisted of differential admissions standards for Tamil and Sinhalese students and then of a system of district quotas, both of which had the effect of dramatically reducing Tamil participation in higher education (De Votta 2005, p. 137). The Official Language Act was superseded by section 7 of the 1972 Constitution, which constitutionally entrenched the status of Sinhala as Sri Lanka's sole official language.

Over the years, there have been a series of unsuccessful attempts to reverse the Sinhala-only policy. One year after the adoption of the Official Language Act, the GOSL and leaders of the Tamil Federal Party (FP) negotiated the Bandaranaike–Chelvanayakam (B-C) Pact of 1957. The FP abandoned linguistic parity for Tamil across Sri Lanka, settling instead for Tamil becoming the language of public administration in the North and East of the island, where Tamils predominated. Although the pact was abrogated in the face of Sinhalese opposition, it was followed by the adoption of the Tamil Language (Special Provisions) Act in 1958. On paper, the Act established many minority language rights for Tamils, including the right to Tamil-language primary and secondary education, to use Tamil in the University of Ceylon, to sit for the public-service exam in Tamil, and to communicate with government officials in Tamil. Tamil would become the internal working language of the North and the East. However, the Act required implementation through regulations, which were not adopted until 1966.[2] Furthermore, these regulations were largely unenforced. The Language of the Courts (Special Provisions) Act, which established the right to use Tamil in the courts in the North and the East, was adopted in 1973. Although Sri Lanka's 1978 Constitution (which established its current semi-presidential system of government) also declared Sinhala to be Sri Lanka's sole official language, it nonetheless constitutionalized many of the existing statutory provisions on the use of Tamil.[3] In 1987, these provisions were significantly enhanced through the Thirteenth Amendment to the 1978 Constitution.[4] The obvious goal was to make the whole of Sri Lanka home to Tamils by enabling them to interact with government institutions in Tamil throughout the island. But as President Mahinda Rajapaksa acknowledged in 2005, many of these provisions remain largely unenforced, with Tamil speakers still unable to communicate with government offices and the police in Tamil.[5] To many Tamil nationalists, this has given rise to the view that the GOSL is a colonial government dominated by Sinhala speakers, as opposed to a government for all Sri Lankans.

Federalism and independence: In 1956, Tamil politicians shifted the emphasis of their efforts to federalism, an option that had long been discussed. One reason for this shift was the adoption of Sinhala as the official language, which ended the possibility of linguistic parity for Tamil. The

[2] Sections 2–5, Tamil Language (Special Provisions) Act, 1958 and associated regulations (1966). These regulations were adopted after the conclusion of the Senanayake–Chelvanayakam Pact of 1965, which was also abrogated by the government.

[3] s. 18 (Sinhala sole official language), s. 21(1) (minority language primary and secondary education), s. 21(2) (higher education), s. 22(1) (Tamil internal working language of government in the North and East), s. 22(2) (right to communicate in Tamil), s. 23 (laws enacted in both Tamil and Sinhalese), and s. 24 (right to use Tamil in courts).

[4] The amended provisions include s. 22(1) (Sinhala and Tamil internal working languages of government GOSL throughout Sri Lanka and of provincial governments except in North and East, where Tamil shall be used), s. 24 (right to use Sinhala and Tamil in courts throughout Sri Lanka).

[5] Policy Statement of President Mahinda Rajapaksa at Ceremonial Opening of Parliament (November 25, 2005).

more practical alternative was to create a federal Sri Lanka with Tamil as an official language in any province with a Tamil majority. Another reason was the GOSL's use of violence against Tamil civilians and its failure to protect Tamils from mob violence, first in response to campaigns of civil disobedience against the Sinhala-only policy and later in response to the launching of armed attacks by the LTTE. The failure of the GOSL to extend to Tamil civilians the equal protection of the law destroyed the faith of many in the legitimacy of the Sri Lankan state, and reinforced the demand for political institutions controlled by a Tamil majority. A third reason was provided by GOSL policies that encouraged the settlement of Sinhala speakers in the East, which altered the region's demographic and linguistic balance. Thus, along with the demand for linguistic autonomy came demands for control over policing and the use of public lands for settlement.

The B-C Pact of 1957 called for the creation of directly elected regional governments, created by and exercising delegated jurisdiction over policy areas pursuant to statute. The Senanayake–Chelvanayakam Pact of 1965, entered into by the Prime Minister and the leader of the Federal Party, similarly called for the establishment of District Councils exercising delegated powers. Neither proposal was implemented in the face of Sinhalese opposition. As Rohan Edrisinha has recounted, the 1972 Constitution was a watershed in the Tamil demand for a federal Sri Lanka (2005, pp. 244–9). One of the first moves of the Constituent Assembly tasked with drafting the 1972 Constitution was adopting a resolution defining Sri Lanka as a unitary state in the Constitution. Sections 2 of both the 1972 and 1978 Constitutions declare Sri Lanka to be a unitary state. The Federal Party argued against the resolution, arguing instead in favor of adopting a federal constitution. After the resolution was adopted, Federal Party MPs walked out of the Constituent Assembly. Ultimately, the Federal Party merged with other Tamil organizations to form the Tamil United Liberation Front (TULF). In 1976, the TULF adopted the Vaddukoddai Resolution, which called for the creation of an independent Tamil Eelam. The Vaddukoddai Resolution plays a critical role in the constitutional arguments of the Tamil nationalists. Although Tamil politicians had been calling for secession as an option since the debates over official language policy in the 1950s, the idea entered the political mainstream in 1976.

To be sure, there have been various constitutional initiatives to decentralize power. The leading effort is the Thirteenth Amendment to the Sri Lankan Constitution, adopted in November 1987. The terms of the Thirteenth Amendment had been spelled out in the Indo-Sri Lanka Accord between the GOSL and India in July 1987. In outline, the Thirteenth Amendment confers both exclusive and concurrent legislative jurisdiction on nine provincial councils. The principal criticism of the provincial council system is that it leaves a great deal of executive and legislative authority in the hands of the central government. Each province is structured in a semi-presidential manner, but with a Governor appointed by the President as opposed to being elected, as is the case for the national government. The appointed Governor nonetheless holds wide powers, such as the power to prorogue and dissolve the Council, possesses the provincial executive power, and is not bound to follow the advice of the Chief Minister of the Province. Finally, the Governor is subject to the direction and control of the President, placing the provincial executive in a subordinate relationship with the national executive, rather than in a coordinate relationship as would be the case in a true federation. On the legislative side, the Thirteenth Amendment allows the President to suspend the operation of a Provincial Council and transfer its jurisdiction to Parliament, which may in turn transfer it to the President, if the President concludes that the administration of the province cannot be carried out. Moreover, the Thirteenth Amendment allows a two-thirds majority in Parliament to legislate in exclusive areas of provincial jurisdiction over the objections of a Provincial Council. Finally, it appears unnecessary to have recourse to these provisions, because the Ninth Schedule to the Constitution reserves to Parliament the jurisdiction to enact "National Policy on all Subjects and Functions," which would seem to encompass any topic falling within exclusive provincial jurisdiction.

Indeed, the fact that the Thirteenth Amendment has not altered the unitary character of Sri Lanka was confirmed by the Supreme Court.[6] Under the 1978 Constitution, there are two procedures for constitutional amendment: (i) a two-thirds majority in Parliament, and (ii) a two-thirds Parliamentary majority and approval in a referendum. Amendments to the unitary nature of the state require a national referendum. The Thirteenth Amendment was passed under the first procedure, and the Supreme Court ruled that this was the correct procedure, stating that the Thirteenth Amendment did not alter the unitary nature of the country because of the subordinate character of provincial legislative and executive authority. Not surprisingly, the TULF opposed the Thirteenth Amendment, as did the LTTE, precisely for this reason. To compound dissatisfaction with the constitutional status quo, the system of Provincial Councils was inoperative

---

[6] Thirteenth Amendment to the Constitution and the Provincial Councils Bill, (1987) 2 SLR 312.

in the Northern and Eastern Provinces after 1990 (Loganathan 1998). However, the GOSL held a Provincial Council election in the Eastern Province in May 2008 after taking military control of the area, and since the defeat of the LTTE has promised to hold elections in the Northern Province after defeating the LTTE.

Put simply, Sri Lanka faces a clash between the two conflicting constitutional visions captured by the exchange between the Tamil delegation (consisting of the LTTE and other Tamil political parties) and the GOSL at the first (and unsuccessful) round of peace negotiations in Thimpu, Bhutan, in July and August, 1985. The Tamil delegation set out four principles in what has become known as the Thimpu Declaration.[7] The principles call for "recognition of the Tamils of Ceylon as a nation," "recognition of the existence of an identified homeland of the Tamils in Ceylon," "recognition of the right of self-determination of the Tamil nation," and "recognition of the right to citizenship and the fundamental rights of all Tamils in Ceylon." These principles were issued in response to a proposal released by the GOSL at the talks a few days earlier. In brief, the proposals would have devolved certain powers to over two dozen District Councils, which could then have combined into larger provinces. The President would have had the power to disallow District or Provincial legislation. The TULF had rejected these proposals because they provided an insufficient degree of regional autonomy. The Thimpu Declaration, in essence, fleshes out the theory underlying this rejection, by grounding its principles in the right of peoples (or nations) to self-determination and deriving from that right a claim to a specific territory and right to choose the political status of that territory and the population attached to it.

The GOSL rejected these principles outright, at a conference session the next month. The response bears careful examination:

[W]e must state emphatically that if the first three principles are to be taken at their face value and given their accepted legal meaning, they are wholly unacceptable to the Government. They must be rejected for the reason that they constitute a negation of the sovereignty and territorial integrity of Sri Lanka, [and] they are detrimental to a united Sri Lanka ...[8]

The GOSL clearly interprets the right of peoples to self-determination as the right to *external* self-determination, and that right encompasses

---

[7] Discussion of the "Thimpu Talks" of July–August 1985 is available at: http://www.tamilnation.org/conflictresolution/tamileelam/85thimpu/850713thimpu declaration.htm [accessed January 13, 2010].

[8] Discussion of the "Thimpu Talks" of July–August 1985 is available at: http://www.tamilnation.org/conflictresolution/tamileelam/85thimpu/850812phase2 sri lanka opening statement.htm [accessed January 13, 2010].

the right to an independent, sovereign state. But the Thimpu principles are notably ambiguous on whether they are to be realized *within* or *outside* Sri Lanka. Indeed, the Tamil negotiators noted that while they had demanded a separate state, "[d]ifferent countries have fashioned different systems of government to ensure these principles" and they would be open to reviewing proposals in that light.[9] The principles could in fact be satisfied through *internal* self-determination – in other words, a federal form of government with real regional autonomy, within the context of a united Sri Lanka. So the GOSL draws an implicit but crucial inference about the internal constitutional structure of a state from the fact of external sovereignty – that to enjoy true sovereignty, a state must have a unitary constitution because sovereignty is indivisible. A united Sri Lanka is necessarily unitary. For the Tamils to demand any kind of sovereign authority would be radically incompatible with the ongoing sovereignty of Sri Lanka over its territory. Furthermore, to the extent that sovereignty and statehood are grounded in the right to self-determination, the holder of that right is the people of Sri Lanka as a whole, of which the Tamils are a part. The Tamil nationalist claim that there are two nations on the island was rejected, because of the existential challenge it poses to the Sinhalese nationalist constitutional vision.

This constitutional vision is reflected in the 1978 Constitution, which provides in sections 3 and 4 that "sovereignty is in the people and is inalienable" and "[t]he sovereignty of the people shall be exercised" by the various institutions of the unitary state – the Parliament, the President, and the courts. The origins of Sinhalese nationalism, however, do not lie in a deep constitutional vision, but rather in political and economic competition over white-collar public sector employment. Why has economic competition for white-collar jobs been such an important driver of official language policy? There is a cluster of mutually reinforcing reasons. Demand for these kinds of employment opportunities increased dramatically in post-independence Sri Lanka because of increased social mobility, which in turn was a function of increasing rates of participation in education, especially secondary education. The increasing proportion of youth completing advanced studies was made possible by a deliberate public policy decision to expand the availability of public education in Sinhala. The result was a marked increase in the demand for white-collar employment. Education also fueled the migration of the newly literate, with youth flocking to urban centers in search of employment opportunities

[9] Ibid.

not available in rural areas. Once they arrived, they found that access to those opportunities was in short supply. It was this demographic – unemployed, newly educated youth, literate in the vernacular and concentrated in urban areas – that fueled demand for access to white-collar employment opportunities. The new entrants into the labor pool were predominantly Sinhalese, which created the political incentives for Sinhalese political parties to compete with each other on modifying the rules governing access to universities and government employment.

These demands first manifested themselves in debates over official language policy. The choice of an official internal working language of public administration creates unequal access to white-collar public sector employment. As economic competition for these kinds of employment opportunities emerged, it was translated into a political demand for policies to redistribute those opportunities by modifying the linguistic policy status quo. Prior to independence, the rates of participation of the Tamil minority in the colonial administration were much higher, either a deliberate product of a colonial divide-and-rule strategy or the rational response of Tamils from the North-East to the relatively poor prospects for agriculture on that part of the island. In the post-independence period, the dominance by Tamils in white-collar public sector employment continued. In the 1950s and 1960s, when Sinhalese nationalist parties took power and mobilized the Sinhalese majority around a project of linguistic nation building, Sinhala became the official internal working language of government and of the civil service examination, which had the effect of restricting access to state employment to Sinhala speakers. Tamil nationalism arose as a defensive response to these policies, which in turn fueled the development of the unitary state mindset among Sinhalese nationalists.

Notwithstanding its origins in economic and political competition, this unitary state mindset is now firmly set. President Rajapaksa of the Sri Lanka Freedom Party (SLFP) illustrated the durability of this mindset in a policy statement, "Peace with dignity in an undivided country," released in November 2005 shortly after he was elected. The goal of the peace process should be the "[c]reation of a government infrastructure that will safeguard Sri Lanka's sovereignty, territorial integrity, and the unitary nature of the state."[10] Predictably, the LTTE responded by stating that President Rajapaksa had taken "shelter in a rotten unitary

[10] Policy Statement made by President Mahinda Rajapaksa at the opening of the New Session of Parliament, November 25, 2005. Available online at: http://www.president. gov.lk/sinhala/html/speeches/2005/new_session_of_parliament.htm [accessed April 21, 2009]. He also reaffirmed this view in the most recent round of negotiations.

constitutional concept."[11] It is against this backdrop that the true significance of the apparent concessions made by the parties at the outset of
the Norwegian-mediated peace negotiations becomes clear. In the Oslo
Declaration (issued in December 2002), the parties agreed "to explore a
political solution founded on the principle of internal self-determination
in areas of historical habitation of the Tamil-speaking peoples, based on
a federal structure within a united Sri Lanka."[12] The equation of external
sovereignty, statehood and an internal unitary constitution was broken.
To be sure, this was not the first time that Sinhalese politicians had been
willing to make that move. In 1996, President Chandrika Kumaratunga
presented a set of constitutional proposals that would have stated that
Sri Lanka is "a united and sovereign Republic" that is "an indissoluble
Union of Regions."[13] Faced with opposition from Sinhalese nationalists,
Kumaratunga eventually dropped the term "Union" when she introduced
the draft constitution in Parliament.

CONSTITUTIONAL POLITICS: PROCESS

Alongside this disagreement over substance has been a parallel disagreement over the constitutional *process*. The basic disagreement concerns
the precise character of constituent power in Sri Lanka. On the one hand,
the GOSL views the population of Sri Lanka as a whole as the relevant
constitutional actor – as a single nation which expresses its consent to
constitutional change through procedures spelled out in the constitution.
Although the Sri Lankan demos may be linguistically, culturally, and
religiously diverse, the groups defined by those differences do not enjoy
national status. On the other hand, defining the people of Sri Lanka as a
whole as the constituent actor denies what Tamil nationalists contend –
that Sri Lanka is not a nation-state but a multinational state, and the constituent power does not reside in one, undifferentiated Sri Lankan nation
but in its constituent nations. The state is not an association among
citizens considered free and equal, but a union among different nations
or peoples, each of which is such an association. As a consequence, the

[11] "LTTE Responds to Rajapaksa's statement", February 15, 2006. Available online
at: http://www.tamilnation.org/conflictresolution/Tamileelam/norway/060215ltte.htm
[accessed April 21, 2009].
[12] Statement of the Royal Norwegian Government at the conclusion of the third session
of peace talks between the Government of Sri Lanka and the LTTE in Oslo, December
5, 2002. Available online at: http://www.norway.lk/peace/peace/talks/third.htm [accessed
April 21, 2009].
[13] See section 1 of Sri Lanka Draft Constitution, March 1997.

Tamil negotiators participate in the process of constitutional change, not as mere agents of political interests, but as agents of a nation or people whose agreement is required for constitutional change.

This basic disagreement over the character of constituent power within Sri Lanka has played itself out in a number of particular disputes, as described below:

The relative status of the negotiating parties: Although Sri Lanka was from in a state of civil war 1983 to 2009, there have been numerous sets of peace negotiations – in Thimpu, Bhutan in 1985, in Colombo in 1989–1990, in Jaffna in 1994–1995, and the Norwegian-facilitated peace talks which began in 2002 and ended in 2006. In each of these rounds of negotiations, a preliminary question was the relative status of the negotiating parties. The hybrid nature of the discussions complicated the answer to this question. On the one hand, the discussions were ceasefire discussions between combatants, and therefore proceeded on a basis of formal equality. But they were also constitutional negotiations in embryo, and so the question of relative status required the parties to address what gave them standing to participate in the negotiations. For the GOSL, its standing was not in question – it represented the interests of the state of Sri Lanka, which asserted sovereignty over the entirety of the island. But the status of the Tamil negotiators was an ongoing source of debate. Did the Tamil negotiators simply represent a set of political interests within the Sri Lankan polity? Or did they instead represent a nation, and were the negotiations to be conducted "nation-to-nation" on a basis of equality? In the Thimpu talks, for example, the GOSL described the Tamil delegation as merely "six groups representing interests of certain Tamil groups in Sri Lanka,"[14] in contrast to the GOSL delegation, which represented "all communities in Sri Lanka," including Tamils.[15] The LTTE responded by stating that they were "not mere negotiators representing a clientele," but rather representatives of "the Tamil Nation," and that the face-to-face negotiations between the parties were the embodiment of their national and coequal status.[16] The government responded by changing its terminology, drawing a distinction between "Tamils of recent Indian origin" and other Tamils, arguing that it represented the former and by implication conceding that it did not represent the latter, but nonetheless acknowledging that the Tamil groups present represented

[14] See note 10.
[15] Ibid.
[16] Ibid.

"the Tamil people" and hence possessed the capacity "to reach a negotiated settlement."[17] This was a grudging concession of parity of status.
This issue arose again in 2002, when the LTTE demanded at the outset of
the Norwegian-facilitated negotiations that the GOSL remove the LTTE's
designation as a terrorist organization. This move had little or no practical impact on the LTTE's operations. As Anton Balasingham writes in his
memoirs, it was important to the LTTE because it was an acknowledgment of its status as the representative of the Tamil nation, which could
only negotiate with the GOSL "on a status of parity" if its representatives were not deemed to be criminals by the GOSL (2004, pp. 372–3).
GOSL Foreign Minister Mangala Samaraweera responded in June 2006
"there can never be 'parity of status' between a legitimate, democratically elected Government and a group practicing terror that has yet to
renounce violence or show any willingness to enter the democratic process." As I suggest in the conclusion, although the LTTE may have been
defeated on the battlefield, the issue of process and the relative status of
the negotiating parties has not gone away.[18]

   The (il)legitimacy of existing constitutional arrangements: The GOSL
and Tamil nationalists have offered competing constitutional historiogra-
phies of the legitimacy of existing constitutional arrangements. In part, this
has been a debate over substance. Tamil nationalists argue that the existing constitutional order lacks legitimacy because it is majoritarian and has
offered no protection to Tamils from a mixture of linguistic discrimination
and repressive power of the state. But this debate has also been joined on the
issue of process. The GOSL proceeds on the assumption of the legitimacy
of existing constitutional arrangements because they have been enacted in
accordance with the correct legal procedures. Thus, the 1978 Constitution
was adopted pursuant to the rules for constitutional amendment in the
1972 Constitution; the latter in turn derived its legitimacy from the fact
that it was adopted by a Constitutent Assembly, and deliberately not in
accordance with the amending procedure in the Soulbury Constitution,
severing the link with the imperial origins of Sri Lanka's post-independence
constitutional order. It is a constitution that the Sri Lankan people (singular) gave themselves, through an exercise of constituent power. The preamble to the 1972 Constitution captures this claim:

[17] Ibid.
[18] Address by Hon. Mangala Samaraweera to the Standing Committee on Foreign Affairs
   of the Storting (Norwegian Parliament), June 14, 2006. Available online at: http://www.
   peaceinsrilanka.org/peace2005/Insidepage/Pressrelease/GOSLreleases/GOSLmediaRel140606.
   asp [accessed April 21, 2009].

We the people of Sri Lanka being resolved in the exercise of our freedom and independence as a nation to give ourselves a constitution ... which will become the fundamental law of Sri Lanka deriving its power and authority solely from the people ...

Tamil nationalists challenge this account by arguing that Sri Lanka is a multinational polity, and each of its constituent nations possesses the inherent power to grant or deny consent to the constitution. For Tamil nationalists, the existing constitutional order lacks legitimacy because it did not receive the consent of the Tamil nation. Thus, in the Vaddukoddai Resolution, the TULF recounted that Tamil representatives boycotted the proceedings of the constituent assembly that drafted the 1972 Constitution. And the LTTE subsequently stated that the "Tamils did not participate in the making of the 1972 and 1978 constitutions," and by implication were not bound by it. The main Tamil political party, the Federal Party, took the same position (Wilson 1988, p. 88). Indeed, the Tamil Congress argued that Tamil voters rejected the Soulbury Constitution in the general election of 1947, because it won an overwhelming majority of seats in Tamil areas and had campaigned on a platform that opposed the Soulbury Constitution (Wilson 1988, p. 73).

The procedures necessary to adopt a final constitution: The issue that has generated the most debate is the procedures necessary to adopt any constitutional amendments – including a new constitution – as part of a settlement of the Sri Lankan conflict. The rules governing constitutional amendment in Sri Lanka have changed over time, as has their ability to protect minority interests. The Soulbury Constitution vested the power of amendment with Parliament, requiring a two-thirds vote of all members. At the time of independence, it was predicted that approximately 43 of the 101 members of Parliament would come from minority communities, thereby giving them a collective veto over constitutional amendments supported by the Sinhalese majority (Wilson 1988, p. 19). However, new citizenship laws adopted immediately after independence withdrew citizenship from Indian Tamils, and gave Sinhalese MPs a two-thirds majority. As a consequence, the two-thirds rule offered much less protection to the Tamil minority. The two-thirds rule was carried forward into the 1972 and 1978 constitutions. But the 1978 Constitution made two important changes that have converted the two-thirds rule from a mechanism that fails to protect minorities into an obstacle to a constitutional settlement to the Sri Lankan conflict. First was the introduction of a system of proportional representation, which has fractured the Sinhalese electorate and made it

nearly impossible for any one party to command a two-thirds majority in
Parliament (Shastri 2005, p. 55). As a consequence, it has become difficult
for a party forming the government to deliver on the terms of a constitutional package negotiated with the Tamils. A personal account of the
1989–1990 negotiations by Bradman Weerakoon, an advisor to President
Premadasa, reveals that he was unable to meet the LTTE's demand for the
repeal of the Sixth Amendment because he could not secure a two-thirds
majority in Parliament (1998, pp. 127, 151). The issue is not whether
Sinhalese nationalist parties control one-third of parliamentary votes. It
is rather that under proportional representation, it is exceedingly unlikely
that any one party would control two-thirds of the seats. Moreover, the
two leading parties – the United National Party (UNP) and (now) the
People's Alliance – have not been reluctant to politicize the peace process for electoral advantage, which thus far has prevented the two from
coming together on a consensus position (Uyangoda 2005a, pp. 953–60).
Second, as explained earlier, amendments to the constitutional provision
stating that Sri Lanka is a unitary state, in addition, require approval in
a referendum. Thus, any federal settlement of the conflict would go to an
island-wide vote. In that volatile context, with a focus on a single issue,
Sinhalese nationalist parties may be able to mobilize public opinion to
block approval of the requisite constitutional amendments.

   The real difficulties of working the existing procedures of constitutional amendment have produced a range of reactions. Sinhalese
nationalists, including many politicians, have demanded that any constitutional changes take the form of amendments to Sri Lanka's unitary
constitution, pursuant to its established amendment procedures. In his
memoirs, GOSL negotiator John Gooneratne – who negotiated with
the LTTE under both UNP Prime Minister Ranil Wickremasinghe and
SLFP President Rajapaksa during the Norwegian-facilitated talks – suggests that this was an assumption that both parties shared (Gooneratne
2007, pp. 108–19). Indeed, shortly after President Rajapaksa was elected,
he publicly stated that "[c]onstitutional reforms will be proposed and
approved according to proper legal procedures in order to include the
objectives reached through a broad consensus" – an indirect reference to
the need for approval by Parliament and a referendum.[19] A particularly
extreme variation of this position has been taken by H. L. de Silva – now

[19] "Sri Lanka President's First Policy Statement Calls for Revision of Ceasefire and Transparent
   Peace Process," November 25, 2005. Available online at: http://www.peaceinsrilanka.org/
   peace2005/Insidepage/PressRelease/GOSLreleases/GOSLmediaRel251105.asp [accessed
   April 21, 2009].

a constitutional advisor to President Rajapaksa – relying on the notion of a single Sri Lankan nation. He argues that, in addition to the procedural barriers to the adoption of a federal constitution, the 1978 Constitution imposes substantive barriers on constitutional amendments that make it impossible to adopt federalism, because the people cannot divest themselves of their sovereignty, which is inalienable and indivisible.[20] An intermediate option advanced by President Kumaratunga in her 2000 Sri Lanka Constitution Bill was to adopt a mixed member proportional system that would increase the chances of a future government being able to muster a two-thirds majority for constitutional amendments. However, the Bill did not attract sufficient support in Parliament to be passed, and so was never put to a vote.

However, there have been more radical proposals to evade the procedures for constitutional amendment entirely – that is, to step outside the constitution and to engage in a revolutionary constitutional change. These have come from both the Sinhalese and Tamil sides and, accordingly, proceeded from different premises. Sinhalese pragmatists proceed from the assumption of a single Sri Lankan nation, and argue that the procedures for constitutional amendment are too rigid a mechanism for the nation to exercise its inherent, constituent power to amend the constitution. President Kumaratunga advocated this strategy when it became clear that the 2000 Constitution Bill would not secure a two-thirds majority in Parliament (Shastri 2002, p. 177). Indeed, in her speech introducing the Bill, she complained that "[e]ven when we had won 80 percent of the electorates in the Parliamentary elections, we have only a single vote majority in Parliament … [b]ecause of this peculiar constitution."[21] Kumaratunga's strategy was to take the issue to the people directly in a referendum, which although formally consultative, would allow her to take the result as a mandate to summon a constituent assembly which would adopt a new constitution through a simple majority (De Votta 2003, p. 115).[22] The LTTE, by contrast, proceeded from the assumption that Sri Lanka is a multinational polity. The problem with the existing amending formula is twofold – that it sets too high a threshold, but also

---

[20] See de Silva, H. L. (2003, March 9). Are Ill-Conceived Understandings Reached at Negotiating Table? *Sri Lanka Sunday Island*. Colombo.

[21] Speech of President Chandrika Kumaratunga on new Constitution Bill in Sri Lanka Parliament, 7 August 2000. Available online at: http://www.tamilnation.org/conflictresolution/tamileelam/cbkproposals/oochandrika.htm [accessed April 21, 2009].

[22] Kumaratunga abandoned this plan in exchange for the support of the Sinhalese nationalist JVP in Parliament, which enabled her party, the SLFP, to remain in power.

that it presupposes the existence of one nation in Sri Lanka whose consent is required, as opposed to two. So running constitutional amendments through a Parliament that will always have a Sinhalese majority is illegitimate because it reflects and reinforces the majoritarian and unitary character of the Sri Lankan constitutional order. The solution is a bilateral mechanism for constitutional amendment. Notably absent from the LTTE's case for stepping outside the constitution was any popular participation or democratic accountability for such an approach to constitutional reform, either in areas under its control or under the control of the GOSL. It appears that the consent of the GOSL executive and the LTTE would have been enough.

Before the military defeat of the LTTE in 2009, these issues were central to the debate over the creation of an interim Self-Governing Authority (ISGA) in LTTE-controlled areas in the North-East. This was an LTTE objective since at least 1995.[23] Prime Minister Wickremesinghe campaigned in the 2001 parliamentary elections on a platform that included the creation of an interim administrative structure in the North-East. The topic was one of the first items on the agenda at the first round of the Norwegian-mediated negotiations in 2002. After the formal, face-to-face talks were suspended by the LTTE in April 2003, negotiations on the structure and powers of an interim authority continued for much of 2003, with the exchange of increasingly detailed proposals.[24] Ultimately, these negotiations ended in failure, although as discussed below, they were revived after the 2004 tsunami.

The background to the LTTE ISGA proposal is that until 2009, for nearly twenty years, the LTTE exercised de facto authority over large tracts of the North and until 2005, the East. As Kristian Stokke recently argued, the extent of the LTTE's de facto authority was considerable, and the pattern of its control complex (Stokke 2006, p. 1021), although the extent of this control was disputed (Sarvananthan 2007; Stokke 2007). In some LTTE-controlled areas, local civil administration, while formally part of the GOSL, actually reported to the LTTE. Moreover, even in areas under formal control of the GOSL, the LTTE asserted considerable control over local administration. Finally, the LTTE operated a parallel state which managed a number of core policy areas, including policing, criminal

[23] Address by Hon. Mangala Samaraweera to the Standing Committee on Foreign Affairs of the Storting, June 14, 2006. Available online at: http://www.peaceinsrilanka.org/peace2005/Insidepage/PressRelease/GOSLreleases/GOSLmediaRel140606.asp [accessed April 21, 2009].
[24] For the full text of these proposals, see Gooneratne (2007, pp. 191–246).

and civil courts, and, to a lesser extent, resettlement and housing, health, education, nutrition, microcredit, vocational training, and taxation. By contrast, while the GOSL still asserted de jure authority over the entire island, it was for the most part only present as "a coercive military entity that engaged in war and occupation" (Uyangoda 2005a, pp. 963–4). If the basic test of sovereign authority is a monopoly of force, the GOSL did not meet that test for over two decades (Smith 2007, p. 69). Over time, this gap between constitutional theory and the facts on the ground became increasingly glaring. But despite its de facto control, the LTTE lacked legitimacy. Thus, although a stated goal behind the establishment of the ISGA was to utilize the ceasefire to launch the reconstruction of the North-East (Balasingham 2004, p. 380), the more important goal was to obtain the GOSL's explicit consent to these arrangements, which would legitimize the LTTE as a governmental entity. Another stated goal was for the ISGA arrangements to serve as a floor for the degree of regional autonomy under a federal constitution. And although the LTTE denied that this was its goal, in the event of the failure of the peace negotiations, the ISGA could serve as the stepping-stone to a unilateral declaration of independence, secession, and recognition by other states, since the LTTE would be exercising effective governmental authority over a defined territory and population.

The GOSL opposed the formal establishment of a full-fledged "interim" regional government in LTTE-controlled areas precisely because of its longer-term implications. However, this debate quickly became a debate over constitutional process. The LTTE's de facto authority meant that a fundamental change in the institutions of public power had occurred in Sri Lanka without recourse to formal constitutional amendment. The concern was that for the GOSL to sign off on the ISGA would have been to legitimize extralegal conduct and participate in the subversion of the Sri Lankan constitutional order, by circumventing the formal processes of constitutional change.[25] The Balasingham memoirs from the Norwegian-facilitated peace talks confirm that the constitutional obstacles to the establishment of the ISGA were front and center in the government's response to the LTTE's proposals. Unfortunately, he provides no details regarding the content of these arguments, other than to say that the GOSL negotiator, constitutional scholar G. L. Peiris, stated that "the present entrenched constitution could not provide space for the institutionalization of such

---

[25] See de Silva, H. L. 2003. Are Ill-Conceived Understandings Reached at Negotiating Table. *Sri Lanka Sunday Island*. Colombo, March 9.

an administrative structure" (Balasingham 2004, p. 383). However, it is not hard to piece together this argument. Under the 1978 Constitution, all legislative power is vested in Parliament, whose legislative authority, subject to the constitution, is plenary.[26] Taken on its own, however, this provision does not explicitly prohibit Parliament from *delegating* its legislative powers to a subordinate body, which is a widespread practice in many developed democracies. But the Constitution goes on to explicitly provide that "Parliament shall not alienate its legislative power, and shall not set up any authority with any legislative power" – which would clearly prohibit the enactment of a statute vesting an interim authority with formal legislative powers.[27] For the ISGA proposal to have been implemented, a constitutional amendment would appear to have been required. According to a member of the GOSL negotiating team, the LTTE rejected these constitutional objections and "took the position that [*sic*] they were not constrained by these limitations, as they were an extra-constitutional structure, and so did not accept the writ of the Sri Lanka Constitution." (Balasingham 2004, p. 384; Gooneratne 2007, p. 25).

The subsequent exchange of detailed proposals through Norwegian mediators in 2003 proceeded from these radically different constitutional premises. The first move was made by the LTTE, which requested the GOSL to generate a proposal for "a new innovative structure for the North-East with adequate authority and legal status for the rapid implementation of humanitarian and development activities." The response of the GOSL was something much less ambitious.[28] Its proposals called for the creation of a "Reconstruction and Development Council," which was principally a body to coordinate the efforts of the GOSL and LTTE, with no clear decision-rules, which was far from an interim administration for the North-East. The LTTE rejected these proposals.[29] Prime Minister Wickremesinghe responded a few days later with a second set of proposals for the creation of an "Apex Body," which would be "a policy advisory and review board" and would have LTTE membership, but which nonetheless reaffirmed that the "[a]dministration of the North-East is the responsibility both of the [defunct] North-East Provincial

---

[26] Sri Lanka Constitution 1978, s. 3 (legislative power exclusively vested in Parliament), s. 75 (plenary power of Parliament).

[27] Sri Lanka Constitution, s. 76(1).

[28] The GOSL's proposals were communicated to the LTTE on May 17, 2003. A partial text of this first set of proposals can be found in Gooneratne (2007, pp. 198–204).

[29] Letter from Balasingham to Helgesen, May 21, 2003. See Balasingham (2004, pp. 445–9).

Council and the Central Government."[30] Balasingham raised the constitutional issues squarely in the LTTE's frustrated response, accusing the
GOSL of taking "refuge under ... an entrenched constitution that allows
no space for manoeuvre."[31] The Apex Body would have "no administrative powers" and would "only [be] an advisory council."[32] By "[s]
ituating the development structure within the parameters of the constitution," the GOSL had "effectively placed the proposed institution
under the authority of the central government," as opposed to acknowledging "the stark reality that the LTTE [ran] a de facto administration of
its own in vast tracts of territories under its control in the North-East."[33]
He asked rhetorically "[h]ow long can our people wait and tolerate their
hardships if your government seeks refuge under legal and constitutional
obstacles?"[34] Wickremesinghe responded by asserting the primacy of the
constitution, stating that any proposal must "not be in conflict with the
laws of Sri Lanka."[35] Balasingham's response could not be more direct,
calling upon the GOSL to "find a radical and creative method to overcome the legal and constitutional impediments."[36]

Just how radical the LTTE expected the GOSL to be was revealed by its
own ISGA proposals, which it released some months later.[37] Before setting
out the substance of the proposed arrangements, the LTTE took pains to
justify proceeding outside the processes of the Sri Lankan Constitution.
Thus, it asserted that "the Tamils did not participate in the making of the
1972 and 1978 constitutions, which institutionalized discrimination and

[30] Letter from Prime Minister Ranil Wikremesinghe to Jan Petersen, Foreign Minister of
Norway, May 27, 2003. The proposal was entitled "Agreement between the Government
of Sri Lanka (GOSL) and the Liberation Tigers of Tamil Eelam (LTTE) regarding administrative and financing arrangements to expedite efficient implementation of programmes
and projects relating to relief, rehabilitation and development in the North-East".
Available online at: http://www.peaceinsrilanka.org/Downloads/Pmdocs/31May03%
20-%20PM%20ltr%20Annex1%20GOSL-LTTE%2026May03.doc [accessed April 21,
2009].
[31] Letter from Anton Balasingham to Prime Minister Ranil Wickremasinghe, May 30, 2003.
See Balasingham (2004, pp. 449–53).
[32] Ibid.
[33] Ibid.
[34] Ibid.
[35] Letter from Prime Minister Ranil Wickremasinghe to Anton Balasingham, June 1, 2003.
See Balasingham (2004, pp. 453–56).
[36] Letter from Anton Balasingham to Prime Minister Ranil Wickremasinghe, June 4, 2003.
See Balasingham (2004, pp. 456–58).
[37] The Proposal by the Liberation Tigers of Tamil Eelam on behalf of the Tamil People for
an Agreement to Establish an Interim Self-Governing Authority for the Northeast of the
Island of Sri Lanka, October 31, 2003. See Gooneratne (2007, pp. 234–46).

denied them an effective role in the decision-making process," thereby indicating that the procedures created by that constitution lacked legitimacy.[38] As an alternative, it referred to "the practice in international relations over the last decade of solving conflicts between Peoples through agreement between the parties to the conflict on terms of equality," including agreements "for establishing interim governing arrangements in war-torn countries *having the force of law based solely on pacts or agreements between the parties* recognized by the international community."[39] Thus, the LTTE proposed discarding the existing process for constitutional amendment with a bilateral process that accorded the LTTE and the GOSL parity of status and required the consent of both parties. The proposals themselves would have created a regional government in the North-East with powers approaching that of an independent state. They called for an absolute majority of members to be from the LTTE, for the ISGA to "have plenary power for the governance of the North-East" including "all powers and functions ... exercised by the GOSL in and for the North-East ... control over the marine and offshore sources of the adjacent seas and the power to regulate access thereto" and "control over the natural resources in the North-East region."[40] Confirming that both the substance of the proposals and the procedure for adopting them were extra-constitutional, the ISGA proposals called for disputes over its interpretation or implementation not to be settled by the Sri Lankan courts, but by an arbitration panel appointed by both parties.

The radical nature of the LTTE's proposals was immediately apparent. One commentator referred to them as "an exercise of revolutionary constitutionalism," and linked the unique process that had been proposed to "the fractured state of the Sinhala polity where no party is capable of obtaining a [*sic*] two third majority necessary for meaningful constitutional change."[41] Another described the creation of the ISGA as "a fascist move" that "by-passes Parliament and the constitution" and would lead to the creation of "two sovereign states."[42] The GOSL's reaction to the proposals quickly fell pray to broader political forces. Since

[38] Ibid.
[39] Ibid. (italics added).
[40] Ibid.
[41] D. B. S. Jeyaraj 2003. "D.B.S. Jeyaraj on Draft LTTE proposals", *Sri Lanka Sunday Leader*, October 26; D. B. S. Jeyaraj, 2003. "Details of LTTE Draft Proposals", *Sri Lanka Sunday Leader*, October 26.
[42] G. Weerakoon, 2003. "Reinventing the Sri Lankan State or creation of two states?," *Sri Lanka Island*, October 28.

the parliamentary elections of 2001, Sri Lanka had been governed by a Prime Minister (Wickremesinghe) and a President (Kumaratunga) from two different parties, the UNP and SLFP, respectively, in French-style "cohabitation." The President had been excluded by the Prime Minister from the Norwegian-facilitated peace negotiations, and took advantage of the controversy surrounding the LTTE's proposals to undermine the Prime Minister. The SLFP released a lengthy critique of the ISGA proposals, arguing that they were unconstitutional because they contravened the provisions of the constitution that vested exclusive legislative, executive, and judicial authority in the institutions of the unitary state.[43] On the same day, the President suspended Parliament and seized control of the defence ministry – thereby rendering it impossible for the Prime Minister to negotiate with the LTTE (DeVotta 2004, p. 49)· She dissolved Parliament in February 2004. In the April 2004 elections, the SLFP came to power in a coalition with the Sinhalese nationalist People's Liberation Front (JVP) (DeVotta 2004, p. 98). The new SLFP government reiterated its rejection of the ISGA proposals, although it kept open the door to negotiations.[44] While the LTTE continued to demand negotiations for the creation of an ISGA, the GOSL responded that it wanted to proceed directly to negotiations on a final settlement.[45]

But an important shift occurred as a consequence of the tsunami of 2004. The tsunami produced devastation across the island, including in

---

[43] Lakshman Kadirgamar, Statement by the Sri Lanka Freedom Party on the LTTE's proposals for an interim self-governing authority (ISGA), November 4, 2003. Available online at: http://www.satp.org/satporgtp/countries/shrilanka/document/papers/freedompty_northeast.htm [accessed April 21, 2009]. For a response to some of these arguments, see M. Sornarajah, "ISGA and the Law", July 3, 2005. Available online at: http://www.tamilnation.org/conflictresolution/Tamileelam/norway/050703sornarajah.htm [accessed April 21, 2009].

[44] Lakshman Kadirgamar became Foreign Minister in the SLFP government, and reiterated its opposition to the ISGA proposals. See, e.g., "ISGA blueprint for a future separate state – Kadirgamar," Tamilnet, May 13, 2005. Available online at: http://www.tamilnet.com/art.html?catid=13&artid=11974 [accessed April 21, 2009].

[45] Press Release, Government of Sri Lanka, June 12, 2004. Available online at: http://www.peaceinsrilanka.org/peace2005/Insidepage/stories/PressRel130604.asp [accessed April 21, 2009]; Press Release, Government of Sri Lanka, September 21, 2004. Available online at: http://www.peaceinsrilanka.org/peace2005/Insidepage/stories/PresidentSpeech220904.asp [accessed April 21, 2009]; Press Release, Government of Sri Lanka, December 1, 2004. Available online at: http://www.peaceinsrilanka.org/peace2005/Insidepage/stories/GOSLPressRel011204.asp [accessed April 21, 2009]; Press Release, Government of Sri Lanka, March 3, 2005. Available online at: http://www.peaceinsrilanka.org/peace2005/Insidepage/PressRelease/GOSLreleases/GOSLmediaRelease040305.asp [accessed April 21, 2009].

areas controlled by the LTTE. There was a desperate need for both short-term relief to house and feed the homeless, and for longer-term reconstruction efforts. The tsunami gave the GOSL and the LTTE strong incentives to cooperate. Foreign governments had promised massive financial assistance to assist in reconstruction. However, because the LTTE had been banned as a terrorist organization in many donor countries, it could not receive aid (Uyangoda 2005). For the GOSL, cooperation with the LTTE gave it indirect access to areas that it did not control and a significant role in determining priorities for expenditure and the direction of rehabilitation efforts. In addition, it preempted the possibility that donor agencies might deal directly with the LTTE and could even increase the total amount of aid, since donors would be confident that it would reach the North-East.[46]

The agreement between the GOSL and the LTTE creating the Post-Tsunami Management Structure (P-TOMS) established a complex set of institutions for overseeing rehabilitation and reconstruction efforts. The most important were a set of regional committees in the North-East whose members were appointed by the GOSL, the LTTE, and the Muslim community, with half of the members of each committee (including the chair) appointed by the LTTE.[47] These committees would have power over "project approval and management" and "management" of a regional fund. Needless to say, the vesting of governmental authority in joint institutions apparently operating without legislative basis and outside the formal institutions of the Sri Lankan state sparked outrage from Sinhalese nationalists, who argued that the P-TOMS was an ISGA in disguise. And so, not surprisingly, the debate over the P-TOMS quickly "brought to the centre of attention issues that go far beyond a mere administrative response to the tsunami" (Uyangoda 2005b, pp. 350–1). The debate over the P-TOMS quickly became a constitutional debate. In anticipation of these objections, the GOSL took pains to distinguish the P-TOMS from the proposed ISGA, explaining that it had a joint administrative structure, whereas the ISGA would have been a governing authority.[48] However, the GOSL was initially silent on the potential unconstitutionality of the

---

[46] Statement tabled by GOSL in Sri Lanka House of Representatives, June 24, 2005. Available online at: http://www.tamilnation.org/conflictresolution/tamileelam/norway/050624jmsrilanka.htm [accessed April 21, 2009].

[47] Memorandum of Understanding for the Establishment of a Post-Tsunami Operational Management Structure (P-TOMS), June 27, 2005. Available online at: http://www.satp.org/satporgtp/countries/srilanka/document/papers/P-TOMS.htm [accessed April 21, 2009].

[48] Statement tabled by GOSL in Sri Lanka House of Representatives, *supra* note 47.

P-TOMS. It argued a few days later that "[a]ll existing laws and financial regulations" would "strictly apply to the Regional Fund," that the fund would "operate under the authority of the Treasury," which would "allocate and disburse the relevant funds."[49] However, given that the P-TOMS made no reference to the laws or constitution of Sri Lanka, it appears that pragmatics overwhelmed constitutional concerns. The strength of these pragmatic considerations is underlined by the fact that the P-TOMS was negotiated and signed by the SLFP, which had expressed constitutional concerns with the ISGA while they were in opposition.

Sinhalese nationalists turned to the courts to reassert the centrality of Parliament and constitutional orthodoxy. Thirty-nine MPs from the JVP, who were members of the governing coalition, brought a constitutional challenge to the P-TOMS within days of it being signed. Indeed, the petitioners included cabinet ministers. The motion was for interim relief to suspend the operation of the P-TOMS. The Supreme Court held that key provisions of the P-TOMS governing the powers of regional committees raised significant constitutional concerns.[50] The basis of the court's ruling was a constitutional provision that requires all monies received by Sri Lanka to be paid into the Consolidated Fund of Sri Lanka, with disbursements governed by the constitution and relevant statutes.[51] The regional fund created by the P-TOMS appeared to circumvent these constitutional arrangements, which gave Parliament the central role in supervising public expenditure through statutes and the passage of budgets. In essence, the court had held that the president had attempted to usurp the authority of Parliament and transfer some of its powers to a new institution operating entirely outside of the structures of the unitary state. The unstated implication of the judgment was that a constitutional amendment would be required to effect such a change. The Court temporarily suspended the operation of the P-TOMS. Faced with the near certainty of P-TOMS being struck down as unconstitutional, the GOSL walked away from the agreement.

Since the peace process between the GOSL and LTTE is now over, one could argue the Supreme Court's intervention has no long-term significance. However, that would be a mistake. The involvement of the

[49] "Government Dispels Apprehensions", Press Release, Government of Sri Lanka, June 29, 2005. Available online at: http://www.peaceinsrilanka.org/peace2005/Insidepage/PressRelease/GOSLreleases/GOSLmediaRel290605.asp [accessed April 21, 2009].

[50] P-TOMs Judgment, Supreme Court of Sri Lanka, July 15, 2005. Available online at: http://www.tamilnation.org/conflictresolution/tamileelam/seminar_06_Zurich/factsheets/factsheet8.pdf [accessed April 21, 2009].

[51] Constitution of Sri Lanka 1978, s. 149(1).

Supreme Court in the constitutional politics of the peace process promises to complicate any future efforts at a political settlement.[52] On the
one hand, it has reinforced skepticism on the part of Tamil nationalists of
reaching settlement from within the constitutional order, and the need to
step outside of it. An editorial in one Jaffna daily stated in response to the
Court's ruling on the P-TOMS that

[t]here is no point in condemning the high court. All it can do is to operate within
the law on which it is set up and give rulings and explanation based on them.
That is all.... To search for a solution under the present constitution is like searching in the river for what is lost in the sea. To find what is lost in the sea one must
look for it in the sea.[53]

The LTTE leader, Prabhakaran, offered a similar assessment in his annual
"Hero's Day" address, suggesting that the P-TOMS judgment meant that
the ISGA was a constitutional nonstarter under "the entrenched majoritarian constitution and in the political system built on that constitutional
structure."[54]

[52] Another issue that has recently been the subject of a successful constitutional challenge
is the merger of the Northern and Eastern provinces, a basic LTTE demand. The LTTE
asserts that the North-East constitutes the traditional Tamil homeland, and that a united
Northeastern province should serve as the unit for regional autonomy in a future Sri
Lanka. Sinhalese nationalists have long opposed the merger, because of concerns regarding the large Sinhalese minority in the Eastern province, and because together, the merged
Northern and Eastern provinces constitute nearly one-third of Sri Lanka's territory. As
part of an Indian supervised peace process in 1987, the President ordered the merger of
the North and East provinces in 1988. Although the Constitution authorized legislation
to govern such a merger, a statute set out as a condition for the merger that there be a cessation of hostilities and a surrender of arms. Constitution of Sri Lanka 1978, s. 154A(3);
Provincial Councils Act No. 42 of 1987, s. 37(1)(b). This condition clearly could not be
met, so the President attempted to amend this condition without recourse to Parliament,
through the use of his emergencies powers. The Court held that the President had acted
unconstitutionally, since the constitution had vested Parliament with the exclusive
authority to enact legislation governing the merger of provinces. Jayantha Wijesekera,
Mohamed Buhari, Wasantha Piyatissa vs Attorney General, SC (FR) Application Nos
243–245/06, Supreme Court of Sri Lanka, October 16, 2006. The effect of this decision
has been to reassert the centrality of Parliament, to create the need for recourse to constitutional amendment and to vest such a power in the President.
[53] "Lessons from the High Court Decision (Editorial)," *Uthayan Daily*, July 15, 2005. For
a similar reaction to the ruling on the merger of the Northern and Eastern provinces,
see "Sri Lanka: De-merging the Tamil homeland (Editorial)," *Uthayan Daily*, October
18, 2006; Satheesan Kumaran, "Demeger: lessons for the future," *Tamil Guardian*,
November 1, 2006.
[54] Velupillai Prabhakaran, "'Heroes Day' speech," November 27, 2005. Available online
at: http://www.satp.org/satporgtp/countries/shrilanka/document/papers/LTTE_chief_
Heroes_Day_peech.htm [accessed April 21, 2009].

On the other hand, it emboldened the JVP to reassert the primacy of the unitary constitution and to render unconstitutional attempts to circumvent Parliament in a pragmatic effort to evade the constitutional constraints and reach a negotiated settlement. Subsequent to its victory in the P-TOMS case, the JVP brought a constitutional challenge to the Ceasefire Agreement (CFA) entered into by the LTTE and the GOSL in March 2002.[55] Sinhalese nationalists long argued that the CFA was unconstitutional because the GOSL has a constitutional obligation to reassert its authority over and protect the integrity of the entire territory of Sri Lanka, and therefore cannot through agreement, inaction, abandonment, and acquiescence accept the de facto authority of an armed force acting in breach of the law – the LTTE – over parts of the country (de Silva C. 2007). Indeed, the LTTE fueled this argument, expressly stating that the CFA "was entered into outside the scope of the Constitution"[56] and "transcended the parameters of Sri Lanka's majoritarian constitution" by recognizing "Tamil Eelam's de facto existence."[57] The Court of Appeal dismissed the case on procedural grounds in March 2007. The JVP decided to not take the case to the Supreme Court, perhaps because of a tacit understanding with the Rajapaksa government that the latter would abrogate the CFA, which it did in January 2008.[58]

But had the Court found the CFA to be unconstitutional, it would have held by implication that even interim measures that themselves do not constitute a final settlement of the Sri Lankan conflict require constitutional amendment. Given the practical reality that a ceasefire is, by its very nature, a bilateral arrangement between combatants on a basis of parity of status, this would have rendered nearly any plausible ceasefire to be unconstitutional. The unconstitutionality of the CFA would have closed the legal space for a cessation of hostilities and could very well have been the death knell for any attempt to restructure Sri Lanka through a negotiated settlement. But the broader significance is that it

---

[55] Agreement on a Ceasefire between the Government of the Democratic Socialist Republic of Sri Lanka and the Liberation Tigers of Tamil Eelam (March 18, 2002). See Gooneratne (2007, pp. 123–34).

[56] LTTE Communiqué, Oslo, Norway, June 9, 2006. Available online at: http://www.tamilnet.com/art.html?catid=13&artid\=18454 [accessed April 21, 2009].

[57] Statement by LTTE on 5th Anniversary of Ceasefire Agreement, February 22, 2007. Available online at: http://www.tamilnation.org/conflictresolution/tamileelam/norway/070222ltte.htm [accessed April 21, 2009].

[58] I owe this information and analysis to Asanga Welikala.

would have only confirmed the Tamil nationalist view that the procedures for constitutional change under the Sri Lankan constitution are a barrier to the peace process.

CONCLUSION

In late 2005, Sri Lanka slid back into civil war. The reasons for this are complex. In 2001–2002, both the GOSL and the LTTE had good reasons to agree to a ceasefire (Ganguly, Höglund, & Svensson 2003; Saravanamuttu 2003; Shastri 2002). For the GOSL, there was general weariness of the war. The UNP – which won the parliamentary elections in 2001 – had campaigned on the promise of launching direct negotiations with the LTTE and appeared to acknowledge the extent of the LTTE's de facto control of the North-East. In addition, the GOSL had suffered humiliating military defeats at the hands of the LTTE – the loss of Elephant Pass, an unsuccessful attempt to retake Elephant Pass, and a surprise attack on the Colombo airport. The costs of war were beginning to mount. September 11 gave renewed impetus to the GOSL's international campaign to have the LTTE declared a terrorist organization, which in practical terms made it much more difficult for the group to finance its war against the GOSL. In addition, in the post–September 11 environment, the GOSL was able to secure military supplies and training from the United Kingdom, the United States, and India, which made an LTTE military victory over the GOSL an impossibility. More generally, the ideology of the "war on terror" undermined the legitimacy of the LTTE's recourse to force, since it left no space for armed struggle by national liberation movements. Both sides concluded they had fought, not merely to a tactical, but also to a strategic stalemate, and armed force would not resolve the conflict. Desertions from the GOSL and the recruitment of child soldiers by the LTTE, underlined the difficulty both sides had in sustaining their military campaigns.

The peace began to unravel in 2004, when an LTTE commander in the East, Colonel Karuna, broke ranks and indicated his willingness to negotiate a separate peace with the GOSL, leading to armed clashes within the LTTE (de Silva C. 2007; ICG 2008; Smith 2007). Low-level conflict broke into open war in April 2006, with the attempted assassination of the GOSL army's chief of staff, Sarath Fonseka. The infighting between factions of the LTTE eventually allowed the GOSL to retake the East by July 2007. The GOSL then turned its attention to the North for the remainder of 2007 and 2008. Although it met stiff resistance from the LTTE, the GOSL made considerable progress on the battlefield, seized the initiative and put the LTTE on the defensive. In May 2009, the GOSL declared victory over the LTTE and paraded the body of Prabhakaran on television, after a final battle in the Vanni, in which many civilians were trapped in the field of battle, producing a humanitarian catastrophe.

As Chris Smith (2007) has argued, the strategies of the LTTE and the GOSL were unclear. Prior to its defeat, the LTTE still demanded a federal Sri Lanka. Yet in the 2005 presidential election, it pressured Tamils to *not* vote for Wickremesinghe, who led the GOSL into the Norwegian-facilitated peace process (de Silva C. 2006). It thereby guaranteed victory for Rajapaksa, who supported the view that central provisions of the CFA were unconstitutional and that any settlement to the civil war must occur within the parameters of a unitary state.[59] This was a dramatic departure from the Oslo declaration, which had committed both sides to exploring a federal solution. Supporting the election of Rajapaksa reduced the prospects of a negotiated peace. This apparently contradictory strategy of the LTTE highlights that it was unable to accept the consequences of a negotiated solution to the conflict. A peace package would entail not only federalism, but also the return to competitive party politics, democratic accountability, respect for human rights, and the rule of law in the North-East after an absence of many decades. The LTTE was an authoritarian organization, which had over two decades eliminated other armed Tamil groups and moderate Tamil politicians, and whose control over the North-East was buttressed by extortion and physical violence. In spite of its close alliance with the Tamil National Alliance (TNA), which contested national elections in 2001 and 2006, the LTTE continued to favor military means and showed no signs of making the transition to a political party because this would necessarily have involved a reduction in its authority.

The GOSL's position shifted as well. After President Rajapaksa was elected, he claimed that the CFA was unconstitutional and should be amended accordingly. But at the first round of peace negotiations after he took office, in Geneva in February 2006, the GOSL walked away from these positions and stood by the CFA for 2006 and 2007, even though the country had in fact returned to war. However, on January 2, 2008, the GOSL formally abrogated the CFA.[60] In the place of a negotiated settlement with the LTTE was a new strategy to destroy the LTTE as a

---

[59] Agreement between SLFP Presidential Nominee, Mahinda Rajapaksa and JVP, September 8, 2005. Available online at: http://www.tamilnation.org/conflictresolution/tamileelam/norway/050908mahinda.htm [accessed April 21, 2009].

[60] "Government to withdraw from CFA". Available online at: http://www.peaceinsrilanka.org/peace2005/Insidepage/PressRelease/GOSLreleases/GOSLmediaRel030108.asp [accessed April 21, 2009].

military force and achieve a political solution through the political process, centered on Sri Lanka's parliament and the political parties represented therein. However, it was far from clear that the GOSL could
completely defeat the LTTE militarily. Moreover, since the LTTE originated as a guerrilla movement, it was predicted that the LTTE would
"bomb themselves back onto the agenda"[61] by simply reverting to these
tactics in the jungles of the North with strikes on military targets, and by
terrorizing civilians through bombings in the Sinhalese-majority areas of
the south. Nonetheless, contrary to expectations, the LTTE was defeated,
and has not turned to such type of warfare.

Thus, in these circumstances, given that both sides chose to return to
armed confrontation, and that the GOSL prevailed, it would seem that
the law is of marginal importance. This would appear to be a case where
competing nationalisms within a multinational polity can be understood
without reference to legal materials. But the Sri Lankan civil war is ultimately a constitutional conflict. Law is fundamental to understanding
the causes of the conflict and the possibilities for its resolution. Tamil
grievances have been framed in terms of the defects of Sri Lanka's post-
independence constitutions, and their demands – to the extent that they
call for regional autonomy within a united Sri Lanka – have translated
into calls for the restructuring of the Sri Lankan constitutional order.
Likewise, constitutional arguments have figured centrally in Sinhalese
nationalist discourse. The prominence of legal argumentation in the Sri
Lankan conflict demonstrates how fundamental the law has been to the
parties' understanding of the conflict. And so, even after the civil war had
recommenced, when the parties met in Geneva in October 2006, constitutional issues were raised by the LTTE once more. Recounting the saga
of the ISGA proposals and the unconstitutionality of the P-TOMS, the
LTTE boldly stated that "a solution to the ethnic conflict cannot be found
within the current Sri Lankan constitution."[62]

Examining the Sri Lankan crisis through various legal materials and
texts sharpens our understanding of this case. It vividly illustrates the
value of taking the law seriously in the study of multinational polities.
Moreover, examining the legal materials with the assistance of analytical
categories furnished by constitutional theory illustrates that the descent

---

[61] "Sri Lanka's war: Closing in on the Tiger's Lair", *The Economist*, 4 September 4, 2008.
[62] LTTE Opening Statement, Geneva Peace negotiations, October 28, 2006. Available online
at: http://www.tamilnation.org/conflictresolution/Tamileelam/norway/061028solheim.
htm#LTTE_Opening_Statement [accessed April 21, 2009].

into civil war in Sri Lanka ultimately arose from not one, but two different kinds of breakdown of the Sri Lankan constitutional order. One arose from a fundamental difference over the substance of the constitutional arrangements to frame the relationship between the Sinhalese majority and the Tamil minority – electoral representation, official language policy, federalism, and so on. But there has been an equally fundamental disagreement over the constitutional procedures that should govern that debate over constitutional substance. Constitutional procedures allow the constitutional politics of substance to occur. Without a shared understanding of the process of reform, the constitutional politics of substance may be impossible.

An enormous amount of attention continues to be given to questions of substance – what the shape of a future Sri Lanka should be. But issues of process require much more careful attention than they have received thus far. The critical issue is the process whereby a new constitution would be adopted. Until the LTTE's military defeat, the principal issue was the collision between the internal logic of the unitary constitution and the de facto control by the LTTE of portions of the North. As illustrated by the Supreme Court's judgment striking down the P-TOMS, and the prospect of a successful challenge to the CFA, the constitutional order stood in the way of a negotiated settlement between the LTTE and the GOSL on the basis of a relationship of parity. Indeed, there was a danger that insisting on constitutional orthodoxy could have pushed the LTTE to issue a unilateral declaration of independence.

The end of the war with the LTTE, and the insistence of the GOSL that any political solution to the conflict will be achieved through existing constitutional process, would not appear to raise the same existential concerns. On the one hand, the electoral success of the JVP and the Jathika Hela Urumaya (JHU) make it less likely than ever that the demanding procedures set out in the Sri Lankan Constitution – a two-thirds majority in Parliament, and a simple majority in a national referendum – could ever be satisfied. But on the other hand, the downside risk of a failure of constitutional process would appear to be minimal, since the constitutional status quo would prevail. However, the political situation is in fact much more volatile because the constitutional status quo is deeply unstable. The military victory over the LTTE has not resolved the Sri Lankan constitutional conflict. The LTTE arose after the failure of Tamil political parties to achieve constitutional change through the political process to respond to long-standing Tamil grievances regarding official language status, discrimination in government employment, university admissions, and the failure of the state to protect Tamils from private violence. The defeat of the LTTE has left unaddressed the concerns that initially gave rise to Tamil nationalism and the turn to violence. Recent polling data reveals that Tamils continue to hold these concerns (Irwin 2008). Moreover, the same data shows that Sinhalese do not perceive these issues to be nearly as significant as Tamils, which highlights the degree of political imagination that will be required for the Sinhalese majority to address these concerns. If the political process does not yield a new set of constitutional arrangements that fairly address the legitimate concerns of Tamils, a violent movement would arise again, triggering a further cycle of violence and repression. The fact that the GOSL, after its victory over the LTTE, has called for an increase in the size of the military, to maintain a large and permanent presence in the north and east, may suggest that the GOSL itself is aware of this possibility.

Indeed, the available evidence suggests that Tamils in the north – now free to participate in national elections – are disengaged from the national political process. In the municipal elections held in Jaffna and Vavuniya in August 2009 – now possible because of the defeat of the LTTE – turn-out was extremely low, the government-allied candidate secured insufficient preferences to get elected, and Tamils appear to have supported the LTTE-allied TNA. Moreover, it is not at clear whether Tamils will vote in the 2010 presidential election. Although in theory they possess the balance of power, they do not appear to have a real choice, as both candidates are Sinhala nationalists. The opposition alliance's candidate is General Fonseka – a Sinhalese nationalist who led the GOSL to military victory, has been accused of committing war crimes against Tamil civilians, and has stated that Sri Lanka belongs to the Sinhalese. While President Rajapaksa, by contrast, has called for a "political solution" to the national question, he has reaffirmed that this must occur within the structure of a unitary state and has categorically rejected federalism. The true test will be the parliamentary elections that must be held in 2010, and in which Tamil parties will contest.

To put the point another way, Sri Lankan constitutional order has set in motion a long-term process of self-destruction that has at best been delayed by a military victory over the LTTE. It may be necessary to proceed outside the constitutional order to save the prospect of constitutionalism in Sri Lanka. A useful starting point is V. K. Nanayakkara's recent proposal to step outside the 1978 Constitution by convening a constituent assembly that would draft a constitution to be approved in a national referendum (Nanayakkara 2006). The challenge is to ensure that the membership and voting rules of such a body reflect a conception of Sri Lanka as a multinational, not a mono-national, polity. Two overarching principles should guide the structure of such a body. First, a stable political settlement requires representation from all those with affected interests. A major shortcoming of the various rounds of GOSL–LTTE peace negotiations is that they were bilateral ceasefire negotiations between combatants that did not include all interested parties. These representatives would include other parties that principally represent the South, who have acted as spoilers in Parliament because they were not invested in the process and have turned peace negotiations into questions of partisan political cleavage. But it would also include other Tamil parties in the North-East, who were not at the table.

Second, the voting rules for a constituent assembly should simultaneously reflect the multinational character of Sri Lanka and encourage crosscutting alliances across national boundaries. An important tool for Sri Lanka is the notion of "sufficient consensus" (Haysom and Choudhry, forthcoming). This concept originated in the South African constitutional negotiations in the early 1990s. These negotiations involved two principal parties, the African National Congress (ANC) and the National Party (NP), whose joint agreement was necessary for any negotiated settlement. The ANC and the NP decided early on to invite a large number of smaller political parties in order to secure broad buy-in to the final agreement. However, instead of extending the requirement for the ANC's and the NP's agreement into a decision-rule of unanimity (which would encourage holdouts), the parties agreed to a super-majority rule that was never defined numerically – that is, sufficient consensus. The parties to the Northern Ireland peace negotiations in the mid-1990s adapted the notion of sufficient consensus to multiparty negotiations in a multinational polity. In Northern Ireland, sufficient consensus came to mean majority support within each national bloc – that is, a double-majority rule. This ensured that each national community consented to the final peace agreement. But each national bloc was recognized as consisting of a plurality of voices, and unanimity within each national bloc was not required. Moreover, it encouraged agreement between representatives of different national communities. The notion of sufficient consensus holds promise for Sri Lanka. The parity of status that was long sought by the LTTE would be present, not between the LTTE and the GOSL, but between the Tamils and the Sinhalese.

6

The Dilemmas of Burma's Multinational Society

Ardeth Maung Thawnghmung

Since Burma won its independence in 1948, successive Burmese governments have confronted claims of multiple sub-state nationalist groups to the right of greater autonomy and separate independent states. The common position taken by all Burmese central governments is that appeasing such demands could create a domino effect leading to the breakup of the country, and thus it is believed that these movements must be contained as much as possible. Concern over losing political power and control of economic resources is another reason why the Burmese governments have been reluctant to devolve power to the sub-national levels.

This chapter assesses policies and practices implemented by successive governments toward sub-state nationalist groups in post-colonial Burma. It stresses, in particular, the Shan, Kachin, Karen, Kayah, Mon, Arakan, and Chin – the seven largest sub-state nationalist groups, whose names correspond to the current seven states in Burma. The first

I use the term "Burman" to refer to the country's ethnic majority; "Burma" or "Myanmar" in reference to the country; and "Burmese" in reference to its citizens. In 1989, the military junta replaced the existing English names that had been given to the country, its divisions, townships, cities, streets, citizens, and ethnic groups with what they considered to be more authentic Burmese names. Thus Burma became Myanmar, and its citizens Myanmars; Rangoon became "Yangon," and ethnic groups such as the Karen were renamed Kayin. The use of either the old or new names has become a way of indicating one's political stance toward the Burmese junta. I use "Burma" when discussing pre-1989 situations, but will use Burma and Myanmar interchangeably in the post-1989 period. However, I will use the pre-1989 terms for Burma's ethnic groups throughout to avoid confusion since these terms are commonly used in writings in English, particularly in the books, journals, and published sources cited here.

part of the chapter sets out historical paths that laid the foundation for Burma's multiple nations and analyzes the emergence of sub-state nationalist movements. The period after independence saw the central authorities attempting to appease secessionist demands by forming three ethnically based states and by giving them considerable civil and political freedom and the right to express ethnic identity. However, a lack of consensus within the ruling coalition (the majority of whom later took up arms against the state), failure to implement greater autonomy at the regional levels, and weak state infrastructure handicapped the government's ability to handle competing claims made by sub-state nationalist groups.

This chapter shows how the Burmese military (*tatmadaw*), which perceived itself as a panacea for national unity by staging a coup in 1962, has become a stumbling block for the creation of a multinational state. In addition, while the military junta in general has been less accommodating to ethno-national groups, it has followed diverse policies toward different segments of nationalist groups, depending on the nature of domestic dynamics, the external environment, and the relative strengths of the military and the armed opposition groups. General Ne Win's socialist government (1962–1988), for instance, practiced a scorched-earth policy toward insurgent groups while giving some symbolic recognition to minority ethnic groups that remained "quietly" within legal boundaries. The socialist government's isolationist policies, which provided fertile ground in which communist and ethnic insurgent organizations could prosper in the rebel-controlled areas by taxing goods that crossed the borders and by exploiting natural resources, led to deteriorating economic situations and eventually to the downfall of the regime in 1988. The military government, which took power in 1988, was able to sign ceasefire accords with the majority of the ethnic armed insurgent groups and oversee the drafting of a new constitution, which envisions a quasi-elected and military-controlled government and a referendum on that constitutional proposal.

The second part of the chapter evaluates two constitutional drafts that have been proposed respectively by the SPDC and the opposition movement, and analyzes their various implications for future political reform and national reconciliation. The chapter presents what might be called a "liberal integrationist" policy as an alternative to the creation of ethnic-based states and power-sharing schemes in order to more fully address the nature of Burma's ethnic makeup as well as the various effects of six decades of civil war.

BURMA'S MULTINATIONAL ORIGINS

The territory that now makes up Burma, or Myanmar, is host to a diverse array of ethnic, cultural, religious, and linguistic groups. The eight largest ethnic groups are the Burman, Shan, Karen, Rakhine, Mon, Kachin, Chin, and Kayah, which are respectively estimated to make up 66.9, 10.5, 6.2, 4.2, 2.4, 1.4, 2, and 0.4 percent of the total population, even though an official census based on ethnicity has not been conducted since 1983 (Than 2005, p. 67). There are also several smaller linguistic groups, a majority of whom are subgroups within each of these dominant ones. Burman, along with Mon and pockets of Karen, live in lowland areas in the delta, central, and southern Burma, surrounded by minority populations who live in the highland areas bordering India, China, Laos, and Thailand.

In pre-colonial times the Burman, Arakanese, and Mon occasionally engaged in war against each other for greater control over manpower and territory, but there was also a degree of cultural assimilation and intermarriage among these groups, facilitated by their shared Buddhist religion (Silverstein 1997, p. 169). The Burmese monarchy had always looked down upon minority hill tribe populations as illiterate and uncivilized, occasionally recruiting them for their armies and using them as protective shields against their enemies from neighboring countries (Selth 1986, p. 488; Silverstein, 1997, p. 170). Generally speaking, however, the Burmese kings allowed these hill tribe populations (specifically the Kachin, Shan, and Kayah) to retain their autonomy as long as they recognized suzerainty of the Burmese monarchy and paid tribute to it (Silverstein 1997, p. 169). Thus the territory that came to be known as Burma had never been fully integrated or controlled by a single, central state in pre-colonial times.

The geographic and cultural separation between the mainland peoples and the hill tribe populations continued after the British occupation of Burma in 1885. The colonial regime divided the country into two administrative zones. The central area, called "Ministerial Burma," where most of the ethnic Burmans lived, was put under direct colonial rule. The "Frontier Areas" or the "Excluded Areas," located along the newly drawn borders and populated by other minority groups, were left largely untouched by the British. As a consequence, very little interaction took place between residents of central Burma and those of the Frontier Areas.

The British further separated the Burman from other minority groups by resorting to classic "divide-and-rule" policies. Minority groups, such as Chin, Kachin, and Karen, were deliberately recruited for the army and police. Before the separation of Burma from India in 1935, there were no Burman in the regular army and, for the most part, none in the military police (Selth 1986, p. 488). At the outbreak of World War II in 1939, Burma's regular armed forces had 1,448 Karen (9.3 percent of the population), 868 Chin (2.3 percent), 881 Kachin (1.05 percent), and 168 members of other ethnic groups. There were only 472 Burman (including a few Mon and Shan), although together they constituted 75.11 percent of the country's population (Selth 1986, p. 489).

The Burmese nationalist and resistance movements against British rule were initiated and dominated by Burman populations. Except for two Shan, only ethnic Burman comprised the "thirty comrades" who were smuggled out to Japan and China for military training in the campaign against the British in the early 1940s (Selth 1986, p. 490). In January 1942, the group formed the Burma Independence Army (BIA), and returned to Burma at the head of the invading Japanese. Although quite a few Shan and Mon joined the movement, most members of the BIA, which soon swelled to 10,000, were Burman. On the other hand, some groups such as the Karen, Lahu, Chin, Naga, and Kachin remained loyal and fiercely defended the British. Others such as the overwhelming majority of Shan, Wa, Akha, and other local hill peoples "preferred to try and sit the war out in their remote highland homes" (Selth 1986, p. 496; Smith 1999, p. 64). Those who fought for the British were under the impression that they would be rewarded for their services and sacrifices (Selth 1986, p. 502). Many Karen civilians were slaughtered by the members of the BIA for their perceived privileged status and close association with the British. This resulted in serious outbreaks of racial violence that led to the deaths of members from both Karen and Burman communities in the Salween district in the East and, to a greater extent, in the Irrawaddy delta (Selth 1986, pp. 491–2).

When Aung San and his fellow nationalists realized that the Japanese had made false promises, they formed at the end of 1942 a loose coalition known as the Anti-Fascist People's Freedom League (AFPFL) made up of communists, trade unions, youth groups, and women's and religious organizations. They established secret contacts with the Allies to push back their new oppressor (Selth 1986, p. 495).

After the end of the war, the Burman nationalist leaders were able to eventually negotiate with the British government for the country's independence. Initially, Frontier members, such as Shan, Karen, Kayah, and Chin, preferred to remain autonomous under British rule. They attempted to provide legitimacy to their claims by saying that they had been independent peoples with unique languages and cultural practices before the British occupation and had been conquered separately by the British. Even the Chin, smaller in number and divided along tribal, linguistic, and regional lines, noted that the Chin are "not a minority group but a nation with its own distinctive culture and civilization, language, literature, names and nomenclature, sense of value and proportion" (Sakhong 2003, p. 223). Those who lived in the plains, the Mon and Arakanese (who were occupied by the British as the subjects of the Burman kings) also expressed their desire to establish separate states by tracing their historical origins as independent kingdoms or states before the invasion of the Burmese kings in 1754 and 1784, respectively.

The emergence of the Karen nationalist movement, however, is very much a product of British colonial rule. The Karen, according to official data, constitute 6.2 percent of the country's population, but they are dispersed over a wide area that stretches from the Irrawaddy delta region to the central area of the Pegu Yoma mountain range, and to the eastern hills along the Thai border of the Karen and Tenasserim division. The Karen in particular welcomed the British as protectors against the Burman and as a source of opportunities that were previously lacking. Many of them were also more inclined to accept Christianity, which seemed to fulfill the prophecy of an ancient Karen myth that foretold the return of a white brother bringing the lost book. Many Karen became early beneficiaries of a Western education and of a system of writing developed by American missionaries. Soon they began to foster the idea of pan-Karen nationalism, disseminated in the Karen language through missionary-sponsored Karen schools and churches, and Karen-vernacular newspapers. This nationalism linked the dispersed Karen villages that previously had no sophisticated political organization (Cady 1958, pp. 42–3, 137–8). Karen nationalists claimed that the Karen – a naturally quiet, peace-loving, and hospitable people – were united by their common (historical) origins, kinship, language, national costume, cultural practices, high moral standards, and shared experiences as an oppressed people.[1]

It should be noted, however, that Chin, Kachin, and Karen are collective names for the various ethnic subgroups of the main mother-language groups. Karen, for instance, is the collective name of twenty or so ethnic subgroups of the Karen who joined four different armed nationalist movements (Smith 1999, pp. 30–1). The term "Kachin," which was

---

[1] See Karen National Union, *History of the Karens and KNU*. [Online] Available at http://www.karen.org/knu/KNU_His.htm [accessed April 12, 2009].

consolidated as a primary ethnic category and geopolitical boundary by the 1947 Burma Constitution, represents a collective category of six principal lineages. While the Sgaw Karen Christian dominated a broader Karen identity and played a leading role in the Karen armed-resistance movement in 1949, Jinghpaw dominated the broader identity of Kachin and led a Kachin revolt in 1961.

Despite their previous opposition, after a series of lengthy meetings with Burman nationalist leader Aung San at Panglong in the Shan state, some ethnic leaders, such as the Shan, Kachin, and Chin leaders, agreed to be a part of an independent Burma. Generally speaking, the Panglong Agreement was based on a concept of nations within a nation; it laid the basic principles for the establishment of a future federal union that would recognize political and economic equality and self-determination of non-Burman and Burman ethnic nationalities. For these people the Panglong Agreement was simply a means of securing their independence.[2] Many of the leaders expressed their faith in Aung San, who took a public position in favor of "unity in diversity": "the Hill People would be allowed to administer their own areas in any way they pleased and the Burmese would not interfere in their internal administration" (Silverstein 1980, p. 141). Many ethnic leaders, however, felt that the Panglong spirit was violated by the 1947 constitution and by various practices adopted by the U Nu government after Aung San and his colleagues were assassinated on July 19, 1947.

PARLIAMENTARY DEMOCRACY (1948–1962)

The 1947 constitution established a parliamentary democracy and bicameral legislature composed of a 250-seat Chamber of Deputies and a 125-seat Chamber of Nationalities, some of which were reserved for non-elected hereditary chieftains of the nationalities, especially the Chin, Kachin, and Shan. For many leaders from sub-state nationalist groups, this constitution fell short of expectations.

First, the constitution did not give equal treatment to groups such as the Kachin, Chin, Karen, Mon, and Arakan who had long expressed the desire to have states of their own. It created three new states from the former Frontier Areas – the Kachin, Shan, and Kayah states – which had remained relatively autonomous under traditional rulers in the

---

[2] The preamble of the Panglong Agreement declares "believing that freedom will be more speedily achieved by the Shan, the Kachin, and the Chin by their immediate cooperation with the interim Burmese government." Burma gained independence in January 4, 1948.

pre-colonial period. It also gave the Shan and Kayah states the right to secession after ten years (Silverstein 1980, pp. 22–5). The Kachin relinquished the right to secession in return for incorporation of two major cities into their state. The Chin, who were quiescent, ethnically divided, and always ready to acknowledge their dependence on "Ministerial Burma" (Smith 1999, p. 80), opted to stay in the Union where they were promised economic aid. One Chin nationalist, however, claimed that the Chin had to merely contend with the status of "Special Division" because they misunderstood the term for "state" and because of the opinion of the only Chin delegate who happened to be a college graduate (Sakhong 2003, p. 215). The Chin people were given a designated Minister of Chin Affairs who was endowed with the authority to make decisions relating to schools and cultural institutions.

The status of the territorial authority over three other major ethnic groups – the Mon, Karen, and Arakanese – was left open to be decided after independence in January 1948. The Burman nationalists initially rejected the idea of separation for Arakan and Mon from Burma Proper because the British had conquered them as part of the Burman Empire and because of their "racial identity and characteristics" deemed indistinguishable from Burman.[3] The Karen, dispersed all over Burma, were unable to settle the status and territories of a Karen state and agreed to resolve the matter after independence. Before questions of the status and borders of a Karen state were resolved, the Karen were guaranteed "minority rights," which included twenty-two reserved legislative seats in the Chamber of Deputies, a Karen Affairs Council, and a Karen minister who would have control of all administrative, educational, and cultural affairs relating to Karen (Smith 1999, p. 82). These reserved rights, however, were abolished when the Karen state came into existence in 1956. U Nu took the position that the Karen must surrender the special privileges associated with their minority rights in exchange for the new state, even though the majority of Karen people lived outside of the Karen state's boundaries.

Second, not only were these three newly formed states given different rights because of "their desires, particular background, and social composition," but their institutions were subordinated to those of the Union, or Burma proper. State laws were inferior to Union legislation and states were financially dependent on the Union, which was "the ultimate owner of all the lands" and which appropriated an annual lump sum to the

---

[3] See NMSP, *History of Mon.* [Online] Available at: http://www.nmsp.info/monhis.php [accessed April 12, 2009].

states on a 5-3-1 basis, under which the Shan received the most and the Kayah the least (Silverstein 1980, pp. 186, 203).

Despite these setbacks, the 1947 constitution gave considerable autonomy to new states and guaranteed individual rights. In Kachin, Kayah, and Shan states, both elected and hereditary leaders were allowed to exercise a certain degree of executive, judiciary, legislative, and economic authority. For instance, the State Councils were empowered to raise money through taxation and to make laws, which were subject to the approval of the Union's institutions. At the local level, the Shan and Kayah chiefs were given administrative, judicial, and taxing power over their traditional domains (Silverstein 1980, p. 201). There was also a rotation of the Union presidency from a Shan, who served as the first president, to a Burman, and then to a Karen.

From the very beginning of independence, the first post-colonial government led by an independence movement-turned-coalition party (the AFPFL), experienced internal dissension. It was caused especially by its left-leaning members, who complained that post-colonial economic and political structures had been compromised in favor of the British imperialists' interests. The AFPLF leaders proved to be unwilling and unable to accommodate the demands by various ethnic groups for greater autonomy and independence. An Arakan rebellion began in 1947 (Smith 1999, p. 80). At least one-third of the army joined a communist insurrection in 1948, as did the majority of the nationwide People's Volunteer Organization, ostensibly a veterans' affairs group but in reality, the paramilitary wing of the AFPFL (Callahan 1998, p. 11). By this time, Burma was confronting the threat of multiple insurgencies and most neighboring countries in East and Southeast Asia (particularly Vietnam, Cambodia, Indonesia, Malaysia, and China) were mired in civil wars or still struggling to gain independence from their colonial rulers. The Burmese government had relied heavily on the support of leaders from newly independent India with whom they had shared long historical, cultural, and political ties.

The Karen National Union (KNU) took up arms in 1949 over disagreement with the status and boundaries of the Karen state, and the need to protect Karen populations from the violence that had begun between the Karen and Burman communities during and after World War II. The constitution initially confined the Karen state largely to the backward Salween district and the adjacent areas where Karen formed a majority but the KNU wanted more territory, including a large part of the delta region (where Karen and Burman were intermixed). Angered by constitutional arrangements that did not even give them minority rights, the

Mon, the Pao, and other groups also revolted. The Karenni took up arms to demand a separate, independent state. U Nu faced armed rebellion from all sides and his government was called the "Rangoon government," which referred to the limited areas under its control.

U Nu made various efforts to address the demands of sub-state nationalist groups while carefully balancing his actions so as not to upset the majority Buddhist Burman population. On the one hand, his government promoted Buddhism by passing an amendment in 1961 to make it a state religion, creating the Ministry of Religious Affairs and sponsoring Buddhist holidays and celebrations. It also introduced the teaching and learning of the Burman language and sponsored Buddhist missionary works in minority areas. On the other hand, U Nu's government allowed minority ethnic groups to teach their languages in pre-university-level classes as well as to freely publish books, newspapers, and magazines (Hlaing 2007, p. 156). In early 1958, U Nu offered an "arms for democracy" program that would allow ethnic armed-resistance groups to form political parties and run elections after giving up arms. Many, particularly the Mon and Arakan, exchanged their arms for the right to establish ethnically based political parties to fight for the creation of their respective states. U Nu also agreed in principle to the creation of Mon and Arakan states. The KNU was unwilling to lay down arms before an agreement was reached on the territories and status of a Karen state (Oo & Min 2007).

U Nu sought to treat the Karen insurrection as an action of "bad" citizens, as distinguished from the "good" citizens – those who were loyal and supported the Union. Although he initially suspended Karen from the police and military, he later reinstated Karen officers who had proved their loyalty to the Union (Silverstein 1980, p. 217). He also successfully incorporated a number of aboveground Karen political parties into his party's alliance. Support from this segment of the "other" Karen populations had led to the creation of the Karen state, which came into existence in 1956.

By the end of the 1950s, however, the Shan and Kachin joined the rebellion in response to what they perceived as a breach of the Panglong Agreement. The Shan were incensed by the army's interference into their local administration and its mistreatment of the local population during the military effort to repel the encroaching Karen and Chinese Nationalist armed forces in the Shan areas. In 1959, under pressure from the caretaker military government (1958–1960), the Shan Sawbwa (traditional chiefs) gave up their constitutional right to govern in return for a cash payment and maintenance of their hereditary titles and personal property. The Kachin, having been pressured by the government to give up three villages to China in a border settlement, were frustrated by its failure to provide economic assistance and infrastructure, and by its promotion of Buddhism. Several smaller minorities rebelled over the lack of political and economic autonomy and over fears of Burman assimilation.

Faced with a possible Shan secession and the emergence of insurgent groups in the Shan and Kachin states among other areas, U Nu met in 1961 with Shan leaders, who demanded greater autonomy and called for Burma proper to be treated as separate from the national government and coequal with other states. In the end, when U Nu decided in 1962 to convene a federal seminar to allow various ethnic leaders to discuss their grievances and to pave the way for the creation of Mon and Arakanese states, the military took over power. The junta saw these concessions as a precursor to the breakup of the Union of Burma as they could stimulate comparable demands for other minority groups and lead to state disintegration. Secessionist activities in Indonesia and growing communist movements in the neighboring countries (China, Vietnam, Cambodia, Laos, Philippines, Thailand) may have also added a sense of urgency precipitating the military takeover.

The U Nu civilian government (1948–1962) demonstrated a gap between the expectations of ethnic leaders who felt cheated by the Panglong Agreement and Burman nationalists who opposed the creation of nations within a nation. U Nu, though he never approved of the idea of separate ethnic states, attempted for political reasons to accommodate sub-state nationalist demands. A lack of consensus within the ruling coalition (the majority of whom later took up arms against the state) and weak state infrastructure, however, had handicapped the government's ability to handle competing claims made by sub-state nationalist groups that had relatively strong military forces and bargaining power. All major sub-state nationalist groups took up arms against the state by the time the military took over power in 1962. This history served as a warning sign to the military junta that was then determined at all costs to bring the country under its strong grip.

THE REVOLUTIONARY COUNCIL (1962–1974) AND THE BURMA SOCIALIST PROGRAM PARTY (1974–1988)

Upon seizing power, General Ne Win opened peace talks with various armed-resistance groups, but most of these rejected his terms and conditions, which they considered tantamount to demands for outright surrender (Oo & Min 2007, p. 9). The Revolutionary Council soon launched a military campaign against these resistance groups and implemented a "four-cut policies" which forcibly relocated villages in areas controlled by the insurgents to deny them a source of recruits, food, intelligence, and finance. These strategies succeeded in wiping out communist and KNU resistance groups in the Irrawady and Pegu Yoma divisions. The continuing civil war resulted in thousands of deaths, displacements, and violations of human rights that were well documented by several human rights organizations.

Despite massive casualties, these various sub-state nationalist insurgencies continued to control a large area along the border, thanks to its abundant natural resources, taxes imposed on goods that crossed the borders between Burma and its neighbors, and an opium economy. By the late 1970s, the Burmese military was confronting a multitude of armed resistance groups. The largest sub-state nationalist armed organizations, which controlled large base areas, included the Kachin Independence Organization or KIO (8,000 troops) in the north, the Karen National Union or KNU (6,000), the New Mon State Party or NMSP (1,500) in the south and southeast, the Shan State Progress Party or SSPP (2,500), the Tailand Revolutionary Council or TRC (3,000), and the Shan State Nationalities Liberation Organization or SSNLO in the Shan state (Smith, 1999, chart 1). Most operated like states within a state by administering local populations, dispensing justice, distributing social services (health care and education), and exercising control over the monopoly of force. They ran schools that offered courses taught in their respective minority languages and carried out anti-Burman propaganda (Hlaing 2007, p. 166). In addition, since the 1960s, the Thai government had practiced a "buffer policy" of using Burma's insurgent groups as barriers against the expansion of communism into Thailand and against the Burmese government, with which Thailand had historically hostile relationships. Thailand had maintained close ties with various anti-Rangoon insurgents along the Thai-Burma border. It allowed them to operate on Thai soil and to have access to arms, communication equipment, foreign contacts, and medical care for the troops (Myoe 2002, 47). China also provided support to the Communist Party of Burma, which had recruited minority ethnic leaders among its rank and file members. In addition, General Ne Win's authoritarian political system and isolation policy had alienated Burma from the rest of the world, particularly from democratic India.

Territories of Burma were now divided into government-controlled areas (white areas), rebel-controlled areas (black areas), and contested areas (gray areas) under which different authorities exerted control. Ethnic civilians who lived in rebel-controlled areas developed anti-Burman sentiments through their experience as objects of harsh military campaigns and through nationalist discourses constructed by their respective ethnic, armed organizations.

None of these armed organizations, however, were ethnically exclusive. SSNLO had Pao, Shan, and Kayan groups and the SSPP had the Shan and Palung, while the Karenni National Progressive Party (KNPP) had Kayah, Kayan, Bre, and Shan. In the Shan state alone, there were numerous armed factions led by smaller groups such as Wa, Pao, and Palung. All the larger ethnic armed organizations, such as the KIO, KNU, NMSP, and KNPP, had explicit goals to fight for self-determination and greater autonomy (Smith 1999, chart 1). However, some individuals or groups operated like warlord and criminal gangs, prospering on border trade, the exploitation of natural resources, and the cultivation and trade of opium. These remarks are not meant to belittle the many groups who had genuine grievances or held a vision of ethnically homogeneous communities. By 1984, many of these ethnic armed organizations (particularly members of the National Democratic Front) had dropped demands for secession to establish a unified Federal Union with all the ethnicities, including the Burman (Smith 1999, p. 386).

While the government resorted to harsh treatment toward insurgent groups, their co-ethnic counterparts who remained "quietly" in the government-controlled areas were left alone as long as they did not pose a threat to the socialist and military institutional order. On the other hand, Ne Win's Revolutionary Council closed down all missionary schools; made Burmese the only medium of instruction in all university and pre-university classes, except for English language classes; and allowed the teaching of minority languages only up to the second grade. At the same time, these nationalities could develop and promote their respective cultures and languages as long as their activities did not have adverse consequences for national unity and socialist projects (Hlaing 2007, p. 161). Thus, Buddhist monasteries and Christian churches continued to offer minority language courses after school and during summer holidays. In addition, public schools in the Chin state, Palung, and other remote areas continued to use their mother tongues as their medium of instruction and, in many minority areas, ethnic minorities were able also to resolve some legal problems, such as rape, divorce, and inheritance, using their respective customary laws and practices. The Ministry of Education also published textbooks, folklore, and historical and anthropological studies of Mon, Shan, Karen, Chin, and Kachin national groups, and encouraged nationwide celebrations of Union Days and ethnic national days (Hlaing 2007, p. 162; Silverstein 1980, pp. 236–7). Article 21 of the 1974 constitution gave "the national races" the "freedom to profess their religion, use and develop their language, literature, and culture, follow their cherished traditions and customs, provided that the enjoyment of any such freedom does not offend the laws or the public interest." Other well-intended but failed projects during the Revolutionary Council and Socialist eras included the creation of the Academy for the Development of National Groups, which recruited and trained representatives from all ethnic groups to spread the new ideals of socialism and national unity, and to help improve living standards of people in the remote areas by educating them on basic health, social, and educational subjects (Silverstein 1980, pp. 235–6).

These actions were obviously an attempt to suppress demands for self-determination by institutionalizing the government's version of what were acceptable cultural and political practices. Most ethnic nationalities were fully aware of the contrast between the military's harsh campaign against ethnic armed-resistance groups and the official portrait of national harmony. Whereas the previous government had made Buddhism a state religion, its successor reversed this policy. The Revolutionary Council ended Buddhist religious holidays, lifted the restrictions on animal slaughter and other proscriptions sanctioned by Buddhism, and no longer encouraged proselytizing among the non-Buddhist minorities (Silverstein 1980, p. 239).

Under the new constitution for the Socialist Republic of the Union of Burma in 1974, Burma was territorially and administratively divided among seven states (designated for seven sub-state nationalist groups corresponding to the major ethnic groups – which included the Kachin, Shan, Karen, Kayah, Chin, Mon, Rakhine) and seven divisions in the areas where Burmans constituted the majority population (the Tenasserim, Irrawaddy, Rangoon, Pegu, Sagaing, Magwe, and Mandalay divisions). Ne Win became the chairman of the Burma Socialist Program Party, while the top-ranking positions in these states and divisions were filled by people with military backgrounds.

The 1974 constitution, however, was intended to depoliticize ethnic identities by abolishing ethnic identities as a basis for political mobilization and by diffusing the majority Burman populations into the seven divisions, giving these newly formed states and divisions equal power and authority (in practice, governments of these states served merely as implementers of central policies, thereby making these constitutional powers meaningless). Silverstein notes that "the states no longer belonged to any ethnic group.... the new constitution solved the problem of national unity by emphasizing the equality of all as Burmese and not as representatives of separate and distinct groups" (Silverstein 1980, p. 242).

Policies were made at the central level and carried down the various administrative ladders. Any indigenous populations, regardless of their ethnicity, origin, religious backgrounds, were allowed to run for the uni-cameral People's Assembly (the Pyithu Hluttaw) and People's Councils (executive organ) at different administrative levels. The constitution made no mention of reserved seats for various groups in the legislative body. Eligibility and access to professional schools or higher education was now based mainly on merit and partly on personal networking and economic status rather than on ethnic criteria (Thawnghmung 2008). There were thus a few minority ethnic leaders who occupied high-profile government offices at the regional and national levels, but the major and important decisions were made by General Ne Win and his close colleagues, a pre-dominantly Burman-elite group. Burma's national army, which had been organized along ethnic lines until the Karen insurrection in 1949, was gradually transformed into a Burman-dominant institution, using Burmese as a medium of instruction to promote a curriculum exhorting national unity and extolling the heritage and traditions of the majority group.

These practices produced a number of consequences. First, by "sym-bolically" acknowledging the existence of seven ethnic-based states, the socialist government attempted to appease the demands of sub-state national groups, which in reality legitimized its actions to maintain strong central power and suppress armed-resistance movements while denying opportunities for the pursuit of genuine self-determination. In addition, real power and major decision-making authority were still concentrated in the hands of a few Burman military leaders. Second, the socialist gov-ernment's inability and lack of willingness to provide the needed support and resources to promote minority culture led to a gradual assimilation of minority populations (including members of sub-state nations) into the majority population (Hlaing 2007, p. 164). A number of surveys indi-cate that a significant proportion of minority groups are now more accus-tomed to Burman history, language, music, and culture than to their own, and they appear to interact more intensively with the majority Burman population (Hlaing 2007, p. 177; Thawnghmung 2008). Despite these trends, however, minority languages and cultures continued to survive thanks to the initiatives of private citizens and religious institutions. Third, the emphasis on socialist, non-ethnic values led to the depoliticization of ethnic identities, and promoted inter-ethnic interactions and peaceful coexistence among different cultural groups. Fourth, the government's inability to crack down on insurgencies left under insurgent control a significant number of areas where minority languages have thrived and anti-Burman sentiments have been instilled.

SLORC/SPDC (1988–PRESENT)

In 1988, the military assumed the name State Law and Order Restoration Council (SLORC) in order to stage another coup and crack down on popular demonstrations against failing political and economic policies. In 1988 and 1989, over 10,000 students and civilian activists fled underground into the insurgent-controlled mountains. Of these, an estimated 5,000 went to the KNU; 1,300 to the NMSP in the south; 2,000 to the KIO; and a few hundred to the Communist Party of Burma in the north (Smith 1999, p. 371).

Mired in domestic crises and stung by international criticism, the SLORC "opened up" its economy to foreign investments, removed restrictions on some imports and exports, and held a multiparty election in 1990. The main opposition party, the National League for Democracy (NLD) led by Aung San Suu Kyi, the daughter of Aung San, won a landslide victory. The military junta refused to defer to pressure from international forces and domestic opposition groups to hand power over to the NLD, and instead cracked down on opposition parties. A dozen members who had been elected and were from the NLD fled into KNU-held territory in the early 1990s, where they formed the exiled National Coalition Government Union of Burma (NCGUB). This led to the formation of the National Council Union of Burma (NCUB), an umbrella organization of anti-government groups that included ethnic armed-resistance groups, elected members of parliaments, and students.

In government-controlled areas, minority religious groups have complained of discrimination in government services, education and job promotion, increased restriction on freedom of worship, as well as the inability to build new churches. A process of "Burmanization" and "Buddhization" has appeared in a number of public places and spaces (Houtman 1999). The highest-ranking government and military positions have been exclusively reserved for Burman Buddhists. Government-controlled media have covered daily stories and pictures of high-ranking military officers prostrating themselves in front of Buddhist monks, donating gifts, and visiting monasteries. Furthermore, the government has changed all English names for the country, towns, major cities, well-known streets, and ethnic groups to Burmese names.[4] Thus "Burma" became "Myanmar" and "Rangoon" became "Yangon."

By the early 1990s, the geopolitical situation was no longer favorable to armed-resistance groups. The Thai government adopted a "constructive engagement" policy toward Burma to secure lucrative logging, fisheries, and gas pipeline deals offered by the SLORC.[5] Funds from this emergency sell-off of natural resources to Thailand enabled the Burmese junta to buy much-needed arms, ammunitions, and aircraft from neighboring countries, particularly China. The Chinese government had supported the Communist Party of Burma, and then became friendly with the Burmese government in order to take advantage of Burma's resources, energy, and economic opportunities. China has become Burma's major arms supplier and has blocked punitive UN Security Council measures against the Burmese military government. Concerns about China's growing power in the region, its troubled northeast region in the Burma-India border, and the need for energy and natural resources have prompted India to pursue a pragmatic approach by abandoning its initial support for the establishment of a democratically elected government in Burma. India has not only established trading relationships and provided economic aid and investment to Myanmar, but it has also offered military training and arms supplies to the Burmese army.

The mutiny of ethnic commanders against the Burman-dominant Communist Party leadership also favored the SLORC (Oo & Min 2007, p. 12). The SLORC took advantage of the situation and successfully negotiated ceasefire agreements with these various ex-communist groups. The ceasefire agreements involved seventeen main groups by the mid-1990s, including such important groups with strong ethno-nationalist aspirations as the KIO, NMSP, and SSA (Shan State Army). This enabled the SLORC – which became in 1997 the State Peace and Development Council (SPDC) – to concentrate its resources on mounting a stronger military campaign against the remaining insurgencies. This period also witnessed increasing numbers of refugees and displaced populations due to intensified military campaigns, the continuing implementation of four-cut policies in rebel-controlled areas, as well as intense and widespread natural

---

[4] It should be noted that the government's actions are based more on "political" rather than "ethnic" considerations. This was evident in its ruthless crackdown of the Burmese Buddhist monks during the 2007 September demonstration against the military regime.

[5] This policy, however, was reversed in 1997 by Prime Minister Chuan Leekpai, who revived the Thai buffer policy vis-à-vis the ethnic minorities along the border in the name of democracy promotion. See Myoe (2002, p. 13).

resource exploitation in the ceasefire areas. At present, there remain only four non-ceasefire groups with strong ethno-nationalist agendas: the KNU, the Karenni National Progressive Party, the SSA-South, and the Chin National Front, all of which maintain military forces on dwindling economic and manpower bases (Smith 2007, p. 48).

According to Zaw Oo and Win Min, many ethnic groups agreed to the ceasefires because of battle fatigue, intense military pressure, governmental agreement that they continue bearing arms, temporary territorial concessions by the government, incentives for local development, economic interests over drug trafficking and natural resource extractions, border trade, pressure from neighboring countries, pressure from the local population, and the hope that a political settlement would later be reached (Oo & Min 2007, p. 14). Ceasefire groups, such as the Mon and the Karen, however, have recently come under increased pressure to disarm and have faced growing military buildup in their areas after the SPDC leadership changed at the end of 2004 (Graver, 2007, p. viii). Some groups, such as the PSLP (Palung State Liberation Party) were successfully forced to disarm, while others, such as the Shan State National Army, returned to armed resistance in response to forcible disarmament (Oo & Min 2007, pp. 32, 55).

On the one hand, ceasefire agreements with various armed groups since 1989 have benefited the local ethnic population by allowing people to return to normal life and to live, work, and move with relative safety (Oo & Min 2007, p. xii). Residents in ceasefire areas enjoy better health care, education, transport, and more economic opportunities. In many areas, ethnic civic groups have engaged in various tasks of community development (South 2007; Oo & Min 2007, p. 3). National groups are allowed to continue their work in social, cultural, and humanitarian activities as long as these activities do not pose a threat to government power. For instance, Mon schools run by the NMSP were closed down because of their critical stance against the government, whereas the Mon cultural association in Yangon and the departments of Myanmar language and literature in universities were allowed to continue offering courses on the Mon language (Hlaing 2007, p. 170). Nevertheless, this period also witnessed increasing numbers of grassroots organizations that were attempting to deal with social, cultural, and humanitarian concerns.

Ceasefire situations have enabled the KIO to increase its troops from 7,000 at the beginning of the ceasefire to over 10,000 today, and the United Wa State Army (which mutinied against the Communist Party of Burma) to increase from 12,000 to over 20,000. (Oo & Min 2007, p. 24). In other areas, such as the Kachin and Mon states, however, ceasefire

agreements have led to increased environmental destruction, land confisca-
tion, and displacement, which has occurred as a result of resource extrac-
tion such as logging, jade and gold mining, infrastructure development,
and incursions of the Burmese army into previously contested areas. Many
residents in the Northern Wa region have faced food shortages and economic insecurity after a ban on opium cultivation (Kramer 2007, p. 36).

Mary Callahan sheds light on this new complex political landscape, which
has emerged from agreements between former armed insurgent groups and
the SLORC/SPDC. Consequences include a "near devolution" in some parts
of the Shan state (under areas controlled by the Kokang Democratic Army
and United Wa States Army) where cross-border traders, financiers, former
insurgent leaders, and ethnic Chinese syndicates, rather than the SPDC,
exercise control, and authority (Callahan 2007, p. 25). She notes, in fact,
that "this arrangement represents the most extreme concession of central
control over Burmese territory in modern history, even more extreme than
U Nu's plans in 1962 to grant statehood to the Mon and Arakanese and to
consider seriously Shan and Kayah efforts to exercise their secession rights"
(Callahan 1998, p. 18). What differentiates this situation from the years
under U Nu is that some of these ceasefire groups, which are growing in
strength and are given considerable autonomy and economic opportunities,
are not necessarily the ones that would be recognized as sub-state nationalist groups in the first constitution of independent Burma.

The other extreme forms of political reconfiguration, which Callahan
terms as "occupation and exclusion" occur in Rakhine state where
Rohingya Muslims are subject to the most comprehensive forms of government restrictions and oppression, such as forced relocation, restriction
over movement and trade, as well as heavy taxes on registration of births
and requests for permission to marry (Callahan 2007, p. 31). Callahan
refers to areas that are still controlled by the non-ceasefire insurgencies as
"occupation: ongoing – but de-territorialized – war." These include pockets in the Shan state, where the SSA continues to fight; Karenni regions
where the Karenni National Progressive Party still fights; and the Karen
state where the KNU continues to fight (Callahan 2007, p. 35). They have
been subject to intense military campaigns and four-cut policies, and have
been home to hundreds of thousands of refugees, and several competing authorities (ceasefire and non-ceasefire groups, as well as the SPDC)
(Callahan 2007, p. 38).

Between "near devolution" and "occupation" lies a space of coexist-
ing relationships between the SPDC forces and ceasefire groups, either in
the form of "resignation" (in Chin state where economic opportunities

have been minimal and local elites have little leverage to negotiate
autonomy with the regime) or "contested" space, or "accommodation"
(in Kachin areas where significant natural resources, flourishing trade,
and business enable local leaders to maintain their cultural, political,
and economic autonomy) (Callahan 2007, p. 39). Kachin areas, for
example, are divided among three competing factions: NDA-K (Kachin
National Democratic Army), the KIO, and the SPDC (Callahan 2007,
p. 43), each of which attempts to exert control over the population and
imposes taxes on traders who pass through territories under their control (Callahan 2007, p. 44). Finally, there is a situation of "pragmatic
acceptance," which can be observed in southern Shan state where the
ceasefire PNO (Pao National Organization) leadership has accepted a
diminished, unequal role in its relations with the SPDC (Callahan 2007,
p. 47).

This ad hoc arrangement reveals that claims of sub-state national
groups based on shared culture, language, experiences, and historical
precedence no longer serve as a basis for "who gets the most economic
and political benefits." It depends largely on the timing of the ceasefire
agreements, the nature of economic opportunities that are available in
ceasefire areas, and the military strength of these groups. Two ceasefire
agreements with the KIO and NMSP have seemed better in terms of
enabling grassroots cultural and humanitarian activities, increasing military forces, and allowing continued publicity of their nationalist vision.
Meanwhile, ceasefire sub-state nationalist groups that have not agreed
on a ceasefire, such as the KNU, KNPP, CNF (Chin National Front), continue to survive on meager manpower resources.

THE POST-SPDC CONSTITUTION IN BURMA

Two different constitutional options have thus been proposed to serve
as a basis for governance in the post-SPDC period in Burma. The first,
proposed by the SPDC and now enacted, was completed in September
2007 at the National Convention (NC), which was been held on and off
since 1993. Under the Seven-Step Road Map formulated by the SPDC,
the regime's constitution was submitted to a popular referendum in May
2008, and will eventually result in the holding of elections for the legislative body in 2010. The Constitutional Drafting National Convention was
attended by 1,074 delegates of whom 633 were from the non-Burman
ethnic groups and those ethnic organizations that have entered into a
ceasefire with the regime.

Many groups that have accepted a ceasefire welcomed and attended the national convention and collectively received over 100 seats, or 10 percent of the total delegates. These included, in particular, groups that have been politically quiescent, weak, numerically small, and without strong and clear nationalist goals. Smaller groups, such as the Myanmar National Democratic Alliance Army (Kokang) and the National Democratic Alliance Army (eastern Shan state), have made few political demands and have seemed more focused on business opportunities. The New Democratic Army-Kachin has operated like a border police force and has seemed mainly interested in maintaining the status quo, which has allowed it to control its territory relatively undisturbed, maintaining its arms and pursuing its economic interests (Kramer 2007, p. 47). Likewise, the United Wa State Party (UWSP) has preferred dealing directly with the central government in Rangoon and has avoided interacting with many different actors (Kramer 2007, p. 52). Larger ethno-national groups that have agreed to a ceasefire, such as the NMSP and KIO, have been more vocal and critical of government policies. However, all their demands for greater political and economic benefits were dismissed by the SPDC.[6] Thus the SPDC's new constitution, which is most likely to influence the course and direction of Burma's future political and economic path, fails to include demands of several important political stakeholders in Burma and may perpetuate military rule. For instance, it emphasizes as its main objectives "genuine and disciplined democracy," "non-disintegration of the union," "non-disintegration of national solidarity," "perpetuation of sovereignty," and a leading role for the *tatmadaw* in the state.[7] It proposes that the president must have a "military outlook" and that the military be given 25 percent of the seats in both houses of parliament, another quarter in state and regional assemblies, and key Cabinet positions. The SPDC's version of administrative and territorial structure is based on a federal model comprising fourteen regions and states having equal status and authority. In addition to the existing seven states and seven major divisions, new self-administered zones will be created for the Pao, Kokang, Palaung, and Danu minorities in the Shan state, as well

---

[6] On June 9, 2004, the thirteen ethnic groups – KIO, PSLO, NMSP, SSA, KNLP, SNPO, KNPLF, KDA, NDA-K, KNG, KNPP collectively asked for decentralization of power to the state level.

[7] Robert Taylor, the author of the widely read book "The state in Burma," argues, however, that other autonomous zones for ceasefire groups of certain sizes, and state and divisional governments with Pyithu Hluttaws look like a "form of federalism without using the word." Personal e-mail communication with Robert Taylor, September 2007.

as the Naga in the Sagaing division. A larger self-administered division will be created for the Wa, and special participation rights will be given to smaller groups such as the Akha and Lahu also in the Shan state. In fact, the SPDC makes it known that Myanmar has "135 national races" in its attempt to diffuse and dismiss the eight big "races" its predecessors identified. These attempts are aimed at achieving the twin objectives of manipulating nationalist demands by allocating greater authority to the units that were not historically considered as "nations" and denying recognition to those who have historically been considered as "nations." For instance, although many groups with a population of over 50,000 in the Shan state, including Danu, Inntha, Pao, Akah, Kokang, and Wa, have sought self-administered areas from the NC, few were granted self-administered areas and the criteria for selection remain unclear (Sai Kham Mong 2007, pp. 272–3).[8] This has created confusion among many groups within the Shan state. One businesswoman and community leader, a member of the Danu, which expects to be granted a self-administered district, stated: "We don't really need it. And I don't see how things will be changed significantly by gaining self-administered status." The Lahu, who feel they have been used by government to fight other insurgent groups, deeply resent their failure to be granted self-administered areas.[9]

The Shan state, with its abundant natural and mineral resources as well as numerous insurgent organizations, has always been strategically important. As a result, the SPDC has been intent on pre-empting or crushing any potential unifying force within the state and on encouraging divisions that would undermine any broad-based national movement. Although it is unprecedented for the smaller ethnic nationalities to be given self-administered areas under the new constitution, it seems to be no coincidence that five of the six entities to be granted self-administered districts or divisions are in the Shan state.

There has been a rival constitution drafted by the opposition movement, which includes the NCGUB, the NCUB, the National Democratic Front (composed of forces that have rejected a ceasefire, including groups such as the KNU, the KNPP, the CNF, and the SSA-South (Shan State Army South), the United Nationalities League for Democracy Liberated Areas and the Women's League of Burma. Contrary to the SPDC draft,

---

[8] The constitution implies that to qualify for a self-administered district, groups must form a majority in a minimum of two townships; and, for a self-administered division (as in the case of Wa), they must form a majority in a minimum of six townships.

[9] Author's interviews, Myanmar 2008.

the constitution of the Federal Republic of the Union of Burma emphasizes the subordinate role of the military under a popularly elected government. It is based on a principle of equal opportunities across different
nationalities or ethnic-based states. It proposes a minimum of eight
"national states," where one ethnic group has a clear majority (thus,
the existing seven states plus a "Bama" state), and "nationalities states,"
where various groups are intermixed (such as Taninthayi and Irrawady).
It gives member states of the Federal Union greater autonomy and independence by granting them the right to draft and enact their respective
state constitutions.

THE DILEMMA OF NATIONAL UNITY

As Josef Silverstein (1997, p. 196) once noted, "a careful reading of the
opposition draft shows that it includes many of the ideas of Aung San.
These ideas and principles convinced many of Burma's minorities to join
the new union in 1947. They are still valid in 1997 and could form the
basis for ethnic policies that could rebuild national unity." Is that really
the case?

Although they are almost diametrically opposed to each other, neither of the two options deals with the exact allocation of power between
federal government and state government or the treatment of minority
populations in each of the main ethnic states, an important issue that
must be addressed in light of the nature of Burma's ethnic composition
and the evolution of ethnic identities and alliances.

First, none of the existing seven ethnic states is ethnically homogeneous (Smith, 1999). Shan, Kayah, Mon, and Rakhine are the names
of the majority ethnic groups in each territory. The Shan, for instance,
constitute approximately 60 percent of the population in the Shan state
of the northern and eastern part of Burma, which is also home to the
Kachin, Pao, Palung, Wa, Padaung, Lahu, Akha, Danu, and other groups
(Smith 1999, p. 47).

Second, six decades of civil war have transformed the nature of conflict and produced new forms of identities, positions, and alliances. The
strongest armed organization is currently the UWSP, which has an ethnic
nationalist agenda to build a Wa state within Burma, but has never in
the post-colonial era been recognized as a separate nation by Burman
nationalists. According to the UWSP, sixteen different ethnic groups live
in the areas under its control, including Wa (72 percent), Lahu (13 percent), Shan (7 percent), Chinese (4 percent), Akha (2 percent), and Lisu

(2 percent). One analyst notes that the extent of the UWSP's demand for the formation of a future Wa state seems to be based more on current territorial control than on ethnicity since it would incorporate significant non-Wa populations that are currently under its control, while excluding other Wa-inhabited areas not under its control (Kramer 2007, pp. 30–1). The UWSP has come into conflict with various ceasefire and non-ceasefire Shan factions as well as Lahu militias in the southern Shan state. Its logging and mining activities in the Kachin state also provoked resentment from Kachin residents and ceasefire groups (Kramer 2007, pp. 52–3). Burma's ethnically mixed nature, divided along linguistic, religious, and ideological lines, is also complicated by the emergence of new forms of identity and alliances throughout the sixty years of civil war. Not only did co-ethnic members develop different political stances toward the Burmese government but their alliances and political allegiances have changed depending on internal dynamics within each group, the changing nature of domestic and international environments, and the availability of options and resources. A small portion of these minority groups is either assimilated into the majority population or is fighting with the government against its co-ethnic members. For instance, General Ne Win introduced the Ka Kwe Ye (KKY) program in 1961 to form local militias against the insurgents, including the SSA. In return, the KKY militias were allowed to rule their areas relatively undisturbed. Most of them became heavily involved in the opium trade, which eventually led to the KKY's demise in 1973. Lo Hsing-han, the leader of Kokang KKY, went underground and joined its former enemies, the SSA, but he later served as a mediator in talks between the government and his co-ethnic members who broke away from the Communist Party of Burma in 1989.

Likewise, not everyone who joined the armed-resistance movement has sided with his or her co-ethnic members against the military government. For instance, the Communist Party of Burma, the largest insurgent army in the country until 1989, incorporated into its ranks local ethnic Kokang, Wa, Kachin, and Shan leaders, whom it used to fight against their co-ethnic members in its long-standing armed conflict with some National Democratic Front members, including an eight-year-long war with the KIO in northern Shan state (Kramer 2007, pp. 13, 16).

Decades of civil war in Burma have produced a motley array of various armed factions that broke off from their mother organizations, or defected to the government, in addition to those that continue to fight. In the Kachin state, several Kachin armed organizations such as the Kachin Defense Army (KDA), the New Democratic Alliance-Kachin (NDA-K), and the KIO have often competed over control of territory and resources, with the regime playing one side against the other (Oo & Min 2007, p. 45). Likewise, the Kayah (Karenni) state has recently seen fights between groups supported by the SPDC and the still insurgent Kayan New Land Party (KNLP), which was forced out of its territory. The oldest Kayah organization, the Karenni National Progressive Party (KNPP), broke its ceasefire after a few months, while the third organization, the Karenni National Peoples Liberation Front (KNPLF) has maintained its ceasefire and financed its activities from logging and tin mining (Graver 2007, p. ix).

The majority segments of these ethno-national populations, in fact, have shunned armed resistance and have lived quietly inside the Union of Burma. Some of them have been involved in aboveground social networks and engaged in non-violent activities to promote their social and economic activities within the parameters set by the authoritarian government. In fact, there are a few ethnically based political parties, including the Shan Nationalities League for Democracy (SNLD), the Arakan League for Democracy (NLD), and the Mon National Democratic Front (MNDF), that ran and won in the 1990 elections (South 2007, p. 166).[10] Although continuing to see themselves as separate nations and holding anti-SPDC sentiments, these leaders have oftentimes questioned the legitimacy of armed resistance and challenged the armed revolutionary leaders for leadership of their respective communities (South 2007, p. 168). Younger generations in particular have little awareness of the dynamics of ethnic politics in Burma and lack knowledge of armed-resistance groups that claim to speak for them. Many of them no longer speak the language of their ethnic group, are completely ignorant about the history of ethnic politics, and are more interested in finding jobs and education overseas. The best and brightest members of Burma's national groups, who would have been at the forefront of nationalist movements sixty years ago, are now leaving the country in search of new opportunities.

So far, very little interaction has taken place among the various segments of co-ethnic groups with different levels of political positioning and varying degrees of identity. Although ethnic ceasefire groups are restricted from contacting their co-ethnic members from anti-government organizations inside Burma, some such as the Pao and Mon have gained greater access to their community groups, gathered tremendous public

[10] In 2002, ethnic parties that participated in the 1990 election formed United Nationalities Alliances and advocated for the establishment of a Federal Structure in Burma. See Smith (2007, p. 49).

support and enjoyed contacts with their respective political parties (Oo & Min 2007, p. 44). Others, however, have met severe repercussions. For instance, Shan ceasefire leaders and SNLD leaders who held a meeting in Taunggyi in February 2005 were arrested (Oo & Min 2007, p. 41) and are now serving long prison sentences in remote jails.

It is not clear how these co-ethnic members who belong to different organizations such as ethnic-based political organizations, ceasefire armed groups and non-ceasefire armed groups will be brought into play in a new post-SPDC political arena.

Most importantly, not all issues that require urgent attention involve ethnic politics. Martin Smith observes that he frequently witnessed the political indifference of many villagers in the Tenasserim division (who from one valley to another may vary from Karen to Mon, Tavoyan, Burman, Shan, and even Salum sea gypsies (to the "political enticements of the Burmese Socialist Programme Party (BSPP); the CPB, KNU; NMSP or Parliamentary Democracy Party (PDP); remnants" (Smith 1999, p. 323). A researcher and human rights activist notes that many Karen villages perceive "sovereignty" as the freedom of their village to live without interference. Most villagers see the KNU not as a government, but as a force to drive the Burmese out of their area so they can live in peace. Thus village heads would ask the KNU forces to move out of their areas if they were perceived to be attracting the *tatmadaw* into their area (Heppner, 2005, p. 18). A Karen refugee in Umphien defines "equal rights" as the opportunity to "stay in peace" (Brooten 2004, p. 182). Another researcher also noted that the yearnings of many Karen old villagers are "not for a nation-state yet-to-be, but a return to their villages and local communities, to live their way of life as they knew it, free from predation by the Burmese armed forces" (Rajah 2002, p. 533). It is not clear whether these views represent the majority non-combatant members of sub-state nationalist groups, but they do bring out the perspectives of ordinary people whose goals and vision may be different from those of the leaders of ceasefire and non-ceasefire armed organizations.

The situation of residents under the UWSP reflects the way grassroots populations continue to be alienated from the emergence of new political processes in Burma. For instance, one researcher notes that UWSP leaders, who were military commanders in the Communist Party of Burma's people's army, have very little communication and consultation with the communities the UWSP aims to represent, and these communities are not allowed to take part in decision-making processes (Kramer 2007, p. 40). In addition, the agreement between the military government and the UWSP that has led to the relocation of tens of thousands of poppy growers and impoverished villagers from their mountainous homelands in the Northern Wa region to the fertile valleys in southern and northern Shan state has resulted in the fleeing of some 4,000 Lahu, Akha, and Shan inhabitants of southern Shan state to Thailand, and another estimated 4,500 who have moved to other areas in the Shan state (Kramer 2007, p. 42).

Last but not least, the current status reveals that the conflicts have gradually shifted from the multiple demands for great political autonomy and the preservation of minority culture to competition over resources and business opportunities, although this is not to deny that these two objectives were not necessarily mutually exclusive. In addition, there are strong nationalist visions that continue to be upheld by non-ceasefire and ceasefire sub-state nationalist groups. Many smaller groups that have now been appeased with various economic opportunities are more likely to cling to the status quo. A few sub-state nationalist groups that started out with legitimate claims and strong popular support now appear to be struggling with meager resources and manpower and are increasingly alienated from their constituencies.

AN ALTERNATIVE TO THE MILITARY AND
OPPOSITION DRAFTS

One alternative approach to addressing the current situation is to revisit U Nu's vision of a multinational society in Burma, which is very much in line with a liberal integrationist approach. U Nu was fundamentally opposed to the idea of separate states. Instead he favored a unitary state administered by a staff selected on a meritocratic basis. U Nu was quoted as saying that he wanted leaders with the required qualifications, whether they were Karen, Shan, Chin, Kachin, Karenni, Mon, or Burman. He argued that the solution to the minority problem lay in the cementing of racial bonds between all communities rather than in dismembering the union and creating separate states (Silverstein 1980, p. 150). Silverstein notes that "U Nu's twin ideas – a unitary state and equal political rights for all were the basis of his concept of national unity. It implied the submersion of local identities and mutual mistrust in favor of creating a new identity equally shared by all and based on new community values and ideas" (Silverstein 1980, p. 151). U Nu's vision, which would avoid the politicization of ethnic identity, shares many features with a US-style mononational, non-ethnic, territorial, or administrative unit. This approach would give civil and political rights to all individuals (such as freedom of speech, association, and conscience) regardless of group membership or ethnic or religious affiliation. This ethnically blind policy would address the nature of ethnic identity and composition by eliminating ethnicity as a basis for political mobilization, encouraging political parties to appeal to broader constituencies across different nationalities, creating cross-cutting allegiances among different ethnic groups, and encouraging inter-ethnic cooperation. At the same time, it would promote the culture and language of different nationalities, and would address the needs of grassroots populations since religious tolerance and human rights would protect ethnic and national groups indirectly, by allowing them to engage in their livelihood, practice their culture and religion freely, as well as simultaneously paving the way for social integration across ethnic and national boundaries.

CONCLUSION

The current, confusing array of ethnic armed organizations shows that the end of military rule will not necessarily bring the end of Burma's age-old problems of managing ethnic relations. The British and the post-colonial parliamentary democratic governments promoted ethnicity as a basis for political representation by favoring some groups at the expense of others. These periods witnessed increased politicization of ethnic identity and antagonistic communal relationships. The civilian government under parliamentary democracy failed to meet the expectations of many sub-state nationalist groups. Its willingness to accommodate various groups' demands, however, was even further undermined by the military coup in 1962. Ne Win's socialist government resorted to a scorched-earth policy against secessionist movements and did very little to help promote minority culture and language. Its adherence to a socialist ethos, however, depoliticized ethnic identities and created an atmosphere for peaceful coexistence among ordinary citizens of different nationalities, who have shared similar experiences as economically deprived and politically oppressed populations. Despite massive deaths and casualties, the harsh military and counterinsurgency campaign has done very little to suppress or appease the demands of armed insurgent groups that have continued to thrive on abundant natural resources, the opium economy, and taxes on border trade.

The current junta's ceasefire agreements were based on ad hoc arrangements that have not produced a long-term solution to Burma's age-old problem. The arrangements also favor smaller groups that were not conventionally regarded as "nations" and weaken the status and strength of some groups that had historically been considered as such. The harsh military campaign against non-ceasefire groups and commercial exploitation in ceasefire areas has led to the displacement of populations (including former insurgent leaders and soldiers) who later sought refugee status in Australia, Europe, and North America. Members of these diaspora have become strong critics of the military regime and some provide support to armed movements. Burma's poor economy has also led to the outflow of migrant workers to neighboring countries. Among these are younger, highly educated members of ethnic nationalities, who now seek jobs, education, and other opportunities rather than the creation of separate states in Burma.

The past forty years of military rule have demonstrated that coercive measures have not worked to appease or suppress sub-state nationalist sentiments, nor have they resolved Burma's age-old problem. At the same time, it is not clear whether the Panglong Agreement's principles of ethnic-based states in a federal structure would have worked since they were and would never be implemented due to strong resistance by segments of Burman nationalists and the military. In the meantime, one should also begin to assess the feasibility and applicability of a more liberal integrationist model, particularly in light of the complex nature of Burma's ethnic composition and the emergence of new forms of identities, alliances, and positions.

7

The Double-Edged Sword of Autonomy in Indonesia and the Philippines

Jacques Bertrand

Sub-state national groups usually seek some form of self-determination and recognition of their special status. Self-determination is sometimes expressed in calls for an independent state that would coincide with the territorial homeland of the nation. For the most part, however, such goals are unattainable. Instead, most groups settle for some form of autonomy or for federalism, where such structures already exist.

Autonomy allows the accommodation of ethno-nationalist demands by creating a new territorial unit with special powers, or by decentralizing additional powers to an existing territorial unit that corresponds to the group's homeland (Gurr 2000; Horowitz 1985). Asymmetrical federalism accomplishes the same goals. Groups not only obtain political control over their territorial homeland, but also, with their control of a sub-state government, they obtain the leverage to negotiate with the central government.

Autonomy also provides a territorially grounded recognition of national status, although this is mostly implicit. Many states are reluctant to formally recognize sub-state national groups as "nations." The recent recognition of the Catalan nation by the Spanish state is a rare exception. Some states in Asia have recognized "multination" status but, as Laliberté and Thawnghmung have noted in the cases of China and Burma, they have, ironically, done so against a backdrop of strong centralizing tendencies and an actual denial of significant powers to accompany such recognition. This kind of recognition is typical of the Soviet-style model of recognition. In most Asian states, the extension of some form of autonomy provides an implicit recognition of national status, in a limited way.

Yet, autonomy can sometimes become an empty shell. Powers may exist in law, but are subsequently undermined by the central state. For instance, the central state can enact other legislation that might contradict the autonomy law. By various bureaucratic or extra-institutional means, it might also slow or stall the autonomy law's implementation. Repressive policies might be launched after the autonomy law is passed, thereby reducing its meaning and ultimately its legitimacy. There are various ways in which autonomy, therefore, can be significantly eroded or even nullified after it is extended as symbolic recognition.

The reasons for this are mostly strategic. To some extent, all states are likely to view sub-state nationalist groups as potential threats to their integrity. As a result, they are likely to pursue a number of strategies to undermine sub-state nationalist claims. When the state chooses accommodation, however, it might be costly to offer the sub-state nationalist groups powers, which might subsequently reduce its own effectiveness, particularly in a democratic state. The short-term gain achieved by significantly reducing the mobilizational capacity of the sub-state national group may be offset in the long run if the group rejects concessions by the state and decides to mobilize once again. However, strategic reasons in themselves are insufficient to explain why state elites would take such risks, particularly in new, fragile democracies.

There are deeper issues that can explain why these contradictory tendencies might appear. In particular, the way state elites conceive of the state and nation can be an important constraint on the state's ability to accommodate sub-state nationalist demands. As Bhargava has articulated in the case of India, the concept of institutionalizing autonomy for some groups might fall beyond the "mindset" of state elites and make it very difficult to make concessions to particular types of groups. This mindset has been conditioned by historical trajectories, some of which are more likely to reinforce a unitary state and nation view.

In Indonesia and the Philippines, such tendencies have been clear, yet we would have expected more flexibility. Both countries are somewhat unique in Asia; their territories were an inheritance of colonial administration and do not strongly correspond to any particular ethnic group. They have no history of the large-scale state consolidation and civilizational unification that has characterized China and India, for example. Lacking an ethnic core, the unifying thrust of both the Indonesian and Filipino nationalist movements relied heavily on the shared colonial experience and the building of a common, modern society. This differentiates them

from the Thai state, for instance, where the building of a core Thai identity
was closely linked to a group with a historically strong sense of identity,
a common language, and the Buddhist religion. This, of course, does not
mean Thai identity is fixed; it has continued to expand its boundaries and
has been reshaped by evolving historical circumstances (Connors 2003).
We should expect, however, that Indonesia and the Philippines, given their
immense diversity, would have more flexibility than a country such as
Thailand.

To some extent Indonesia and the Philippines have been flexible but not
toward sub-state national groups. Significant accommodation has been
extended, mostly in the form of de-ethnicized administrative decentralization. In the Philippines, the 1991 Local Government Code decentralized fiscal and administrative power to the municipal level. In Indonesia,
two sets of laws have provided autonomy to the districts and greater
powers to the provinces. Furthermore, with elections of provincial governors and district heads, both levels of government now enjoy stronger
popular backing. Some of this autonomy has coincided with traditional
homelands of particular ethnic groups, particularly where new provinces
and districts were carved out to reflect closer coincidence between administrative and ethnic boundaries. In principle, however, autonomy laws in
Indonesia were not devised as a tool for accommodating ethnic groups
and were integrated to constitutional frameworks that emphasize the
existence of a single Indonesian nation.

In the case of sub-state national groups, both states have been very
reluctant to extend meaningful autonomy, even when there are few viable
alternatives. In both countries, significant groups have contested the idea
of a single nation and claimed, instead, their own national status. This
has been the case for the Moros in the southern Philippines, as well as
the Acehnese and Papuans in Indonesia. Sub-state nationalist organizations have mobilized and resisted state attempts to integrate their regions
within a unitary mold, and to subscribe to an imagined community of
single nationhood.

In response to this resistance, both states have reluctantly granted
autonomy in various guises, which is often followed by measures to
undermine it. Out of several instances where they have granted autonomy, only once has it been extensive and, at least on paper, very empow-
ering: the Law on Aceh of 2006. Given that the experience is relatively
new, it is too early to tell whether it will be implemented successfully. This
single case of success occurred, however, against a backdrop of several
cases of relative failure: Aceh (2001), Papua (2001), Mindanao (1996),

and the Cordilleraus (1990, 1998).[1] In the case of the Cordillera, who never really developed a sense of a "Cordillera nation," autonomy was twice rejected for its lack of expected real devolution of power. More significantly, autonomy had been extended to Mindanao, Papua, and Aceh (prior to 2006), but in each case, there were obstacles to implementation that significantly reduced its effectiveness.

The major reason for this poor record is the persistence of the unitary nation-state model as a dominant paradigm. Central states in Indonesia and the Philippines have extended concessions to sub-state nationalist groups only to preserve stability and without accepting the principle of multiple nations within one state. Although de facto recognition is provided by extending autonomy to sub-state national groups, a single-nation discourse is maintained. Furthermore, legislation that contradicts the powers extended by autonomy is introduced; administrative hurdles prevent the flow of resources or the implementation of institutions; and sometimes repressive measures are used alongside the concession of autonomy.

This dominant paradigm expresses itself in two ways. First, in states with histories of strong nationalist tendencies at the center, such as Indonesia, autonomy has been undermined because of a persistent perception among state elites that autonomy contradicts Indonesia's core as a "nation." Second, as is the case in the Philippines, state elites also retain strong beliefs in a unitary state system despite a weaker sense of a single nation. The undermining of autonomy serves central state-elite interests, but there is a conceptual dimension by which the Filipino nation, over time, has failed to be sufficiently inclusive to accommodate the Moros. From its inception, Christians dominated the Filipino state, while the Moros were perceived as backward tribes under both the Spanish and American colonial regimes as well as under the post-independence Filipino state. Over several decades, this dominance has strengthened the perception that the Filipino state is a Christian-dominated state, at least in the eyes of the Muslim Moros. The failure of the Moros to participate significantly in the Filipino state has strengthened the sense that the Philippines is a single nation, strongly dominated by Christian Filipinos, rather than a fully integrative nation. As a result, the Filipino state has moved somewhat closer to the stronger Indonesian nationalist imagery where some exclusion has persisted despite its fundamentally diverse foundation.

---

[1] For purposes of this chapter, I will not discuss the case of the Cordillera, which represents a slightly different case. There is a debate concerning the extent to which "Cordillerans" ever saw themselves as a single, united group, and even less as a nation.

SETTING THE STAGE FOR NATION BUILDING: REVOLUTION
AND THE ANTI-COLONIAL STRUGGLE

Indonesia and the Philippines share a common experience as colonial
constructions. Prior to the advent of colonial rule, there were no strong
centralized states. Instead, in both archipelagoes, small principalities and
kingdoms were occasionally amalgamated into larger political units after
periods of conquest. Yet, these disintegrated and were replaced, once
again, by constellations of small states throughout the region. This pattern only changed with the consolidation of administrative units under
Dutch and Spanish colonial rule, respectively. It was out of these colonies
that the current states emerged, and new nations were constructed.

The Filipino nation and state was born out of a struggle against Spanish
and American colonial rule. The Philippines had a short, failed revolution
against Spanish colonial rule. Two main streams of the revolution never
coalesced to form a strong, united front against neither the Spanish nor
their successors. The Kapitunan movement organized by Andres Bonifacio
gained ascendancy among the lower and middle classes when it declared
a revolution in 1896. It failed to gain adherence among the *ilustrado* elite
(Philippine intelligentsia), however, which had been advocating reform
of Spanish colonial rule but found the Kapitunan to be too radical. The
Spanish quickly repressed the Kapitunan movement, along with the
reformist movement of the *ilustrado* elite (Stanley 1974, pp. 45–6).

The second wave of the revolution, under the leadership of Emilio
Aguinaldo, had better success. Supported by the *ilustrados*, this revolutionary movement was better armed and organized than its predecessors.
More importantly, it capitalized on the weakness of the Spanish, who were
occupied by the Spanish-American war. Supported by the Americans, the
revolutionaries were able to control vast areas of the Philippines by the
time the United States gained control of the archipelago.

Nevertheless, the revolution proved insufficiently powerful to mobilize
large numbers of Filipinos against the Americans. Faced with superior
military strength, the revolution faltered, and the United States gained
control over the archipelago by 1902. Internal division within the revolutionary movement was also an important factor in its defeat. As Stanley
states: "...centrifugal forces of regionalism, tribalism, language, religions,
and class interest proved stronger than the centripetal power of nationalism, racial identification, and revolutionary fervor. The revolution fragmented, and the Americans won both a military and a psychological
victory" (Stanley 1974, p. 267).

American imperialism allowed the Filipino national identity to consolidate itself. Ironically, American colonial rule co-opted the revolution, implementing significant reforms that had been demanded by the *ilustrados*, including a vast expansion of education, development of infrastructure, and the establishment of a civilian government that included representation at the local and regional levels. It allowed the *ilustrado* elite to organize political parties and expand their business interests, in exchange for loyalty to the American imperium. Consequently, Filipinos became increasingly connected through a common curriculum, common representative political institutions, and the English language as the lingua franca (Stanley 1974, pp. 83–4, 267). Linguistic convergence made some major languages become regional lingua franca, such as Ilocano, Tagalog, and Visayan. Neither English nor Spanish could develop as "national" languages as they remained primarily spoken by a small, educated elite and contained the negative connotations of colonial legacy. Still, English provided a broader lingua franca, which avoided the potentially divisive political decision of choosing a national language from among the three major ones.

Although a new Filipino identity was coalescing, it persistently failed to include the Muslims of the South. There is some contention about the degree to which a "Muslim" or "Moro" identity existed prior to American colonial rule, or to even the Commonwealth years. While Muslim scholars such as Majul (1973, pp. 113–14) have traced such an identity back to the resistance against the Spanish, more recent scholarship has contested such claims. McKenna, for instance, revisits the historical evidence on the so-called Moro wars and argues instead that there is little evidence to support the idea that the Moro engaged in a sustained, broad effort to resist the Spanish or that there was a broad ethno-religious identity among the various Muslim ethno-linguistic groups of Mindanao and the Sulu archipelago (McKenna 1998, pp. 81–3). Nevertheless, such an identity did emerge during the American colonial occupation and, to some degree, was crystallized by colonial policies. After a brief period of indirect rule in which local *datus* (traditional rulers) helped to pacify the South as they bolstered their own position, American colonial administrators contributed to the strengthening of local leadership roles while also helping to create "Morohood." Local *datus*, who had collaborated with the Americans, were integrated into the new structure of elected political offices (in municipalities and as assemblymen), and they encouraged a broader Muslim identity as a means, in the end, to integrate the Muslim population into the Filipino polity (McKenna 1998, pp. 105–7). A Moro province was created as the administrative structure including all Muslim areas. The integrative strategy proved illusive but its consequence was to create a much more self-conscious Moro identity.

Among the dominant Filipino elite, Christian identity persisted and, to some extent, became increasingly polarized in relation to a consolidating Moro identity. Although the Revolution had been anti-clerical as well as nationalist, opposition was directed at the Spanish not the Filipino clergy (Wurfel 1988, p. 8). It did not constitute a rejection of the Church or Christian identity, only its elements that were closely related to Spanish colonial rule. Even after a more formal separation of church and state was introduced during American colonial rule, it remained difficult to dissociate Filipino identity from the Christian majority.

Equally a colonial construction, Indonesia was created out of a strong nationalist movement that challenged the long colonial domination by the Dutch. It was built around a regional lingua franca, *pasar* (market) Malay, which Indonesian nationalists renamed *Bahasa Indonesia* (Indonesian language). The Indonesian language, the common experience of Dutch colonialism, and to a lesser extent the Islamic religion, became cultural markers of the Indonesian nation. Shared language and common experience provided a relatively "neutral" set of characteristics, whereas Islam proved capable of unifying only parts of the archipelago. Unlike the Filipino nationalists, the Indonesian nationalists realized the need to downplay religion as a source of unity in order to attract areas with a minority religion, in this case, these were the Christian areas.

Even though the Indonesian motto later became "Unity in Diversity," Indonesian nationalists emphasized national unity over diversity. From its early days, Indonesian nationalism was imbued with the primacy of unity in the fight against the Dutch, and diversity was seen as a potential divisive force. In an archipelago made up of thousands of islands, more than fifty different ethnic groups, where 200 languages were spoken, and at least five major religions practiced by significantly large numbers of people, the challenge of creating a single nation was great indeed.

Yet, many groups adhered strongly to the concept of a single Indonesian nation. After the Japanese retreat at the end of World War II, the Dutch returned to Indonesia and sought to reestablish their dominance. The war between Dutch and the proclaimed Republic lasted from 1945 to 1949. During the Dutch occupation, the territory was reorganized along federal lines, where the units were more or less constituted along ethnic lines. The Republic of Indonesia adopted the principle of a unitary state in the territory it occupied. After several failed agreements, a compromise was finally reached. Under international pressure, the Dutch accepted leaving but only once it was agreed that Indonesia would be constituted as a federation and that Dutch-created federal unity would be preserved. A federal United States of Indonesia was created in 1949, and the Dutch left. Only a few months later, however, most of the federal units were dissolved in the midst of widespread support for a single-nation, unitary state, encouraged by the Republic (which was one of the constituent units by then). Only one region, which included Central and South Maluku, rejected the reintegration to the Republic of Indonesia. By 1950, however, this resistance had been overcome by force. In 1950, the federation was officially dissolved and a new, unitary state, the Republic of Indonesia, was proclaimed with the adoption of a new constitution. The concept of a single Indonesian nation underlies the Republican state and was broadly accepted by almost all ethnic groups across the archipelago.

There are two main reasons why Indonesian nationalism was comparatively stronger than Filipino nationalism. First, the Indonesian nationalist movement managed to mobilize large segments of the population. Although primarily revolving around a small elite that was Dutch-educated or that served in the colonial bureaucracy, the movement nevertheless spread through various organizations. Some of the most important included the *pemuda* (youth movements) across various regions of Indonesia that formed in support of the revolution. Also, the early nationalist movement was represented by the *Sarekat Islam*, an Islamic merchants' association that expanded its focus and formed the basis of an emerging anti-colonial movement. Out of this association were formed, not only the main nationalist stream that would later lead to the creation of the Indonesian Nationalist Party, but also its Communist and Islamic streams. Nationalism spread within different ideological currents and therefore reached more deeply into society.

Second, the Revolution was longer and more widespread. Armed resistance to the Dutch organized itself around the *pemuda* and later out of the nascent Indonesian army that was trained by the Japanese occupying forces. The years of resistance to the returning Dutch after 1945 solidified the ideological mold of the nationalist movement, as Reid argues in Chapter 2. The armed resistance fostered the creation of a strongly nationalist army that would become a pillar as well of the Indonesian nation.

Nevertheless, despite its strength, Indonesian nationalism could not overcome some sub-state nationalist aspirations that would arise to maintain Indonesia as a multination state. Resistance to the Indonesian nation would come primarily from groups that were only later integrated to the Indonesian state. Papuans were formally integrated in 1969 and the East Timorese in 1975. Neither group participated in the Revolution nor the binding years of common resistance to colonial rule. Because they were integrated much later to the Republic, they did not share a common experience with other groups in Indonesia. As a result, they formed sub-state nationalist movements that demanded independence.

The Acehnese are a more complex case. They had clearly developed a strong sense of being a separate Acehnese nation but had joined the Revolution and embraced the Republican ideal. The Acehnese always had strong political identity because they had their own sultanate, which prospered and dominated a large area of Sumatra. They successfully resisted Dutch colonialism until the early twentieth century, when they were finally defeated. They had fought fiercely, however, in the Aceh War (1873–1904) and further consolidated their own identity. Furthermore, they created a strong regional culture based on the local Acehnese language and on a strong adherence to Islam, an inheritance of the sultanate years. Yet, the Acehnese supported the Revolution and refused the Dutch offer to make them a separate federal state under Dutch influence. They fought instead alongside the Republic. They began to resist a few years later when it became clear that the Islamist stream of the nationalist movement had lost and that the new Republic rejected the Islamic state. Nevertheless, in its initial stages under the Darul Islam resistance in the 1950s, Acehnese opposition to the Indonesian state was joined by similar groups from Sulawesi, west Java, and other parts of Sumatra that wanted an Islamic state for all of Indonesia. It was not yet a sub-state nationalist movement.

DEEPENING NATIONAL DEFINITION THROUGH ACCULTURATION

The Philippines and Indonesia both had periods of state-directed attempts at intensifying the assimilation to the core nation. In the case of the Philippines, because of a relatively weak sense of Filipino nation, the state sometimes pursued policies to assimilate and integrate the Moros and at other times pursued policies to isolate them. In Indonesia, it was the strong confidence in the success of the Indonesian revolution and in the initial unity provided by a national ideology that motivated strong assimilationist policies, particularly under the New Order regime after 1965.

The integrative character of the Filipino national model was reinforced during the Commonwealth years (1935–1946), when the Philippine government essentially governed as an independent state, with close ties to the United States. When the Americans relinquished control of the government to Filipinos after 1920, Christian Filipinos remained dominant. The elite persistently either excluded the Moros or attempted to assimilate them through administrative control and migration. Religious polarization contributed to the increasingly bitter division between the Muslim Moros and the perceived "Christian" Filipino national identity. As Anderson has argued:

...indeed the Philippines is the only place in Southeast Asia where such a powerful, consolidated landed upper class exists [a Chinese-mestizo latifundist upper class]. And precisely because of its power and ability to claim a huge majority base in Filipino Catholicism, it found it easy to acquire political independence from the Americans less than fifty years after the latter had seized the colony from the Spanish and the anti-Spanish revolutionaries. The same factors made the upper class indifferent to any need to build a strong coalition with the Muslim minorities in the south. Indeed it is striking that these people were mishandled, not as ethnicities, but as religious deviants. Unsurprisingly, this produced in the end one of the few genuinely secessionist movements of modern Southeast Asian history. (Anderson 1998, p. 328)

Assimilation and integrative strategies were reflected in the government's policies toward the Moros. Christians held most of the administrative positions in the Muslim areas, even under American colonial rule. Of particular importance, they controlled the Bureau of Lands, which issued land titles. After 1935, the government of Manuel Quezon accelerated the appointment of Christians to administrative positions and Christians were encouraged to migrate to Mindanao from Luzon (Wurfel 1988, pp. 29–30). Unregistered land was declared part of the public domain, and therefore Muslims were denied the customary land rights by which Muslim communities had previously governed their territory. Suspicious of the government's intentions and high processing fees, and uncertain about procedures, Muslims failed to register their lands and did not take advantage of new land on offer. The Bureau of Lands did not make much effort to socialize Muslims to this new regime and, instead, favored the migrating Christians. Loans and assistance were also offered to new Christian settlers (Gowing 1983, p. 339; McKenna 1998, p. 117). Christian migration and related land registration were sufficiently high to marginalize Muslims in many areas of Mindanao, where they were once dominant. Muslims in Cotabato declined, for instance, from 64.53 percent in 1918 to 34.64 percent of the population of Cotabato in 1960 (O'Shaughnessy 1975, p. 377).

After the Philippines obtained independence in 1946, some of the Moro elite were integrated into the state through elected offices, but this had little effect on the broader Moro population. The structure of the government was based on the U.S. system and gave no special representation to Moros in the central government. Instead, Moro *datus* and other members of the elite gained access to local and regional offices, occasionally gaining seats in the national congress. Yet, while they were integrated within the patronage structures of the state, there was little effect on the broader Moro population, which remained isolated and poor.

In Indonesia, the core nation was reaffirmed in the first decade after independence but tension remained, with divided views over the basic principles underlying the state as well as regionalist pressures. The first president, Sukarno, upheld a revolutionary rhetoric and nationalist imagery to foster and deepen the national bond. Divisions grew, however, between his vision of nationalism, which was imbued with a secular orientation, and alternative views espoused by Islamists and Communists. The Darul Islam rebellion, involving several regions of Indonesia, primarily represented a rejection of Sukarno's nationalist perspective and favored Islam as the core of the Indonesian nation. These divisions were only resolved when Sukarno abandoned liberal democracy and declared a regime of Guided Democracy in 1959, under which he reaffirmed an adherence to his original conception of the Indonesian nation and a centralized, unitary state structure that most represented this vision.

Regional tensions emerged in Maluku, Sulawesi, and Sumatra but were mostly concerned with modifications to, rather than a replacement of, the Indonesian nation and state structure. Only the South Moluccan Republic movement was a direct challenge to the Indonesian state. Mainly fostered by former soldiers of the Dutch colonial regime, it rejected the abandonment of the federalist state in favor of a unitary one, and therefore attempted to secede. The movement lasted only a few months and never obtained deep support, as most Moluccans were favorable to the Republic. In the late 1950s, as the democratic regime was crumbling and Sukarno sought to centralize the state, military commanders from Sumatra and Sulawesi rebelled against the central state. The rebellion was perceived as regionalist resentment against the centralizing tendencies of the central government and the increasing attempts to strengthen the central command of the armed forces. The regionalist rebellions did not gain strong support, however, and failed. There was no subsequent revival of these movements in the following decades.

If these failures showed, in a sense, the success of Indonesian nationalism, this nevertheless worried the new regime that came to power after 1965. The New Order regime of President Suharto developed an even deeper conception of the Indonesian nation and policies designed to strengthen it. Rising out of a failed coup attempt from the Indonesian Communist Party, the regime's initial consolidation eliminated its two strongest alternative centers of power: communism and Islam. The Communist movement had become one of the largest in Asia, and its growing power clashed with the nationalist-oriented armed forces. After the failed coup attempt, the armed forces eliminated the Party by disbanding and arresting its leaders, followed by a purge throughout the country. In order to prevent the rise of Islamic forces, which had been galvanized by the elimination of the Communists, the regime also prevented the recreation of the Islamist political party, Masjumi, and increasingly repressed its attempts to remobilize. As a result, the armed forces consolidated their power, and the regime strongly reaffirmed the unitary principles of the state and the nationalist vision of the Indonesian nation, as one, single nation under the ideology of *Pancasila* – a quasi-secular ideology developed by President Sukarno.

In addition to the fear of Communism and Islamism, the New Order regime was also worried about signs of regionalist sentiment. It viewed the rebellions of the late 1950s as strong threats to the unity of the state, not surprisingly given that the armed forces had been involved in these rebellions. It therefore reinforced the centralization of the state by strengthening its core institutions, including the armed forces and the bureaucracy.

The centralization of state structures was accompanied by strong attempts to homogenize policies, programs, and institutions across the country, while also fostering a common "Indonesian" culture. Policies were not only designed to address problems, such as family planning and agricultural subsidies, but were also homogenized and presented as national development efforts aimed at strengthening the unity and common purpose of the nation. As a result, policy planning was highly centralized, and the lower levels of government simply implemented directives from above. The educational curriculum was homogenized and included very little regional content, emphasizing instead the state's mythological history of revolution and national heroes. The state ideology *Pancasila* – meaning "five principles," consisting of general societal values such as social justice, consensual democracy, and belief in one supreme God – was taught in school and university curriculum. A whole set of symbolic rituals were repeated daily in schools and in the public service, where the national anthem was sung and national symbols prominently displayed. Museums reproduced the state's own recasting of diversity in displays of colorful material culture blended into an overarching national culture.

To unify their diverse populations, the state in both countries promoted the single-nation model. This single nation was defined in ways that included cultural components. In the case of Indonesia, *Bahasa Indonesia* provided a core cultural bond that did not impose any group dominance. The attempts to forge deeper cultural attachments and to inculcate values associated with the state's vision of the unified nation, however, led to some exclusion. While most groups in Indonesia may have found some of the policies excessively centralizing but not at the cost of their own individual cultures or interests, to some groups that were forcibly integrated and repressed, the same policies appeared as aggressively assimilationist.

To a lesser degree, results were the same in the Philippines, although perhaps through a more accidental process. The gradual creation of a common Filipino identity was a product partly of the failed revolutionary imagery, but also of the American colonial policies and institutional structures that left a powerful elite, sharing common interests, in control of the state. Disparities were gradually reduced between groups in Luzon and the Visayas. The Catholic religion was a strong common bond that, although not made officially a religion of state, nevertheless imbued the political life of the nation and its broad population. Language did not provide the same bond, since major linguistic groups continued to be divided among regional lingua franca. Efforts, however, to raise a modified version of Tagalog to the status of a common language, Filipino, reveals persistent efforts to increase such bonds. State policies favored the Christian majority and made integration difficult for non-Christians. Integrationist policies on the one hand, and marginalization through migration on the other, laid a path by which the Moros refused to consider themselves Filipinos, and perceived any further attempts at integration as threats to their own aspirations and interests.

RESISTANCE TO NATION AND THE EXTENSION OF AUTONOMY

Sub-state nationalist rebellions in the Philippines and Indonesia rejected the single-nation model. Instead, they demanded recognition of their status as "nations" and, consequently, a right to self-determination. Their reasons for rebelling against their respective states varied and involved the complex interaction of factors that were converging toward violent outcomes. Nevertheless, they faced states intent on assimilating groups to a common national core and that escalated repression when groups mobilized against them, and, eventually, settled for some form of autonomy to accommodate grievances and reduce conflict.

In both countries, autonomy appeared to extend to recognition of more than one nation, but the states' attempts at implementation showed as much willingness to undermine the subgroups as to accommodate their demands. Autonomy agreements were signed and institutions were established, but they were often accompanied by contradictory legislation, a lack of resources, or by the continued use of repressive instruments.

Moros

After several decades of attempts in the Philippines to assimilate the Moros, an armed movement was formed when the Marcos government declared martial law and it became increasingly evident that the regime would use military force to further repress Moro demands. Young secular-educated Moros formed the Moro National Liberation Front (MNLF) in 1969, and armed resistance began in 1972. By 1973, the MNLF, under the leadership of Nur Misuari, was asking for a withdrawal of government troops from the southern Philippines, a return of the lands taken away from the Moros, more autonomy, as well as the practice of Islamic law in Muslim areas. In 1974, MNLF demands went even further when the movement declared the establishment of the Bangsa Moro Republic with the stated goal of full independence.

In reaction to the escalation of the conflict, the Marcos government, for the first time in the history of the Philippines, agreed to territorial autonomy for the Moros. The Tripoli Agreement of 1976 became the first document to recognize the Moros' right to political representation on the basis of their distinctive cultural and historical background. It granted the Moro autonomy over a region comprising thirteen provinces and nine cities in Mindanao. Foreign policy, national defense, mines, and mineral resources remained under the jurisdiction of the central government. In the autonomous areas, it was agreed that the Muslims would establish courts based on Shari'ah law and would have the right to establish schools and universities, their own administrative, economic, and financial systems, as well as Special Regional Security Forces.[2]

---

[2] *Agreement between the government of the Republic of the Philippines and the Moro National Liberation Front with the Participation of the Quadripartite Ministerial Commission Members of the Islamic Conference and the Secretary General of the Organization of the Islamic Conference*, Tripoli, December 23, 1976.

Negotiations stalled over the details of the accord, and Marcos insisted on holding a plebiscite to ratify it. Against the wishes of the MNLF, he unilaterally proceeded with the plebiscite and decreed the creation of two autonomous regions. The MNFL rejected the agreement and fighting resumed. Marcos had used the Tripoli Agreement to temporarily defuse the armed conflict and weaken the MNLF, with no intention of actually implementing it (McKenna 1998, p. 168).

After the 1985 "People Power" revolution and a return to democracy, a new opportunity arose. A new constitution included a clause recognizing autonomy for "Muslim Mindanao" (May 1990, p. 50). The Aquino government's negotiations with the MNLF, however, failed because of disagreements over territory. The MNLF included fourteen provinces (based on the thirteen provinces of the Tripoli Agreement) while the Aquino government considered only the five provinces that had a Muslim majority (May 1990, p. 50). The government nevertheless organized a plebiscite unilaterally in thirteen provinces and nine cities of Mindanao, but only four opted for autonomy. The "Autonomous Region of Muslim Mindanao" (ARMM) therefore included only those four provinces (Magdalena 1997, p. 250).

Once again, the central government's ineffectiveness and unilateral implementation undermined autonomy. Although support had been sought among some of the Muslim elite, most Muslims supported rebel organizations. The MNLF rejected the agreement, and the Moro Islamic Liberation Front (MILF), a splinter group of the MNLF formed in 1977 in the aftermath of the Tripoli Agreement, was gaining ascendancy.

Under the government of Fidel Ramos, an agreement with the MNLF was reached in September 1996. It created a temporary administrative body, the Southern Philippines Council for Peace and Development (SPCPD), to supervise the implementation of the agreement during a three-year transitional period. This 1996 agreement also provided for the integration of 7,500 MNLF fighters into the Philippine armed forces and the national police. Second, ARMM and the SPCPD were to be replaced by a new autonomous government after its approval through a plebiscite in the fourteen provinces and nine cities. The agreement also made provisions for the region's representation in the institutions of the national government, the creation of special regional security forces, the inclusion of Islamic curriculum in the education system, as well as the integration of Islamic schools (*madrasah*) to the education system of the regional autonomous government. Finally, the regional government was given the right to establish Shari'ah courts.[3]

Although the September 1996 agreement was the best one that had ever been reached for the Moros, it also failed to be adequately implemented. The plebiscite on the formation of a new autonomous region was never held. Lacking legitimacy and adequate funds, the SPCPD was unable to have a strong impact on the region's socioeconomic problems. Although many of these problems arose out of local ineptitude and corruption on the part of the former MNLF leaders who were in charge of the ARMM and the SPCPD, there were nevertheless other obstacles to the exercise of autonomous government since the SPCPD depended directly on the central government for funding, and the ARMM was similarly weak (Bertrand, 2000).

Furthermore, the MILF gained greater strength as it rejected the agreement and continued to fight. Although the MNLF had disbanded, the MILF grew stronger militarily. Several attempts were made to reach a peace agreement with the MILF. Under the government of Fidel Ramos, ceasefire agreements were reached and preliminary discussions were held. The government of Joseph Estrada, however, lost patience with the MILF and resorted to greater military repression to attempt to crush it. Under President Arroyo, ceasefires were again implemented and peace talks resumed, but the conflict remained at a stalemate. New proposals included an expansion of the ARMM, and the creation of a Bangsa Moro Development Agency, along similar lines as the previous SPCPD.[4] Overall, however, repeated attempts to implement different versions have all led to stalemate, and autonomy has proved very difficult to reach.

East Timorese

In Indonesia, ethno-nationalist rebellions have come from three groups: the East Timorese, the Papuans, and the Acehnese. The East Timorese and the Papuans resisted as soon as they were integrated into Indonesia. At the time, the government was fully launched into a deepening of acculturation to the Indonesian nation, with strong exclusionary effects for both groups. In addition to repressive policies that triggered staunch resistance, the

---

[3] *Manila Chronicle*, Sept. 9, 1996; *Business World*, Sept. 9, 1996; *Philippine Daily Inquirer*, Sept. 10, 1996; *Asiaweek*, Sept. 13, 1996; *Singapore Straights Times*, May 12, 1997.

[4] "Government offers MILF new development agency, bigger ARMM," *Philippines Star*, 22 July 2004.

government took few accommodative measures to represent these groups. Among the Acehnese, an original adherence to the Indonesian Republic was eroded by increasing repression and lack of accommodation. Again, the government's policies were aimed at integrating the Acehnese, on its own terms of inclusion, to the Indonesian nation, which left little room for addressing the particular demands and grievances of the Acehnese. Only after repeated periods of intense violent conflict did the Indonesian government finally provide a significant set of autonomous institutions, which represents a unique and very recent success.

The East Timorese perhaps most strongly rejected the single Indonesian nation because of the way they were integrated and their lack of common historical experience with the rest of the archipelago. The period of 1945–1949 marked the period of institutionalization of the Indonesian nation, at a time when groups across the archipelago were united in their common struggle against the Dutch and a desire to create a new, common nation. But because the Portuguese had colonized it, East Timor shared neither a similar past nor a history of regular contact with the other Indonesian groups. Instead, it was integrated into Indonesia by force and much later, in 1975. No democratic process was used; the local population was not consulted.

State repression, intimidation, and force were used, as elsewhere, to implement the New Order's vision of the Indonesian nation. Except that in East Timor, the state was even more violent and repressive. For the East Timorese, being part of the Indonesian nation meant losing their own identity and freedom, and therefore their perspective differed considerably from that of the liberating, modernist conception of the Indonesian nation with which other groups identified (Joliffe1978; Taylor 1991).

The East Timorese were expected to be a part of not only the Indonesian state but also the nation, adopting Indonesian as their official language and the structures and symbols of the Indonesian nation and state. The Indonesian government emphasized education, internal migration, and the repression of Timorese culture and development. Schools were built, but the education curriculum was exclusively Indonesian. Many primary-level courses emphasized the national ideology *Pancasila*, as well as Indonesia's national history, its heroes, symbols and a common culture promoted by the government (especially elements of Javanese culture). In addition to requiring the East Timorese to use the same textbooks, the government also encouraged the learning of national songs and the wearing of national school uniforms, as a way of promoting unity (Defert 1992, pp. 180–81; Taylor 1991, p. 128). Civil servants were hired from outside the region to fill numerous positions as administrators, technicians, and instructors. Thousands of spontaneous migrants from Sulawesi, Sumatra, and west Timor settled in the territory and increasingly dominated the small-business sector. The use of the local lingua franca, Tetum, was discouraged and displays of Timorese culture were restricted. The government also attempted to gain support by providing large amounts of funding for infrastructural development.

East Timor's future became a central issue when democratic reforms began. As President Habibie acceded to power in 1998 and began to announce political reforms, demonstrations were held in East Timor and Jakarta, demanding a resolution of the conflict. These accompanied waves of demonstrations and riots across the country demanding an acceleration of democratic reforms. Faced with difficulties in consolidating his power, Habibie came to rely on the military's ability and willingness to quell dissent as it arose across the country. The military was overstretched as the government continued to suffer economic downfall in the 1997–1998 Asian economic crisis. East Timor was a thorn in Indonesia's relationship with foreign donors.

To create allies abroad and to solidify his leadership at home, Habibie, in a surprise move, offered a special autonomy package to East Timor, with the possibility of independence if the East Timorese rejected it. In June 1998 he announced that Indonesia was prepared to offer wide-ranging autonomy to the territory, thereby setting a new basis for stalled negotiations between Indonesia and Portugal on the latter's former colony. And then, in response to a lack of enthusiasm from the East Timorese leadership, Habibie proposed on January 27, 1999 that if they rejected wide-ranging autonomy, the government would give East Timor its independence.[5]

In the months leading up to the referendum, which was scheduled for August 1999, violence escalated. The Indonesian armed forces began infiltrating East Timor and arming paramilitary groups in an effort to create a civil war aimed at disrupting the referendum and ensuring that East Timor would remain in the Republic. These pro-autonomy militias stepped up their attacks against the pro-independence groups. A small United Nations mission, UNAMET, was dispatched to East Timor to support the organization of the referendum but did not have the mandate to prevent the mounting violence in the territory.[6]

---

[5] *Tempo Magazine*, 27(18), 1 Feb–8 Feb 1999.
[6] Reports of a systematic campaign by the military and pro-integration militias, called Operasi Sapu Jagad, was reported by Tapol. See "Indonesia's Dirty war in East Timor,"

The referendum was held on August 30 in relative peace, but the results unleashed an unprecedented wave of violence against the civilian population. Of the 451,792 registered voters, 97 percent of whom cast their ballots, 78.5 percent rejected Indonesia's autonomy proposal (21 percent supported it) in a strong endorsement of independence.[7] Hours after the results were announced on September 4, pro-autonomy militias descended on villages, burning, looting, and displacing the local population. Within a few days, 200,000 refugees fled to the mountains and to the neighboring province of west timor, while the militias engaged in vast destruction. Supported by elements of Indonesia's armed forces, and apparently with the tacit approval at the highest levels of military command, the militias undertook to either maintain Timor through violence or, at least, to punish the Timorese for opting for independence.[8] Hundreds of people were killed and thousands became refugees as a result of the systematic destruction of the capital, Dili, and hundreds of villages.

However, the country continued under UN occupation, and secession from Indonesia progressed swiftly. Although Indonesia retained official responsibility for security in East Timor, the territory was under de facto UN rule in the months leading up to the October 1999 session of the People's Consultative Assembly (Majelis Permusyawaratan Rakyat, MPR), Indonesia's highest legislative body. The MPR approved the transfer of authority to a temporary UN body that would oversee the gradual transfer of power to an independent East Timorese government. The newly elected Indonesian president, Abdurrahman Wahid, gave his support to East Timor's independence and offered Indonesia's fullest cooperation.

After twenty-five years of resisting integration into the Republic, East Timor obtained its independence within a little over one year after the fall of Suharto. Secession in East Timor represented the resolution of a

---

Tapol Bulletin, 7 June 1999. Reports of elements of the Indonesian Armed Forces' involvement in the violence was confirmed by the Indonesian and United Nations inquiries on human rights violations in East Timor, following the August 1999 referendum. See International Commission of Inquiry on East Timor, *United Nations Report Of The International Commission Of Inquiry On East Timor To The Secretary-General,* 2000. New York: United Nations, and Commission to Investigate Human Rights Violations in East Timor (KPP-HAM) 2000, *Executive Summary Report on the Investigation of Human Rights Violations in East Timor,* Indonesian Human Rights Commission, Jakarta, 31 January.

[7] "East Timorese Choose Independence," *Associated Press,* 3 September 1999.
[8] The Indonesian Human Rights Commission named high level officers suspected of involvement in the violence following the referendum. See Commission to Investigate Human Rights Violations in East Timor (KPP-HAM) 2000, *Executive Summary Report.*

unique case in Indonesia's history. East Timor had always been different from the rest of the archipelago. It had never been part of the Dutch East Indies, which was the main commonality that brought together the various Indonesian ethnic groups that participated in the anti-colonial revolution and the establishment of the independent Republic of Indonesia. The Timorese, who never felt integrated to the rest of the archipelago, rejected Indonesia's single-nation model that perpetuated their exclusion. The armed forces resisted the move to secession, reacting within the logic of a historical path by which they had been the guardians of the Indonesian nation and state.

Papua/Irian Jaya

Like the East Timorese, Papuans never agreed to the process and means by which they were integrated to the Indonesian nation. Although Irian Jaya[9] shared with the rest of Indonesia the experience of being colonized under the Dutch East Indies, it did not join the Republic during the struggle for independence in the late 1940s. It was integrated in the late 1960s, when the Dutch agreed to depart the country in response to international pressure. Indonesia was given the control of West Papua for a transitional period until Papuans could be consulted on their future. In 1969, the Indonesian government organized a so-called Act of Free Choice. It handpicked all Papuan representatives and, under its pressure, obtained their unanimous support to be integrated to the Republic of Indonesia. Although the UN recognized the results of the consultation, the process was clearly undemocratic and was widely criticized by Papuans and foreigners as well. Thereafter, many Papuans considered integration into Indonesia to be illegitimate (Osborne 1985, pp. 41–48).[10]

However, dissatisfaction with the process of formal integration into the Indonesian state was not the only reason the Papuans resisted. After the formal transfer of power to Indonesia, the New Order government sought to include Papuans into the Indonesian nation. While much of the New Order regime's intervention was self-interested, concerned with the exploitation of natural resources, its policies and actions nevertheless intended to implement its single-nation concept. It aimed at assimilating Papuans,

---

[9] I use names for the province, as they were changed during the different historical periods. Before 1969, the territory was known as West New Guinea. After its integration to Indonesia, it was renamed Irian Jaya, before it was officially changed to Papua in 2001.

[10] Interviews in Jayapura (Irian Jaya), August 2001 confirmed this widespread view.

gradually reducing their attachments to their local cultures, adopting Indonesian characteristics, and espousing the principles of the nation.

Education, cultural repression, and migration fostered assimilation. Education emphasized an Indonesian curriculum with a strong emphasis on *Bahasa Indonesia*, which was the lingua franca of Papua as well, but no local Papuan languages were taught. School courses emphasized local conditions in Java. Pupils were taught Indonesian history, with only a limited reference to Irian Jaya, from an Indonesian perspective. They learned the slogans and songs of Indonesian nationalism, and sang the Indonesian national anthem under the Indonesian flag. They were also taught the principles of Indonesia's national ideology *Pancasila*.[11]

Papuans were also denied the freedom to express their culture and were fed, instead, the symbols of Indonesian culture. Their own province was named Irian, even though local Papuans saw it as an Indonesian fabrication.[12] Using Sanskrit words associated with Javanese culture, the government renamed the province Irian Jaya (Victorious Irian) in 1973 and the provincial capital Jayapura (Victory City). Shortly after 1969, the Indonesians undertook a campaign ("campaign Koteka") in the Papuan highlands to persuade local natives to abandon their penissheaths (*koteka*) and to wear modern clothing instead (Defert 1992, p. 271). Papuan songs or cultural expressions were deemed to be nationalist, and therefore banned for potentially fostering a secessionist threat.

Migration was another means of integrating Irian Jaya. In 1977, the province was named a priority destination for the government's transmigration program. Exact figures are not available, but estimates between 1979 and 1989 vary from 70,000 to 150,000 (compared to an estimated population of 1.2 million Papuans). Spontaneous migrants came in much greater numbers and constituted the greatest threat to the Papuans' livelihood. It is estimated that, out of a population of 2.6 million in 2000, 1.6 million were Papuan and 1 million were spontaneous migrants and transmigrants.[13]

---

[11] Interviews with anthropologist Yos Mansoben, Cendrawasih University, Abepura, 24 August 2001 and Yohanis G. Bonay, Director, ELSHAM-Papua, Abepura, 20 August 2001.

[12] Although originally a word from Biak used to identify the mainland, many Papuans believed that it was an acronym meaning "Ikut Republic Indonesia Anti-Nederland" (Follow the Indonesian Republic against the Dutch), which would have been used by the Indonesians during the 1950s.

[13] Interview with Michael Rumbiak, Lecturer and head of the Population Research Center, Cendrawasih University, Abepura, 25 August 2001.

Resistance to Indonesia mainly took the form of a guerilla movement. After 1969, small groups of armed resistance fighters formed the Free Papua Movement (*Organisasi Papua Merdeka*, OPM). OPM members were equipped with scarcely more than bows, arrows, or the occasional rifle from World War I. However, although it was a weak, divided movement, poorly organized and poorly armed, it became a symbol of resistance to Indonesian rule. Otherwise, there were occasional riots, most frequently near the Freeport–McMoran mine, a vast mining operation jointly owned by foreign investors and Jakarta-based Indonesians.

Despite the weakness of the OPM, the Indonesian armed forces maintained a strong presence, controlled the provincial government, and organized campaigns to weed out the OPM. Military campaigns were regularly waged, especially following local revolts (Osborne 1985, pp. 66–72). As reports of human rights abuses increased, the military diminished the scale of its responses, but violence against civilians, torture, disappearances, and shootings continued. For example, twenty people in Tembagapura were arrested, beaten and tortured during demonstrations in December 1994 (Münninghoff 1995). Several people were killed when troops opened fire on rioters near Timika in March 1996 (Amnesty 1996, pp. 2–3).

When a democratic opening occurred in 1998, the popular appeal of the nationalist movement became clear. In July 1998, demonstrations were organized in major cities throughout Irian Jaya to demand a referendum on independence, raising the Morning Star flag, symbol of Papuan nationalism.[14] In February 1999, a group of one hundred representatives met with President Habibie and bluntly stated that Papuans wanted their independence.[15] The following year, Papuan nationalists formalized their movement by organizing two congresses of the Papuan people. The first Large Deliberative Conference (*Musyarawah Besar*, MUBES), held in February 2000, issued its strong opposition to the Act of Free Choice and the process of integration to Indonesia. It also criticized the Indonesian treatment of the Papuan people, including human rights abuses, impoverishment, and cultural genocide, and reiterated the demands for independence.[16] The Papuan People's Congress (*Kongress Papua*), held from May 29 to June 4, 2000, reaffirmed demands for independence,

---

[14] *Media Indonesia*, 7 July 1998; *Forum Keadilan*, 7, no. 8, 27 July 1998; *Gatra*, 18 July, 1998.

[15] *Gatra*, 6 March 1999; *Forum Keadilan*, 7(25), 22 March 1999; *Tempo*, 28(0): 22, 2–8 March 1999. See also Human Rights Watch (2000, pp. 11–13).

[16] See *Komunike Politik Papua*, signed by Theys Eluay and Tom Beanal as great leaders of the Papuan people, Sentani-Port Numbay (Jayapura), 26 February 2000.

condemned the failure of the international community to recognize past historical injustices in Papua, and demanded its involvement in recognizing the Papuan right to self-determination.[17] A Presidium of the Papuan Congress (*Presidium Dewan Papua*, [PDP]) was elected to represent the Papuan people.

The government responded with an offer of special autonomy. The Special Autonomy Law of 2001 provided autonomy at the provincial level, whereby the Papuan government obtained jurisdiction over all matters except foreign policy, defense, monetary and fiscal policy, religion, and justice. In addition to the Papuan legislature, the Papuan People's Representative Assembly (*Dewan Perwakilan Rakyat Papua*, DPRP), a new assembly was also created. The Papuan People's Assembly (*Majelis Rakyat Papua*, MRP) was meant to represent *indigenous* Papuan groups and included local customary groups, as well as religious and women's groups. It was given the mandate of promoting and protecting the rights and customs of Papuan people. It was also given powers of consultation and assent over candidates for the position of governor and over decisions and regulations relating to the basic rights of Papuans. Finally, the law provided for the creation of a Truth and Reconciliation Commission to investigate the process of Papua's integration to Indonesia, with the objective of reconciling the Papuan people to the Indonesian state and preserving its unity.

In fiscal matters, the law provided large new revenues for the province. The most important source of revenue came from the exploitation of natural resources, particularly mining. Papua was to receive 80 percent of mining, forestry, and fisheries fiscal revenues, and 70 percent of fiscal revenues from oil and gas exploitation. In addition, a greater proportion of other tax revenues were to accrue to the province (Bertrand 2004, pp. 206–7).[18]

Nonetheless, special autonomy was not well received in Irian Jaya. During the process of drafting the special autonomy proposal, the governor's team faced numerous protests. It was unable to hold many special meetings to discuss its contents and, in the end, the proposal was drafted

---

[17] See *Resolutions as agreed by the members of the Papuan Congress, 29 May–4 June, 2000*. Port Numbay (Jayapura), 4 June 2000. Signed by members of the steering committee of the Congress.

[18] Law no. 33, 2004 gave similar percentages to regions for mining, fisheries, and forestry, but less for oil and gas (15.5 and 30.5 percent respectively). Law no. 33, 2004 and subsequent regulations, however, were much more specific about fiscal categories, their definition, and precise methods of redistribution than the Special Autonomy Law for Papua.

by the team without the broad consultation it had intended.[19] It was submitted to parliament and subsequently passed by the DPR, but it received a very lukewarm response. Many groups continued to view any form of autonomy with suspicion.

In the meantime, the military and police began to clamp down on the nationalist movement. They banned flag raisings; there were clashes with the security forces, such as in Wamena on October 6, 2000, in which 37 people were killed. Theys Eluay and several members of the PDP were arrested and jailed for two months in connection with separatist activities linked to the December 1, 1999 flag raisings, the MUBES, and Congress.[20] The local police received orders to stop all separatist activities, repress the activities of the Papuan political elite, and gather intelligence information on the activities of local NGOs, foreigners, and political elites who supported separatism.[21] The Papuan independence movement was paralyzed by a return of repressive measures.

After becoming president in July 2001, Megawati reasserted the government's uncompromising position on the nationalist movement. She continued to support military operations designed to curtail it while supporting the adoption of the law on special autonomy.

At the same time, several measures undermined it. As soon as the Special Autonomy Law took effect, the government revived Law no. 45, 1999 on the division of Papua into three provinces. As part of the strategy to undermine the secessionist movement, the Habibie government had introduced the law to create three distinct provinces. It met with strong local resistance and was not implemented. President Megawati, however, decided to revive the law and passed decree no. 1, 2003 that reaffirmed this division of the province. There were renewed protests, particularly over the creation of the province of Central Irian Jaya, which was postponed indefinitely. The province of West Irian Jaya was nevertheless created.

Other aspects of the law created many problems. There were ambiguous divisions of power between the MRP and the DPRP. Their role was

---

[19] Interview with Yos Mansoben, Uncen faculty member and head of the organizing committee of the Governor's team on special autonomy, Jayapura, 24 August 2001; interview with Frans Wospakrik, rector of UNCEN and member of the steering committee of the team, Jayapura, 20 August 2001.

[20] See Institute for human rights study and advocacy – Irian Jaya (ELS-HAM Irian Jaya). *Laporan "Kasus Abepura 07 Desember 2000"*. Jayapura: ELS-HAM Irian Jaya, December 2000; [HRW Irian, 2001]; *Tempo*, 29, no. 40, 4–10 December 2000.

[21] Kepolisian Negara Republik Indonesia Daerah Irian Jaya. Rencana Operasi "Tuntas Matoa 2000" Polda Irja (Confidential). Jayapura, November 2000, No. Pol.: R/Renops/640/XI/2000, p. 9.

also not clearly distinguished from those of Papuan representatives in the national parliament and the DPD (Regional Representative Council). The language of the law also lacked details on several areas of jurisdiction, and these ambiguities meant that the law could be undermined or diluted through the regulatory process.

In addition, the formation of the MRP suffered many delays. Despite being officially implemented since January 2002, the MRP was only formed after much criticism from local groups, who accused the government of willfully delaying it in order to undermine special autonomy. On August 12, 2005, more than 10,000 people protested over the failure to create the MRP and the creation of the province of West Irian Jaya.

Indonesian security forces continued to increase their presence in the region, despite complaints from local groups. In some gesture of conciliation, plans to create a new strategic reserve command were shelved after protests that this would increase even more the number of regular troops in the area. Nevertheless, military operations along the border with Papua-New Guinea have continued and the government has restricted civilian access to border areas. Internal security matters have increasingly been transferred to the local police, but some units, particularly the *Brimob* (special riot police unit), have overstepped their powers on occasion (International Crisis Group 2006, p. 10).

For the most part, Special Autonomy failed to address the grievances of the Papuans. They continue to vie for a better institutionalization of their self-determination, and remain highly suspicious of any agreement short of independence.

Aceh

The rise of an sub-state nationalist movement in Aceh partly derives from the conception of Indonesia that the Acehnese had initially supported. Unlike the East Timorese and Papuans, the Acehnese participated in the 1945 revolution and actively supported the new republic. They supported the Islamic variant of Indonesian nationalism that was still a potential alternative at the time of independence. Acehnese leaders subsequently joined an Islamic rebellion, under the banner of the Darul Islam, once a secular nationalist model was adopted and the Islamist variant rejected. The Acehnese had developed a strong sense of group identity that was subsequently never fully acknowledged by the Indonesian central government. Instead, rebellions were repressed by the Indonesian state and few concessions were extended. The Acehnese were integrated to the Indonesian nation along the lines followed in other regions, with little recognition or compromise over their sense of distinctiveness. Under the New Order regime, these policies culminated in military campaigns to eradicate the sub-state nationalist movement. The repressive approach under the New Order did not eliminate nationalist sentiment but contributed, instead, to strengthening it among the Acehnese population.

Three rebellions were crushed by the Indonesian armed forces. The first supported the establishment of an Islamic state for Indonesia. Acehnese *ulama* had gained political power during a social revolution that eliminated the power of the former aristocratic elite (*ulèëbalang*) that governed Aceh under Dutch colonialism. When the unitary state was established in 1950, Aceh lost its status as a province. Furthermore, nationalist leaders rejected an Islamic state for Indonesia. For these reasons, Acehnese *ulama* and their supporters rebelled under the banner of the Darul Islam movement, which had originated in west Java. They fought until the late 1950s, when most of the rebel leaders accepted a settlement but were essentially defeated by the Indonesian armed forces (Morris 1983; Reid 1979). In late 1956, the Indonesian government gave Aceh provincial status and designation as "special region" (*daerah istimewa*). It returned to their previous administrative and judicial position members of the All-Aceh Ulama Association (PUSA), the main political association of *ulama* and civil administrators involved in the rebellion. Finally, Acehnese soldiers returned to serve in the region as Aceh obtained, once again, its own military regional command (Morris 1983, pp. 216–24). Most rebels abandoned the goals of an Islamic state for Indonesia and focused, instead, on gains for Aceh, asking for wide-ranging autonomy and the implementation of Islamic law. The government conceded only to extending wide-ranging autonomy in religion, education, and customary law, while remaining vague on the application of Islamic law (Morris 1983, pp. 226–34).

These institutional concessions became meaningless under the New Order. Disillusion set in among many members of Aceh's political elite when it became clear that national imperatives and the central government's objectives superseded any claims on the basis of regional autonomy. The state emphasized military and political control from the center and the application of Islamic law became void. Furthermore, attempts to reconcile Islamic education with the state's secular curriculum were rejected (Morris 1983, pp. 273–81).

These measures were largely responsible for broadening and deepening the Acehnese rebellion, especially during the repressive decade of the

1990s. A second rebellion emerged in the late 1970s under the banner of the Free Aceh Movement (Gerakan Aceh Merdeka [GAM]). It was essentially organized to protest against the central government's control of the province and especially the newly discovered oil and gas. There were few, if any, benefits for the Acehnese population from the exploitation of these resources, whose revenues accrued to foreign investors, their Indonesian partners in Jakarta, and the central government (Kell 1995, pp. 14–16, 22–23). The rebellion remained small and was swiftly crushed by the armed forces. The reemergence of GAM in the late 1980s was different. It was better armed and waged a stronger insurgency but still remained small, with a core of a few hundred active fighters. This time, the movement seemed to enjoy much broader support among the local population, however, even prompting the regional military commander to complain that supporters might be everywhere, in every village (Kell 1995, pp. 66–74). From disgruntled elite members to a broader section of the population, the exploitation of liquefied natural gas, other industrial production and increased military presence showed that the Acehnese had little means to participate, protest, or reap benefits from development in their own territory.

The Indonesian armed forces' response to the GAM rebellion was out of proportion with the estimate of GAM forces. In what became a "shock therapy" approach, the armed forces went much beyond counterinsurgency tactics and used torture, arbitrary killings, arrests, detentions, and other means of weeding out GAM supporters (Kell 1995, pp. 74–77). It was estimated that 2000 people were killed between mid-1989 and mid-1991 (Kell 1995, p. 75). After 1993, the rebellion was crushed but the armed forces continued their operations.

The democratization of the regime led to the formation of a large civilian movement demanding self-determination but it also led to the reemergence of GAM. The Center for Information on the Aceh Referendum (*Sentra Informasi Referendum Aceh*, or SIRA) was created in February 1999 to advance the cause of a referendum. It organized a mass rally in Aceh's capital, Banda Aceh, on November 8, 1999. An estimated 500,000 people descended into the streets, showing strong support for a referendum.

After June 1999, GAM began new operations and clashes with the armed forces escalated. In the following years, many more people died from the violence than all of the previous rebellions combined, as GAM was better organized, more widespread, and enjoyed unprecedented support among the population. Three humanitarian pauses in May 2000,

September 2000, and March 2001 failed. Under Megawati's presidency, the repressive approach was intensified.[22]

To supplement the military approach, a special autonomy law was adopted. In September 1999 a law was passed on the implementation of the special status of Aceh, including elements of Islamic law, Islamic education, and measures to reinforce Acehnese culture.[23] When these proved insufficient to reduce civilian demands for independence and GAM's activities, the central government supported a proposal for a Special Autonomy law. Several institutions were adopted to reflect Aceh's particular distinctiveness – including a flag and other cultural symbols of Aceh's distinctiveness – and Aceh would retain 80 percent of revenues from oil and gas exploration. It took effect on January 1st, 2002.[24] Special Autonomy was deemed insufficient by GAM, and it was eventually abandoned.

Indeed, President Megawati Sukarnoputri continued to use strong repression and insisted on an autonomy that was already offered, in spite of GAM's objections and continued armed resistance. Special Autonomy began to be implemented, but it had little effect on violent clashes. GAM and the armed forces continued the war, while the civilian movement was eclipsed under the intensity of the violence. With a stronger reliance on the military, Megawati supported her predecessors' uncompromising views on national unity. Military repression was the primary means of defending Indonesia's national model and the integrity of the state.

After successive attempts at several ceasefires, a peace agreement was finally reached and formally signed in August 2005. After two years of intense fighting between the Indonesian armed forces and GAM, the latter was beginning to weaken and was losing some of its support as civilians were caught in the violence. The December 2004 tsunami, which had devastated a large area of Aceh, had created a catalyst for a peace agreement to be brokered. As a result of the agreement, GAM disbanded and a new Law on Aceh was passed.

The Law on Aceh constitutes the most significant recognition of distinctiveness for a national minority in Indonesia, and it provides detailed and precise powers for Aceh.[25] A vast improvement over the Special

[22] *Tempo*, 30(7), 16–22 April 2001.
[23] *Forum Keadilan* 8(31), October 17, 1999.
[24] *Tempo* 29(5), 3–9 April, 2000; *Jakarta Post*, November 27, 2000; *Jakarta Post*, May 18, 2001; *Jakarta Post*, January 2, 2002.
[25] Undang Undang Republik Indonesia nomor 11 tahun 2006 tentang Pemerintahan Aceh [*Law no.11, 2006 of the Republic of Indonesia on Aceh Government*].

Autonomy Law of 2001 as well as the Law for Papua, the Aceh law provides jurisdiction to the Acehnese government over all matters except foreign relations, defense, national security, monetary and fiscal policy, and justice. Legislative and executive powers, as well as obligations, are much more clearly specified, including obligations and forbidden practices of the governor and legislative members. The Law on Aceh extends Islamic law to the region, giving the Aceh provincial government the responsibility for its implementation and enforcement.

It also allows the Acehnese to create a local political party to run in provincial and regency elections, a provision that departs from the law on political parties, which bans such local parties in the rest of Indonesia. Also under the new law, the province gained more oversight powers with regard to the security organizations operating in Aceh, including consultation and approval for the appointment of the Aceh chief of police and for military troops stationed in the province. Additionally, there are provisions for the creation of a truth and reconciliation commission to investigate past abuses by the armed forces (Bertrand 2007).

In fiscal terms, Aceh receives 80 percent of the equalization payments relating to a specified subset of tax revenues on forestry, mining, fisheries, and the oil and gas sector.[26] As an autonomous government, it also obtains additional revenues from the exploitation of natural resources, including a 70 percent of oil and gas revenues from the state's portion of exploitation of these resources (in addition to taxation revenue specified above) and 80 percent of revenues from all other resources in the province. This is a much greater proportion than the previous law had granted. Finally, the law is much more specific in terms of the source of these revenues.

For the first time, a law on autonomy addresses local grievances, recognizes the unique character of a people within Indonesia (even if it does not go so far as to recognize the Acehnese as a nation), and is being implemented without many obstacles. Because the law specifically supersedes other legislation, it has not been embroiled in the legal ambiguities caused by the overlapping and contradictory legislation in Papua. Elections were held and the Free Aceh Movement, now a political party, gained a majority in the provincial parliament, and a former GAM activist was elected governor.

---

[26] Equalization payments are allocations to various levels of government (central, provincial, regency) calculated according to fixed percentages of tax revenues, state revenues from exploitation of natural resources, and other budgetary funds specified by legislation and arising from various sources of state revenue.

The implementation of the Law on Aceh is still at a relatively early stage, but it might constitute the most significant movement away from Indonesia's past emphasis on a strong single nation. By not recognizing the Acehnese as a nation within Indonesia, the Constitution and the central government can still present Indonesia as constituting a single nation. The leverage to enforce this concept through institutions and laws that can further implement it, however, has been significantly curtailed. The Law on Aceh gives to the Aceh government the power to conduct its own affairs and to tailor its institutions and laws to the specific needs of the Acehnese. As such, it constitutes a de facto recognition of Aceh as a nation.

CONCLUSION

Nations within states often demand autonomy as a form of self-determination, yet such demands can become a double-edged sword. Autonomy enhances the recognition of sub-state nations. Short of recognizing equal rights for them, as well as equal power at the center, autonomy provides wide-ranging powers over the territorial homeland of a nation and the ability to manage its own affairs, while also participating in the central government. Autonomy can often be the best form of representation where, in democratic settings, acceptance of an equal status might be difficult to obtain if a nation's population is significantly smaller than half of the total population of the state.

Autonomy, particularly in an asymmetrical form, provides a degree of recognition of a nation within a multination state. By delineating a territory where autonomy will apply, by providing institutions that will be controlled by the national group, and sometimes by including clauses in autonomy laws that specifically address cultural or group distinctiveness, autonomous status is an important and widespread form of recognition. It does not provide the same degree of acceptance of multinational status as a constitutional clause that specifically recognizes a group as a nation, but it provides a platform from which a nation can exercise its self-determination and negotiate with other nations within the state.

At the same time, autonomy can be a dangerous form of recognition for sub-state national groups. It can be used by central governments as a form of appeasement to defuse violent conflict, to divide sub-state nationalist movements, or to co-opt its leaders. In the cases of Indonesia and the Philippines, several experiments with autonomy failed. They were either never implemented, or they were highly criticized for their weakness. As in the case of the Special Autonomy Law for Aceh (2001) or the 1996 peace agreement with the MNLF, autonomy provisions can simply be insufficient to lead to the demobilization of an armed nationalist movement if the legislation itself is weakly crafted in order to exploit ambiguities, or if subsequent legislation undermines it.

In Indonesia and the Philippines, autonomy has constituted a strong departure from past conceptions of the nation. Their respective historical trajectories highly influenced state elites who were not only reluctant to adopt autonomy laws but were deeply imbued by the idea of building single nations. In both countries, state elites pursued integrationist and assimilationist policies to reduce regional distinctiveness and to create a cultural core in order to preserve state unity. A common language and a strong nationalist movement provided Indonesian state elites with the material to implement policies that sought even greater cultural convergence among groups, thereby alienating latecomers such as East Timorese and Papuans, as well as the Acehnese, who had developed a strong regionalist identity. In the Philippines, a relatively weak nationalist movement and the lack of a common language notwithstanding, the dominant elite created sufficiently strong bonds of common interests within an American-inspired integrationist political system to overcome many regionalist tendencies. Built around support from Christian Filipinos, however, this integrative process was never able to include Muslims, who had developed a stronger sense of common ethnic identity, in part because of American colonial policies. Muslims remained marginalized as they continued to reject the Filipino state and nation.

Autonomy, therefore, has been in tension with a historical path that has upheld and reinforced over time a concept of single nation. In the cases of Indonesia and the Philippines, which were constructed out of the borders of colonial administration with little or no previous history of common political community, such a path was perceived as an imperative to safeguard fragile new states with only a thin social and political bond among its diverse populations. They could not, however, avoid excluding groups that developed their own nationalist course in resistance to these centrifugal forces. Repression and further assimilationist attempts only reinforced this resistance and solidified national alternatives, as was clearly the case in Aceh.

Nevertheless, the principle of autonomy has now been enshrined in both countries. Despite its weakness and failings, the Autonomous Region of Muslim Mindanao emerged as a result of a clause inserted in the Constitution of 1987 at the height of the People Power Revolution. In Indonesia, successive autonomy laws have mollified the state elites' resistance to its concept, thereby opening up the door for the landmark autonomy agreement in Aceh. Despite a strong historical path reinforcing the unitary nation-state idea in both countries, there are signs that autonomy may well move both countries in the direction of institutionalizing and acknowledging their multinational status. In the meantime, the record remains mixed, and paths can still be reversed.

8

China and the Virtual Taiwan Nation

André Laliberté

Since Taiwan embarked on its democratic journey in 1987, close to 90 percent of its citizens have refused the offer from the Beijing authorities for peaceful reunification. They know that they will not be recognized as a nation within the People's Republic of China (PRC). They also know that the Chinese Communist Party (CCP) will never give Taiwan even the symbolic form of recognition of the kind Tibetans receive, let alone the substantive powers of a real autonomy. These misgivings are grounded in the reality of the CCP's repeated position on the issue of "reunification" with Taiwan, which denies the Taiwanese any right of self-determination and promises military intervention if Taiwanese leaders declare independence. The PRC authorities' response to the Taiwanese aspirations for recognition of their distinctiveness highlights the limitations of an authoritarian government peacefully managing a multination state. It also points to the difficulty of defining a national identity that is determined by narrow cultural criteria. Although the PRC is officially a multinational state, it is also a unitary state in which one nationality, the Han Chinese, stands above the others. This unequal relationship between the Han and the other fifty-five nationalities in China is addressed in Chapter 9. This chapter discusses an equally problematic dimension of the Chinese national identity: the narrow definition of Han identity itself.

THE PROBLEM OF A TAIWANESE NATION FOR A MULTINATIONAL CHINA

In 1992, when a public opinion poll on the subject was taken for the first time, a majority of Taiwanese declared that they belonged to a nation that is distinct from China. A majority also hoped that this nation could coexist peacefully with the PRC. Based on the remote possibility that China would become a liberal and prosperous democracy, up to a quarter of the Taiwanese said that they would accept being part of a Chinese nation. Still, for more than a third of the Taiwanese population, this would not change their belief that they belonged to a distinct nation that is deserving of recognition. If a military campaign by the People's Liberation Army (PLA) were to forcefully incorporate Taiwan, this would in all likelihood generate a strong opposition from the most determined parts of the Taiwanese population, and China could experience the kind of unrest that the United Kingdom faced in Northern Ireland for decades.

The Republic of China (ROC), as the state in which the Taiwanese live is officially known, was created in 1912 and has existed since 1949 within the current frontiers. This is a virtual existence, however, because its sovereignty is denied by an ever increasing number of states. PRC authorities do not recognize this nation on the international scene and hope to govern it within the framework known as "one country two systems," which recognizes Taiwan as a province with its own distinct institutions but not as a nation with an inherent sovereignty and a right to self-determination. The CCP refuses to accept the case for a Taiwanese nation within the PRC, despite the fact that the PRC's constitution proclaims that China is a unitary multinational state. To put it another way, the PRC recognizes – at least on paper – the existence of a Tibetan nation and fifty-four others, but it denies such recognition to the Taiwanese, who have all the trappings of a nation-state except international recognition by major powers. This attitude is all the more difficult to understand given that the CCP's refusal to recognize a Taiwanese national identity within the PRC diminishes its ability to peacefully assert its sovereignty over Taiwan. The alternative is the continuation of a military stand-off between the two polities' armies: the PRC seeking to prevent a declaration of Taiwanese independence, and the ROC trying to protect its virtual sovereignty. The argument that is made in this chapter is that the disagreement between the PRC and the ROC rests on two radically different views of the nation, which cannot easily be reconciled.

The government of the PRC asserts that there is only one China and that Taiwan is part of it, a point of view known as the "One China Principle." The "one country two systems" formula that the PRC government proposes represents, in principle, a more generous offer than the institutional model of accommodation discussed elsewhere in this book that other sovereign states offer to their sub-state nations. It offers Taiwanese the right to keep their political and economic system, and even their own armed forces, as long as they agree to renounce the sovereignty of the ROC and acknowledge they are citizens of the PRC (Deng 1984). The Taiwanese, however, reject that model because, they argue, Taiwan is not a province within the PRC but a nation with its own sovereign state, albeit one that does not receive international recognition. They do not see why they should risk jeopardizing their hard-won democratic institutions. This chapter does not discuss Taiwanese aspirations to nationhood, which has received considerable attention elsewhere (Corcuff 2002; Tsai 2006; Wachman 2007), but rather focuses on the reasons it is impossible, conceptually, for the current leaders of the CCP to recognize Taiwan as a nation within the PRC, even less one that could live peacefully alongside it.

In a recent book on the subject, Alan Wachman argues that China's growing assertiveness on the international scene has led its leaders to revise the traditional views on China's imagined geography (2007). Taiwan, his argument goes, was seen by Chinese rulers in the past as an outpost from which China's enemies could attack the continent, but since the defeat of Japan in 1945 and the renunciation by the Nationalist Party (*Guomindang*, hereafter GMD) of recovering China by force from Taiwan, the island does not represent a strategic threat anymore. The island, asserts Wachman, now represents a strategic location from which China can assert its influence in the western Pacific and beyond. Although this argument is valid, I propose that China's concern over Taiwanese independence has more to do with domestic concerns than any geostrategic ambitions. This is the discussion of Chinese nationalism used for internal consumption. Therefore, this chapter does not address the issue of nationalism in Chinese foreign policy, which has also been covered elsewhere (Sautman 1997; Zhao 2005; Zheng 1999).

I argue that the CCP's categorical rejection of Taiwanese sovereignty results from the perception that such a possibility challenges its fundamental claim that it can best defend China's national integrity. Moreover, Taiwanese independence challenges the current definition of the Chinese nation the CCP promotes, in its multilayered dimensions. It questions the cultural unity and coherence of the Han people – as ethnic Chinese are known – and it casts doubts about China's political unity as a multinational unitary state. It also challenges the foundation of the CCP's political legitimacy as the guarantor of national unity.

Perhaps even more importantly, Taiwanese aspirations to nationhood, either as a hypothetical Republic of Taiwan or as the existing ROC, rely on a definition of the nation that is incompatible with definitions promoted by the PRC elites. Taiwanese have come to espouse a civic nationalist view of their nation, an idea that rests on the practice of democracy (Schubert 2004; Wong 2001). As long as the CCP promotes the idea of a nation defined by language, culture, or a state-sponsored definition of history, and as long as they postpone the development of democracy and reject the concept of a civic nation, they cannot accept the idea of a Taiwanese nation, distinct from China. For the same reasons, they can accept even less the idea of such a sub-state nation within the PRC.

The rest of the chapter explores these points as follows: I first highlight the fact that even though the CCP today speaks about a perennial Chinese nation, that idea of China is remarkably recent, and it failed to coalesce into a viable political entity in the early twentieth century during the Republican era (1912–1949). This is also true of the first three decades of the PRC regime, when the CCP promoted an internationalist ideology that was inimical to nationalism. I then present three definitions for the nation based on ethnicity, culture, and history, which Chinese intellectuals have proposed in recent years and the authorities have endorsed to various degrees, and then discuss the way these concepts rule out the idea of a sovereign Taiwan. I present another concept of the nation that is embraced by a few Chinese intellectuals in the PRC and by many in Taiwan. It rests on the idea of political participation, and it could help to overcome the limitations seen in the previous approaches. The virtual independence of Taiwan, I argue in a third section, represents a challenge to the first three approaches because it implicitly questions the concept of a homogeneous Han core nation, makes it even more difficult for minority nationalities to accept the unitary nature of the state, and openly challenges the claim that the CCP can enforce national unity. I then discuss some of the possibilities that are opened up by the idea of civic nationalism, concluding with a discussion of some of the consequences of that approach.

NATION BUILDING IN REPUBLICAN CHINA

Nationalism in Republican China (1912–1949)

The construction of Han ethnicity today represents a remarkable example of ethno-genesis, with few parallels. It has evolved faster than the French state's success in transforming "peasants into Frenchmen," to borrow from Eugene Weber's felicitous expression (1976), and in terms of the speed and the number of people concerned, it compares to the

Indian anti-colonial movement's spectacular success in turning "locally and regionally oriented folks into Indians (Varshney 1998, p. 39)." The Han people stand out as an ethnic category comprising many different populations that do not share the same language, beliefs, customs, and so on (Chow 2001; Ramsey 1987). Yet, few people in China today doubt that the Han are anything but a single people, even in Taiwan (Hsieh 1998). This belief in the unity of the Chinese people, however, was not widely shared in Republican China between 1912 and 1949.

A problem that plagues intellectuals in most post-colonial societies has been how, after the colonial rulers have left, to create new national identities out of populations speaking different languages, sometimes adhering to different religions, and following different customs (Chatterjee 1986). China has not been spared this predicament since the collapse of the Qing dynasty in 1911. After that regime change, Chinese revolutionaries tried to build on the remnants of a multiethnic, multicultural, and multinational polity a new principle of political legitimacy based on nationalism, but this proved extremely difficult. Although a majority of people in Republican China realized that they were not Manchus, Mongols, Tibetans, or Muslims because of their language, religious beliefs, or kinship ties, most did not develop a consciousness of being part of a distinct people. For many people, their collective identity did not extend beyond their local communities (Duara 1995). Sun Yat-sen had conspired with his colleagues in the Chinese United Alliance (*Tongmenghui*) to abolish the imperial regime on the grounds that it was led by the alien rule of the Manchus – as people in the West also knew the Qing (Schiffrin 1970, pp. 311–12). Despite the creation of the nationalist GMD, Sun failed to counter the divisive influence of the warlords in the first twelve years of the Republican regime. Shortly before his death in 1924, he lamented that Chinese lacked a sense of solidarity beyond family and clan and said that China was like a "loose heap of sand," in need of a sense of national unity if it wanted to successfully repel foreign control (Sun 1927, pp. 1–6).

The rulers of the ROC who were committed to the unity of their country wondered how to define their nation and which relevant markers of identity they could use to define who qualified as a Han. In nineteenth-century Europe, and even in neighboring Japan, this seemed a very simple and straightforward process. Language, as the carrier of a tradition, represented the central characteristic of a nation, a point that has been reiterated since by many historians of nationalism (Anderson 1991; Breuilly 1993; Gellner 1983; Hobsbawm 1990). This approach, based on linguistic markers of identity, however, could hardly work in China because Han Chinese then – and today – speak a wide variety of dialects and languages (Ramsey 1987). In the area it controlled in Han China, the GMD sought to unify the language of China and adopted Mandarin, the language used by civil servants in Beijing, as the national language (*guoyu*). The task, however, was daunting. Weak communications, little investment, a lack of political unity, and the circumstances of war made very difficult the imposition of a unified linguistic norm.

Another source of national unity that inspired Chinese intellectuals was religion, which, at about the same time that the Qing collapsed and the ROC emerged, represented an important marker of identity for the Irish, the Jews, and the Serbs. Kang Youwei, for example, was inspired by the European states' experience with state religions. He believed that religion could provide a form of cohesiveness that could transcend regional differences and provide some purpose to the whole nation. He therefore, in 1923, proposed that China adopt Confucianism as a state religion (Hao 1987).

This project, however, proved unfeasible. It is true that most Chinese adhere to a diffuse form of religion, which usually comprises the "three teachings" (*sanjiao*) of Confucianism, Daoism, and Buddhism (Yang 1994). Yet, these practices vary from region to region, and many religious movements have evolved outside this parameter. That proposal was also bound to fail because many Chinese, including the GMD leaders, who were themselves Christians, were repudiating traditional Chinese religions as something that kept the nation weak vis-à-vis western powers and Japan.

Another strategy that many intellectuals adopted to justify the claim that a single state must rule the disparate population of China, following the zeitgeist of the time in the Americas, western Europe, and Japan, relied on pseudoscientific racial theories. According to a view that was popular at the end of the nineteenth century, Han Chinese, despite their linguistic and religious differences, all belonged to the same race (Dikötter 1992; Sautman 2000). As they plotted to overthrow the Qing, the early revolutionaries in the Chinese United Alliance claimed that, once in power, they would preserve the demarcation of the existing frontiers. They proclaimed, accordingly, that the new Republic they aspired to create would be a multiracial entity formed by the union of five "races": Chinese (*Han*), Manchus (*Man*), Mongols (*Meng*), Tibetans (*Zang*), and Muslims (*Hui*) (Schiffrin 1970, pp. 295–6). This project was a well-meaning but futile exercise. The GMD's authority never extended durably and effectively to the territories of Tibet, which was under British influence; Mongolia[1];

---

[1] Outer Mongolia became a sovereign state in 1911.

east Turkestan – as people then knew Xinjiang; or Manchuria – which fell under Japanese control in 1932. The GMD's authority and its ability to engage in nation-building in the Han Chinese territory was also limited. In 1928 at the end of the Northern Expedition against the warlords, the latter still controlled more territory than the GMD government located in Nanjing. In 1937, after the beginning of the Sino-Japanese War, the GMD had to relocate the capital to Chongqing, in the western province of Sichuan. In sum, throughout the Republican era, the idea that there existed one China may have been an ideal for some members of the revolutionary elite, but it did not translate into political reality.

CONSTRUCTING THE CHINESE NATION IN THE PRC

The Absence of Nationalism until 1978

When the CCP took power in 1949, the world was recovering from a devastating conflict that was blamed on the ideology of nationalism. Between 1937 and 1945, the CCP had fought along the GMD in World War II against the Japanese militarism which was seen as an extreme consequence of nationalism. Then, after the Chinese civil war resumed, the CCP triumphed over a political party that had explicitly labeled itself as nationalist. Finally, one of the core tenets of the CCP ideology was internationalism, or the view that the target of political struggle is not fellow workers or peasants in different countries but the bourgeoisie, the landowners, and their allies in state bureaucracies both abroad and within China (Hunt 1996; Sheng 1997). The CCP made an exception to that rule when it realized that it needed the support of industrialists and overseas Chinese to develop the country, and despite their suspicious class origins, deemed these social categories "patriotic" and therefore deserving of friendship. Overall, however, the CCP was not nationalist. The leaders of the PRC did not frame the return of Taiwan to Chinese sovereignty within a nationalist discourse, but as part of a narrative on social transformation and resolution of the Chinese civil war between the CCP and the GMD.

One exception to the prevailing view that nationalism was absent from the politics of the CCP before 1949 – and presumably from the PRC under Mao Zedong – was voiced by Chalmers Johnson, who argued that the CCP could succeed against the Japanese invaders because of its ability to mobilize the Chinese peasantry (1962). Otherwise, there is little in the literature about the importance of nationalism in the PRC state-building effort. Most of the literature on Chinese nationalism focuses on the influence of that ideology on foreign policy. The scholars who were paying attention in the 1990s discussed the nature of Chinese nationalism as government officials understood it and have tried to analyze its influence on Chinese foreign policy, but they do not say much about its content to domestic audiences (Guang 2005; Townsend 1992; Zhao 2005; Zheng 1999). Others have looked at it within a framework of opposition between the state and the popular ideology of nationalism but have not looked at relations between Han and national minorities or relations among Han people who come from different regions (Gries 2004; Xu 2001; Zhang 1998; Zhao 1997; Zheng 1999).

In what follows, we shall focus on the Han's self-definitions, which are intrinsically linked with the definitions of the Chinese nation currently approved by the regime, and which intellectuals close to the government articulated in the 1990s. These different versions of nationalism and different definitions of nationhood have found resonance among students and urban residents. Although there is no reliable way to test how popular they are, indirect evidence such as blogs, online discussions, and articles in the press suggest that they are largely supported and that there is little point in creating an artificial cleavage between state-sponsored and popular nationalisms (Gries 2005). These views generally support the "One China Principle" and none of them is compatible with the idea of a civic nation. Schematically, those who hold the most prominent views advocated by the PRC base their definitions of nationhood on the idea that China is the homeland of the distinctive Chinese people, the promoter of a specific culture, or the carrier of a unique historical tradition. The first view promotes the idea that the Chinese nation has a core Han nation; the second view justifies the inclusion of national minorities within the Chinese nation; the third tries to address the lacunae of the first two conceptions.

For the sake of comparative analysis, we can use these definitions in ways commensurable with nationalist approaches used by governments and elites elsewhere. Borrowing from Greenfeld (1992, p.7), Wang Shaoguang, an intellectual of the nationalist New Left, has identified four possible forms of nations and looked at the Chinese self-definitions of their nation within that framework (2004). First, people can identify as members of an ethnic nation that shares attributes such as language, customs, or belief, and that nation controls a state promoting these attributes. This is the situation in nations such as Japan, Korea, or Portugal. Another type of nation is more inclusive, the bearer of a cultural tradition that encompasses patterns of behavior, norms, and myths beyond the attributes of a specific civilization. Wang looks at traditional China as the example of such a state (Harrison 1969; Wang 2004). A nation can also be a sovereign state that is culturally heterogeneous but unified by a shared legal and political culture: India and Indonesia, states with populations speaking different languages and adhering to many faiths, are examples of this, at least at a conceptual level. Finally, a nation can be a free association of citizens linked by adherence to a shared political culture: the United States and the countries of western Europe tend increasingly to define themselves in this fashion. Wang believes that only the last type of nation cannot be relevant to China.

An Ethnic Nation

The discussion of the Chinese ethnic nation excludes two groups of people. It does not include overseas Chinese, despite the fact that the PRC and the ROC have until recently both appealed to this group as "compatriots." The government of the PRC has solemnly absolved itself of any responsibility to protect self-identified Chinese living in foreign countries or being targeted by foreign governments as ethnic Chinese. Even though the PRC authorities call on their support when it comes to investing in China, they accept their foreign citizenship. For different reasons, this chapter does not discuss the situation pertaining to the former colonies of Hong Kong and Macau. The final status of these territories was never in dispute, and their situations differ fundamentally from Taiwan in one crucial respect: the latter has not been a colony since 1945, although the more radical Taiwanese independence activists claim that until Taiwan drops the name ROC, it is still a Chinese colony.[2]

The official China that CCP leaders want to present to the world is not an ethnic nation *stricto sensu*: the constitution defines it as a multinational unitary state where national minorities enjoy large degrees of autonomy. Early on, the CCP adopted a policy against "big nationalism," or Han nationalism, to convince the national minorities to abandon their own "little" or "narrow" nationalisms (Zhao 2004, p. 108). However, the way the CCP has implemented the policies toward national minorities over five decades has shown that the PRC is not a multinational state where each nation enjoys recognition and the smaller and weaker ones receive some measure of self-government. The nationalities of the

[2] See World United Formosans for Independence (WUFI) 2007. Available at: http://www.wufi.org.tw (accessed September 11, 2007).

PRC are unequal in status. The Han nationality, as the state defines it, represents over 91.6 percent of the PRC population[3] and, as result of that demographic predominance, controls the machinery of the state. The other fifty-five minority nationalities, which are nominally recognized by the constitution, exercise very little effective autonomy. If anything, the relations between the Han and national minorities in the autonomous regions are discordant, if not hostile (Bhattacharya 2007; Bovingdon 2002; Gladney 1996 (1991); Kolas 1996; Rudelson 1997).

Parallel to the superstructure the state imposed in 1949 to assert Han dominance over other national minorities, it has systematically promoted the homogeneity of the Han nationality and tried to erase cultural differences within this group. The reification of a Han majority nationality, no less than the other nationalities, results from systematic social engineering on a massive scale. This has represented a formidable challenge in the realm of linguistic policy, for example. Most residents of southern China speak Cantonese, Fukienese, and other languages that are unintelligible to their northern compatriots. To that end, the CCP has promoted the use of Mandarin, also known as the "Common Language (*Putonghua*)," thereby improving on the limited advances made by the GMD in that direction. Decades of education in standard Mandarin ensures that all Chinese in the PRC can communicate in the same language. The state promoted the use of characters for only one language, *Putonghua*, while speakers of the other Chinese languages could only rely on oral transmission to preserve theirs. Naturally, Taiwanese should belong to that ethnic nation, since they speak a language written in Chinese characters – albeit in the traditional, more complex form.

Despite all these efforts, however, creating ethnic cohesion among China's Han population remains an unfinished task. If language is a marker of identity that can pave the way to the development of national consciousness, as in Central Europe in the nineteenth century, the unity of the Han majority may well be fragile when one considers the resilience of regional languages in the PRC. Despite progress in public education, the regional languages continue to survive, and many Chinese do not speak Mandarin properly. Taiwan's evolution demonstrates the logical consequence of this resilience. Although Mandarin with traditional characters (*guoyu*) remains the official language of the ROC, the predominance of Southern Fukienese (*Minnanhua*), already serves to reinforce the sense of distinctiveness shared

---

[3] See Chinese Government Official Website, "Fifty-six Ethnic Groups." Available at: http://www.gov.cn/english/2006–02/08/content_182626.htm (accessed April 11, 2009).

by the majority of Taiwanese. The refusal of the Chinese authorities to support the expression of regional languages reminds the Taiwanese of the efforts to erase their culture under Japanese colonial rule and under the GMD's martial law regime for four decades. Conversely, the evidence of nationalist and separatist sentiments in Taiwan reminds PRC leaders of the dangers of letting regional differences develop.

A Cultural Nation

The official Chinese nation that the CCP may prefer to present to the world – and presumably the one that the world would be happy to live with – is the cultural nation. This variant of nationalism promotes the idea of a community defined by a shared cultural heritage of coexistence and respect of differences. People who belong to this type of nation may speak different languages or believe in different religions, but they share some cultural heritage in the domains of customs, norms, and patterns of behavior. This time, the social engineering does not seek to eradicate linguistic or religious differences, but works instead in the realm of values. We have seen before that Chinese speak different languages and that some strong regional identities can emerge from these differences, especially when they relate to provincial and local cleavages. Forging a national identity based on linguistic uniformity is therefore problematic because it can trigger resistance and eventually lead to the formation of divisive regional identities. The diversity among Chinese in the realm of religion, particularly folk customs, does not present this kind of problem. The geographical expanse of Buddhist, Taoist, and folk religious practices among Han Chinese does not coincide with any provincial boundaries – in contrast with linguistic boundaries, which almost espouse provincial boundaries.[4] Basing a national identity on this aspect of Chinese culture, therefore, stands a better chance of generating support among Chinese regardless of the language they speak. Although Chinese practice different religions, most Han share the same references to the values promoted by Confucianism and all identify, despite regional differences, to the same foundational myths on the origins of China (Guo 2003, 2004).

Cultural nationalists envision the creation of a Chinese realm that would encompass three concentric circles with the PRC at its core.

---

[4] This is the case for Jiangxi, were most speakers of the *Gan* language are located; Hunan, where reside *Xiang* speakers; and Zhejiang and Shanghai, where live most speakers of the *Wu* language. Fujian is home to different *Min* languages, and most Guangdong residents are Cantonese speakers. Hakka speakers are scattered in the southern provinces.

A first tier includes Taiwan and the Hong Kong and Macau Special Administrative Regions; a second tier, the overseas Chinese, and finally, a third tier the Asian people influenced by Chinese culture, such as Japan, Korea, and Vietnam. This realm includes five elements: a unique approach to economic development, a specific ethical system based on Confucianism, the Chinese written language, a distinctive aesthetic, and a way of thinking that is specific to Chinese people (Xu 2001; Zhang, Zhang, & Wang 1994). It is not clear on which ground these cultural nationalists can attract Tibetans, Uyghurs, Mongols, and most other national minorities to partake to this Chinese realm. Conversely, it is clear that for these cultural nationalists, Taiwanese *ought* to be included. The Taiwanese have shown the way in their approach to economic development; they share with other Chinese a respect for quintessential Confucian values such as filial piety; they speak languages that are part of the Chinese language family; their aesthetics, in architecture and arts, are Chinese; and their beliefs originate from the same shared Chinese tradition. In sum, cultural nationalism may provide more solid grounds than ethnic or historical nationalism to attract Taiwanese. However, Chinese leaders may be weary of espousing this option because it has little to offer non-Han people.

A Historic Nation

One solution to the contradictions embodied in the ethnic and cultural nationalist projects is the often-repeated argument, based on international law, that the PRC is a successor state to the ROC and its predecessor, the Qing Empire. This assertion serves to support the present territorial claims of the PRC. Accordingly, the PRC represents a solution of continuity with the multiethnic, multicultural, and multinational empire that the Qing rulers built in the seventeenth century, which was a coalition of non-Chinese and Chinese ruling elites governing a vast realm resulting from the military conquests of Ming China (1636–1683); Outer Mongolia (1696); Tibet (1724), and finally Dzungaria and the Tarim (1757). However, the claim that because the Qing Empire ruled Taiwan, and so by rights, the PRC, as the successor state to the Qing via the ROC, should govern it, is problematic. Not only was the Qing Dynasty established by a foreign people – the Manchus – but the future of Taiwan after the Japanese defeat in World War II remains an object of controversy among international lawyers, casting doubts on the view that Taiwan should have been ceded back to the ROC in 1945 (Hara 2001).

To be sure, the PRC carries on the institutional legacy of the ROC in some essential aspects. This reference to the republican regime, however, is also bound to be problematic. When the PRC leaders portray themselves as the successors to the state the GMD built, they claim continuity with a regime that never managed to rule effectively because of political fragmentation or foreign encroachment. When the constitution of the PRC states that China is a multinational state it proclaims a variant of a policy already promulgated in the ROC that the GMD never implemented. The claim that the PRC should control Taiwan because it is a successor to the ROC also rests on shaky grounds for two other reasons. First, the ROC has never relinquished control over the island since 1945, although this control was marred by the massacre of February 28, 1947, in which the GMD killed many members of the local Taiwanese elite (Lai, Myers, & Wei 1991). Second, since 1992, the sovereignty of the ROC has changed in a fundamental way. It is not exercised by an authoritarian party anymore and a majority of the island's population has clearly expressed that it does not want to be governed by the CCP.[5] In sum, the use of history to define Chinese nationhood may provide an effective means to unite different ethnic groups within the Chinese population, but it excludes the possibility of the existing ROC living side-by-side with the PRC.

A Civic Nation in the PRC?

Officials in China do not believe that civic nationalism can be developed in China, and a surprising number of intellectuals agree with them, albeit for different reasons. People on the New Left like Wang Shaoguang and people at the opposite end of the political spectrum, such as the neo-conservative Xiao Gongqin, agree that civic nationalism and liberalism are not appropriate for China. They think that procedural democracy and abstract concepts such as citizenship cannot resonate with Chinese values rooted in community or family. Many of the Chinese intellectuals who share the views discussed on the ethnic, cultural, or historical bases of the Chinese nation hold this position, and many know that to advocate liberal democracy and republican citizenship may not generate lots of support since these ideas are not approved by official authorities. It is therefore difficult to say whether intellectuals genuinely embrace the ethnic, cultural, and historical nationalism or whether they are simply

[5] See Mainland Affairs Council (MAC) (2007). "What is the Government's Position on the Issue of 'One China'?" Taipei: the Executive Yuan, ROC. (Online) Available at: http://www.mac.gov.tw/english/english/qa/1-4.pdf (accessed September 7, 2007).

cautious. Two notable exceptions to this rejection of civic nationalism are Xu Ben (2001), who is weary of populist nationalism, and Zhang Xuding. Zhang believes that Chinese liberal thinkers, who benefit from globalization, are not supportive of civic nationalism because it may ultimately challenge the state on whose support they depend (Zhang 1998, p. 110; Zhao 2004, pp. 130–64).

We have seen that the historical evolution of China from a multinational empire into a modern nation-state has never been the ineluctable telos described by the CCP. The fragile construction of the modern Chinese state and the fungible nature of the nation that it claims to overlay can help us understand the CCP's concerns over national unity. The next section will underline that the existence of a sovereign Taiwan directly challenges the CCP claims that it represents the whole of China and its different nationalities and ethnic groups, that it has a historical mandate to complete the unification of the Han people, and that it therefore embodies the sovereignty of the people in China and Taiwan.

TAIWANESE VIRTUAL SOVEREIGNTY AND CHALLENGES TO THE CCP'S VIEWS OF THE NATION

Taiwan's virtual sovereignty represents a threat to the claim that the Han people represent a homogeneous group. Its existence puts into sharp contrast the relevance of regional cleavages within the Han population, which are defined by languages, customs, and in many cases, distinct local histories. In the PRC, the dogma of the Han people's cultural and ethnic unity still prevails (Wen 2004). Most people, including Chinese scholars, still hold this view despite considerable ethnographic evidence to the contrary (Chu 1998). We can attest the reality of the Han people's diversity along most of the angles used elsewhere to identify and distinguish different ethnic identities. Some of those used by the population remain well known: most Chinese are aware of broad distinctions between northerners and southerners – who, among overseas Chinese communities, refer to themselves as "people of the Tang (*tangren*)" rather than Han.[6] In south China, people are aware of important ethnic and cultural differences that go back centuries for people such as the Hakka, the Cantonese, or the Fukienese (Gladney 1994b; Windrow 2005). These distinctions are invisible in ethnographic maps produced in China, but they are experienced strongly in local politics.

[6] China incorporated the province of Fujian for the first time under the Tang dynasty (618–907).

In the PRC, recognizing ethnic identities within the Han remains dangerous because it evokes the specter of the Warlord Era (1916–1928), when Republican China was divided by competing factions and unable to present a united front against foreign colonial powers. There are fears that recognizing regional ethnic identities, which sometimes coincide with the boundaries of provinces, may encourage the growth of separatist movements. Republican China had briefly experienced that in 1920, when an ephemeral movement for the self-government of Hunan emerged – with a young Mao Zedong as one of its promoters (McDonald 1976). Any hint of an emerging regional center of power in the PRC has been suppressed to prevent a return to this situation of division. This was the case with the Gao Gang affair, for example, in the early years of the new regime (Teiwes 1990; Zhu 1998). These fears still exist today, and they have received increased salience in the reform period, especially during the government of Jiang Zemin, when conflicts emerged between provinces and the central government over taxes and policies (Chung 1994; Zhang 1999).[7] Since then, conflicts between provinces over trade, equalization, and preferential policies have multiplied (Hendrischke 1999; Kumar 1994; Zheng 1994).

These disputes are not framed by discourses of ethnic grievances or specific provinces' alienation, and even less by discourses of nations seeking recognition within the Chinese ethnic majority. Instead, the interregional, interprovincial, and center-province disputes are based on economic issues: inequalities between wealthy coastal provinces on the one hand and the poorer provinces and autonomous regions of the west on the other; disagreement over the creation of Special Economic Zones (SEZ); or fiscal arrangements with the central government (Mackerras 2004; Zheng 2004, pp. 109–19). Yet, this should provide little comfort for the CCP: the modernist approach in the literature on nationalism has long argued that the superposition of uneven development between regions within a state with cultural differences favors the emergence of separatist nationalism (Gellner 1964; Nairn 1981 (1977)). Further aggravating the issue, from the perspective of the CCP's view on the homogeneous nature of the Han people, the ROC has been officially recognizing these divisions since 2001, when it granted the Hakka people the cabinet-level Council of Hakka Affairs to look after their interests in Taiwan (Wang 2004).

Writing about China's vulnerability to separatist sentiments from national minorities, June Dreyer mentioned the breakup of the Soviet

---

[7] See also Delfs (1991) "Saying No to Peking," *Far Eastern Economic Review* 151(14): 21.

Union as a source of inspiration for separatists and the American war on terrorism after 2001 as an encouragement for the central government to clamp down on some of them (2005, p. 69). From the CCP's perspective, the virtual sovereignty of Taiwan in the ROC represents a challenge to the political unity of China as a multinational unitary state. It is thought that tolerating the sovereignty of a population believed to share the same cultural attributes as the Han people in the PRC would a fortiori make even less acceptable control over people with a distinct territory, a totally different culture, and a tradition of separate statehood, such as Tibet, and up to a certain degree, Xinjiang.[8] The CCP has made it abundantly clear that it could not countenance the independence of these autonomous regions and place the issue within a framework of non-negotiable national security (Baranovitch 2003). Furthermore, there is little doubt that the construction of otherness through the representation of national minorities in the PRC serves to reinforce the reification of a homogeneous and united Han ethnic majority (Gladney 1994a). The challenge raised by Taiwanese independence is even more pressing in this respect.

Finally, the virtual sovereignty of the ROC undermines the CCP's foundation of political legitimacy because it reminds Chinese that the party has not achieved its proclaimed goal of achieving national unification. CCP leaders base their claim of legitimacy on the doctrine of the successor state, whereby the PRC supersedes the authority of the previous regime, the ROC, ruling the same territory.[9] This principle of historical continuity, evoked to justify that Taiwan is an inalienable part of China, is openly challenged by Taiwanese authorities. The PRC is certainly the successor to the ROC in Mainland China, but it has never exercised its authority over Taiwan, where the ROC still holds sway.[10] In addition, PRC authorities' claim that Chinese on both sides of the Taiwan Strait all oppose Taiwan's independence is rhetoric on the part of the CCP instead of actual fact. Chinese are not democratically consulted on this or any other matter. Furthermore, the CCP even denies this right to Taiwanese

---

[8] Inhabitants of Xinjiang identify with different ethnic groups.

[9] The Taiwan Affairs Office mentions the PRC is a successor state to the ROC, not the Qing. See Taiwan Affairs Office (TAO) (2000) "The One-China Principle and the Taiwan Issue" In *White Papers on the Taiwan Issue*. Beijing: Information Office of the State Council. (Online). Available at: http://www.gwytb.gov.cn:8088/detail.asp?table=WhitePaper&title=White%20Papers%20On%20Taiwan%20Issue&m_id=4 (accessed September 7, 2007).

[10] See MAC (2007) "What is the Government's Position on the Issue of One China?"

when it threatens to attack Taiwan if its government attempts to organize a referendum on any change to the ROC's political status.[11]

The CCP, of course, bases its legitimacy on other issues besides national unity. Its achievements in economic development certainly rank as one of the most important sources of stability (Guo 2003; Wang & Zheng 2000; Yang 2006a). However, this last achievement is fragile: economic growth has led to rising social inequities (NHDR 2005 and UNDP 2005), environmental degradation (Economy 2004), land expropriation (Guo 2001), labor exploitation (Chan 2001; Wright 2004), and a decline in social services (Finer 2003). Growing corruption aggravates the resolution of these problems (Hsu 2001; Wedeman 2004). Finally, the numerous instances of social disturbance, unrest, and upheavals has made governing China increasingly difficult (Hurst & O'Brien 2002; Perry & Selden 2006,). In sum, an independent, prosperous, and relatively stable Taiwan would put into sharp relief the lacunae of CCP governance.

RECONCILING THE PRC WITH THE IDEA OF A
TAIWANESE NATION

The variants of ethnic, cultural, and historical nationalism promoted by the leaders of the PRC are problematic because they do not appeal to the Taiwanese. The existing definitions of the Chinese nation appeal to different justifications that are incompatible with the ways in which Taiwanese are presently constructing their own narrative of national identity and destiny. In other words, whether the CCP proclaims solemnly that Taiwanese are "the flesh and blood of the Chinese race," that they should partake to an illustrious global "Chinese civilization," or that they should "go back to the fold of the motherland after the century of humiliation," Taiwanese simply do not recognize themselves in these schemes. The discourse they are relating to in increasing proportion has to do with their democratic practice. Even if this is imperfect, they still look at it as a collective source of pride (Lin 2001; Tsai 2006; Wong 2003).

As discussed above, logical inconsistencies mar the concept of an ethnic nation for the PRC. To start with, it promotes congruence between an ethnic group and its own state, but the definition of the core ethnic

---

[11] Taiwan Affairs Office (TAO) 2005. "Anti-Secession Law Adopted by the NPC (National People's Congress)" In *One China Principle*. Beijing: Information Office of the State Council (Online). Available at: http://www.gwytb.gov.cn:8088/detail. asp?table=OneCP&title=One-China%20Principle&m_id=28 (accessed September 7, 2007).

group, the Han Chinese, has negative consequences for a population classified in the official taxonomy as Han. Cultural diversity, especially in the realm of language, is not encouraged. The PRC can claim some degree of success in implementing the unification of the language in media, education, and government, but this comes also at a price: it marginalizes the languages spoken by non-native Mandarin speakers within the Han population. This trend goes against the evolution observed in the ROC. After four decades of an authoritarian cultural assimilation policy that imposed Mandarin on a population whose overwhelming majority – over 85 percent – spoke other mother tongues,[12] Taiwanese are now free to use *Minnanhua* or *Hakka* in public spaces. Understandably, the prospect of an ethnic nationalism that erases all forms of particularity is unlikely to attract a population that only recently gained the right to express its cultural diversity.

The concept of an ethnic nation also suffers from another contradiction that the idea of a cultural nation tries to overcome. The notion of an ethnic nation cannot appeal to non-Han, for it suggests that because of their small number, national minorities are destined to obey the will of the ethnic majority and have little power of self-determination. The result is that the PRC is a state controlled by its core ethnic group, the Han, which adopts a paternalistic relation with the other ethnic groups. The idea of a coexistence between different nations within a state inspired by values transcending different cultures remains a difficult proposition. Imperial China could rely on one or many religious institutions to sanctify the authority of the emperor for its subjects, but the leaders of the CCP have failed to convince national minorities that socialism and its scientific theory of history perform a similar function. Many national minorities that remain attached to their own cultural tradition see socialism as just another expression of the Han cultural chauvinism between 1949 and 1978. The effective repudiation of socialism in the policies adopted by the CCP since the beginning of the reform policy does not change this equation. People in the national minorities, especially in areas with well-established distinct cultural traditions such as Tibet, experience the Han Chinese's embrace of market forces as another form of cultural imperialism with which they do not see much in common (Crombe 2002). Although there are no national minorities in Taiwan, aboriginal people are different from the Han, and they are moving towards some measures

---

[12] The proportion was even higher before the GMD relocated its government in Taipei, bringing with it over 1 million immigrants into a population of less than 10 million.

of self-government (Stainton 1999). For them, cultural nationalism is unlikely to have much appeal.

Other proponents of Chinese nationalism do not embarrass themselves with the above nuances and make use of history. In their concept of the nation, the CCP bases its claims of legitimate rule over Taiwan on the principle of succession. According to this principle, the CCP leaders claim that the PRC has successfully completed the task of modernization in the mainland that the ROC failed to do because it could never politically unite the ethnically diverse population of the former Qing Empire. Although nominally the PRC has for the most part recovered the territories ruled by the Qing, and that the ROC claimed in vain, the virtual sovereignty of that regime in Taiwan suggests that the unification of the Chinese nation remains incomplete. Taiwanese leaders of all political parties, however, view things differently. Whether they are satisfied with the fact that the ROC is limited to Taiwan and a few offshore islands, or whether they should call this polity the Republic of Taiwan, they all recognize that the PRC has established its sovereignty in Mainland China. However, they also agree that the PRC has never ruled the territory of the ROC administered since 1949 and therefore has no legitimate claim to it.

The concept of the Chinese civic nation makes relevant discussions that have been shelved for years (Zheng 2007). Many forms of arrangements have been proposed, from a federation uniting all provinces – with the ROC being relegated as one province among others – to the idea of a federation between the PRC and the ROC. None of these proposals, however, has been considered seriously. Federalism comes with some heavy baggage in contemporary China: many still associate it with the weaknesses of the Republican period. Many are also uncomfortable with the basic principle that the federal state results from the free association of sovereign entities. Furthermore, it is difficult to see the incentive for national minorities to stay in a federal Chinese state if they have been oppressed by its ethnic majority. If it is suspected that the central government might change policy and reassert centralized authority, they might just follow the precedent of the former Soviet or Yugoslav republics that seceded as soon as they sensed an opportunity to achieve independence at a low cost. A federal solution could appeal to most Taiwanese, but PRC leaders are unlikely to grant Taiwan the recognition of sovereignty required by the institution of a meaningful federal state.

The potential of asymmetric federalism represents an interesting variant of this position. This form of institutional arrangement exists already in virtual form, via the multiple regimes of autonomy that the PRC has put in place over the years, to solve different issues (Ghai 2000a). This constitutional arrangement has been proposed to resolve tensions between the central government and national minorities with a territorial base – namely Tibet (Sautman 2000) – or to ease the integration of former colonies that had different legal and economic systems, such as Hong Kong and Macau (Ghai 1999, 2000b). Taiwanese do not see any interest in the regime of autonomy granted to regions, prefectures, and counties populated by national minorities to nominally accommodate their cultural needs and favor their development. They see no autonomy in these different territories. Neither are they attracted to the Special Administrative Region (SAR) status granted to Hong Kong and Macau. Taiwanese have seen the central government in Beijing watching closely over the political development in the former British colony and reneging on previous promises of letting Hong Kong residents extend their electoral franchise. They do not trust that, under PRC control, they could preserve their recently gained democratic rights.

Taiwanese are also skeptical that the "one country two systems" policy will preserve their freedoms when they look at the fate of mild measures of governance reform. One of these reforms, decentralization, has been questioned since its start, and still remains debated (Raman 2006; Yang 2006b). The PRC achieved some measure of decentralization during the 1990s to encourage economic development, but after realizing that it raises enormous difficulties in fiscal matters, the central government changed course and reasserted its prerogatives, albeit with great difficulty. The potential for devolution in attracting Taiwanese into a potential union with the PRC is a hypothesis that remains to be tested. However, as long as China exists in its present form as a unitary state, any form of decentralization will remain hostage to changes of central government policies and fail to attract the majority of Taiwanese. Another measure of governance reform that could have encouraged Taiwanese to believe that the specific character of their society would be preserved in the PRC is the mechanism of village elections. These would serve as a first step towards elections at higher levels, the way the Taiwanese democratic transition evolved. But, like decentralization, village elections have stalled and the central government even questions their usefulness (Liu 2000). In light of this limited possibility to accept people's sovereignty, it is no wonder that the Taiwanese remain uninterested by the CCP's proposals to join the PRC.

There are other options that could be explored, although there is no evidence that Chinese decision makers have done so. For example, the formula of "sovereignty-association," explored for Quebec and Canada, and even discussed for Jammu and Kashmir's relations with India, represent an extreme form of asymmetrical federalism between two entities of unequal size. However, because it is predicated on the idea of inalienable sovereignty, it could not work as long as China held onto the "One China Principle," while sovereignty-association is premised on the idea of two sovereign entities. The concept of coalescent nationalism, discussed by Bhargava elsewhere in this volume, could perhaps attract Taiwanese because it is based on the recognition that people within a given polity have an inalienable right to choose their own institutions. The regime of autonomy discussed before could make possible this form of nationalism, if only it has substantial content. So far, the behavior of the PRC government in Tibet and Xinjang does not suggest it wants to move in that direction.

CONCLUSION

The specific nature of the PRC as an authoritarian state, its revolutionary path, and its strategies for nation building go a long way in explaining its inability to accommodate, even theoretically, a nation such as Taiwan within, let alone without, China. The PRC is an authoritarian regime whose leaders fear they would not survive the test of democratic elections, and therefore they can hardly countenance the idea of a nation within that could rest on that mode of selection for its leadership. But this explanation is insufficient because the PRC leaders accept – albeit reluctantly and with reservation – democracy in Hong Kong. After the failure of their revolutionary path to achieve socialism, CCP leaders have determined that economic growth would represent their best source of legitimacy. But in a context of growing social inequities, this is not sufficient, and they have increasingly resorted to nationalism and their success in achieving national unity to assert this claim. In adopting this approach, Chinese leaders must prove their willingness to achieve their self-proclaimed goal of "reunification," which means denying the existence of a sovereign Taiwan. Yet, this explanation does not suffice either. It does not explain why the CCP refuses to recognize the idea of a Taiwan nation within the PRC, an idea that could presumably encourage a majority of Taiwanese to consider becoming citizens of the PRC. This can be explained by the nature of Han identity itself. If the cultural characteristics of the Tibetans, the Mongols, and most of the other fifty-four national minorities in the PRC clearly set them apart from the Han, reinforcing the latter's own sense of identity, the concept of a Taiwanese nation seriously changes that sense of self. If Taiwanese constitute a distinct nation, what would prevent Fukienese, Cantonese, or Hunanese from eventually thinking the same thing?

This chapter has shown that PRC elites have moved away from a negation of any nationalist ideology – a defining characteristic of socialist internationalism – to the promotion of different variants of ethnic, cultural, and historical nationalism. In sum, definitions of the Chinese nation are changing, and so presumably is the demarcation of its boundaries. As long as rigid definitions of ethnicity, cultural heritage, or historical legacy determine the nature of Chinese nationalism, it will be arduous for the CCP to countenance the possibility of a sovereign Taiwan existing along the PRC because this would challenge all the claims that form the basis of these different definitions of the Chinese nation. A concept of the nation based on a more abstract concept of procedural democracy would be acceptable for Taiwanese, but most Chinese intellectuals who interact with the PRC government do not show support for this concept, or if they do, the CCP has not shown any inclination to agree with this view.

This comment, however, calls for an important caveat. There is no guarantee either that a democratic China would be more accepting of a sovereign Taiwan. Overseas Chinese asked about this possibility usually reject it, even if they live in countries where they are free to speak out their mind. The emotional identification with China still matters to them. In a hypothetical democratic China with multiparty elections, we should not exclude the possibility that a political party standing for the inclusion of Taiwan in China at any cost may get more support than political parties that would tolerate Taiwanese independence. Mansfield and Snyder's research on the consequences of rapid democratization in ethnically divided societies gives us food for thought on that matter. They have argued that rapidly democratizing or newly democratizing states are more likely, not less, to engage into more extremist nationalist politics (2005). Eventually, a democratic China that faces difficulties with economic management and ethnic unrests in its boundaries may provide opportunities for politicians who look after quick fixes and propose populist resolutions of ethnic disputes that could escalate into violent conflict.

On the other hand, we should not discard another possibility: a democratic and prosperous China may very well represent a most interesting proposition for Taiwanese residents (Friedman 2000). That is, Taiwanese residents may be proud to become citizens of the second, or even the most, important economic powerhouse in the world if they believe they can benefit personally from it. If such circumstances were to prevail, the issue of a Taiwanese nation may become irrelevant or decline in importance if residents of Taiwan do not feel threatened in their identity or security. Recognizing the legitimacy of a Taiwan nation in this perspective would deserve the support of Chinese who advocate democracy because it serves as a constant reminder that democracy is compatible with societies with a Chinese cultural heritage. Conversely, Chinese who favor the prospect of a China that includes Taiwan may want to ponder how much the democratization of China would make their goal more attainable, and at a much lower cost.

9

The Failure of Ideologies in China's Relations with Tibetans

Gray Tuttle

This chapter considers China's relations with Tibet, one of the most intractable problems faced by the Chinese Communist Party (CCP) in its minority nationalities policy. Among the fifty-five minority nationalities that are recognized by Chinese officials, Tibetans come the closest to constituting a sub-state nation seeking self-determination. Like all the other groups discussed in this book, Tibetans have made demands for the protection of their language, way of life, and culture. But in this case, religion has played a major role in Tibetan national identity, and, as this chapter argues, has represented a central element of Tibetan–Chinese relations for decades, even before the CCP took power. In addition, the Chinese state, under both the Republican regime and under the CCP since 1949, has made many promises to the Tibetans that, for the most part, have not been kept.

THE CREATION OF TIBETAN NATIONALISM

Since this volume focuses on the instability of multination states, it is especially appropriate to consider the issue of Tibet as a part of China. Like the long struggles of Palestinians and Kurds, the Tibetan sub-state nationalist movement has proven to be an enduring international issue in the contemporary era. While the Chinese state has asserted the primacy

My thanks to André Laliberté, Robbie Barnett, Sarah Jacoby, Katherine Kerr, and anonymous reviewers for helpful suggestions they provided to improve this chapter. The conclusions and any errors are, of course, my own. Thanks to Thierry Dodin for permission to reprint the map from www.TibetInfoNet.com.

FIGURE 9.1. Tibetan autonomous units of government in the People's Republic of China. Base map from TibetInfoNet: http://www.tibetinfonet.net/static/map_of_tibet

of a unitary nation-state, the strong tradition of an independent narrative history of Tibet largely revolving around its distinct religio-political system (as well as the de facto Tibetan independence from 1912 to 1951) has provided a powerful intellectual resource for the current Tibetan nationalist movement. The fact that some 50 percent of Chinese territory has traditionally been dominated by non-Han Chinese people has also lent some strength to this sub-state nationalism. One quarter of the People's Republic of China (PRC) is formally recognized as being under Tibetan autonomous control (see map, Figure 9.1).[1] Tibetans are recognized by the Chinese state as a nationality with legal rights within and beyond these autonomous divisions, although their ability to enforce these rights is very limited (Fiskesjö 2006, pp. 33–4 on the 1984 Law of Regional Nationality [=Minority] Autonomy). For this reason, it would be too strong a claim to say that Tibetans have been totally denied any ethnic accommodation, at least compared to groups like the Kurds in Turkey.

---

[1] Aside from the Tibetan Autonomous Region, large portions of Qinghai and Sichuan provinces, as well as smaller portions of Gansu and Yunnan Province, are designated as autonomous Tibetan divisions, and together these autonomous areas make up around 25 percent of the People's Republic of China (PRC), an area roughly the size of western Europe or the American southwest.

Although it is seldom acknowledged in the West, the Chinese party-state arguably has done more to create a unified sub-state Tibetan national movement than any amount of exile activity could ever have accomplished. First, the introduction of Chinese armed forces and Communist reforms, as well as the influx of Chinese into Tibet since 1951, have given the diverse and historically divided peoples now called Tibetans an "other" against whom to define themselves. Second, the Chinese state classification of Tibetans (*Zangzu*) as a single ethnic group (*minzu*) has given this formerly fragmented group a more cohesive sense of identity. The Communist Chinese created this identity and enforced it through various state mechanisms (governance, education, etc.), but then tried to limit regional autonomy (*zizhi qu*) to the Tibetan Autonomous Region (TAR) (*Xizang zizhi qu*), while asking the majority of Tibetans to submit to other provincial authorities in areas dominated by Han Chinese (Qinghai, Gansu, Sichuan, and Yunnan). Given the history of nationalism (*minzu zhuyi*) in China, it is hardly surprising that Chinese-educated Tibetans aspire to have an ethnic regional autonomy that embraces all the areas inhabited by ethnic Tibetans.

Remarkably, Tibetans were so divided prior to 1950 that they did not have a single term that referred to all Tibetan people, especially not one that was acceptable to eastern Tibetans. While today some Tibetans in eastern Tibet might willingly call themselves "Bömi" (*bod mi*) or, less likely, "Böpa" (*bod pa*), such terms historically meant people from central Tibet, a region at the center of the current TAR, including Lhasa, Shigatsé, and parts of Lhoka and Kongpo (see Figure 9.1; Tsering Shakya 1993, p. 9). In fact, at the beginning of the Tibetan popular nationalist movement in 1957, no term could be agreed upon by all of those whom we today call "Tibetans," so they called themselves simply "tsampa eaters" as this conveyed a distinct sense of their shared identity (as opposed to the Chinese "rice eaters"), without privileging any one regional designation (Knaus 1999, 145). However, this food-based designation did not endure, and the armed Tibetan resistance movement that lasted from 1957 to the early 1970s was soon known by a regionally specific name: "Four Rivers, Six Ranges (*chu bzhi sgang drug*)," which describes only the region of Kham, and definitely not all of ethnic or even all of eastern Tibet, and reflects the dominance of Khampa Tibetans in the resistance (Tsering Shakya 1999, pp. 66–7). Despite these internal differences, the Chinese chose not to make separate nationalities for Khampas and Amdowas because they saw Tibetans as one nationality.

Although paying attention to the details of the generation of a Tibetan ethnonym may seem tedious to those who don't know Tibetan or Chinese, the creation of a single term for all Tibetans has been crucial in shaping Tibetan resistance to the Chinese state. The spread of modern education, with its key role of creating citizens for the state, has had a significant impact on Tibetan youth since the late 1970s, when modern secular education became available for many Tibetans for the first time in history.[2] Tibetans were instructed that an ethnicity is defined by having a shared territory; language (at least in written form, as with Chinese and Tibetan), economy; and "psychological nature" (i.e., culture, including religion).[3] Given this ideological formulation, it seems likely that the situation might have been the same in Tibetan areas as Michael Coleman found for the schooling that the British imposed on the Irish from the 1820s to the 1920s: that it "may actually have stimulated Irish nationalism" (Coleman 2007, p. 241). The shift toward a single term for Tibetan was one essential element of pan-Tibetan nationalism that could be best inculcated through state education; it was part of learning to be a citizen. To illustrate this point, Tibetans in exile (only some 2 percent of the Tibetan population in any case) have generally already embraced this term as an ethnonym applicable to all Tibetans regardless of regional origin. However, even aside from those in exile, it is exceptional that some young PRC Tibetans today are probably the first in history to have embraced the previously regional-specific terms Böpa or Bömi (*bod mi*) as self-descriptive for Tibetans from all over the Tibetan plateau, including those from the eastern Tibetan regions (Amdo and Kham).[4] Previously, terms such as Böpa or Bömi (*bod mi*) would only have been used to describe people from central Tibet (near Lhasa and Shigatsé for instance).

Thus Tibetans' status as ethnic Tibetans, *Zangzu* in Chinese, is equated with being Tibetan, literally Börik (*bod rigs,* also *bod mi rigs*). For some Tibetans, these terms seem to have become synonymous, even in eastern Tibet, with terms that used to be reserved for central Tibetans

---

[2] On the role of mass campaigns in spreading such ideas from the 1950s, see Makley (2007, pp. 79–81).

[3] For more on CCP policy on nationalities, and its Leninist-Stalinist origins, see Dreyer (1976) and Harrell (1995).

[4] Zhang (1998 [1993]: 1852) gives just such a typical Chinese state definition of *Bod rigs*. This dictionary, a more or less "official" project of the state, also does not define *bod pa* or *bod mi*, almost as if these were unacceptable terms, at least in the 1980s, when the dictionary was last revised. This date of the 1980s is based on the fact that the entry on *bod rigs* gives the Tibetan population as 3.9 million, which accords with the 1982 census.

(*bod pa*).[5] This would be equivalent to Southerners in the United States being comfortable being called "Yankees." Even as late as 1994, I heard older Tibetans from the Gansu part of eastern Tibet (Amdo), who were most likely not raised in modern secular schools, refuse to allow themselves to be designated as "Böpa." On the other hand, the broadening adoption of such previously regionally specific terms may simply be the result of the need for unity in the face of the Chinese majority finally overriding a sense of loyalty to regional designations (Sperling 1994, p. 277).[6]

In addition to adopting the Chinese state's conception of Tibetans as a unified group to challenge the state, Tibetan sub-state nationalists in the PRC "often use rhetoric that is part of a vocabulary common to both Chinese Marxism and anti-colonial movements in general," such as calling Communist China "Imperialist" (Sperling 1994, p. 278). This follows a long trend of Chinese-educated Tibetans using the nationalist forms to which they were introduced by modern Chinese education to argue against the Chinese state's failure to deliver on promises made to Tibetans.[7]

CHINESE PROMISES AND TIBETAN HOPES

The role of the Chinese state in actually generating a pan-Tibetan identity and thus the basis for Tibetan sub-state nationalism creates a challenging trajectory for China's efforts at dislodging such nationalism. It is obvious that if China fails to better accommodate the Tibetans, there seems no way short of the imposition of martial law to suppress this movement. It is hardly surprising that such efforts to suppress dissent, like U.S. efforts to quell the insurgencies in Afghanistan and Iraq, seem to generate even more resistance. Of course, there is one significant difference: there is no armed Tibetan resistance, but instead mainly civic protest.

While martial law was imposed for a time after the demonstrations of the late 1980s, the Chinese state dismantled this regime fairly quickly (by

---

[5] For instance, see the young Tibetan students who use the term when talking to a Tibetan from the exiled community, Kalsang Dolma, in the 2004 film, *Ce qu'il reste de nous* (*What Remains of Us*), produced by François Prévost, written and directed by François Prévost and Hugo Latulippe. Others, especially people who spend time in Kham, say that Khampa people still refuse to use these overarching terms for Tibetans.

[6] For some of the specific terms in actual use, see Sperling (1994) and Gayley (forthcoming).

[7] See Tuttle (2005, pp. 147–55) for earlier instances of Tibetan efforts to push the Chinese state to live up to its own rhetoric on Tibetan affairs.

1990) and shifted strategies: first, China incorporated as many Tibetan elite as possible in the state's labor pool, and second the government made a new promise to broaden the benefits of inclusion in the Chinese state to all Tibetans (in principle) through the plan to "Develop the West" (*xi bu da kai fa*).[8] In short, this campaign poured money into Tibet, mostly for infrastructure projects, and the effects were felt throughout the Tibetan economy. By 2001, over 100,000 Tibetans in the TAR alone worked in state-owned units and were paid salaries higher than those of state workers at equivalent levels in Beijing and only surpassed by those in Shanghai (Fischer 2005, pp. 113–115). This number would be much higher if one included all of the various Tibetan autonomous areas, since the TAR is home to less than half of the Tibetan population.[9] Likewise in the TAR, over 600 representatives of religious groups (abbots, incarnate lamas, and so forth) occupied government positions at the provincial level and below, often with a salary but not much responsibility (Hillman 2005, p. 36), and this number too would be much higher if it included all Tibetans in the PRC. These elite Tibetans clearly benefited from the state support granted to them. However, for the majority of Tibetans the promise of a better future as part of the PRC is centered on the ongoing Develop the West plan, which is supposed to improve Tibet's overall economic prospects.

Today the Tibetan areas within the PRC are among the very poorest in China by any measure and are on a par with the poorest areas in the world (Fischer 2005, p. 119). Yet the Chinese state and average Chinese citizens who know anything about Tibet seem very frustrated that Tibetans do not recognize "everything that the state has done" to develop Tibet. It is certainly true that modern infrastructural developments (roads, electricity, modern schools, and hospitals) were almost entirely introduced to Tibet after the Chinese takeover. And in recent decades, there have been dramatic improvements on all these fronts (Fischer 2005). However, the poverty is extreme, and between 1999 and 2001 "over a third of rural households [over three-quarters of all Tibetans live in rural areas] in both

[8] For more on this campaign, see Tibet Information Network (2000); Lai (2002); Goodman (2004); Holbig (2004); Tian (2004).

[9] In 1965 there were only 7,508 Tibetan cadres, and this number had grown to at least 29,406 in 1986; see Tsering Shakya (1999, p. 390). For fuller details, including a much larger number of cadre in Tibet, see Conner and Barnett (1997). My thanks to Robbie Barnett for sharing an electronic copy of this out-of-print book with me. Unlike this latter work, I treat any institution that is sponsored by the PRC government as part of the government, and do not limit the use of this term to the executive bodies that directly exercise power in the PRC.

the TAR and Qinghai were either in poverty, or else just marginally above it" (Fischer 2005, p. 108).[10]

It is clear that development has been driven by the priorities of the Chinese state and not by local interests. In fact, "most outside government funding is being spent on the state itself, either directly through government administration, or indirectly on state-owned units" (Fischer 2005, p. 77).[11] For instance, the costs of the high-tech train to Tibet that started to operate in July of 2006 were more than three and half times what the Chinese state spent on all health and education measures in the TAR from 1952 to 2002 (US $4.1 vs. $1.16 billion).[12] To put this into perspective, China spent US $3.8 billion just to build a new terminal at the Beijing international airport to impress visitors coming for the Olympic games; it is the largest building in the world.[13] When the Chinese state is willing to spend three times more funds to erect a single building in Beijing than it is to improve the health care and education of Tibetans in the TAR over a half century, Chinese at home and abroad should not be surprised that Tibetans and their supporters are critical of state claims of substantial financial support for Tibet. Tibetan health care costs have skyrocketed (up 75 percent in Qinghai from 1997 to 2001) and the growth of education spending has slowed since 2001 (Fischer 2005, pp. 48–9). Even Chinese state-supported scholarship on Tibet recognizes that according to the internationally accepted Physical Quality of Life Index (PQLI), which measures infant mortality, life expectancy, and adult literacy rate: "(the PLQI for) Tibet's population and the Tibetan population in the country[side]…are not only lower than the world average, but also lower than the average for Asian countries. They are 29 percentage points lower than the national average of China."[14] If Tibetans had truly been consulted about how funds should be spent in Tibet, it is

[10] This percentage is also accepted by the Chinese authorities, see Zheng (2001, p. 501).
[11] While the Tibetan elite who work for the government benefit from these state funds, this represents less than 5 percent of all Tibetans, even assuming some 200,000 Tibetans work for the state.
[12] International Campaign for Tibet (2003, p. 44), citing the Chinese state's *Tibetan Statistical Yearbook 2001*; International Campaign for Tibet (2007, p. 30), citing the Chinese state's *China Daily, Oct. 15, 2005*. Zheng (2001, pp. 492–3) noted that from 1950 to 1990, the Chinese government had transferred over 25 billion *yuan* in grants, construction investments and industrial goods to Tibet, but he did not specify how much of this was spent on education and health, as opposed to roads, airports, barracks, and other infrastructure essential to the military occupation of Tibet.
[13] See Barboza, D. (2008). Going All Out for the Games. *The New York Times*. May 2.
[14] Zhang (1997, p. 120). This work also discussed education and health care in Tibet without listing expenditures in these fields.

almost certain that they would have requested further development of education and health services, which are totally inadequate at present, as opposed to this train-line, which reduces the time (compared to road travel) or cost (compared to flights) of travel by a modest amount simply for the relatively few Tibetans who use it.

All of these issues point to the fact that the Chinese state continues to make promises to minority nationalities in general, and Tibetans in particular, but fails to fully deliver on these promises. In a social contract, if the more powerful party constantly changes the terms of the agreement, it is hardly surprising that the other party dissents. Over the course of decades of failed promises, the Tibetan people, who probably have more of a voice now (even with all the current restrictions in the PRC) than they had prior to Communist rule, are exercising the very rights that China's constitution and education system has taught them they should have. In the context of a failing social contract that the Chinese and Tibetans have negotiated, such dissent should be taken as an opportunity to correct course and restore the terms.[15]

STEPPING BACK TO THINK AHEAD: PAST SUCCESSES AND FAILURES

It is useful to look to the past to learn from prior failures when trying to gain some perspective on more recent events, the effects of which are still unfolding.[16] This is especially true when considering the events of March and April 2008 when Tibetan demonstrations, and at least one event that can be characterized as a riot, made world headlines as China prepared to host the summer Olympics.

In the first two decades of the modern Chinese nation-state from 1912 to 1933, the failure of secularization policies led the Chinese state to reconsider its relations with Tibet. Thus, by the 1930s and 1940s, relations between Chinese and Tibetans had been reconfigured more along religious lines that were acceptable to Tibetans. Similarly, the demonstrations in the spring of 2008 were the culmination of two decades of

[15] This idea of a contractual relationship between the Chinese state and the Tibetan people comes from a presentation given by Robert Barnett at an event entitled "Will the Tibetans Follow the Kosovars: Special Roundtable on the Events in Tibet," Association for the Study of Nationalities, Harriman Institute, Columbia University, April 11, 2008 and chaired by André Laliberté.

[16] See Tuttle (2005) for additional background on some of the figures and events described below. Excerpts here are printed with permission of Columbia University Press.

misguided policy that followed the last wave of Tibetan demonstrations in 1987 and 1988. The policy outcomes of the 2008 demonstrations have yet to be determined, but a look back to the past may be helpful in imagining possibilities for the future.

The secularization of government in early-twentieth-century China at first blush appeared to have been an unmitigated success. In China, the main role of religion in the middle and late Qing period is most commonly understood as providing a messianic outlet for the frustrations of rural society, from the White Lotus rebellions at the turn of the late 1700s to the Taiping Rebellion (1850–1864). Communism would later channel much of these energies with its own promises of salvation. Work by Qing scholars (Crossley 1999; Naquin 2000; Rawski 1998) has demonstrated what a vital role religion played in the life of the empire and the imperial family. But Republican leaders of China lost this vital mediator between state and society when they adopted the modernist secular policies of the Western nation-state as their model. From 1912 to 1933, China very nearly ruptured the historic basis for relations with Inner Asia, especially Tibet. While military might had been critical to Qing rule of Inner Asia, the religiously inflected ideological underpinnings of Qing emperorship, as outlined by the recent works mentioned above, were crucial factors in allowing the threat of military force to rest lightly on the subject territories as well as on the imperial finances. Likewise, while a military occupation of Tibet was critical to the Chinese Communist incorporation of what had been a de facto independent state for decades, real rule of Tibet has more often depended on the cooperation of the Tibetan elite with the CCP (see Fisher 2005; Goldstein et al. 2008; Hillman 2005; Tsering Shakya 1999).

In the past, one of the most critical religious roles the Qing emperors played (some better than others) was as patrons of Tibetan Buddhism. This patronage was essential state policy as Tibetan Buddhists (both ethnic Tibetans and Mongols) inhabited roughly one-half of the Qing dynasty's domains. Yet with the secularization of the government after the 1911 Revolution, for the first two decades of the Chinese Republic the role of patron of Tibetan Buddhism was basically relinquished by the leaders of China. It is no coincidence that Tibetans' current claims for an independent state focus their attention on this period. With no patrons among the rulers of China – as there had been consistently in the Yuan and Qing, and intermittently in the Ming – the Tibetan elite had no incentive to become a part of the newly conceived secular Chinese nation-state.

In Nationalist China (1927–1949), the National Government (*Minguo zhengfu*) initially pursued only political, and not religious, ways of relating to the Tibetans. The ideologies of nationalism and racial unity were central to the government's efforts to work with exiled Tibetans to resolve what the government saw as the problem of Tibet's independence. Some Tibetans, like the 9th Panchen Lama and Norlha Qutughtu, who had both been driven out of Tibet by the centralization efforts of the 13th Dalai Lama, chose to embrace these modern ideas and tried to implement them in Tibetan regions. However, in the late 1930s the Chinese government failed to live up to the dual promise of such rhetoric: national autonomy and racial equality. This failure destroyed Chinese hopes of employing secular ideologies of nationalism and race to incorporate Tibet. Instead, when these secular ideologies failed to engender Tibetan cooperation, Chinese officials were eventually forced to embrace religion in an effort to include Tibet within the modern Chinese nation-state. While contemporary China has to some degree incorporated Tibetan Buddhist religion in its efforts to maintain a stable government in Tibet, the repeated Chinese Communist promises of autonomy (enshrined in various constitutions and statutes and the subject of a great deal of rhetoric) and the more recent promise of economic development (equality in a manner that really counts) have not been fulfilled.

Under the leadership of the Nationalist Party (*Guomindang*), the Northern Expedition seized power in central and northern China in 1927–1928, replacing the Beijing government with the National Government in Nanjing. After the death of Yuan Shikai, the old Beijing government focused its concerns mainly on retaining power in North China. In contrast, the new administration envisioned centralized rule of all China, including the former frontier territories of the Qing Empire. Through the party-state system and a rational reorganization of the government structure, the Nationalist Party led a government more unified than China had seen for decades. Sun Yat-sen's work, especially the Three Principles of the People, was elevated to the guiding ideology of the new state. In the process, the early Republican idea of the unity of the five races (*wuzu gonghe*) was replaced by a Sino-centric (Han chauvinist) nationalism. This shift was marked by such signs as the replacement of the five-barred flag of the Beijing government (with each color representing one of the central "races" of China) with the National Government's flag featuring a white sun on a blue and red background. Nevertheless, the Nanjing administration continued to find multiracial rhetoric useful when dealing with the borderland peoples outside of its control.

Inclusion of Tibetans in the Chinese administration, though part of the multiracial rhetoric of the Chinese Republic from its early years, only started to become a reality in the late 1920s. Initially, the context of these early-twentieth-century Tibetan exiles' understanding of nationalism predisposed them to oppose such modern ideologies. For the Tibetan Buddhist leaders of small polities on the borders of central Tibet, the arrival of nationalism in their homeland constituted a particular challenge. From 1913, the Lhasa government embarked on a program of state building characterized by a strong centralized administration. Backed by a British-armed military, the thirteenth Dalai Lama Tupten Gyatso (Thub bstan rgya mtsho, 1876–1933) refused to accommodate the interests of lamas accustomed to local autonomy and ousted those who resisted the imposition of the nascent Tibetan nation-state's power.[17] Thus, when Tibetans went into exile in China, they were wary of the ideologies that would subordinate their interests as the centralizing Tibetan administration had done.

Partially to circumvent this resistance from Tibet's traditional elite, the Chinese government developed educational institutions to train Tibetan youth in the prevailing secular ideologies, a practice that would be greatly developed under Communist rule. The record shows an acceptance of parts of Sun Yat-sen's principles by some Tibetans. However, the Chinese government's refusal to give real political positions to these Chinese-educated Tibetans or to grant even regional autonomy to Tibetans in the Kham (*Xikang*) region demonstrated to the Tibetans that promises of real autonomy (implied in the ideology of Sun Yat-sen) were only rhetoric (Goldstein 2004, pp. 7–21; Stoddard 1985; pp. 69–94; Tuttle 2005, pp. 147–55). Of course, even if the Chinese government had supported these Chinese-educated Tibetans from the borderlands, they would have had little influence on the religious center of Tibetan culture in Lhasa.[18]

In the early 1930s, the Republican Chinese government only gained effective and influential support from prominent Tibetans when the National Government recognized the religious, as well as the political, roles of Tibetan lamas exiled in China. Despite their eventual cooperation with Chinese politicians, these exiled Tibetans were also pursuing their own goals. In order to return to their previous positions of power

[17] For details on this, see Tuttle (2005, pp. 51–6).
[18] By contrast, the Chinese Communists were later to pursue a different approach, at least in dealing with Central Tibetans, by reaching an accommodation with the Tibetan government in Lhasa in 1951, as the Seventeen Point Agreement effectively granted very real autonomy to Central Tibet. See Goldstein (1989, pp.763–72).

in Tibet, they sought the financial and military backing that only the Chinese government could provide (Tuttle 2005, pp. 132–5, 183–92). In fact, as religious figures cooperating with the Chinese government, they established an important pattern for the future of Sino-Tibetan relations. As is still the case today, Chinese politicians were drawn to work with the religious leaders of Tibet to try to maintain control over the populace in the region (Hillman 2005). At the same time, these Tibetans invented and adapted strategies for dealing with the new challenges of a globalized world. For instance, they dealt with Chinese government ideology by judiciously employing the government's multiracial or nationalist rhetoric when addressing the Chinese. However, there is little indication that this rhetoric made much of an impact on the lives or thoughts of the leading Tibetan lamas exiled in China.[19] Successful dialogue with the Chinese government only came after 1931 when the National Government embraced the dual religious and political system that these lamas represented. Until that time, the effort to engage prominent Tibetans solely as political figures who could be included in a secular Chinese nation-state set the stage for the substantive Sino-Tibetan dialogue that followed in the 1930s.

The Communist People's Republic of China (PRC) went through a similar cycle as the Nationalist Republic of China. Initially, with the advice of Chinese who had lived in Tibet in the 1920s and 1930s, the government, recognizing the very different state and social structure in Tibet, granted central Tibet real autonomy, as outlined in the Seventeen Point Agreement of 1951 (the only such agreement made with any nationality that became part of the PRC).[20] But from the late 1950s to the late 1970s, the PRC (like the Guomindang before them) tried to follow secular policies in Tibet. As with the Guomindang, after two decades they recognized that this policy had failed. The Communist government has also realized, as the popular saying goes, "a month of talking by a government cadre is not worth one word uttered by a lama" (Hillman 2005, p. 40). Therefore, some elements within the Chinese state returned to a model of patronage, at least for some prominent monasteries and lamas. There is strong evidence that since the reforms of the late 1970s, Chinese government leaders, especially on the local level, have again cultivated connections

---

[19] For further elaborations on this impact, see Tuttle (2005, pp. 139–47; 2008). For a different interpretation of the impact of these ideas on the Panchen Lama, see Jagou (2004, pp. 139–66).

[20] See Goldstein (1989, pp. 763–72) for details. As the Chinese dissident Song Liming (1998: 59) said: "If China had sovereignty over Tibet before 1951, why did China need to conclude the Seventeen Point Agreement?"

with local monastery leaders similar to past patronage relations (Hillman 2005, pp. 44–9). The state has also tried to train patriotic lamas with varying degrees of success. Most recently, the PRC has enshrined the institution of incarnate lamas in new legal framework.

Tibetans in exile and their supporters decry such policies, but the real surprise is that a Communist state would ever allow, much less embrace, such traditions. This illustrates very well the success the Tibetans have had in asserting the relevance of their cultural standards into the Chinese vision of how Tibet should be governed, especially the joining of religion and politics (*chos srid zung 'brel*), the bedrock of Tibetan social ideology.[21] Of course, Tibetans have cause for concern, since non-believers who get involved in this Tibetan Buddhist tradition obviously do not have the same stake in the legitimacy of the selection of incarnations. But inasmuch as the state still allows Tibetan Buddhist religious leaders to direct this process, it is a remarkable testament to the endurance of a tradition that flies in the face of the declared ideology of a strictly secular state. A genuine respect for Tibetan culture, which necessarily includes religion, has been and remains critical to China's most successful policies toward Tibet. Accepting Tibetan Buddhist religion means accepting its role in politics, which is very different than the secular model that was adopted in China through Marxist-Leninist ideology. This approach also harkens back to policies that worked for the dynasties that ruled China from the thirteenth century and proves as true today as it did in the early twentieth century.

HISTORICAL TRAJECTORY OF CHINA'S CONTRACT
WITH THE TIBETANS

For eighty years the regime type has not changed in China, which has been ruled by an authoritarian party-state since the Nationalists took Beijing in 1928 (Kirby 2000, 2004). There has been remarkable continuity between the Nationalist and Communist party-states in terms of the approach to borderland peoples. The most important aspect of this continuity is that the Han Chinese majority has consistently made unilateral

---

[21] See McCartney (2007). "China tells living Buddhas to obtain permission before they reincarnate." *The Times* [Online] (Updated August 4, 2007). Available at: http://www. timesonline.co.uk/tol/news/world/article2194682.ece [accessed June 17, 2008]; and International Campaign for Tibet (2007, pp. 10–13, 89–98). On the joining of religion and politics, see Ruegg (1995); Dung dkar Blo bzang phrin las (1991). For specific information on the Chinese state embracing this notion in the Republican period, see Tuttle (2005, pp. 160–92).

decisions about policies that affect other nationalities that they have defined as being included within the Chinese state.

The earliest promise of real autonomy made to the Inner Asian peoples was the 1922 manifesto of the (then powerless) CCP, which "proclaimed Mongolia, Tibet, and Turkistan [Xinjiang] to be autonomous states (*pang*) and envisioned their voluntary unification with China proper in a Chinese Federated Republic" (Dreyer 1976, p. 63). Sun Yat-sen's declaration of the Guomindang platform in 1924 echoed this sentiment: "We hereby repeat solemnly that we recognize the right of self-determination for all peoples in China, and that a free united Republic of China based upon the principles of free alliance of the different peoples will be established after the fall of imperialism and militarism" (Smith 1996, p. 326). This platform was clearly incorporated, at least for the Tibetans and the Mongolians, in "the 1925 draft constitution [which] gave a right of Mongolia and Tibet to have separate governance, and separate constitutions, as long as these did not conflict with that of the Republic" (Fiskesjö 2006, p. 21).

Shortly thereafter, in 1931 the Communists in Jiangxi drew up a constitution that offered ethnic groups even more latitude in relation to the Han Chinese. The constitution stated:

The Soviet Government of China recognizes the right of self-determination of the national minorities of China, their right to complete self-determination from China and to the formation of an independent state for each national minority. All Mongols, Muslims [Hui], Tibetans, Miao, Yao, Koreans, and others living in the territory of China shall enjoy the full right of self-determination, i.e., they may either join the Union of Chinese Soviets or secede from it and form their own state as they prefer. (Fiskesjö 2006, p. 26)

This was again reinforced in May 1935, when the CCP leader at that time issued the declaration: "the basic policy of the CCP and the Chinese Soviet government toward national minorities is to recognize unconditionally their right of national self-determination, namely the political right to be independent and free, should they wish, from the oppressor nationality, i.e. the Han nationality" (Fiskesjö 2006, p. 26). Then in 1938, Mao himself spoke of "equal rights ... given to the various nationalities in the country, under the principle of their own volition to unite and establish a united government" (Fiskesjö 2006, p. 27). In Mao's statement we see the presumption that the decision will favor joining with the Chinese state. In all these statements we can detect traces of Sun Yat-sen's "kingly way" (*wang dao*). Sun had asserted that the Chinese race/nation (*minzu*) had been created naturally through the kingly way, while the state had been created through military force. Following the logic that a race/nation must coalesce naturally without the introduction of force, Tibetans would be expected to *agree* to join the Chinese Republic.[22]

Ultimately, Asian studies have neglected the fact that both the Nationalist and Communist parties insisted that Tibet become a part of China by choice, and not through force. But ignoring almost three decades of persuasive rhetoric on the part of the Chinese limits our ability to understand why the Tibetans made some of the choices they did. Sun's follower and the leader of the Guomindang, Chiang Kai-shek, embraced the same idea in the 1940s publication of *China's Destiny* (*Zhongguo zhi ming yun*), where he stated, with regard to "the Chinese nation ... at no time has it used military force to expand" (Chiang 1947, p. 29). We also clearly see the paternalism associated with this sort of view in his 1945 speech on National Independence and Racial Equality:

As regards the political status of Tibet, the Sixth National Kuomintang Congress decided to grant it a very high degree of autonomy, to aid its political advancement and to improve the living conditions of the Tibetans. I solemnly declare that if the Tibetans should at this time express a wish for self-government, our Government would, in conformity with our sincere tradition, accord it a very high degree of autonomy. If in the future they fulfill the economic requirement for independence, the National Government will, as in the case of Outer Mongolia, help them to gain that status. But Tibet must give proof that it can consolidate its independent position and protect its continuity so as not to become another Korea. (Chiang 1946)[23]

All of the above statements were made in the absence of any control over Tibet, so in this sense they were promises made to attract not just the Tibetans, few of whom probably ever heard them, but also other borderland peoples with whom both the Communists first and the Nationalists soon after found themselves living when they had been pushed to the frontiers of China proper (in Yan'an and Chongqing, respectively).

Much more significant for the Tibetans were the negotiations of late 1950 and early 1951. These negotiations decided the specific ways in which the Chinese state was willing to accommodate the de facto independent state of Tibet in order to gain the Tibetan government's legal

---

[22] See Sun Yat-sen (1929, pp. 6–8). Even the Communists kept up this strategy, as Tibet was the only region of the former Qing empire which signed an agreement, albeit at gunpoint, with the Communist government.

[23] For full reference, Chiang (1946 vol. II, p. 857).

agreement to become part of the modern Chinese state. This was embodied in the Seventeen Point Agreement, signed May 23, 1951, which guaranteed Tibetan autonomy on a number of specific fronts (see Goldstein 1989, pp. 763–72):

Point 3: "the Tibetan people have the right of exercising national regional autonomy under the leadership of Central People's Government";
Point 4: "central authorities will not alter the existing political system in Tibet";
Point 7: "religious beliefs, customs, habits of the Tibetan People shall be respected, and lama monasteries shall be protected. The central authorities will not effect a change in the income of the monasteries";
Points 9 & 10: "school education of the Tibetan nationality …. [and] the people's livelihood shall be improved step by step in accordance with the actual conditions in Tibet";
Point 11: regarding "matters related to the various reforms in Tibet, there will be no compulsion on the part of the central authorities."

These were significant concessions if, as the Chinese state and Chinese nationalists around the world like to argue today, Tibet has been an inalienable part of Chinese territory since the thirteenth century.[24] But more significant for the Tibetans and their place in China today is the fact that "the Communists, after taking power in 1949, cancelled the promise they had made early on, in the 1930s … the explicit right to formal secession [for borderland polities]" (Fiskesjö 2006, p. 18). Once this right was taken away from Tibetans, the Chinese state proceeded to implement

---

[24] For instance see the YouTube video, posted March 15, 2008: "Tibet WAS, IS, and ALWAYS WILL BE a part of China". Available at: http://www.youtube.com/watch?v=x9QNKB34cJo [accessed 19 June 2008], which has received over 3 million hits in its first four months online. For an official view see the article "China publishes historical records that show Tibet an inalienable part of country." *Xinhua* [Online]. (Updated April 8, 2008). Available at: http://news.xinhuanet.com/english/2008–04/08/content_7935999.htm [accessed June 17, 2008]. This article describes a new China's State Archives Administration website, which supposedly used "historical records that showed Tibet had been under jurisdiction of the central government for more than 700 years since the Yuan Dynasty (1271–1368)." However, the first two documents are concerned with other matters. The first addresses religious freedom in Tibet by citing two 1950s telegrams from the Fourteenth Dalai Lama to Mao Zedong stating that the CCP "has implemented the policy of freedom of religious belief" in Tibet. The second set of documents (sales contracts of serfs, 1914–1943) addresses the principle justification for China's current rule of Tibet: that Tibet was a feudal society that needed to be liberated. Ironically, the latter documents clearly demonstrate that China did not have control of Tibet at the time they were written, or it would not have permitted such transactions. Or see the state archives site at: http://www.saac.gov.cn/. [accessed April 11, 2009]. These sites were all responses to the Tibetan demonstrations of March and April 2008, and the ensuing support for Tibetans expressed around the world.

reforms in Tibetan areas outside of where the Lhasa government controlled in 1950. This led quickly to an open revolt in Kham and Amdo in
the mid-1950s, which spread to central Tibet by 1959. It is remarkable
how little has been written about the Tibetan uprisings in eastern Tibet
in the 1950s, but the Chinese state has been systematic in preventing
publications and research on this topic in Tibetan regions. This sensitivity
about events already half a century past shows just how tense relations
still are between Chinese and Tibetans in eastern Tibet, as the events of
the spring of 2008 also demonstrate. In any case, once the revolt spread
to central Tibet, the Dalai Lama fled into exile and both parties reneged
on the Seventeen Point Agreement.[25]

The next significant milestone in the trajectory of Chinese accommodation of Tibetan sub-state nationality interests came only after the
end of the Cultural Revolution, when General Secretary Hu Yaobang
went to Tibet on May 22, 1980, to celebrate the 39th anniversary of the
Seventeen Point Agreement. On May 29, he made a speech to thousands
of party cadre in Lhasa outlining six tasks, the first of which was: "To
exercise nationality autonomy in the region fully – that is to say, to let
Tibetans really be the masters of their own lives" (Wang 1994, p. 287).
Even more remarkably, Hu went on to both accept blame, on behalf of
the party, and to place blame especially on the Chinese cadre in Tibet for
the failures of the Chinese party-state up to that point, as quoted and
analyzed by Tsering Shakya:

'We feel our party has let the Tibetan people down. We feel very bad! The sole
purpose of our Communist Party is to work for the happiness of the people, to
do good things for them. We have worked nearly thirty years, but the life of the
Tibetan people has not notably improved. Are we not to blame?' The harshest
words were reserved for the Chinese cadre working in Tibet. He asked what
they had done with the millions of yuan in grants the Central Government had
made to the TAR ... comparing the situation in Tibet with colonialism. (1999,
pp. 381–2)

Other points in his speech pledged new economic policies to benefit
Tibetans and a renewed openness to Tibetan culture (clearly including
religion), language, and education (Tsering Shakya 1999, pp. 381–2).
This elevated rhetoric looked, for a time, like it might be backed up with
action. Already in January of 1980, a new law was promised, one which

---

[25] Song (1998, p. 65) asserts that "the Tibetan government ... repudiated the agreement in
1959, while the Chinese government still regards it as legal," though the government is
clearly not honoring the agreement.

would at last "realise the right to autonomy" for Tibetans, which had been an unfulfilled promise since 1967 (Tsering Shakya 1999, p. 391). These changes were finally made in 1982 in the constitution, which asserted that:

Regional autonomy is practised in areas where people of minority nationalities live in compact communities; in these areas organs of self-government are established for the exercise of the right of autonomy... The people of all nationalities have the freedom to use and develop their own spoken and written languages, and to preserve or reform their own ways and customs.[26]

Since the Chinese constitution is not a legally enforceable document, in 1984 these rights were defined in the Law of Regional Autonomy, among other statutes (Fiskesjö 2006, p. 34; Tsering Shakya 1999, p. 291). But as is well known in the Tibetan case, once the demonstrations of 1987–1989 took place, Hu's policies were stopped, martial law was enacted, and the hardliners have resisted making substantial concessions to accommodating Tibetan sub-state nationality interests ever since.

TWENTY-FIRST CENTURY DEVELOPMENTS
AND THE SPRING OF 2008

The most significant new promise the Chinese state has made to Tibetans – along with other peoples on the old frontiers of the Qing Empire that were incorporated into the modern state – is the plan to "Develop the West" (*xi bu da kai fa*) announced in 2000. This plan has affected Tibetans across the plateau, though those near large infrastructure projects (mostly in urban areas, but also in some rural areas near train lines, hydroelectric dams, etc.) have obviously been most affected (Fischer 2005, p. 69). Some of the changes are quite remarkable, especially in rural areas, such as the relative ease of transportation (travel times are generally much shorter than they were a decade ago), the growing availability of electricity and the internet, and cellphone coverage better than that in the United States. Nevertheless, in Tibetan regions, "the provinces that account for about three-quarters of the Tibetan population and territory emerged as the leading laggards amidst exceedingly rapid national economic growth" (Fischer 2005, p. 17). Once rural Tibetans have a television, they can see what they do not have, and what

---

[26] Full text: http://english.people.com.cn/constitution/constitution.html [accessed April 11, 2009].

they can access only with great difficulty and tremendous shifts in their ways of life (Goldstein et al. 2008). The grand promises have remained unrealized while the unfulfilled vision of a better life seems to have only frustrated many Tibetans, especially the youth. Earlier generations know that life is better now than under the harsh political campaigns of the past, but anyone born after 1980 has grown up with the constant promise of a better life, especially a financially better life, since the oldest of them were twenty years old when the plan to "Develop the West" was announced. At the same time, the influx of workers with greater economic empowerment who have come to develop Tibet make Tibetans feel acutely aware of being second class citizens in their own autonomous territories (Fischer 2005, pp. 133–49). Thus this most recent social contract that Chinese have offered the Tibetans, the promise of a booming economy in exchange for a less restive population, has failed to deliver a satisfied Tibetan public.

Thirty years after reforms and almost twenty years since the last major demonstrations in Lhasa, the demonstrations throughout Tibetan regions in the spring of 2008 show that a broad range of Tibetans are dissatisfied with China's rule. Though it has been difficult to gather reliable information in recent months, both monks and lay people, adults and youth, students and nomads, farmers and urban dwellers – in other words every type of Tibetan – seems to have been involved in the demonstrations. What exactly these Tibetans are dissatisfied with will be hard to discover until and unless the Chinese government lives up to the rights promised in the Chinese constitution:

Article 35. Citizens of the People's Republic of China enjoy freedom of speech, of the press, of assembly, of association, of procession and of demonstration.
Article 36. Citizens of the People's Republic of China enjoy freedom of religious belief.
Article 41. Citizens of the People's Republic of China have the right to criticize and make suggestions to any state organ or functionary.

But these freedoms are strongly tempered by another article, which puts the party-state's interests over the rights promised above.

Article 51. The exercise by citizens of the People's Republic of China of their freedoms and rights may not infringe upon the interests of the state, of society and of the collective, or upon the lawful freedoms and rights of other citizens.[27]

---

[27] Full text: http://english.people.com.cn/constitution/constitution.html, bold font in the original [accessed April 11, 2009].

As I have argued above, I think that it is in the interest of the state to be able to hear the voice of the Tibetan people, through the exercise of "freedom of speech, of the press, of assembly, of association, of procession and of demonstration" and especially "the right to criticize and make suggestions to any state organ or functionary." The restrictions on these freedoms has led the Tibetans, like other peoples in China proper and around the world, to become frustrated, and that pent up frustration did lead to at least one deplorably violent episode, on March 14, 2008 by Tibetan demonstrators reacting to police beating monks, arresting students, and halting a range of nonviolent demonstrations.[28]

While many in the West regretted and called for an end to the violence in Tibet, the world did not share the same level of outrage as Han Chinese about the attacks on Chinese and Hui (Muslim) and their shops in Lhasa, which included arson and as many as nineteen deaths (whether ethnic Han Chinese, Hui, or Tibetan was not clear, though the majority of them seem to have been deaths by people trapped in the shops set on fire).[29] But Chinese people also probably do not feel terrible remorse

---

[28] As frequently noted, ethnic Chinese are responsible for most of violent and non-violent demonstrations in China, amounting to hundreds of thousands of instances before the government stopped reporting the statistics after 2005. See for instance, French (2005) Anger in China Rises Over Threat to Environment. *New York Times*, July 19. This author states (2005): "the number of mass protests like these skyrocketing to 74,000 incidents last year from about 10,000 a decade earlier, according to government figures." In early 2006, the Chinese Ministry of Public Security issued a press release that stated that the number of instances of "public order disturbances" (as opposed to mass incidents) had risen to 87,000 in 2005. The Chinese state's own English language newspaper, *China Daily*, has described this ministry report as describing the number of "mass incidents" so the discrepancy between the terms used to described such incidents seems not to be a major concern to the Chinese state. "China strives to handle mass incidents." *China Daily* [Online] (Updated December 9, 2006). Available at: http://www.chinadaily.com. cn/china/2006–12/09/content_754796.htm. [accessed October 3, 2008]. Many thanks to Andrew Nathan in alerting me to these latest figures and the discussion about how these terms and numbers are understood and often misreported.

[29] It would be interesting to know whether the shops that were burned were mostly owned by Chinese and Hui or whether the Tibetans indiscriminately targeted these stores, even when they were owned by Tibetans who were just renting to the other nationalities. Unfortunately, at present, it is extremely difficult to get permission from the Chinese state to do basic research on the Tibetan economy. For an assessment of some of these difficulties see Yeh (2006); for an exception to this rule, see Goldstein et al, (2008). See "13 civilians burned or stabbed to death in Lhasa riot," *Xinhua* [Online]. Available at: http://news.xinhuanet.com/english/2008–03/20/content_7826369.htm [accessed June 19, 2008]; "17 jailed for Lhasa violence," *Xinhua* [Online] (Updated April 29, 2008). Available at: http://news.xinhuanet.com/english/2008–04/29/content_8073067.htm [accessed June 19, 2008]. I can find no information on the cause of deaths on the Chinese state's English language website on Tibet. The closest reference to the riot that I

about the American soldiers killed in Iraq. They view the soldiers' presence as interference in another country's internal affairs, so they are more sympathetic to the Iraqi deaths.[30] And likewise many Westerners have come to feel that the Chinese presence in Tibet also reflects interference with a formerly independent country's internal affairs, so they are more sympathetic to the Tibetans who have been beaten and imprisoned and killed by the Chinese state. (Westerners also probably wrongly assume that all this activity is only being perpetrated by Chinese, which is incorrect, since many Tibetans work for the state, as prison and border guards, undercover police, and in many other positions, including high officials.)

Of course, part of the problem with assessing the level and nature of the violence in Tibet (whether inflicted by Tibetans or Chinese) is that the Chinese state would not allow open access for media coverage of this event, despite promises of media freedom leading up to the Olympics. In fact, in China foreign media (and domestic media in different ways) was and remains (in December, 2009) almost totally restricted in its access to Lhasa and Tibet, except for press visits coordinated by the state. What is so remarkable about these limitations on the press is how widespread they are, covering the entire Tibetan plateau (roughly equal to one quarter of the territory of China).

In the absence of the ability of scholars and journalists to hear openly and directly from Tibetans to gain their perspective, I think that the Tibetans in China are trying to realize the promise of Article 41 of the

could find was a note about tourism resuming after "[t]ourism to Tibet was halted after the March 14 riots" in the article: "Local officials: Lhasa to reopen to foreign tourists soon" [Online] Available at: http://eng.tibet.cn/ [accessed June 19, 2008]; and a note about unemployment for workers in the tourism industry: "First batch of compensation issued to 3.14 victims in Tibet." [Online] Available at: http://eng.tibet.cn/. [accessed June 19, 2008]. The clearest account of the count of the injured and the dead is the article "18 civilians, 1 police officer killed by Lhasa rioters," *People's Daily* [Online] (Updated March 22, 2008) Available at: http://english.people.com.cn/90001/90776/6378824.html. [accessed January 5, 2008], but this article also does not distinguish between the ethnicities of the dead and injured or the exact causes of the deaths or injuries. A search of the People's Daily English edition online brings the reader to a special page that addresses the "Truth behind the March 14 Lhasa Riots" which aims to "Tell You a True Tibet." *People's Daily* [Online]. Available at: http://english.people.com.cn/90002/93607/index. html. [accessed January 5, 2008].

[30] In fact, the Chinese official website on Tibet had this to say: "The casualty [sic] during the [Lhasa] riots there is far less than that of the daily loss of lives in Iraq." See: Graefin von Borries (2008). "Tibet a ploy to run down China and Olympics," *China Daily* [Online] (Updated June 13, 2008) Available at: http://eng.tibet.cn/news/opinion/200806/ t20080613_406244.htm [accessed June 18, 2008]. Though this article for the English language version of China's official Tibet website was written by a non-Chinese, it clearly represents a position of which the Chinese government approves.

Chinese constitution: the right to criticize and make suggestions. When they wave the flag of the Tibetan government in exile and call for a return of the Dalai Lama, they might well be harkening back to the period in which the Dalai Lama still lived in Tibet and the flag still flew in Tibet (until 1959), a period when the Seventeen Point Agreement still meant something and there was real autonomy for the Tibetans (at least those in what was to become the TAR), though I think it is safe to say that no one wants a return to everything as it was in the 1950s. Tibet was not a perfect place in the 1950s, but most Tibetans, and many outside observers believe that things could be better there today. Even in the face of such changes, if the Chinese state continues to fail to deliver on promises it has made for over eighty years, then the radical elements of the Tibetan independence movement may gain strength and overturn the Dalai Lama's tradition of non-violence.

CONCLUSION AND LOOKING AHEAD

I have attempted to trace here the various aspects of the process through which the Chinese have tried to attract and employ Tibetans in their effort to incorporate Tibet into the Chinese Republic. The earliest efforts involved the application of ideologies of race and nationalism, which though tempting to some Tibetans ultimately proved ineffective, principally because the Chinese government was not willing to live up to its promises of racial equality and national autonomy. Greater success in working with prominent Tibetans exiled in China was enjoyed once the National Government recognized – with titles, offices, and financial remuneration – the importance of religion. Religious recognition of these exiled lamas was critical to their willingness to support the Chinese government. It may be that the Nationalist Chinese government, like the Communist government today, was able to grant this religious recognition precisely because no other religious element played a major role in governing China.[31] In negotiating the relations with Tibet, China's modern rulers, like earlier Mongol and Manchu emperors, are constantly drawn into the tradition of political and financial support for particular lamas in order to maintain their control over Tibet. But accommodating Tibetan Buddhist practice is only one of the many promises the Chinese government has made to the Tibetans and failed to fulfill. For a positive

[31] For the weakness of Chinese Buddhism as force in China's politics, see Welch (1968).

outcome in the future, a realization of the promised political autonomy and economic development will also be essential.

For instance, in the introduction of this book the editors note that multination states are characterized by the fact that they contain more than one group seeking equal status, especially the power of self-determination, which precisely describes the Tibetans' aspirations. Despite the rhetorical titles ("autonomous," Ch. *zizhi*, Tib. *rang skyong*) attached to all political divisions of the Chinese state (regions, prefectures, counties, etc.) that have significant populations of Tibetans, the Chinese party-state clearly recognizes that there is no real political self-determination allowed in Tibetan regions. Until the party-state is willing to accommodate more Tibetan autonomy, unrest will continue in Tibet. Although the Chinese government chooses to see Tibetans' attention to religion and the dictates of their religion as threats to China's territorial sovereignty, some state officials have started to realize that Tibetan Buddhist religion could also be a resource to draw on in order to integrate Tibet as part of China. As discussed in the editors' introduction, Chinese leaders also fear the idea that "giving administrative autonomy to particular groups ... can create a new set of resources that can enhance the group's mobilization and claims, thereby leading to sub-state nationalist mobilization, instability, and secessionist tendencies in some cases."[32] But this is not realistic in the Tibetan case, which is different than the case of the Soviet Union's Central Asia republics for a number of reasons. The massive presence of armed forces in this border region, infrastructural integration, and the large presence of Tibetans in government who share the state's interests would make such secession nearly impossible.

While it is true that Tibetan Buddhism has provided multiple opportunities for resistance to the Chinese state in the face of failed promises, this religion is also a cultural resource that is flexible in its ability to adapt. Tibetan Buddhism, as a foundation of Tibetan society, can constitute a resource for legitimizing resistance to the state. Yet, with the right incentives, such as genuine respect for religious freedom, the same body of knowledge could be turned to other ends, as when the Fourteenth Dalai Lama understood Marxism positively through a Buddhist interpretation of that ideology. But to reach this point, Chinese officials will have to stop the practice described in the introduction of this book of only giving symbolic or rhetorical autonomy to the Tibetans. Of course, the Chinese state also needs to live up to its past promises of development in Tibet as well, starting with spending as much on health and education as they do on

---

[32] See the introduction of this volume (Bertrand and Laliberti, p. 14).

transportation and communication infrastructure. The best hope for the future would be to develop a federalist system that allows Tibetans real cultural and religious autonomy within the framework of the People's Republic of China, which would no doubt solve many of the problems of Tibet and be an attractive demonstration of a new system to Taiwan as well.

But at a more practical level, some of the first concrete steps the Chinese government might take towards realizing the latest promise of prosperity through the campaign to Develop the West would be to invest significantly in education and health care for Tibetans all over the plateau. I have already mentioned the disparity between what the Chinese government has spent on infrastructure development (both inside and beyond Tibetan regions) and the paltry funds spent on education and health care in Tibetan regions over the last fifty years. One very easy step the government could take to address this past discrepancy would be to commit significant resources (at least a billion *yuan*) to create four central institutes of higher and continuing education for Tibetans, each with an associated medical clinic. These institutes and clinics could be strategically located around the plateau to reach the widest number of Tibetans. Each of these four centers would be responsible for outreach to a broad section of the relevant surrounding communities, which would be explicitly designed around reaching common dialect groups.

The idea for such new institutions would be to reach the majority of (rural) Tibetans, without requiring them to move to expensive, ethnically Chinese urban centers to gain access to continuing or higher education. Thus, these centers would be entirely Tibetan language medium schools. Among other fields, these institutes and teaching clinics would focus on providing medical clinics that could also serve as education centers in public health and specific training for basic surgeries (such as those given by the Seva Foundation). They would bring together the best Tibetan language textbooks, especially those in science and health care, and spread this knowledge to local teachers and clinicians. These regional institutes for continuing and higher education could offer formal degrees (associates, bachelors of arts, and bachelors of science), but they could also serve as centers for continuing education for teachers from the local schools in their region. Thus, on a regular basis, during periods of school vacation, teachers could be brought to these centers to be introduced to the latest developments in Tibetan language education for rural youth.

Chinese government support for such medical and educational initiatives would provide the centralized and long-term planning that is necessary to reach millions of Tibetans across a vast and sparsely inhabited region. Such initiative on the part of the Chinese government would also demonstrate the state's real concern for practical matters facing the Tibetan people on a daily basis. Massive urban and infrastructure developments are of limited use to most (rural) Tibetans. To truly fulfill the state's latest promise to Tibetans, the promise of material development, better use of state funds will have to be made. The Chinese state must reach out to rural Tibetans in ways that make a real difference.

10

Leninism's Long Shadow in Central Asia

Edward Schatz

Those who study state policies toward sub-state national minorities typically focus on how *responsive* the state is to minorities that are already politically mobilized. This book is no exception; it follows a venerable tradition of examining groups that seek self-determination to consider the extent to which and the forms by which such groups are accommodated.

An already mobilized minority and degrees of state responsiveness are an important theoretical possibility, but one among many. States do more than react; they also act, sometimes decisively and with clear initiative and agency. When they do, their actions may be viewed as preceding, rather than following, the political mobilization of cultural groups.

If it is difficult to discern the empirical outlines of such *proactive* policies in some Asian cases, ex-Soviet Central Asia (Kazakhstan, Kyrgyzstan, Turkmenistan, Tajikistan, and Uzbekistan) brings them and their impact into sharp relief. The Leninist state in the Soviet Union sought – as a part of its ideological and coercive agenda – to be *proactive* in attending to minority groups, even in those regions where levels of nationalist mobilization were low, popular national identities were practically nonexistent, and local identities prevailed. In this chapter, I argue that these policies set in motion political processes that were ultimately beyond the ability of the Soviet state to control. Central Asia's political development since the Soviet collapse has been deeply conditioned by this Leninist legacy.[1]

---

[1] Central Asianists and other scholars of the Soviet period have written much on the topics summarized in this chapter. See, for examples, Edgar (2004); Hirsch (2005); Khalid (2006, 2007); Martin (2001); Schatz (2004); Slezkine (1994); Suny (1993).

This chapter begins by addressing the blind spots in a literature that assumes that groups are already mobilized. In a second section, I introduce the Leninist project in Central Asia, characterizing it as an example of proactive policy making. Third, I consider some crucial outcomes of this project that had become visible by the late-Soviet period. Fourth, I highlight how these outcomes continued to shape politics after the Soviet collapse. Finally, I ask whether and in what ways proactive policy making about identity politics might be rescued from its historically Leninist manifestations.

REACTIVE STATES AND ALREADY MOBILIZED GROUPS

Those interested in policies to ameliorate intergroup tensions, accommodate group interests, or protect group rights often assume that a group's existence is unproblematic, uncontested, well established, and normatively legitimate. Moreover, they tend to assume that such group identity more or less automatically drives the members of such groups to mobilize. Whatever their analytic utility, such axioms are often descriptively inaccurate.[2]

As the constructivist turn has taught us, group identities tend to be more fluid, variable, multifaceted, and contingent than was once thought. It is not, of course, that a sense of Kachin or Uighur or Tamil group identity never crystallizes or becomes substantial; collective sentiments can become powerful and even rigid. But, the degree of group feeling is a variable, not a constant.[3] When ethnic or national group identity, for example, becomes more salient than other, competing (and perhaps crosscutting) identities, we should ask why this occurs and how long it might reasonably be expected to last (Megoran 2007).

Some analysts imply that national identities, once constructed, become bedrock – more or less permanent, factual, and inevitable. Walker Connor (1994a), for example, famously problematized the primordialist assumption of ancient nations, asking, "When is a nation?" His scheme, however, suggested that once a critical mass of people has identified with the nation, no meaningful evolution of the field of identity relations takes place. Connor's is a classic teleology; his version of history moves perhaps complexly and sometimes unevenly but always inexorably toward

---

[2] Brubaker (2004) goes further than I do here, calling into question the analytic utility of such assumptions.

[3] See Schatz (2004) for my attempt to grapple with continuity and change in group identification.

the nation's apotheosis. The logic by which modernity hardens collective identities and reduces the range of salient sentiments is tempting; one recent study presents compelling evidence that mass literacy tends to solidify national identity, searing the content of nationalist myths in the popular imaginary (Darden & Gryzmala-Busse 2006). From such a perspective, even if nations are historically constructed, they are experienced by individuals as primordial (Geertz 1973).

One need not accept premature depictions of a "post-national" world (Appadurai 1993) to recognize that, whatever narrowing of the field of identities that occurs with modernity and the rise of the nation, this is unlikely to be a permanent state of affairs. From emerging supranational identifications (European and transnational Muslim come to mind) to resurgent class narratives in parts of Latin America in the mid-2000s, the ways in which human beings potentially understand themselves are far more varied than the nationalist narrative and many analyses of nationalism imply. Even if we still live in an era characterized by nationalism, we should be careful not to project the present indefinitely onto the future, nor read it inappropriately back onto the past.

Just as the existence of discrete groups is rarely straightforward, groups do not automatically translate existing collective identity into political mobilization. Mobilization requires selective incentives to overcome collective action problems, a way for elites to bridge identification gaps with masses, and political opportunities (McAdam, McCarthy, & Zald 1996). Ethnic or ethno-nationalist mobilization, more specifically, requires that individuals align their identity and interests with those of their leaders; therefore, as Giuliano (2000, p. 296, emphasis added) points out, "A more accurate assessment of ethnic mobilization must examine how voters *come to support* particular issues and the role of politicians in *constructing* that support." Among other things, elites must deploy their persuasive arsenal to allow their rhetoric to take root (Cruz 2000), and they must tap into prevailing resentments against other groups – groups that ordinary people deem comparable (Horowitz 1985). A full theory of mobilization cannot assume that these things happen.[4]

Analytic convenience may dictate that we opt for the language of already mobilized groups; after all, treating already-mobilized groups as independent variables allows us to view their impact on political and

---

[4] We should also not assume the veracity of accounts of successful mobilization. As Commercio (2004) details, in some cases the state may have an interest in exaggerating the magnitude or success of mobilization for domestic political purposes. See also Brass (1996).

social life. I do not call into question these analytic decisions. I do, how-ever, argue a point that the Central Asian cases make clear: state action may precede the *problématique* covered in this volume. While states may view their projects as accommodative and as reacting to the normatively justified needs of groups, in the process their policies reify groups and structure mobilization. We need to recognize how states "see" but at the same time avoid seeing like a state ourselves.[5]

In the hypothetical absence of Leninist proactive policy making, some form of mobilization might still have occurred in Central Asia. The *forms* such mobilization assumed, however, were deeply conditioned by the Soviet experience in the region. This Soviet experience was one thing in cases where a strong sense of national solidarity (Georgia and Armenia) or state-like structures (the Baltic states) predated Soviet rule. In a Central Asian context that lacked well-consolidated pre-existing states and well-established ethno-national identities, the Soviet imprint was deep.

LENINIST PROACTIVE POLICY MAKING

Recent historiography makes clear that Leninism in Central Asia rested on two pillars – an ontology of ethnic belonging and a high-modernist ideology of state-led transformation.[6] In the early years of Soviet power, of course, other principles had competed for prominence; for example, some state actors under Lenin and at the beginning of Stalin's rule force-fully argued that Soviet governance should be constructed on a logic of economic rationality – even if it contravened other logics (Hirsch 2005). After the uncertainties of Lenin's rule and the tumults of Stalin's were in the past, however, the ethnic ontology and state-led transform-ism suffused social and political behavior in the region. Particularly with Brezhnev's "trust in cadres" policy, when Central Asian first secretaries enjoyed long tenures in office, state and society developed stable pat-ters of interaction that institutionalized these two pillars for decades to come.

That the Soviet state institutionalized a sense of ethnic attachment has been well documented (Brubaker 1996; Edgar 2004; Hirsch 2005; Martin 2001; Slezkine 1994). Before the Soviet period, Central Asia was

---

[5] "Seeing like a state" is from the title to Scott (1998). My injunction is consistent with Scott's – to recognize how states see is neither to endorse them in a normative sense nor accept their "viewpoint" in an analytic one.

[6] The apt term "high modernist" is from Scott (1998).

characterized by a wide range of group identities, most of which were local and regional in character (Edgar 2004) and existed in a patchwork of crosscutting and overlapping configurations that defied easy categorization (Schoeberlein-Engel 1994). Ethnicity was among the possible articulations of identity, but its resonance was largely confined to an elite attuned to nationalist ideologies that were filtered through the writings of the Russian national intelligentsia.[7] An overstated version of the argument – one that posits that the Soviets created ethnically defined nations ex nihilo – is justifiably dismissed as unfounded and ignorant of the region's deep history (Weller 2007), but the truth remains that the Soviet period fundamentally altered the landscape of identity relations.

Soviet authorities did not understand their efforts as creating ethnicity. Especially from the mid-1920s, Soviet ideologues understood ethnic groups as "really existing" – as the essential building blocks for the construction of a socialist society. Theirs was an ontology of fundamental ethnic belonging, and Soviet planners and administrators commissioned entire armies of ethnographers to "map" the region's really-existing ethnic terrain. From this perspective, the impossibly complex republican (and now international) boundaries of the Ferghana Valley only *seem* to be evidence of Stalin's "divide-and-rule" strategy; in fact, the region's cultural demography was such that, if one assumed ethnicity to be fundamental and were committed to draw boundaries to reflect these fundamental communities, they could only be drawn complexly.[8]

Ethnicity became perhaps *the* crucial taken-for-granted of Soviet-era life in Central Asia. As across the entire Union of Soviet Socialist Republics (USSR), large-scale territorial divisions followed an ethnic logic, with each major ethnic group assigned a federal unit that bore its name. Affirmative action, as Martin (2001) describes, occurred along ethnic lines. In each ethnically defined context, language policies coalesced around the codification, standardization, and promotion of a single language that was normatively understood to define each group. Even state coercion often followed an ethnic logic, with authorities punishing entire ethnic groups with deportation and internal exile, citing traits and behaviors assumed

[7] To a lesser extent, ethno-nationalist sentiment among elites was inspired by developments in the waning years of the Ottoman Empire and the early years of Republican Turkey. See Khalid (1998).
[8] See Hirsch (2005) for an in-depth discussion of the role of early Soviet-era ethnographers in providing information on cultural background that would serve the purposes of Soviet administration.

to be inherent to them (Conquest 1970). For the Soviets, ethnicity was the defining feature of the existing order and the raw material with which the next one was being built.

Moreover, the fact that ethnic sentiment was weak in Central Asia was an unimpressive obstacle to socialist construction. Lenin's Bolsheviks (later the Communist Party) was, first and foremost, a vanguard; its historical destiny was to reimagine and reshape the region on behalf of Central Asians. At the forefront of historical and evolutionary change, only the Party could attend to the essential needs of really-existing ethnic groups, even when Central Asians themselves were beset by false consciousness that had them believing otherwise.

Ultimately, reification and promotion of ethnicity were not pursued for their own sake. Rather, they became valuable when hitched to Soviet ideologues' notions of evolutionary progress, which Hirsch (2005) aptly calls "state-sponsored evolutionism." As Edgar (2004, p. 44) describes, "Put simply, a people had to become a nation before it could move on to the more advanced socialist and internationalist stages of human existence. By promoting national distinctiveness, the Soviets would ensure a speedier passage through this stage; eventually…the promotion of nationhood would lead to the disappearance of nations and the emergence of a united humanity." Thus, the promotion of ethno-national categories would facilitate the evolutionary progression of history toward a socialist future that would inevitably be transethnic.[9]

Engineering evolutionary progress through the reification of ethnicity and the accoutrements of ethnic culture naturally required the dismantling of the preexisting order, which was considered anathema to socialist construction. The Leninist role in Central Asia thus was predicated on the heavy-handed eradication of the public role of Islam, an undermining of the place for sub-ethnic clan and tribal ties and behaviors, and the overturning of pre-Soviet systems of gender relations. This *destructive* side of Soviet power accompanied the profoundly *constructive* transformations that Soviet rule brought.[10] I attend to these alternative forms of identity below. For now, the central point is that clan and religion were deemed competing forms of identity and allegiance that needed to be rooted out. The proactive logic of Soviet governance seemed to require it.

[9] In Soviet parlance, "international" (*mezhnational'nyi*) would have been more common.
[10] On this *destructive* aspect, see Schatz (2004). The adjectives "destructive" and "constructive" are meant to be descriptive, not normative. Both sides of Soviet power were fundamentally coercive.

EMERGING CHALLENGES TO GOVERNANCE IN
LATE-SOVIET CENTRAL ASIA

By the late-Soviet period, these proactive policies had left their mark in several ways. First, they had legitimated and privileged ethnicity, producing both entitlements and resentments understood through an ethnic lens. Second, they had delegitimized and stigmatized non-ethnic attachments, producing the potential for anti-hegemonic discourses to be enacted in the name of these attachments. Third, they had helped to create disembedded elites who existed in separation from their societies. All these outcomes – privileged ethnicity, stigmatized non-ethnicity, and disembedded elites – presented crucial challenges to governance in the late-Soviet period.

First, as elsewhere in the USSR, the reification of ethnicity generated a sense of ethno-nationalist entitlement (Brubaker 1996, pp. 23–54). In some parts of the USSR, this ethno-nationalism was "quiet," while in others it was "noisy" (Beissinger 2002); but it was everywhere the most prominent taken-for-granted category of practice.[11] Western and Moscow-based analyses that had anticipated Islamist movements in Central Asia proved to be far from the mark; ethnic categories were deeply institutionalized, and they edged alternative categories from the landscape of identity relations (Khalid 2007).

While it is true that ethno-nationalism in Central Asia was weaker than in other parts of the Union (Beissinger 2002), it was nonetheless the most important type of mobilization in the region. In 1986 Almaty, the capital city of Kazakhstan, was seized by riots after an ethnic Russian, Gennadyi Kolbin, replaced Dinmukhammed Kunaev, the long-standing ethnic Kazakh first secretary of the republican Communist Party. Disturbances spread to other cities in the republic. While Kazakhs were not agitating for independence (since this was well before the early-riser nationalists in the Baltic republics began to advance their claims), they strongly objected to the violation of a deeply institutionalized arrangement of ethnic accommodation whereby the first secretary was always a Kazakh. Moscow's late-coming attempt to recentralize authority faced ethnically defined patronage networks that had become deeply entrenched. Republican, titular, first-party secretaries ruled for at least twenty uninterrupted years in all the Central Asian cases except Turkmenistan (where Muhammetnazar Gapurov ruled for sixteen years). Violence that occurred in 1990 in Osh, Kyrgyzstan, between ethnic Uzbeks and ethnic Kyrgyz serves as another example. Although Megoran

---

[11] On ethnicity as a "category of practice," see Brubaker (2004).

(2007) is correct to suggest that the violence can be understood through lenses other than that of ethnicity, most people in the region nonetheless articulated it as "ethnic," and state authorities marshaled ethnic categories to record the events and prosecute perpetrators (Tishkov 1995).

Societal-level ethno-nationalism was weaker in Central Asia than in the Baltic cases, but Central Asia's state elites nonetheless championed ethno-nationalist logics as the Soviet apparatus crumbled. As Smith et al. (1998) document, the Central Asian regimes of the 1990s were classic "nationalizing states"; they were assumed to exist *for* the titular, ethnically defined nation. In Kyrgyzstan and Kazakhstan, which had significant ethnic Russian minorities, this focus on the titular group was overlaid with civic principles that were designed to appease the international community (as well as the Russian Federation), while in the other cases, something closer to a purely ethnic logic prevailed. Even in the former cases, however, formal civic protections meant fairly little in the context of a state apparatus that was plagued by corruption, lack of resources, and a lack of will to uphold them.

The flip-side of ethnic entitlement was a sense of displacement among those deemed not entitled to accommodation. In large part due to Stalin-era deportations, Central Asia was home to a striking variety and large number of cultural groups. Germans (who had been moved from the Volga region of Russia) lived alongside Koreans (who had been deported from the Far East); Chechens (who had been coercively resettled en masse in 1944); Uighurs (who had migrated from the borderland with China);[12] Slavs (who had migrated in large numbers beginning in the nineteenth century);[13] and titular groups. During the Soviet period, many of these non-titular peoples had lived adequately in the region,[14] but as the Soviet state began to lose its capacity and eventually collapsed, their situation became less secure. Many of those with the means emigrated to their titular "homelands" (or, less often, from less hospitable locales within the region to locales they perceived to be more hospitable). The iron-clad logic of ethnic entitlement meant ipso facto that non-titulars belonged elsewhere. At best, they could be the guests of their rather generous titular hosts.

It is worth trying to capture some of the psychology of this displacement. The Soviet state, alongside its emphasis on ethnicity, propagated a

---

[12] On the Uighurs of Central Asia, see Roberts (1998).
[13] See Commercio (2004) and Laitin (1998).
[14] This was especially the case for Slavs, who were the emissaries, technical specialists, and administrators of Soviet rule, and therefore came to enjoy disproportionate privileges.

strong ideology of equality. The reality, of course, was more checkered (Derlugian 2005), and something of an ersatz equality prevailed, wherein even small differences in wealth, status, or entitlement contradicted the propagated state ideology, thus fueling resentments. This led some ethnic groups – particularly within Russia proper (where the *matrioshka*-like administrative structure was most pronounced) – to envy the status of other groups and to agitate for whatever administrative arrangement (or, later, outright independence) their luckier neighbors enjoyed.[15]

A rejection of ersatz equality and demands for greater input into governance were key elements in the descent of Tajikistan into civil violence in the early 1990s. Tajikistan, a Soviet socialist "union republic" since 1929, was the site of a variety of autochthonous cultural groups who were all glossed as "Tajik" – a category that Soviet power made increasingly meaningful, but one that belied significant cultural and linguistic diversity on the ground. During the descent into civil war, parts of the Gorno-Badakhshan Autonomous Region (which is today still notable for the broad use of numerous regional and local languages from the eastern Iranian subgroup alongside Tajik as a lingua franca)[16] expressed their frustration with ongoing domination by a Soviet-backed Leninabad elite and declared independence. One might call this "status envy" – to emphasize the psychology of displacement and a feeling of relative deprivation that, once the opportunity presented itself, could mobilize a region that felt disadvantaged by its position in a culturally defined hierarchy.

Grievances, as a variety of scholarship makes clear, are not enough to spur mobilization; the fact that socialist reality belied the language of socialist equality did not generate mobilization among every minority ethnic group. Ethnic Uzbeks outside of Uzbekistan, for example, harbored significant grievances but engaged in limited political mobilization. In the Leninabad region of Tajikistan (which is topographically linked to the Uzbekistani parts of the Ferghana Valley), Uzbeks remained largely quiescent. This was also the case with Uzbeks in the Osh region of southern Kyrgyzstan (also linked topographically to the Uzbekistani Ferghana Valley).[17] The same quiescence characterized ethnic Tajiks of the Bukhara and Samarqand regions of Uzbekistan; there was little political

---

[15] The *matrioshka* is the nesting doll associated with traditional Russian culture. On so-called *matrioshka* nationalism, see Bremmer and Taras (1993).

[16] Gorno-Badakhshan is also known for large numbers of adherents to Ismaili Islam – a feature that further distinguishes its inhabitants from those elsewhere in Tajikistan.

[17] In 2006 some Uzbeks issued public demands that the Uzbek language be placed alongside Russian and Kyrgyz as an official language of Kyrgyzstan.

opportunity to mobilize in the context of hard authoritarian Uzbekistan. Nonetheless, these groups often experienced a sense of displacement and marginalization – an insufficient though necessary factor for political mobilization.

While ethnicity was promoted publicly as the vessel through which socialist modernity would arrive, Central Asians, of course, harbored additional forms of identity. A second outcome of Leninism's proactive policies concerned these non-ethnic categories. Here the picture is more complex and varied; I limit myself to a brief discussion of two alternative forms of identity – sub-ethnic clans and Islam.

As I have detailed elsewhere (Schatz 2004), the Soviet state intended to eradicate all manifestations of sub-ethnic clan behavior, but its command economy generated ongoing functional utility to kin-based networks that could provide access to goods in limited supply. This was particularly true in Kyrgyzstan and Kazakhstan, where the oral tradition of former nomads preserved cultural space for the sub-rosa transmission of genealogical information. The Soviet privileging of ethnic categories had a perverse effect: clans were deprived of space for their public expression, and their function was reduced to instrumental utility. By the late-Soviet period, they had become a resource by which networked individuals could strip the state's assets. Their main expression was anti-state, not because of qualities inherent to clans, but because Soviet rule had constructed them as such.

Islamic identities were similarly targeted for removal from public space, but here the outcome was different. Unlike clan ties, which helped individuals to navigate the complexities of the late-Soviet "shadow" economy, Islam in the late-Soviet period acquired a position as part of each ethnic tradition. That is, what distinguished an ethnic Kazakh from an ethnic Ukrainian was, among other things, the religious tradition associated with each reified ethnic culture. Islam thus was a marker of identity – often one with little identifiable religious content (Khalid 2007). For a tiny minority that was exposed to ideological currents from the global resurgence of Islam in the 1970s and 1980s (via the Afghanistan conflict or via the limited links that the Soviet state allowed between Soviet Muslims and the outside world), the religion potentially served as a mobilizing ideology. Generally, however, Islam inspired little political mobilization until the late 1990s in Central Asia. But the Soviet state's reification and promotion of ethnicity lent a particular coloration to identity as Muslim; to be Muslim in a transethnic sense and to infuse that identity with any religious content was understood to be threatening to the Soviet state. As I examine below, the assumption that transethnic religious sentiment is inherently anti-state has its roots in Soviet-era understandings of legitimate and illegitimate vessels for identity.

A third outcome of Leninism was the creation of disembedded elites across Central Asia. The Soviet promotion of ethnicity was not felt equally across lines of status within each territory. The Soviet state relied significantly on indigenous elites from the region to staff high-level administrative posts. These Central Asians learned, in Kotkin's (1991) felicitous phrase, to "speak Bolshevik," which meant important degrees of linguistic and cultural Russification, especially in Kazakhstan and Kyrgyzstan. The irony is this: while these indigenous elites claimed to speak on behalf of their ethnically defined populations, they themselves often had a tenuous grasp of the language and culture associated with their ethnic traditions. The fact that they were disembedded from their ethnic society generated ongoing tensions that played out within ethnic groups that were assumed by outsiders to be internally homogenous.

Whereas disembeddedness was characterized as cultural in many cases, in Tajikistan it was spatial, and this particular Soviet legacy crucially and tragically distinguished the case from others in the region. The ruling Leninabad elite remained relatively well connected vertically to ordinary Leninabadis within the northern Leninabad region. At the same time, however, in part due to a divisive mountain topography, the ruling elite functioned at a fundamental disconnect from the other regions of the country. Moreover, its position was strengthened by ongoing and unwavering support from Moscow (Collins 2006). As a result, the Leninabad elite perceived itself to be invulnerable, doing little to address grievances that were mounting in the late 1980s and early 1990s outside Leninabad (Akbarzadeh 1996).

This disembeddedness was among the factors contributing to the Tajik civil war (1992–1997). Likewise, the ethnic ontology and state-led transformism were key Soviet practices at play in the descent to conflict. Because Soviet categories held that Tajiks constituted one cultural community, the Leninabad elite mistakenly imagined its interests to be coterminous with those of the rest of Tajikistan. It was therefore blindsided by, for example, demands from the Badakhshan region for greater autonomy. Moreover, the Leninabad region was both relatively more advanced economically and culturally Russified – signs of its privileged position in leading Tajikistan to a better future. While a full explanation of the civil war is beyond my scope, these Soviet practices, taken together, produced an arrogance of power that made compromise unlikely in the early 1990s as Tajikistan progressively became less stable.[18]

These three outcomes of Leninism in the region – privileged ethnicity, stigmatized non-ethnicity, and disembedded elites – produced challenges to governance in the late-Soviet period. Ethnicity proved a mobilizing discourse in the late 1980s, as ethnic nationalist groups in Kazakhstan, Kyrgyzstan, and Uzbekistan agitated to remake the Soviet social contract. Notwithstanding riots in Almaty in 1986 and in Osh in 1990, this was often a "quiet" nationalism, but as massive, nationalism-inspired falsification of cotton receipts in Uzbekistan makes clear, it was far from insignificant as a challenge to governance.[19] Similarly, the asset stripping of late-Soviet kinship-based networks exacerbated the erosion of state power in the waning years of Soviet rule.[20] Even Islam, although stigmatized by the Soviet experience, was on occasion the language through which emergent protest was articulated.[21] Finally, the disembeddedness of elites, combined with the state's emphasis on ethnic authenticity, produced a crisis of legitimacy for indigenous elites in the late-Soviet period. In Kazakhstan, Turkmenistan, and Uzbekistan, the indigenous leadership (with varying degrees of success) transformed itself from a communist elite that "spoke Bolshevik" to a nationalist one attuned to the ethnically defined nation. In Kyrgyzstan and Tajikistan, the indigenous elite was unable to make this transformation, and a new elite emerged in the wake of the old.

It is not, as Malia (1995) has forcefully argued, that the Soviet Union had planted the seeds of its own demise; for Central Asia (at least), such an argument is too strong. On the other hand, it remains true that the Soviet state structured groupness and generated mobilizational possibilities that posed novel challenges to governance. Proponents of Lenin's vanguard party would have been appalled at the Party's inability to keep pace.

---

[18] Much later, in the mid-2000s, the Rakhmon regime would unfortunately proceed with similar arrogance – conflating its interests with those of the entire ethnically defined "nation" and constructing for itself an image of its own progressive role. The likelihood that civil war would resume was diminished because Rakhmon was less disembedded than his Leninabadi predecessors had been and because the international community enjoyed a strong presence and a deep interest in keeping Tajikistan stable.

[19] On the so-called Rashidov affair, see Gleason (1983). On how small-scale, sub-rosa subterfuge matters, see Scott (1992).

[20] On asset stripping in the Soviet collapse, see Solnick (1999).

[21] In the late 1990s, Islam would become more resonant as a counter-hegemonic discourse.

LENINIST LEGACIES

In the post-Soviet period, both state and society in Central Asia continued to be deeply conditioned by these Leninist legacies; Soviet-era logics and categories of practice animated post-Soviet realities. Beissinger (1995) was among the first to emphasize continuities with the Soviet era, showing how habitus encourages the reproduction of pre-existing patterns of behavior and human relationships. To be sure, the Soviet collapse introduced important ruptures in the realm of formal institutions, but in the context of Central Asia, where independence came largely by surprise, the region as late as 2008 remained "Soviet" in crucial ways. For present purposes, the privileging of ethnicity, the stigmatization of non-ethnicity, and the disembeddedness of elites cast a long shadow on the landscape of Central Asian politics.

The privileging of ethnicity and the logic of ethnic entitlement remained pervasive. As Smith et al. (1998) show, the region's regimes imagined themselves as champions of ethnic culture and ethnically defined statehood. Why else, the logic went, would a "Kazakh-stan" exist if not *for* the Kazakhs?[22] If this principle seems beyond dispute, it is worth recalling that the region's forms of political organization that predated Soviet rule did *not* have an ethnic logic. In the pre-Soviet Ferghana Valley, as Schoeberlein-Engel (1994) has detailed, people defied simple ethnic categorizations; the fact that in the post-Soviet era ethnicity *even in the Ferghana Valley* was among the most, if not *the* most, salient form of identity suggests how much changed in the intervening years.[23] Likewise, precisely because the nineteenth-century khanates at Samarqand and Bukhara combined elements of Persian and Turkic culture among both the elite and general population, they are today hotly contested; they do not fit neatly in an ethno-nationalist narrative that seeks to define them as either essentially Tajik or essentially Uzbek.[24]

---

[22] Only Kyrgyzstan eliminated the so-called "fifth column" of the passport – the line that indicates ethnic background. In Kazakhstan, citizens had the right to indicate or not to indicate their ethnicity in their passports, but most people (including passport-issuing authorities) were unaware of this right.

[23] Megoran (2007) highlights how ordinary people in the Ferghana Valley call upon ethnicity in complicated ways and understand it to be intertwined with a striking array of other identity categories. As true as this is, the real puzzle is why ethnicity – whatever its complex entanglements in concrete empirical situations – matters so much in the first place when it once mattered so little.

[24] See also Shnirelman (1996).

Historiography in the post-Soviet period was ethnicized. Scholars and state-sponsored mythmakers were called upon to demonstrate the antiquity of ethnically defined nations, even when this produced historiographical absurdities, such as the claim of one Kazakh historian that Genghis Khan was a Kazakh, or the broad Uzbekistani state's hagiography and iconography of Tamerlane as the father of the Uzbek nation. Such depictions were consistent with Soviet legacies of ethnicization. That these depictions in many senses exceeded those of their Soviet predecessors suggests a logic of ethnic outbidding generated by insecurity over the elite's legitimacy. Just as their juridical statehood and empirical capacity to govern were in question in the early 1990s, the elite's legitimacy was uncertain, at best.[25]

The pervasive ethnic logic that characterized the post-Soviet period suggested the contours of what "accommodation" of minority ethnic groups would look like. Kazakhstan and Kyrgyzstan adopted the Soviet-era discourse of "internationalism," laying it over the discourse of titular entitlement. Thus, while the titular group in each case was normatively understood to be the beneficiary of state redress for Soviet-era atrocities committed against co-ethnics, non-titular groups were nonetheless to be treated with fairness and respect. That they "belonged" to another state bearing the name of their ethno-national group did not absolve anyone of this basic responsibility. Emigration of ethnic Slavs from the region – while counterproductive for these independent states in crucial ways, given Slavs' disproportionate levels of technical expertise – avoided the kinds of ethnic cleansing that characterized the Balkans during the same period. This owes at least something to the discursive legacy of Soviet internationalism.

Like its Soviet-era predecessor, post-Soviet internationalism did not assume that a "melting pot" would dissolve ethnic differences; rather, it was considered to be a bringing together (*sblizhenie*, in Soviet parlance) of reified ethnic communities. Thus, both Kazakhstan and Kyrgyzstan created an unelected body called the Assembly of Peoples, which assembled selected representatives of ethnically defined, corporately understood communities.[26] All Central Asian rulers made strong rhetorical commitments (followed by negligible-to-low levels of financial commitment) to provide education and to support print media in the major ethnic languages of the state they ruled. And, following in the tradition of Soviet-era

[25] This returns us to the question of the elite's disembeddedness, which I consider below.
[26] Kyrgyzstan's new constitution in 2007 eliminated the body.

public displays of internationalism, these states constructed spectacles to showcase the ethnic traditions of major groups, replete with reified understandings of ethnic dress, cuisine, song, and dance.

As in the Soviet era, the flip-side of ethnic entitlement was ethnically defined grievance. Many groups remained quiescent, but resentments simmered. Until the early 2000s, ethnic Russians in Kazakhstan periodically mobilized to air their concerns about the promotion of the Kazakh language, the emphasis on Kazakh ethnic culture, and a de facto affirmative action for ethnic Kazakhs within state structures. Once both the Kazakhstani economy, buoyed by oil receipts, began a period of dramatic growth and the demographic power of ethnic Russians had diminished due to emigration and the ageing of those who remained, grievances were articulated less often. In southern Kyrgyzstan, ethnic Uzbeks – though generally quiescent – began to agitate for greater linguistic recognition and political representation. The potential for ethnic minorities to advance claims was only enhanced by the prominence of state-sponsored schemes that promoted the titular group.

While the logic of ethnic entitlement and resentment was continuous from the Soviet period, one difference was crucial. Whereas the Soviet Union was characterized by an ethno-federalism that provided territory-based administration for the largest of ethnically defined groups, the post-Soviet Central Asian states were unitary, not federal. Uzbekistan provided nominal autonomy for its Karakalpakstan region, as did Tajikistan for Gorno-Badakhshan, but these were the exceptions. Moreover, Karakalpakstan's autonomy was relatively meaningless in the context of a hard authoritarian Uzbekistan that lacked other quasi-federal units. Gorno-Badakhshan's autonomy was perhaps more meaningful, but only by default; the central state in Dushanbe was too weak to enjoy real capacity to penetrate its far-flung regions, whatever their relationships to the central government on paper.

Just as in the Soviet era, non-ethnic categories were considered challenges to legitimate forms of identity and governance. With kinship-based clan networks, this was particularly visible in Kazakhstan and, to a lesser degree, Kyrgyzstan. In both cases, the state no longer sought to *eradicate* clan identities and behaviors, but it still viewed with suspicion any overt, public discussion or manifestation of clan. Given the Soviet and post-Soviet logic of ethnicity and progressive evolution from traditionalism to modernity, any admission of a legitimate, public role for kinship was considered tantamount to undermining the state. Such an ongoing effort to delegitimize clan connections generated destabilizing potential by continuing to drive their expressions underground and to construct their manifestations as counter-hegemonic.[27]

With Islamic identities, the post-Soviet trajectory was different. Islam as a *marker* of ethnic identity during the Soviet period was, as I described above, considered normal and virtuous, as long as it avoided claiming to transcend ethnicity and as long as it contained minimal religious content. As Khalid (2007) details, each of the Central Asian states viewed religion with suspicion and sought to keep close tabs on religious currents, typically via state-sponsored agencies charged with – to varying degrees – monitoring Islam. Even Tajikistan, in which religious political parties were not proscribed by the Constitution, witnessed a progressive marginalization of the Islamic Renaissance Party (IRP) and increasing surveillance of the activities of ordinary Muslims, once the Rahmon regime no longer required the IRP's support.[28] In this sense, Khalid's (2006) comparison of the Soviet transformative project to that of the Turkish republic under Ataturk is apt. In both post-Ataturk Turkey and in parts of post-Soviet Central Asia (especially Tajikistan and Uzbekistan), the state considered public displays of religiosity (such as women wearing the *hijab* (head scarf) to be inherently political acts.

Suppressing forms of religious practice they deemed illegitimate was never simple. For one, these states lacked the resources and capacity to monitor the changing religious currents that wended their way through Central Asian societies.[29] Second, they required outside financial assistance to shore up their own capacity and consolidate their rule. In all cases, this included some reliance on financing or "capacity building" from Muslim-world states. Once Saudi or Egyptian money contributed to mosque construction or *madrasa* creation, and once Turkish money brought Güllen-inspired education to the region, it was difficult to keep foreign influences out. Even Uzbekistan could not remain unchanged; in 2007 Karimov, a strong foe of overt religiosity, accepted the designation of the capital city of Tashkent as a "world capital of Islamic culture" by the International Islamic Educational, Scientific and Cultural Organization (ISESCO), symbolically cementing Uzbekistan's links with the rest of the Muslim world. Thus, while the region's leaders continued

[27] For an in-depth discussion of clans in Kazakhstan, see Schatz (2004). See also the cautions provided by Roberts (2006).

[28] The IRP was a part of the settlement that ended the civil war in 1997 and a part of the coalition government that ruled the country. Gradually, its position became marginal.

[29] See McGlinchey (2007) for a ground-level account of the limits to the Uzbekistani state's ability to monitor Islam.

to be suspicious of religious currents from outside the region, they also recognized that Islamic identities and practices could not be hermetically sealed from what was occurring elsewhere.[30]

For at least some in the region, Islam acted as a language of protest. The more that Uzbekistan's Karimov, for example, ensnared ordinary pious Muslims in his indiscriminating dragnet, the more their friends and family viewed Islam as a legitimate vehicle for protesting Karimov's hard-nosed authoritarianism. Similarly, public policy, such as the banning of *hijabs* in public education produced a steady flow of new members to the Tajik IRP. More generally in Tajikistan, the regional concentration of support for the IRP shifted over the years. While the IRP in the early 1990s had derived much of its support from the Gharm Valley and criticized the Leninabad elite, by 2007 it found the Sughd (former Leninabad) region, which was feeling increasingly marginalized from the central government in Dushanbe, to be fertile ground for recruitment.[31]

How long could these legacies be expected to last? In at least some senses, global Islamic currents offered the potential to become a counter-hegemonic project. As an idiom, global Islam carried at least three crucial discursive moments that articulated a distance from Soviet legacies. First, it was avowedly transethnic and transnational in orientation. It could therefore not be mistaken for a marker of ethnic identity. Second, it aspired to be public in ways that could not be accommodated by Soviet-style governance, which required the privatization of religious practice. Finally, and perhaps most importantly, it was in these senses a disavowal of the Soviet experience and a claim to a lost, pre-Soviet authenticity. It was the only language that protested the normative categories propagated by the Soviet state and the entirety of its transformative project. That this discourse was likely to remain marginal in the region underscores the hegemony of Soviet-era categories of practice.

Finally, elites' disembeddedness showed little sign of abating in the post-Soviet period. In Tajikistan, as mentioned previously, a spatial disconnect of the Leninabad elite contributed to the civil war in the early 1990s. In Kazakhstan, elites championed linguistic Kazakhization of state and society. This commitment was largely rhetorical, however, because ethnic Kazakhs in leadership positions were themselves overwhelmingly

---

[30] The use of the term "Wahhabi" to broad-brush any foreign religious current as alien, radical, and therefore potentially destabilizing is one example of elite suspicion of foreign versions of Islam.

[31] Author's fieldnotes, May 2006 and May 2007, Khujand, Tajikistan.

linguistically Russified and therefore operated at a fundamental remove from the ordinary Kazakhs they claimed to represent (Dave 1996). In Kyrgyzstan, the Akaev regime, which had partially liberalized in the early 1990s, was by the 2000s a study in increasing insularity, as it sought to protect itself from mounting popular criticism (Schatz, 2009). More generally, a region-wide preference among elites for authoritarian rule suggests an ongoing suspicion of popular input, representation, and participation. Like their counterparts across the USSR, they had been socialized to function at a distance from society and ruled accordingly. In Central Asia, this distance was greater than that, for example, in Russia, since it coincided with a cultural and linguistic divide.[32]

Soviet legacies crucially defined Central Asia through the 2000s. State and society could recombine and redefine elements of this past, but they were unable to make a fundamental break with it.

CONCLUSION: CAN PROACTIVE POLICYMAKING WORK?

In this chapter, I have argued that Soviet proactive policymaking, by privileging ethnicity, stigmatizing non-ethnicity, and creating disembedded elites, generated challenges to Soviet rule. Moreover, I have suggested that the legacies of these practices remained visible in the 1990s and 2000s. Leninist policies in Central Asia were miscalibrated in the simple sense that they did not accommodate Central Asian populations and failed to depoliticize questions of diversity in ways that Soviet planners would likely have preferred.

Proactive policies need not, of course, be Leninist. Can the value of pro-action be rescued from its historically Leninist manifestation? Is there something useful in proactive policymaking – that is, in developing policies that might precede rather than react to group mobilization?

Several perils to such policy making appear unavoidable. First, it seems clear that policymaking of any kind generates unintended consequences; proactive policymaking is unlikely to be an exception. In fact, to the degree that pro-action requires that elites accurately *anticipate* future developments more than reactive policy making does, it contains great potential to be miscalibrated and create surprising, and perhaps undesirable, outcomes. Second, proactive policy making is potentially elitist and anti-democratic. If a state generates policies that are *not* designed to meet the

---

[32] On Central Asians' perceptions of the Soviet project as "alien," see Edgar's (2006) discussion of the "women question."

demands articulated by already mobilized groups, then the state is making a claim to knowledge of the essential needs of its population. At best, this is paternalistic; the assumption that people need to be stirred from their "false consciousness" is not unique to Leninist contexts, and everywhere it is problematic. Finally, proactive policy making assumes that elites have both the ability and the will to create farsighted policies that anticipate future developments. Political elites rarely have these traits.

On the other hand, the Central Asian cases remind us that state action constructs groupness and structures mobilization. I would be surprised if the dynamic I have identified were not universal, even if it were usually more subtle than what occurred in the Soviet Union. In this sense, we should admit that state action willy-nilly has an impact on identity politics and proceed to think about policy making accordingly. In at least one case, policy makers have taken this to heart. The European Union has adopted principles of "gender mainstreaming" that require EU policymakers to assess the likely impact on men, women, and on relations between the two of any major policy initiative in advance of creating the policy, *whether or not such a policy explicitly deals with gender issues*. The basic principle is similar to that of an environmental impact statement; it is a "best guess" about the future. Anticipating the ancillary impact or "externalities" of a policy is, of course, hazardous business; nonetheless, it can potentially sensitize elites to the fact that state action matters – sometimes in powerfully transformative ways.

11

Conclusion

Jacques Bertrand and André Laliberté

The creation of unified polities in Asia remains a daunting challenge because of the numerous claims made by nations within state boundaries. None of the states in the case studies included in this book can claim unmitigated success in achieving harmonious reconciliation between the demands of sub-state nations seeking recognition and the goal of the central government to forge polities that transcend differences between these groups. In fact, there is much variance among states in Asia with respect to the willingness to recognize or accommodate sub-state nationalities. Contributors to this book have traced the roots of this variance, as well as the common traits that characterize many Asian states. Together, they suggest broad patterns and explanatory factors that are rooted in the domestic arena, based on which we suggest tentative generalizations based on the Asian experience.

Although we have found that historical trajectories and domestic political factors provide the strongest explanation of similarities and differences among Asian cases, the international environment has also to some extent conditioned the willingness and ability of Asian states to recognize their multinational status. As many of the contributors have shown, colonialism had a determining influence on the institutional choices made by post-colonial states. The Cold War in Asia, which quickly came to the fore with events such as the Korean War (1950–1953) and the Taiwan Strait Crises (1954–1955, 1958), exacerbated or dampened conflicts within multinational states, as the Bangladesh crisis of 1971 has demonstrated. Regional rivalries fed a climate of suspicion that made demands from sub-state nationalities appear subversive and dangerous. Finally, the more recent "war on terror" may have added a layer of complexity to the challenges raised by sub-state nationalist movements.

In this chapter, we first review the variety of approaches Asian states have taken toward the accommodation of sub-state national groups. Second, we discuss some aspects of the international context that may help to explain the resilience of sub-state nationalist movements and the resistance of states to accept the institutionalization of multinational states. In particular, we address the impact of the international context on the (mis-)management of multinationality in Asia, specifically the enduring relevance of the colonial legacy, the Cold War, regional conflicts, and the "war on terror." Although we give some weight to these factors, we generally find that their explanatory reach is very limited. Third, we provide tentative generalizations on domestic conditions that have led to the accommodation of sub-state nationalities and those that have perpetuated conflict.

A POOR RECORD OF ACCOMMODATION

A broad sweep of Asian cases shows that the accommodation of sub-state national groups has been rare and has not always reduced conflict. Where accommodation has been absent, conflicts have persisted or been reduced to simmering cauldrons under the weight of repressive regimes. Where accommodation has been granted, it has often been undermined. Several Asian states have given recognition to sub-state nations and/or accommodated their demands, but more often these are strategic attempts to defuse conflicts rather than sincere attempts to eliminate them. As a result, these concessions have often been devoid of substance or hijacked by contradictory measures.

Refusal to grant concessions can have disastrous consequences. As Ganguly demonstrates in his discussion of Pakistan, the refusal to respond to Bengali demands set in motion a process that led to conflict and, ultimately, to the independence of Bangladesh in 1971 as the only acceptable alternative. The Sri Lankan state's refusal to accommodate Tamils and its persistent attempts to usurp negotiations by insisting on procedures that Tamils rejected created a cycle of protracted conflicts. Intransigence, combined with strong repression, has yielded military successes recently but promises little resolution of the conflict. China's refusal to contemplate the possibility of a sovereign Taiwan fed for decades a military face-off that, thanks to the latter's strategic alliance with the United States, came repeatedly close to triggering a major confrontation.

Not all Asian states have refused to grant any form of accommodation. But they have done so often unevenly. The Burmese state, for instance, has experimented with extending some forms of autonomy. In its recent constitutional proposals, it gives some special administrative rights to some groups but not to others, particularly sub-state national groups. India, as Bhargava discusses, has devised permanent territorial reorganization in response to demands of linguistic groups like the Marathis and the Telugus but has steadfastly refused the same for claims based on different ascriptive criteria, such as religion in the case of the Sikhs in the Punjab and culture in the case of the Naga people of the Northeast. The Indonesian government has granted very substantive autonomy to Aceh but much less to Papua.

In some instance, states have given autonomy but it has often turned out to be meaningless. In its regime of autonomy, China gives constitutional recognition to Tibet as a minority nationality, as well as to fifty-four other such nationalities, but, as Tuttle shows, this has failed to provide Tibetans with a sense of meaningful protection for their culture. The territory of Azad Kashmir ("Free Kashmir" for Pakistanis or "Pakistan-Occupied Kashmir" for Indians), Ganguly notes, has received considerable autonomy on paper but it remains firmly in control of the central government in Pakistan.

The cases of Indonesia and the Philippines demonstrate that the problem is also present in new democracies. Repeated promises of autonomy without proper implementation, argues Bertrand, created deep problems of commitment that fueled nationalist resistance in Aceh, Papua, and Mindanao. Attempts were also made to decentralize to units across the country in order to diminish the importance of granting autonomy to the Acehnese or Papuans. In Papua, moreover, the government divided the region into two provinces as it was granting special autonomy. Although autonomy has recently been extended much more credibly to Aceh in recent years, this occurs against the backdrop of many uses of autonomy as defusing mechanisms without much substance and political commitment.

Despite a general pattern of resistance to accommodation, some variance exists. We note that authoritarian regimes have sometimes provided symbolic recognition without substance, but democracies have also done so. Strong resistance to accommodation of sub-state nationalities has occurred in several countries, but a pattern of unequal accommodation appears to be also frequent. In order to explain this variance, we have looked at historical roots of state and nation-building, as well as domestic political factors. Such processes, however, have occurred against the backdrop of an international context that has had some influence as well.

THE WEAK EFFECTS OF THE INTERNATIONAL SYSTEM

Over the last 200 years, states became ever more powerful and present across the territories under their control. In the introduction, we discussed the extent to which the nation-state system and its normative underpinnings dramatically reconfigured the international system in the nineteenth and twentieth centuries. In Asia, as elsewhere, nationalism provided the ideological tool to further strengthen state identities as belonging to particular groups, however defined. These changes, we noted, swept away former empires while many sections of previously ungoverned territories fell under the purview of centralizing state structures. Notions of unified states and strong single nations clashed dramatically with the existing landscapes of complex group identities.

While these transformations continued to affect and even shape relations between sub-state nationalities and central governments, they did not occur in a void. Major wars and changes at the international level continued to have repercussions on the way states managed sub-state nationalist challenges and the reality of their multinational status. In the following sections, we look at four dimensions of the international context that have influenced relations between central governments and sub-state national groups: the legacy of colonialism, the Cold War, regional conflicts, and the "war on terror."

Colonial Rule

Colonialism had significant, although limited, impact on current configurations of sub-state national groups and the associated conflicts in Asia. Through the establishment of state boundaries, new state structures, mapping, group categorizations, and even museums, colonial states contributed to constructing or solidifying ethnic identities, laying the basis in some places of future nationalist claims (Anderson 1991; Reid 2009). Although it was not a primary focus of this book, some of the chapters made reference to lasting impacts of the colonial experience on the approaches adopted by post-colonial states toward sub-state nationalist groups. Nevertheless, the influence of colonialism has limited reach, and its effects are sometimes ambiguous. Post-colonial trends and state structures, as well as subsequent state policies, have mediated colonial effects and rendered them much less significant than was perhaps expected.

Bhargava notes that, although "the federal idea had some resonance in non-modern traditions, the current federal arrangement in India has its origins in colonial modernity." The centralization of power in the hands of British colonial authorities shaped the political structure of independent India in the initial period of its formation (Bhargava, Chapter 3: pp. 56–67). But beyond this colonial legacy, the Indian Congress recognized that the struggle for independence had to be waged along federalist lines, in ways that were radically different from the centralizing tendency of British rule.

For Ganguly, the colonial government's creation of separate electorates under the 1909 Minto-Morley Reforms was a precursor to the development of a primordial form of pan-Islamic South Asian nationalism, which later became hostile to demands for recognition by sub-state nationalist groups, such as the Bengalis, Sindhis, and Baluchis, within Pakistan (Ganguly, Chapter 4: pp. 86–87; 92). Yet, Ganguly also notes, the colonial notions of "martial races," which fed on the contempt of West Pakistan's elites vis-à-vis their compatriots in Bengal, shows that colonialism's influence could cut both ways: instigating unity against colonial rulers, but also sustaining divisions.

The ambiguous effects of colonialism were obvious in Sri Lanka as well. As Choudhry notes, the divide-and-rule policy of British rulers in colonial Ceylon gave the Tamil minority disproportionate influence, and triggered, as a response, the rise in Sinhala majority nationalism. But the effects of colonial rule were far from one-sided. A few years before independence, in a reversal of previous policies, colonial rulers refused to yield to demands from Tamil politicians who hoped for post-colonial institutions entrenching their privileged position (Choudhry, Chapter 5: p. 107).

Colonialism, in the case of Burma, had limited consequences, and some of the intractable problems faced by the current government have little to do with its effects. Thawnghmung recalls that the Karens were constructed out of twenty different linguistic groups under British colonial rule. But she also points out that the divisions between ethnic Burmans and the other groups, such as the Shan, Kachin, and Kayah, predated colonial rule. The overall structure of ethnic-group relations and future sub-state nationalist movements, therefore, has only tenuous and partial roots in colonial practices (Thawnghmung, Chapter 6: pp. 138–140).

Reid notes that, although there were complex state formations in Java and Bali before colonial rule, the bureaucratic forms of the modern state were imposed in the Malay archipelagoes by British and Dutch colonial rulers. Yet, in his discussion of Acehnese historical memories of pre-colonial sultanate, he suggests that the pre-colonial experience may matter as much as colonial rule itself in helping us understand the resilience of some sub-state nationalist movements (Reid, Chapter 2: p. 47).

In discussing Indonesia and the Philippines, Bertrand also singles out the rather unique experience of these states in Asia in that they had no legacy of a pre-colonial unified statehood, in contrast to India and China. He notes that the Catholicism imposed by Spanish colonial rulers served, in part, as a glue for the consolidation of the Filipino national identity. But if Spanish colonialism contributed indirectly to the emergence of a national consciousness, the case of the Moros, whose adherence to Islam made them feel excluded and alienated in the Philippines, shows that colonialism can also sow the seeds of division (Bertrand, Chapter 7: pp. 168–170).

All the states we have discussed so far have experienced colonialism directly. China is the notable exception because the country did not experience colonialism across all its territory. Direct colonial rule was limited to Taiwan, ceded to Japan. Laliberté shows that this different historical experience of very limited colonial rule did not lead Chinese leaders to adopt a mindset that departs significantly from that of other Asian leaders of previously colonized countries. The leadership of the People's Republic of China, he notes, invokes the collective memory of colonial powers' influence in treaty ports and peripheral territories from the late imperial to the Republican era to justify its refusal to accept Taiwanese sovereignty (Laliberté, Chapter 8: pp. 207–208).

In fact, and leaving aside the contentious argument that China under the Qing Dynasty was itself a colony, China is seen by some as a colonial power itself. Hence, Tuttle underlines that this is the case for Tibetans, who resent Beijing's control of their territory. Moreover, those among them who aspire for greater autonomy, if not outright independence, place their struggle within the framework of an anti-colonial discourse (Tuttle, Chapter 9: p. 223). In this last case, the legacy of colonialism's influence on the mindset of political leaders is not a matter of interpreting history but a highly contentious political matter.

Although Schatz did not make reference to colonialism to explain the emergence of sub-state nationalism in the former Central Asian Soviet Republics, he looks at these states as post-colonial entities. His argument, however, is different from that of the other chapters, which have looked at sub-state nationalism as a bottom-up movement. Not unlike some of the legacies of colonialism embedded in administrative structures, he suggests that we need to understand the emergence of sub-state national groups as resulting, in part, from the very policies of these states and argues that new identities were invented by leaders who wanted to prevent the mobilization from below of populations that could otherwise have contested their regimes (Chapter 10).

In sum, the influence of colonialism was relevant because the playing field was certainly not equal at the time states gained their independence. Obviously, not all states were colonized. But beyond that obvious contrast, the effect of different experiences on the policies of Asian states is not clear. Similarities in the colonial experience have not prevented the adoption of radically different approaches to the accommodation or repression of sub-state nationalism. Moreover, the shared experience of domination by the same colonial power could not explain post-colonial outcomes either. Although India, Pakistan, Sri Lanka, and Malaysia were all colonized by the British, they have adopted very different approaches to the multinationality of their respective polities.

Colonialism can help to explain why sub-state national groups were constructed and, to some extent, why they mobilized against other constructions of the nation (or other groups) in the post-colonial period. It does not explain, however, the variance in the post-colonial state's response to sub-state national groups. The resistance to sub-state nationalist movements, we have suggested in the introduction to the volume, was very strong in the immediate post-colonial period and marked by insecurity over state boundaries and the attractiveness to new leaders of the idea of unitary states. Feeding these insecurities, arguably, were two important factors: the Cold War, which affected the whole region, and regional rivalries. After the Cold War, it is unclear whether the "war on terror" since 2001 has had much of an impact on the accommodation of sub-state nationalist groups.

The Cold War, Regional Rivalries, and the War on Terror

The Cold War and regional rivalries are two important dimensions that have been influencing the Asian context for several decades. Across various regions of the developing world, the Cold War influenced sub-state national movements in three different ways. First, it created strong incentives for the superpowers to maintain the existing boundaries within the satellite states and thus to reinforce their already strong preference for unitary states and the resistance to demands from sub-state nationalist groups. Second, the American containment policy and the Soviet expansionist revolutionary aims under Stalin and Brezhnev meant that sub-state nationalist movements could be seen as "communist" by the United States. Sometimes sub-state nationalist movements used communist rhetoric to obtain funding for their cause, thereby reinforcing that impression. In some other cases, groups believed they could obtain American support to help their cause by casting their struggle as anti-communist. Third, some sub-state nationalist movements became embroiled in proxy wars between the Soviets and the Americans. Examples of these Cold War dynamics abound in cases across Latin America and Sub-Saharan Africa, but they are much less present in Asia.

The expansion of communism in China and Southeast Asia had some consequences in the region. For instance, as Thawnghmung mentions, the 1962 coup by the Burmese army was a reaction to the growth of insurgencies from sub-state nationalist groups as well as the growing communist movement. With growing communist insurgencies in Vietnam and other parts of the region, the Burmese army was uneasy about all insurgencies threatening national unity. Some ethnic leaders had joined the Communist Party of Burma, which was supported by China. Conversely, the Thai state used ethnic insurgents along the border as a buffer in its own struggle to contain the spread of communism to Thailand (Thawnghmung, Chapter 6: pp. 145–146). Despite relationships to communist movements, however, sub-state nationalist movements and government responses to them were motivated by other factors.

Most cases of autonomous movements in Asia, in fact, were not connected with superpower rivalry. The autonomous movements in Northeast India, Punjab, Baluchistan, Aceh, Mindanao, and the Cordillera in the Philippines, as the contributors to this book have discussed, were all sui generis and generally did not receive support from either superpower. One could mention the cases of Bangladesh and Taiwan, which owe their current political status to the Cold War. But not only are these cases exceptional, the complex historical circumstances that led to the independence of Bangladesh and the virtual sovereignty of Taiwan had little to do with the superpowers' rivalry at the beginning. In the case of Bangladesh, it became entangled in the Cold War almost by accident while, in the case of Taiwan, it was a result of the Chinese Civil War that preceded the onset of the Cold War.

Bangladesh's secession from Pakistan was made possible because of the realignment of Great Powers that was underway during the Cold War, when the United States was about to achieve its historic rapprochement with the People's Republic of China at the expense of the Soviet Union. India supported Bangladesh's independence because it felt threatened by a flow of refugees, and it saw an opportunity to weaken strategically Pakistan, which presented a challenge to India's defense. Because of

Chinese and American support to the cause of Pakistan, the government of Indira Gandhi sought, and obtained, strategic support from the Soviet Union (Baxter 1998, pp.145–6). Before the break up of the Soviet Union, however, Bangladesh stands out as an exception: it was the only example of a post-colonial state that successfully emerged from another post-colonial state.

Taiwan, or the ROC, as it is known officially, also represents an exception. It was an established state in 1912, and after the end of the Chinese Civil War, its government relocated to Taipei. Its resilience was first made possible because of the United States' decision in 1950 to establish a security perimeter to contain the expansion of communism in Asia (Clough 1999, p. 17). This influence of the Cold War on Taiwan's de facto sovereignty, however, is rather limited. After the Nixon administration decided in 1971 to normalize relations with China to counterbalance the Soviet Union, the survival of Taiwan as an entity depended on a different set of conditions. No longer did Cold War politics determine policy toward Taiwan but it was the commitment to maintain an American presence in the Western Pacific to provide a balance of power in East Asia that did. At the end of the Cold War, and as relations between China and the United States changed, these commitments were becoming increasingly difficult to enforce (Waldron 1997).

In sum, the Cold War had only a limited impact on the emergence and resilience of sub-state nationalist movements, and can only explain part of the variance in states' responses to these movements. The end of the superpower rivalry has not affected the emergence of recent claims, nor attempts at accommodation. It might explain in part the decrease in the ability to arm resistance movements, but it does not take away the issues, as all the cases discussed in this book remain pressing problems. The end of the Cold War has not led to the abandonment of sub-state nationalist claims, and it has not led to a softening of the governments that have shown greater resistance to them.

Regional rivalries at times have had modest influences on policies toward sub-state national groups. The two largest powers of the region, China and India, have boundaries between them in the Himalayas that remain undemarcated and contested. Populations with numerous grievances against their respective governments are scattered along this joint border. They include Tibetans on the Chinese side and populations in the Indian Northeast and in Kashmir on the other. Although China and Japan do not have a major territorial dispute, the rivalry between the two states for hegemony in Northeast Asia ensures that the status of Taiwan is going to remain a bone of contention. The rivalry between India and Pakistan, poisoned for decades by the dispute over Kashmir, is the third regional dispute with a potential effect on autonomist movements. Yet, in all three cases of enduring rivalries, regional powers have sought to avoid instigating separatist movements in their opponents' territories, for the same reasons mentioned previously with respect to the rivalry between superpowers.

China and India have avoided interfering in issues regarding autonomist or sub-state nationalist groups, despite their border disputes (Sidhu & Yuan 2003). While India has welcomed the Tibetan government in exile in Dharamsala, it has consistently avoided encouraging Tibetan independence, even though it has never stopped pressing its demand to reclaim the territory of Aksai Qin. Conversely, even though China has yet to give up on its claim to the territory of Arunachal Pradesh, there is no evidence that it has encouraged the autonomist rebel movements in neighboring Nagaland and Mizoram. Although each government accuses the other of supporting autonomous movements, neither provides such support for fear of a reciprocal attempt by their adversary.

The future status of Taiwan in the relationship between China and Japan represents an equally complex quandary. Although statements from the Chinese government often blame Japan for covertly supporting Taiwanese independence, most Japanese politicians understand that the national interest militates against such an approach, with the exception of a few right-wing extremists. The Japanese national interest requires access to Chinese markets, and it is clear that supporting Taiwanese independence would have a devastating effect on the already fragile Japanese economy. Conversely, it is clear that despite China's often-repeated resolve to prevent Taiwanese independence, the prospect of a war with Japan over Taiwan, which would inevitably involve the United States, does not appeal to Chinese leaders (Kim 1997, p. 319).

Finally, even the bitter rivalry between India and Pakistan, which has often escalated into actual armed conflicts with considerable loss of life, cannot be held responsible for most of the sub-state nationalist movements' mobilization in both states. With Kashmir arguably standing as an exception, most sub-state nationalist disputes with the Indian central government stem from domestic factors, as is demonstrated in this book by Rajeev Bhargava. The same is true of similar groups in Pakistan, as argued by Sumit Ganguly. If regional rivalries did not instigate autonomist movements, the converse is also true.

Since 2001, the "war on terror" represents a new type of global conflict that could have an impact on the growth of sub-state nationalist movements or on state policies toward them. Pakistan, Indonesia, the Philippines, and Sri Lanka all have groups that were suspected of links to global terrorist networks. Pakistan is perhaps best known for its active Al-Qaeda militants along the Afghan border. Ganguly shows, however, that sub-state nationalist movements long predated the advent of Al-Qaeda and the establishment of the Taliban in neighboring Afghanistan. Pakistan's North-West Frontier Province, which received a lot of attention from the United States after September 11, had a troubled relation with the Pakistani government decades before the war on terror. Obviously, the Pakistani state has received additional aid to suppress these movements, which are accused of harboring terrorist networks.

In Sri Lanka, the identification of the Tamil Tigers as a terrorist organization did have some impact on their strength. After adding them to the list of terrorist organizations, several countries cracked down on networks of financial support the group received from Tamil communities abroad. This contributed to the weakening of the Tamil Tigers and to giving the Sri Lankan government the upper-hand against them. Yet, the state's policies and approach toward the Tamils remained unchanged and largely predated September 11.

In most other cases, the link and impact of terrorist activity is tenuous at best. In Southeast Asia, in spite of alarmist claims by some terrorism experts, the link between the Moro Islamic Liberation Front (MILF) and Jemaah Islamiyah has never been clearly established, and there has been no evidence of significant linkages between the groups. Nevertheless, the government of Gloria Macapagal-Arroyo did use the aftermath of September 11 to invite American military specialists to train Philippine troops, and benefited from increased military aid against the Abu Sayaff group, considered a terrorist group for its highly publicized bombings and kidnappings. These developments also had consequences on operations against MILF camps. In recent years, however, these effects have faded away. There was no mention of linkages between the MILF and Jemaah Islamiyah, and negotiations have continued for a peaceful settlement to the conflict. The recent failures of these negotiations had no linkages to the war on terror, nor did the reversals of concessions made on ancestral domains.

Similarly, in Indonesia, the Free Aceh Movement distanced itself very quickly from international terrorist networks. It refused attempts by

Jemaah Islamiyah leaders to create linkages with GAM. It distanced itself from extremist Islamic groups, and always positioned itself as a secular nationalist organization. As a result, the Indonesian government never accused GAM of terrorist linkages, and the war on terror had no consequences for the conflict.

Colonialism, the Cold War, regional rivalries, and the "war on terror" have framed the international context within which nation-states have managed sub-state nationalist challenges. Colonial rule left a legacy that set the path for independent states to emphasize state and nation-building at the expense of institutionalizing multinational alternatives. The Cold War ensured more rigid state boundaries and had some impact in a few cases where superpower alliances could be exploited. Regional rivalries, at times, either boosted or reduced sub-state nationalist claims in a few instances when these claims became intertwined with regional competition. Yet, the impact of these international factors was limited in the end. While colonial rule left significant legacies in Indonesia and the Philippines, it had far fewer effects in countries such as China that were not fully colonized. After almost a half century since the end of colonial rule, most states have now entered what Jean-Luc Racine has called the "post-postcolonial era," and so the longer the time period since colonialism, the less one can effectively explain any outcome by referring back to such legacies (2006, p. 46). The Cold War and regional rivalries, for the most part, had limited impact in Asia because states were reluctant to exacerbate tensions with their neighbors or invite interference from superpowers.

The international context has affected the mobilization of sub-state national groups, as well as the responses by states. Yet the roots of the latter are much deeper. The international context has provided constraints on the elites of states and sub-state national groups but does not explain their mindsets. It does not shed light on the reasons behind the elites' inability to accommodate demands from sub-state nationalist groups in some cases, or their inflexibility in others. Explaining the variance in these attitudes was the explanatory task taken up by our chapters. They led us to believe that endogenous factors may provide better explanations for the reluctance of many Asian governments to accept the plurality of nations within their state, as the following section demonstrates.

STATE STRUCTURE AND HISTORICAL TRAJECTORIES

The chapters in this book confirm that Asian states are generally resistant to accommodating sub-state national groups, but also that there is still a significant variance in outcome, which requires explanation. We have identified two categories of factors that explain differences between Asian states' responses. We have grouped them according to state structure and regime type, and then to historical trajectories.

State Structure and Regime Type: Important but Insufficient

Variance in state structures and regime type accounts to some extent for greater (or less) accommodation, but they are insufficient. Scholars have argued that federal states in democratic settings best reflect multinational societies (Stepan 1999). Yet, federalism has only partially accommodated sub-state national groups in some Asian cases.

There are only four federal states in Asia,[1] and in the two that qualify as multinational, their responses to demands of national groups do not differ significantly from those of unitary states such as Indonesia and the Philippines. This view receives further support if we accept the claim made by specialists on relations between central and local governments in China that the People's Republic is a de facto federation (Zheng 2007). If that is so, it would appear that federations are as intolerant of the demands for genuine autonomy as unitary states, such as Myanmar.[2] In other words, the difference in state structure did not produce different approaches to the recognition of sub-state national groups.

One consequence of federalism, however, can be inferred from the breakup of the Soviet Union. The quasi-automatic accession to independence from the Union of the former Soviet Socialist Republics was greatly facilitated by the existence of mutually recognized boundaries, constitutions, and state apparatuses. Fictitious and merely symbolic as long as the central authority of the Union was strong, these institutions were "ready-made" for the empowerment of local elites when power collapsed at the center, leaving it unable to assert and enforce its authority. This historical example is likely to serve as a warning for the leaders of unitary regimes

---

1 The Indian Union, the Islamic Republic of Pakistan, and Malaysia have been federations since their independence; the Democratic Federal Republic of Nepal was established only in 2008. The ephemeral United States of Indonesia (1949–1950) does not count as a federation because it was a creation of the Dutch colonial power. It can be argued that Indonesia has moved toward federalism since decentralizing powers to its provinces in 2004 and, asymmetrically, to Papua and Aceh in 2002 and 2006, but this is a recent development and, furthermore, one that has not been entirely successful at accommodating sub-state nations (see Chapter 7).

2 The Union of Burma claimed to be a federation until 1962, but since Ne Win took power in 1962, it has remained so only in name.

that may consider adopting a federal form of government. From their perspective, the experience of the Soviet Union shows how easily even merely symbolic recognition of the multinational character of the state can lead to secessionist mobilization. Yet, where significant autonomy is provided to federal units, the outcome is more often stabilizing rather than divisive.

Democracies should generally be more accommodative of sub-state national groups than authoritarian states but, in Asia, regime type is a weak predictor of such accommodation. A specific problem of state legitimacy arises from the mobilization of different groups asking for recognition as distinctive nations. These groups challenge the basic premise upon which the state is formed, particularly where it is upheld as the representative of a single nation. Although authoritarian rulers can clearly repress attempts to redefine the basis of the state to allow for the representation of multiple nations, it does not necessarily follow that democratic regimes will be more willing to concede on this point. Linz and Stepan (1996) have argued that many recent democracies face a particular problem of consolidation when faced with prior issues of "stateness," by which the very existence of the state and its boundaries are contested. From the democratic state's perspective, nationalist mobilization by sub-state national groups threatens the "national" interest, which is defined by the majority which controls the state itself by virtue of its demographic weight, military might or political mobilization. As a consequence, obfuscation, manipulation, or even repression can be used in democracies to defuse mobilization, at least as much as accommodation.

India, the developing world's largest and most long-lasting democracy, offers two trends (Bhargava, Chapter 3). Generally, it has followed the expected democratic path by responding to early contestations of an overly centralized Indian state and unified Indian nation by creating linguistic federal units and accommodating both nascent and mobilized national groups within that context. However, traumatized by the Partition of 1947 that resulted from the "two nations" theory, it has refused consistently to recognize nations defined by the criteria of religion, such as Khalistan or Kashmir. Over the years, this refusal to grant accommodation has extended to other types of nationalist demands. Further mobilization, as Bhargava shows in the case of Nagaland, has met with repression rather than accommodation.

Authoritarian states in Burma since 1962, the People's Republic of China since 1949, the Philippines under Marcos, Indonesia under Suharto, and Pakistan under the military juntas of Yahya Khan, Mohammed Zia ul-Haq, and Pervez Musharaff have all repressed militarily sub-state nationalist mobilization. Even when these groups are constitutionally recognized under an ambiguous category of "national minorities," the preservation of their culture is difficult. Thawnghmung has shown that military leaders basically denied any actual realization of minority culture in Burma. Tuttle has demonstrated that accommodation has failed to translate into substantial autonomy for Tibetans, despite state promises to the contrary. Moreover, Laliberté has suggested that China categorically refuses to accept the idea of a Taiwanese nation, even though there exists a virtual sovereign Taiwanese state to substantiate that claim. Schatz indicates that in the extreme case of the former Soviet Union, the recognition was not inconsequential; the territorial homeland of national minorities became the basis for the formation of new states in Central Asia.

With the exception of India, and within the limits that we have indicated above, democratic states in Asia have not been strongly inclined to accommodate sub-state national groups. Bertrand shows that autonomy was extended in the Philippines at very early stages after the democratic opening, but it was done unilaterally and was very limited in scope. A subsequent agreement with one faction of the Moros led to a peace agreement and a new framework for a more extended autonomy, but it was never adequately implemented. At the same time, renewed mobilization under the MILF led to both repressive responses and to some attempts at negotiations without reaching a settlement. Indonesia' new democracy extended autonomy to some nations within the state, but its implementation has been mixed. Whereas Aceh appears to have obtained a strong autonomy framework, Papuans have contested the version of autonomy the central government eventually adopted. Choudhry has argued that, while Sri Lanka has also followed a democratic path for many years, it is precisely the democratic process and a flawed constitution that gave strong powers to the majority that led to the exclusion of the Tamils and to the severity of the subsequent conflict. Hiding behind constitutional process in this case has magnified the problem because the process denies the ability to accommodate Tamil grievances.

In sum, the nature of the political system did not appear to make a significant difference. If we take Myanmar/Burma as a historical model of a federal state and compare it to China, the epitome of a unitary state, it is clear that federal states have not been more tolerant of diversity than unitary states. The difference in state structure did not produce different approaches to the recognition of sub-state national groups. Even in India there were limits to the state's ability to imagine "deeply asymmetrical" forms of federalism (Bhargava, Chapter 3).

Whether a state has adopted democratic or authoritarian institutions does not appear to be a determining factor either. India had democratic institutions for decades, but its preference for a centralized form of government and refusal to accept sub-state nationalism was at least as pronounced as that of Pakistan, which had failed to establish a robust democracy. Moreover, China, which has maintained an authoritarian regime, has proclaimed theoretically, if not substantively, that it is a multinational state. Clearly, the nature of political regimes may represent a necessary condition to explain the flexibility or lack thereof of governments in accepting to accommodate sub-state nationalist movements, but it does not explain it sufficiently. Variance in the record of democracies points to the necessity for analysis beyond regime type to explain resistance to accommodation.

Historical Trajectories of State and Nation Formation

Nationalist mobilization, late-colonial state formation, and the path to independence have crystallized certain conceptions of the nation and the modern state that have been anathema to subsequent accommodation of nations within states. These conceptions of the nation, in contrast to those of old European states such as Spain, Portugal, France, and those of the British Isles and Scandinavia, which evolved through centuries of state building, were often nurtured in a very short time frame within colonial states that established their control in areas where, often, more than one state had evolved concurrently over the course of history. In other words, in post-colonial states like India, Indonesia, Pakistan, and Burma, the leaders of the new states faced the challenge of building imagined communities out of populations that identified with different histories, making the constitution of a single, shared memory, all the more difficult.

Paths to Independence: Revolution, Gradualism, Secession. One proposition lies in the manner in which states obtain independence and the degree to which a strong nationalist movement underpinned the initial state formation. Reid, for instance, argues that revolution enabled the nationalist movement in Indonesia to create strong bonds that transcended boundaries across diverse ethnic groups and religious communities, thereby fostering the consciousness of an "Indonesian" nation in the archipelago. Although Indonesian nationalism did create a strong bond among diverse peoples through this revolutionary process, it is precisely this strong concept of an Indonesian nation that would subsequently make some groups develop their own separate national consciousness and mobilize against the homogenizing effects of the post-colonial state. The case of China also demonstrates that the revolutionary path can work both ways. It did transcend regionalist and linguistic divisions among the Han majority that might have otherwise evolved into sub-state nationalist claims, a possibility that the Chinese leadership still fears, argues Laliberté, but this path has also increased the sense of alienation felt by non-Chinese people, as Tuttle demonstrates in his chapter on Tibet.

The Indian independence movement, which has adopted a gradualist approach, did show more flexibility than the Chinese and Indonesian revolutionary movements in the accommodation of diverse sub-state nationalist movements. Yet, as Bhargava reminds us, it is nevertheless important to note that to this day, the Indian central government refuses to consider these movements as being more than regional, linguistic, ethnic, or communal movements, rather than national. Reid presents Malaysia as a contrast to this case. He shows that as the gradualist approach toward independence under British colonial rule allowed for greater asymmetry to be crafted, yet at the same time it seemed to prevent the formation of a "Malaysian" identity. Instead, Malay nationalism led to the creation of a state that serves primarily the interests of the Malays. Bertrand shows that the Philippines had a less revolutionary path than Indonesia and that although the Filipino nationalist movement was weaker, it nevertheless took an exclusivist form.

Secession has been another path that created some significant problems on abilities to build a nation coincidental with the new state. As Ganguly argues, Pakistan has searched for an articulation of shared experience or attributes around which to forge a common nation. Because of its origins in turmoil and religious division, however, its ability to do so has been seriously restrained, and as a result, the state has been unable to find a formula to address diversity. The Central Asian states that have their origins in secession from the Soviet Union face a similar constraint, explains Schatz. Having been constructed out of Soviet categories of national minorities and administrative homelands, he argues, these states lacked any shared experience or set of traits around which nations could be built. As a result, they created elites who had a shared

Soviet experience but few connections to societies, thereby stimulating after secession several mobilization responses in ethnic and clan terms.

The trajectories leading to most Asian states' independence have had tremendous consequences for their conception of national unity. All these states have in common a collective memory of colonial powers that played regional actors against each other to establish their hegemony, and then enforced a strategy of divide-and-rule to prevent the formation of anti-colonial coalitions and maintain their domination. Although China was not colonized, it also suffered from political divisions and became vulnerable to Japanese invasion as a result. These divisions unquestionably reinforced the preference of Asian leaders for strong unitary states. However, these collective memories do not explain the variety of responses to demands for recognition from sub-state nationalist groups that Asian states have adopted.

Basis of the Nation: Culture, Civic Ties, Multiple Coexistence. Whether through revolutionary process, gradualism, or secession, leaders of newly independent states crafted political projects that included attempts to build nations from above. Through what Anderson has called "official nationalism," these leaders tapped into state resources to create bonds between sometimes very diverse groups (Anderson 1991). When they followed strong bottom-up nationalist movements, such as in Indonesia or China, these nation-building efforts often reinforced already existing conceptions of the nation that had been socialized to some extent among a broader population. In other cases, such official nationalist projects were completely designed by state leaders, who were often highly concerned about potential disintegration. Pakistan and the Central Asian states are perhaps most strongly imbued with the absence of such movements from below, leaving state leaders grasping for appropriate formulas to manage diversity.

In cases where a cultural core has been defined at the center, there are often strong reactions from sub-state nationalist groups who define themselves outside of the cultural parameters. The degree to which such concepts of the nation at the state level contain cultural attributes varies considerably. Although it might be useful to classify states on a continuum from more civic to more ethnic forms of nation, each ideal type actually contains more subtle forms of exclusion that can also lead to fairly severe reactions from sub-state national groups.

Some forms of official nationalism have sometimes used religion or language, for example, as cultural "glue." The cases of Pakistan and

Sri Lanka also demonstrate the degree to which nation-building that is defined by religion can serve as the basis for conceptions of nationhood that have proved especially intolerant of national diversity. Despite its secular origins, the Filipino nation could not easily dissociate itself from its Christian majority, thereby making accommodation of the Moro (Muslim) nation particularly difficult. Language as a marker of the nation has sometimes created exclusivist tendencies, although at other times it has been more successful at creating a cultural attribute to which diverse groups could adhere. Indonesia's choice of a particular Malaysian dialect as the official Indonesian language, for example, contributed to creating strong bonds to the Indonesian nation. India recognized early on the importance of accommodating its linguistic diversity rather than choosing a single language upon which to build its nation. By reorganizing the state around a linguistically based federalism, it arguably preempted the emergence of aggrieved minorities that could have sought separate nationhood. China, on the other hand, managed to deny its diversity by successfully imposing a homogeneous ethnic identity within the Han majority.

Each strategy, however, has limits. India, as Bhargava demonstrates, has difficulty accepting identity markers other than language as the basis of claims for nationhood. This is highly problematic, he documents, because many important identities are not defined by language and are thus deprived of recognition. Ganguly shows that Jinnah's decision to adopt Urdu as the national language of Pakistan, which was meant to show that the new state would not be controlled by the powerful Punjabi-speaking majority, in the end alienated Bengalis of east Pakistan, thereby laying the basis of a Bengali nationalist movement and the eventual breakup of Pakistan. In China, Communist revolution further solidified a conception of a single nation around a cultural core. Laliberté also demonstrates that even when a state successfully imposes cultural homogeneity via the adoption of a single language such as Mandarin, this remains insufficient to prevent the emergence of sub-state nationalism within one cultural group. Hence, defining an ethnically homogeneous Han nation within the People's Republic of China has not prevented a resilient sense of national identity from emerging in Taiwan that, albeit culturally Chinese and Mandarin-speaking,[3] refuses forced integration within the Chinese nation as defined by the Communist Party.

---

[3] A majority of the population in Taiwan speaks Fukienese (Minnanhua), but the official language is Mandarin.

Chinese communists reinforced the former nationalist claims that the Han constitute a core nation, with national minorities being recognized in a hierarchical relationship to this core. In his examination of the Tibetans' relations with the Chinese central government, Tuttle reminds us that the ability of the Chinese to construct a Han identity could not go so far as to include a large number of groups that were previously seen as "barbarian," and non-Han. While the Chinese state allowed some form of symbolic accommodation that included the recognition of national minorities, it also preserved a sense of hierarchy between Han and non-Han and its own strong inclinations to deny national minorities any equality of status or to refuse to make significant political concessions. The Indonesian government, as Bertrand argues, developed other markers of the Indonesian nation that contributed to the exclusion of Papuans and Acehnese. Although it was cast in fairly civic terms, basing the nation on the Indonesian language and shared history contributed to the state's reinforcement of particular cultural institutions, educational curriculum, the national ideology of *Pancasila* and practices that reinforced a "national" culture, and alienated Papuans and Acehnese.

We have seen that the definition of a state's identity on the basis of the majority's culture has generated sentiments of alienation from people who do not belong to that majority. Yet, very few Asian states have adopted this approach. Only Sri Lanka fits that ideal type entirely, and as expected, the adoption of a Sinhalese and Buddhist identity has alienated the Hindu Tamil-speaking minority.

The populations within each Asian state are too diverse to allow for a form of national identity based on culture without generating a sense of exclusion for large minorities. Most states have accordingly adopted models of national identity that emphasized civic ties forged through the experience of revolution and anti-colonial struggle. We have seen that China, India, Indonesia, the Philippines, and Burma, have tried to avoid using culture as the defining element of their nation-building project. China's socialist ideal, India's appeal to secularism, and Indonesia's *Pancasila* have not convinced China's Tibetans, India's Nagas, and Indonesia's Acehnese, who have seen in these state-promoted ideals the cultural values of ethnic majorities being imposed on them. The Philippines' civic nationalism has not convinced the Muslim minority that the national identity was more civic than Christian, and the Burmese attempts to create various brands of socialism has failed to convince minorities that the project was a way to impose the values of Burmans on them. States that have tried a mixed approach by using more inclusive cultural markers of identity to transcend other cleavages have not been successful either. Pakistan's reference to the common faith of Islam has not prevented the secession of Bangladesh and continued unrest in Baluchistan.

Bhargava's notion of the political elites' conceptual "mindset" begs further reflection in many cases. Historical paths and elite conceptions of nation that have become crystallized over time, in spite of some gradual changes, appear to strongly limit the ability to make significant conceptual shifts to accommodate certain forms of sub-state national groups in their respective polities. In India, where the elites have been most accommodative, the state still prevents them from imagining deeper asymmetrical forms of federalism that could accommodate religiously defined sub-state national groups or culturally different groups in the Northeast. Deep prejudice and the limitations of elite mindsets create a powerful insight into the ways in which Pakistani political elites have been unable to move beyond viewing Islam as the single mode of unity, the way Indonesian elites have conceived of Papuan mobilization, or the way Philippine elites have seen Moro demands, not to mention the inability of Chinese elites to accept the idea of Taiwanese nationhood.

In sum, the Asian cases should give pause to those who believe that civic nations are more inclusive and tolerant of diversity than ethnic nations. Clearly, the ways in which the lofty principles are implemented matter as much as how they are defined.

CONCLUSION

Asian states have devised a variety of responses to accommodate the demands of sub-state nationalist movements for some measure of self-government. These responses have ranged from an outright resistance to the granting of autonomy in various degrees. The conditions of insecurity and upheaval under which political leaders consolidated post-colonial and post-revolutionary states shaped their negative views about the demands of sub-state nationalist movements, which they saw as a source of division and an obstacle to the creation of strong states. Although the form of the state and the type of political regime mattered, these did not emerge as decisive factors.

Nationalism in Asia was a powerful force that transformed the region and created new political forms. Nations were "imagined" where none existed before, and states used nationalism to create unity and strengthen the integrity of their boundaries (Anderson 1991).

At the same time, it can be said that achieving congruence between nations and states in the region remains an unfinished process. Millions of people believe that their nations do not fit the boundaries of the states within which they live, and would prefer their own government and a seat at the United Nations. It was not the purpose of this book to make comments on the justice of these claims for recognition nor to deconstruct their history and refute them. These nations exist as a pressing political reality in the mind of the millions of people willing to die for them. And more important for the purpose of this book, they exist as a sometimes lethal political reality that existing states must accept. Chapters in this book have shown that brute force alone will not make these claims disappear. The central issue we wanted to examine is the refusal of many Asian states to accommodate the demands for recognition from these groups.

We have tried to understand the rationale of states that refuse to accept the demands for recognition from sub-state nations. We have found that the path-dependency of state formation has played a good part. Collective memories of division and vulnerability to foreign domination have generated a sense of insecurity that makes the state's accommodation to any demands for recognition tantamount to legitimizing these divisions. It may be too early to tell, but the passage of time is likely to erase these memories of division, and as Asian states grow increasingly secure about the integrity of their territories, they may become more accepting of the institutional recognition of diversity within their boundaries. This possibility, obviously, is premised on the ability of Asian states to maintain political regimes that are responsive and not contested by citizens.

More to the point, perhaps, the detailed histories presented here have laid to rest a fallacy that tends to obscure our judgment when reflecting on stateless nations, sub-state nations, or multinational states. Not every ethnic group, ethno-national group, and national minority aspires to be recognized as a nation. Considering the formidable complexity of India's ethno-linguistic cleavages, it is remarkable that so few of the cultural groups in that country have pressed demands for recognition as nations. The limited number of these demands should leave us to inquire about the factors that explain these exceptions.

Finally, if we follow Connor and look at the formation of nations as a process rather than an occurrence (1994, pp. 223–4), there are no reasons to believe that today's sub-state nations will endure as a political reality, but we also have to admit that other ethnic groups may reinvent themselves as nations. The limited number of such groups in as vast a region as Asia, with all of its complexity, should dispel the fear that accommodating a few nations within existing states will open a Pandora's box of demands for recognition. It is absurd to think, for example, that granting genuine autonomy for Tibetans in China will lead to similar demands from all the other national minorities of the People's Republic, who sometimes count only a few thousand individuals. In fact, the relative success of the Indian Union and other Asian states with a complex degree of cultural, religious, and linguistic diversity, show that governments that have managed to be inclusive and accepting of differences may stand a better chance of inspiring allegiance from their diverse citizenry.

References

Ahmed, Feroz 1998. *Ethnicity and Politics in Pakistan*. New York: Oxford University Press.

Ahmed, Samina 1996. "The Military and Ethnic Conflict," in Kennedy and Rais (eds.) *Pakistan 1995*. Boulder, CO: Westview Press.

1997. "Pakistan," in Brown and Ganguly (eds.) *Government Policies and Ethnic Relations in Asia and the Pacific*. Cambridge: Cambridge University Press.

Akbarzadeh, Shahram 1996. "Why Did Nationalism Fail in Tajikistan?" *Europe-Asia Studies*, 48(7): 1105–1129.

Alavi, Hamza 1972. "The State in Post-Colonial Societies: Pakistan and Bangladesh," *New Left Review*, 1(74): 59–81.

Anderson, Benedict 1991. *Imagined Communities: Reflections on the Origin and Spread of Nationalism*. London, UK: Verso.

(ed.) 2001. *Violence and the State in Suharto's Indonesia*, London: Verso.

Anderson, Benedict R. O' G. 1998. *The Spectre of Comparisons: Nationalism, Southeast Asia, and the World*. London and New York: Verso.

Appadurai, Arjun 1993. "The Heart of Whiteness," *Callaloo*, 16(4): 796–807.

Austin, Granville 1966. *The Indian Constitution: Cornerstone of a Nation*. Oxford: Oxford University Press.

Ayres, Alyssa 2002. "Pakistan," in Brown and Ganguly (eds.) *Fighting Words: Language Policies*. Cambridge, MA: The MIT Press.

Azad, Maulana Abul Kalam 1960. *India Wins Freedom*. New York: Longmans, Green.

Balasingham, A. 2004. *War and Peace: Armed Struggle and Peace Efforts of Liberation Tigers*. London: Fairfax Publishing.

Banerjee, Ashis 1992. "Federalism and Nationalism" in Nirmal Mukarji and Balveer Arora (eds.) *Federalism in India: Origins and Development*. New Delhi: Vikas Publishing House.

Banerjee, Mukulika 2000. *The Pathan Unarmed: Opposition and Memory in the Northwest Frontier*. Santa Fe, NM: School of American Research.

Baranovitch, Nimrod 2003. "From The Margins to the Centre: The Uyghur Challenge to Beijing," *The China Quarterly*, 175: 726–750.

Baruah, Sanjib 2003. "Confronting Constructionism: Ending India's Naga War," *Journal of Peace Research*, 40(3): 321–338.

Bastian, Adolf 1884. *Indonesien, oder die Inseln des Malayischen Archipels*. Publication Info: Leipzig.

Baxter, Craig 1998. *Bangladesh: From a Nation to a State*. Boulder, CO: Westview Press.

Behera, Navnita Chadha 2000. *State, Identity and Violence: Jammu, Kashmir and Ladakh*. New Delhi: Manohar.

Beissinger, Mark R. 1995. "The Persisting Ambiguity of Empire," *Post-Soviet Affairs*, 11(2): 149–184.

    2002. *Nationalist Mobilization and the Collapse of the Soviet State*. Cambridge: Cambridge University Press.

Bertrand, J. 2000 "Peace and Conflict in the Southern Philippines: Why the 1996 Peace Agreement is Fragile," *Pacific Affairs*, 73(1): 37–55.

    2004. *Nationalism and Ethnic Conflict in Indonesia*. New York: Cambridge University Press.

    2007. "Indonesia's Quasi-Federalist Approach: Accommodation Amid Strong Integrationist Tendencies," *International Journal of Constitutional Law*, 5(4): 576–605.

Bhattacharya, Abanti 2007. "Chinese Nationalism and the Fate of Tibet: Implications for India and Future Scenarios," *Strategic Analysis*, 33(2): 237–266.

Bhutto, Zulfiquar Ali 1969. *The Myth of Independence*. London: Oxford University Press.

Bin Sayeed, Khalid 1960. *Pakistan: The Formative Phase*. Karachi: Pakistan Publishing House.

Binder, Leonard 1963. *Religion and Politics in Pakistan*. Princeton: Princeton University Press.

Bourchier, David and Hadiz Vedi (eds.) 2003. *Indonesian Politics and Society: A Reader*. London: Routledge/Curzon.

Bovingdon, Gardner 2002. "The Not-So-Silent Majority: Uyghur Resistance to Han Rule in Xinjiang," *Modern China* 28(1): 39–78.

Brass, Paul R. 1990. *The Politics of India Since Independence*. Cambridge: Cambridge University Press.

Brass, Paul R. (ed.) 1996. *Riots and Pogroms*. New York: New York University Press.

Bremmer, Ian and Raymond Taras 1993. *Nations and Politics in the Soviet Successor States*. Cambridge: Cambridge University Press, 1993.

Breuilly, John 1993. *Nationalism and the State*. 2nd edition. Chicago: Chicago University Press.

Brooten, L. 2004. "Human Rights Discourse and the Development of Democracy in a Multi-Ethnic State," *Asian Journal of Communication*, 14(2): 174–191.

Brown, David 1994. *The State and Ethnic Politics in South-East Asia.* London: Routledge.

Brown, Judith 1994. *Modern India: The Origin of an Asian Democracy.* Oxford: Oxford University Press.

Brown, Michael E. and Sumit Ganguly 2003. *Fighting Words: Language Policy and Ethnic Relations in Asia.* Cambridge, MA: The MIT Press.

(eds.) 1997. *Government Policies and Ethnic Relations in Asia and the Pacific.* Cambridge, MA: Harvard Centre for Science and International Affairs.

Brubaker, Rogers 1996. *Nationalism Reframed: Nationhood and the National Question in the New Europe.* New York: Cambridge University Press.

2004. *Ethnicity without Groups.* Cambridge: Harvard University Press

Bunce, Valerie 1999. *Subversive Institutions: The Design and the Destruction of Socialism and the State.* New York: Cambridge University Press.

Byman, Daniel 2005. *Deadly Connections: States that Sponsor Terrorism.* Cambridge: Cambridge University Press.

Cady, John F. 1958. *A History of Modern Burma.* Ithaca, NY: Cornell University Press.

Callahan, Mary 1998. "Democracy in Burma: The Lessons of History," *The National Bureau of Asian Research,* 9(3): 5–26.

Callahan, Mary 2007. *Political Authority in Burma's Ethnic Minority States: Devolution, Occupation and Coexistence.* Policy studies 31, East West Center, Washington DC.

Case, William 2007. "Semi-Democracy and Minimalist Federalism in Malaysia," in He, Galligan, and Inoguchi (eds.) *Federalism in Asia.* Cheltenham: Edward Elgar, pp.124–143.

Chan, Anita 2001. *China's Workers Under Assault: The Exploitation of Labor in a Globalizing Economy.* Armonk, NY: M. E. Sharpe.

Chatterjee, Partha 1986. *Nationalist Thought and the Colonial World: A Derivative Discourse?* London: Zed Books for the United Nations University.

Chauvel, Richard 1990. *Nationalists, Soldiers and Separatists: The Ambonese Islands from Colonialism to Revolt.* Leiden: KITLV Press.

Chiang, Kai-shek 1946. *The Collected Wartime Messages of Generalissimo Chiang Kai-shek, 1937–1945, Compiled by Chinese Ministry of Information.* Vol II. New York: The John Day Company.

1947 [1943]. *China's Destiny and Chinese Economic Theory.* Translated from Mandarin by Philip Jaffee. New York: Roy Publishers.

Chow, Kai-Wing 2001. "Narrating Nation, Race and National Culture: Imagining the Hanzu Identity in Modern China," in Chow, Doak, and Fu (eds.) *Constructing Nationhood in Modern East Asia.* Ann Arbor: University of Michigan Press, pp. 47–84.

Chu, J. Y. et al. 1998. "Genetic Relationships of Populations in China," *Proceedings of the National Academy of Science of the United States of America* [Online], 95(29): 11763–11768. Available at: http://www.pnas.org/cgi/content/abstract/95/20/11763.pdf [accessed June 8, 2007].

Chung, Jae Ho 1994. "Beijing Confronting the Provinces: The 1994 Tax-Sharing Reform and Its Implications on Central-Provincial Relations in China," *China Information,* 9(2–3): 1–23.

Clough, Ralph 1999. *Cooperation or Conflict in the Taiwan Strait?* Lanham, MD: Rowman and Littlefield.

Cohen, Stephen Philip 2004. *The Idea of Pakistan.* Washington, DC: The Brookings Institution.

Coleman, Michael 2007. *American Indians, the Irish, and Government Schooling: A Comparative Study.* Lincoln: University of Nebraska Press.

Coll, Steve 2004. *Ghost Wars: The Secret History of the CIA, Afghanistan and Bin Laden, from the Soviet Invasion to September 10, 2001.* New York: The Penguin Press.

Collins, Kathleen 2006. *Clan Politics and Regime Transition in Central Asia.* New York: Cambridge University Press.

Commercio, Michele 2004. "The 'Pugachev Rebellion' in the Context of Post-Soviet Kazakh Nationalization," *Nationalities Papers,* 32(1): 87–113.

Conner, Victoria and Robert Barnett 1997. *Leaders in Tibet: A Directory.* TIN background briefing papers; no. 28. London: Tibet Information Network.

Connor, Walker 1994a. "When is a Nation?" in Hutchinson and Smith (eds.) *Nationalism.* Oxford: Oxford University Press, pp. 154–159.

  1994. *Ethnonationalism: The Quest for Understanding.* Princeton: Princeton University Press.

Connors, Michael Kelly 2003. *Democracy and National Identity in Thailand.* London: Routledge Curzon.

Conquest, Robert 1970. *The Nation Killers: The Soviet Deportation of Nationalities.* London: MacMillan.

Coppel, Charles (ed.) 2004. *Violent Conflicts in Indonesia: Analysis, Representation, Resolution.* Richmond: Curzon.

Corcuff, Stephane 2002. "'Mainlanders,' New Taiwanese?" in Corcuff (ed.) *Memories of the Future: National Identity Issues and the Search for a New Taiwan.* Armonk, NY: M. E. Sharpe, pp. 163–195.

Cornell, Svante 2002. "Autonomy as a Source of Conflict: Caucasian Conflicts in Theoretical Perspective," *World Politics,* 54(2): 245–276.

Crombe, Xavier 2002. "Tibet between Tibetans and Chinese Migrants," in Godemont (ed.) *China and its Western Frontier.* Paris: Centre IFRI, pp. 111–138.

Crossley, Pamela Kyle 1999. *A Translucent Mirror: History and Identity in Qing Imperial Ideology.* Berkeley: University of California Press.

Cruz, Consuelo 2000. "Identity and Persuasion: How Nations Remember Their Pasts and Make Their Futures," *World Politics,* 52(3): 275–312.

Dahm, Bernhard 1969. *Sukarno and the Struggle for Indonesian Independence.* Ithaca, NY: Cornell University Press.

Darden, Keith and Anna M. Grzymał a-Busse 2006. "The Great Divide: Literacy, Nationalism, and the Communist Collapse," *World Politics,* 59(1): 83–115.

Dasgupta, Chandrasekhar 2002. *War and Diplomacy in Kashmir.* New Delhi: Sage Publications.

Dasgupta, Jyoti Bhusan 1968. *Jammu and Kashmir*. The Hague: Martinus Nijhoff.

Dave, Bhavna 1996. "National Revival in Kazakhstan: Language Shift and Identity Change," *Post-Soviet Affairs*, 12(1): 51–72.

Day, Tony 2002. *Fluid Iron: State Formation in Southeast Asia*. Honolulu: University of Hawaii Press.

De Silva, C. 2006. "Sri Lanka in 2005: Continuing Political Turmoil," *Asian Survey*, 46(1): 114–119.

  2007. "Sri Lanka in 2006: Unresolved Political and Ethnic Conflicts amid Economic Growth." *Asian Survey*, 47(1): 99–104.

De Votta, N. 2003. "Sri Lanka's Political Decay: Analyzing the October 2000 and December 2001 Parliamentary Elections," *Commonwealth and Comparative Politics*, 41(2): 115–142.

  2004a. *Blowback: Linguistic Nationalism, Institutional Decay, and Ethnic Conflict in Sri Lanka*. Palo Alto, CA: Stanford University Press.

  2004b. "Sri Lanka in 2003: Seeking to Consolidate Peace." *Asian Survey*, 44(1): 49

  2005. "From Ethnic Outbidding to Ethnic Conflict: The Institutional Bases for Sri Lanka's Separatist War," *Nations and Nationalism*, 11(1): 141–159.

Defert, G. 1992. *Timor-Est, Le Génocide Oublié: Droit D'un Peuple Et Raisons D'Etats*. Paris: L'Harmattan.

Deng, Xiaoping 1984. "One Country, Two Systems," in *Selected Works of Deng Xiaoping* vol. 3 (1982–1992). Translated from Mandarin by the People's Daily. [Online] Available at: http://english.peopledaily.com.cn/dengxp/contents3.html [accessed August 16, 2007].

DeSilva, K. 1998. *Reaping the Whirlwind: Ethnic Conflict, Ethnic Politics in Sri Lanka*. Delhi: Penguin.

Dikötter, Frank 1992. *The Discourse of Race in Modern China*. London: Hurst & Company.

Drakard, Jane 1999. *A Kingdom of Words: Language and Power in Sumatra*. Shah Alam, Malaysia: Oxford University Press.

Dreyer, June Teufel 1976. *China's Forty Millions: Minority Nationalities and National Integration in the People's Republic of China*. Harvard East Asia Series: 87. Cambridge, MA: Harvard University Press.

  1997. "Assimilation and Accomodation in China," in Brown and Ganguly (eds.) *Government Policies and Ethnic Relations in Asia and the Pacific*. Cambridge, MA: Harvard Centre for Science and International Affairs, pp. 351–392.

  2005. "China's Vulnerability to Minority Separatism," *Asian Affairs, an American Review*, 32(2): 69–85.

Duara, Prasenjit 1995. *Rescuing History from the Nation: Questioning Narratives of Modern China*. Chicago: University of Chicago Press.

Dung dkar Blo bzang 'phrin las. 1991. *The Merging of Religious and Secular Rule in Tibet*. Beijing: Foreign Language Press.

Eaton, Richard M. 1993. *The Rise of Islam and the Bengal Frontier, 1204–1760*. Berkeley: University of California Press.

Economy, Elizabeth C. 2004. *The River Runs Black: The Environmental Challenge to China's Future*. Ithaca, NY: Cornell University Press.

Edgar, Adrienne Lynn 2004. *Tribal Nation: The Making of Soviet Turkmenistan*. Princeton: Princeton University Press.

2006. "Bolshevism, Patriarchy, and the Nation: The Soviet 'Emancipation' of Muslim Women in Pan-Islamic Perspective," *Slavic Review*, 65(2): 252–272.

Edrisinha, R. 2005. "Multination Federalism and Minority Rights in Sri Lanka," in Kymlicka and He (eds.) *Multiculturalism in Asia*. Oxford: Oxford University Press, pp. 244–261.

Elson, Robert 2008. *The Idea of Indonesia: A History*. Cambridge: Cambridge University Press.

Erland, Jansson 1981. *India, Pakistan or Pakhtunistan? The Nationalist Movements in the North West Frontier Provinces, 1937–1947*. Uppsala: University of Uppsala Press.

Feith, Herbert 1962. *The Decline of Constitutional Democracy in Indonesia*. Ithaca, NY: Cornell University Press.

1967. "Politics of Economic Decline," in Tan (ed.) *Sukarno's Guided Indonesia*. Melbourne: Jacaranda Press, pp. 46–57.

Feith, Herbert and Lance Castle (eds.) 1970. *Indonesian Political Thinking 1945–1965*. Ithaca, NY: Cornell University Press.

Fernando, Joseph 2002. *The Making of the Malayan Constitution*. Kuala Lumpur: Malaysian Branch of the Royal Asiatic Society.

Finer, Catherine Jones 2003. *Social Policy Reform: Views from Home and Abroad*. Aldershot, UK: Ashgate.

Fischer, Andrew Martin 2005. *State Growth and Social Exclusion in Tibet: Challenges of Recent Economic Growth*. NIAS Report no. 47, Copenhagen: Nordic Institute of Asian Studies.

Fiskesjö, Magnus 2006. "Rescuing the Empire: Chinese Nation-Building in the Twentieth Century," *European Journal of East Asian Studies*, 5(1): 15–44.

Friedman, Edward 2000. "Globalization, Legitimacy, and Post-Communism in China: A Nationalist Potential for Democracy, Prosperity, and Peace," in Tien and Chu (eds.) *China Under Jiang Zemin*. Boulder, CO: Lynne Rienner, pp. 233–246.

Gagnon, Alain G. and James Tully (eds.) 2001. *Multinational Democracies*. Cambridge: Cambridge University Press.

Ganguly, K., K. Höglund, and I. Svensson 2003. "The Peace Process in Sri Lanka," *Civil Wars*, 5(4): 103–118.

Ganguly, Sumit 1999. *The Crisis in Kashmir: Portents of War, Hopes of Peace*. Cambridge: Cambridge University Press.

2001. *Conflict Unending: Indo-Pakistani Conflicts Since 1947*. New York: Columbia University Press.

2006. "Will Kashmir Stop India's Rise?" *Foreign Affairs*, 85(4): 45–56.

2007. "The Roots of Religious Violence in India, Pakistan and Bangladesh," in Cady and Simon (eds.) *Religion and Conflict in South And South East Asia: Disrupting Violence*. London: Routledge.

Ganguly, Sumit, Larry Diamond, and Marc Plattner (eds.) 2007. *The State of India's Democracy*. Baltimore, MD: Johns Hopkins University Press.

Gayley, Holly Forthcoming. "The Ethics of Cultural Survival: A Buddhist Vision of Progress in Mkhan po Jigs phun's Heart Advice to Tibetan for the 21st Century," in Tuttle (ed.) *The Rise of the Modern in Tibet*. Beiträge zur Zentralasienforschung, International Institute for Tibetan and Buddhist Studies – Wissenschaftsverlag GmbH: Sankt Augustin.

Geertz, Clifford 1973. *The Interpretation of Cultures*. New York: Basic Books.

1980. *Negara: The Theatre State in Nineteenth-Century Bali*. Princeton: Princeton University Press.

Gellner, Ernest 1964. *Thought and Change*. London: Weidenfield and Nicolson.

1983. *Nations and Nationalism*. Ithaca, NY: Cornell University Press.

Ghai, Yash 1999. *Hong Kong's New Constitutional Order: The Resumption of Chinese Sovereignty*. Hong Kong: Hong Kong University Press.

2000a. "Autonomy Regime in China: Coping with Economic and Ethnic Diversity," in Ghai (ed.), *Autonomy and Ethnicity: Negotiating Competing Claims in Multi-Ethnic States*. Cambridge: Cambridge University Press, pp. 77–98.

2000b. "The Basic Law of the Special Administrative Region of Macau: Some Reflections," *International and Comparative Law Quarterly*, 49: 183–198.

Giuliano, Elise 2000. "Who Determines the Self in the Politics of Self-Determination? Identity and Preference Formation in Tatarstan's Nationalist Mobilization," *Comparative Politics* 32(3): 295–316.

Gladney, Dru C. 1994a. "Representing Nationality in China: Refiguring Majority/Minority Identities," *The Journal of Asian Studies*, 53(1): 92–123.

1994b. "Ethnic Identity in China: The New Politics of Difference" in Joseph (ed.) *China Briefing, 1994*. Boulder, CO: Westview Press, pp. 171–192.

1996 (1991). *Muslim Chinese: Ethnic Nationalism in the People's Republic*. Cambridge, MA: Council on East Asian Studies, Harvard University.

Gleason, Gregory 1983. "The Pakhta Programme: The Politics of Sowing Cotton in Uzbekistan," *Central Asian Survey*, 2(2): 109–120.

Godden, Gertrude M. 1897. "Naga and other Frontier Tribes of North East India," *Journal of the Anthropological Institute of Great Britain and Ireland*, 26: 161–201.

Gohain, Hiren 1989. "Bodo Stir in Perspective," *Economic and Political Weekly*, 25: 1377–1379.

Goldstein, M. 1989. *A History of Modern Tibet: The Demise of the Lamaist State*. Berkeley: University of California Press.

Goldstein, M., Dawei Sherab, and A. Seibenschuh. 2004. *A Tibetan Revolutionary*. Berkeley: University of California Press.

Goldstein, M. C., G. Childs, and Puchung Wangdui 2008. "Going for Income in Village Tibet: A Longitudinal Analysis of Change and Adaptation, 1997–98 to 2006–07," *Asian Survey*, 48(3): 513–534.

Goodman, David S. G. 2004. "The Campaign to 'Open Up' the West: National, Provincial-level and Local Perspectives," *The China Quarterly*, 178: 317–334.

Gooneratne, J. 2007. *Negotiating with the Tigers (LTTE) (2002–2005)*. Pannipitya: Stanford Lake.

Gourevitch, Peter 1978. "The Second Image Reversed: The International Sources of Domestic Politics," *International Organization*, 32(4): 881–912.

Gowing, P. G. 1983. *Mandate in Moroland: The American Government of Muslim Filipinos, 1899–1920.* Quezon City: New Day Publishers.

Gravers, Mikael 2007. *Explaining Diversity in Burma.* NIAS, Denmark.

Greenfeld, Liah 1992. *Nationalism: Five Roads to Modernity.* Cambridge, MA: Harvard University Press.

Gries, Peter Hays 2004. *China's New Nationalism: Pride, Politics and Diplomacy.* Berkeley: University of California Press.

2005. "Popular Nationalism and State Legitimation in China," in Gries and Rosen (eds.) *State and Society in 21st-century China,* London: Routledge, pp. 25–43.

Guang Lei 2005. "Realpolitik Nationalism. International Sources of Chinese Nationalism," *Modern China,* 31(4): 487–514.

Guha, Ramachandra 2007. *India Since Gandhi: The History of the World's Largest Democracy.* London: Macmillan.

Guo, Baogang 2003. "Political Legitimacy and China's Transition," *Journal of Chinese Political Science,* 8(1–2): 1–25.

Guo, Xiaolin 2001. "Land Expropriation and Rural Conflicts in China," *China Quarterly,* 166: 422–438.

Guo, Yingjie 2003. "Imagining a Confucian Nation: The Search for Roots and the Revival of Confucianism in Post-Tiananmen China." *The Canadian Review of Studies in Nationalism,* 30: 1–14.

2004. *Cultural Nationalism in Contemporary China.* London: Routledge Curzon.

Gurr, T. R. 2000. *Peoples Versus States: Minorities at Risk in the New Century.* Washington, DC: United States Institute of Peace Press.

Habib, Haroon 2002. "Regrets for 1971," *Frontline,* 19(17): 17–30.

Hao, Chang 1987. *Chinese Intellectuals in Crisis: Search for Order and Meaning, 1890–1911.* Taipei: SMC.

Hara, Kimie 2001. "50 Years from San Francisco: Re-Examining the Peace Treaty and Japan's Territorial Problems," *Pacific Affairs,* 74(3): 361–382.

Hardy, Peter 1972. *The Muslims of British India.* Cambridge: Cambridge University Press.

Harper, T. N. 1999. *The End of Empire and the Making of Malaya.* Cambridge: Cambridge University Press.

Harrison, James P. 1969. *The Communists and Chinese Peasant Rebellions: A Study in the Rewriting of Chinese History.* New York: Atheneum.

Hasan, Mushirul 1997. *Legacy of a Divided Nation: India's Muslims Since Independence* Delhi: Oxford University Press.

Hatta, Mohammad 1954. *Kumpulan Karangan,* 4 vols, Biografi Politik: Jakarta.

Hayes, Louis D. 1984. *Politics in Pakistan: The Struggle for Legitimacy.* Boulder, CO: Westview Press.

Hayson, N. and Choudhry, S. "Mechanisms for Resolving Divisive Issues." Unpublished Paper.

Hechter, Michael 1999. *Internal Colonialism: The Celtic Fringe in British National Development.* New Brunswick, NJ: Transaction Books.

Hendrischke, Hans J. 1999. "Provinces in Competition: Region, Identity and Cultural Construction," in Hendrischke and Feng (eds.) *The Political*

Economy of China's Provinces: Comparative and Competitive Advantage. London: Routledge, pp. 1–30.

Heppner, Kevin 2005. "Sovereignty, Survival and Resistance: Contending Perspectives on Karen Internal Displacement in Burma," Karen Human Rights Group Working paper. Available on-line at: http://www.khrg.org/ papers/wp2005w1.pdf [accessed April 14, 2009].

Hillman, Ben 2005. "Monastic Politics and the Local State in China: Authority and Autonomy in an Ethnically Tibetan Prefecture," *The China Journal,* 54: 29–51.

Hirsch, Francine 2005. *Empire of Nations: Ethnographic Knowledge and the Making of the Soviet Union.* Ithaca, NY: Cornell University Press.

Hlaing, Kyaw Yin 2007. "The Politics of Language Policy in Myanmar: Imagining Togetherness, Practicing Difference," in Guan and Surydinata (eds.) *Language, Nation and Development in Southeast Asia.* ISEAS: Singapore, pp. 160–180.

Hobsbawm, Eric J. 1990. *Nations and Nationalism Since 1870: Programme, Myth, Reality.* Cambridge: Canto.

Hobsbawn, Eric and Terence Ranger (eds.) 1983. *The Invention of Tradition.* Cambridge: Cambridge University Press.

Hodson, H. V. 1969. *The Great Divide: Britain, India, Pakistan.* London: Hutchinson.

Holbig, Heike 2004. "The Emergence of the Campaign to Open Up the West: Ideological Formation, Central Decision-making and the Role of the Provinces," *The China Quarterly,* 178: 335–357.

Hooghe, Liesbet 2004. "Belgium: Hollowing the Center," in Amoretti and Bermeo (eds.) *Federalism and Territorial Cleavages.* Baltimore, MD: The John Hopkins University Press, pp. 55–92.

Horowitz, D. L. 1985. *Ethnic Groups in Conflict.* Berkeley: University of California Press.

Houtman, Gustaaf. 1999. *Mental Culture in Burmese Crisis Politics.* Tokyo: ILCAA Study of Languages and Cultures of Asia and Africa Monograph Series, No. 33. Tokyo University of Foreign Studies.

Hsieh, Shih-chung 1998. "On Three Definitions of Han Ren. Images of the Majority People in Taiwan," in Gladney (ed.) *Making Majorities: Constituting the Nation in Japan, Korea, China, Malaysia, Fiji, Turkey and the United States.* Palo Alto, CA: Stanford University Press, pp. 95–105.

Hsu, Carolyn L. 2001. "Political Narratives and the Production of Legitimacy: The Case of Corruption in Post-Mao China," *Qualitative Sociology,* 24(1): 25–54.

Hunt, Michael H. 1996. *The Genesis of Chinese Communist Foreign Policy.* New York: Columbia University Press.

Huntington, Samuel 1968. *Political Order in Changing Societies.* New Haven, CT: Yale University Press.

Hurst, William and O Brien Kevin 2002. "China's Contentious Pensioners," *China Quarterly,* 170: 345–360.

Hussain, Monirul 1992. "Tribal Question in Assam," *Economic and Political Weekly,* 27(20 & 21): 1329–1332.

International Campaign for Tibet. 2003. *Crossing the Line: China Railway to Lhasa, Tibet.* Washington, DC: International Campaign for Tibet.

International Campaign for Tibet. 2007. *Tracking the Steel Dragon: How China's Economic Policies and the Railway are Transforming Tibet.* Washington, DC: International Campaign for Tibet.

International Crisis Group 2006. *Aceh: Now for the Hard Part. Asia Briefing* [Online], 48(29) March. Available at: http://www.crisisgroup.org/home/index.cfm?id=4049

  2006. *Aceh's Local Elections: The Role of the Free Aceh Movement (GAM).* Jakarta/Brussels: *Asia Briefing,* 57: 29 November.

International Crisis Group. 2007. *Sri Lanka: Sinhala Nationalism and the Elusive Southern Consensus.* Brussels: Asia Report no. 141.

  2008. *Sri Lanka's Return to War: Limiting the Damage.* Brussels: *Asia Report* no. 146.

Irwin, C. 2008. "Peace in Sri Lanka: From Symbols to Substance." Available online at: www.cpalanka.org/research_papers/Peace_in_SrI_Lanka.pdf [accessed January 2009].

Jackson, Robert 1975. *South Asian Crisis, South Asian Crisis: India, Pakistan and Bangladesh.* New York: Praeger.

Jacob, J. F. R. 1997. *Surrender at Dacca: Birth of a Nation.* Delhi: Manohar Books.

Jaffrelot, Christophe 2002. "Nationalism without a Nation: Pakistan Searching for Its Identity," in Jaffrelot (ed.) *Pakistan: Nationalism without a Nation?* New Delhi: Manohar Books.

Jagou, Fabienne 2004. *Le 9e Panchen Lama (1883–1937): Enjeu des relations Sino-Tibetaines,* Monographie 191. Paris: École française d'Extrême-Orient

Jahan, Raonaq 1972. *Pakistan: Failure in National Integration.* New York: Columbia University Press.

Jalal, Ayesha 1985. *The Sole Spokesman: Jinnah, the Muslim League and the Demand for Pakistan.* Cambridge: Cambridge University Press.

  1990. *The State of Martial Rule: The Origins of Pakistan's Political Economy of Defence.* Cambridge: Cambridge University Press

Jetly, Rajshree 2004. "Baluch Ethnicity and Nationalism (1971–81): An Assessment," *Asian Ethnicity,* 5(1): 7–26.

Jha, Prem Shankar 1996. *Kashmir, 1947: Rival Versions of History.* Bombay: Oxford University Press.

Johnson, Chalmers 1962. *Peasant Nationalism and Communist Power: The Emergence of Revolutionary China.* Palo Alto, CA: Stanford University Press.

Jolliffe, J. 1978. *East Timor: Nationalism and Colonialism.* St. Lucia, AUS: University of Queensland Press.

Jones, Reece 2008. "Searching for the greatest Bengali: The BBC and shifting identity categories in South Asia," *National Identities,* 10(2): 149–165.

Kahin, Audrey (ed.) 1985. *Regional Dynamics of the Indonesian Revolution: Unity from Diversity.* Honolulu: University of Hawaii Press.

Keating, Michael 2001. "So Many Nations, So Few States: Territory and Nationalism in the Global Era," in Gagnon and Tully (eds.) *Multinational Democracies*. Cambridge: Cambridge University Press, pp. 39–64.

2001. *Plurinational Democracy: Stateless Nations in a Post-Sovereignty Era.* Oxford: Oxford University Press.

Kell, T. 1995. *The Roots of Acehnese Rebellion, 1989–1992.* Ithaca, NY: Cornell University Modern Indonesia Project.

Keyes, Charles 1997. "Cultural Diversity and National Unity in Thailand," in Brown and Ganguly (eds.) *Government Policies and Ethnic Relations in Asia and the Pacific.* Cambridge, MA: Harvard Centre for Science and International Affairs, pp. 197–231.

Khalid, Adeeb 1998. *The Politics of Muslim Cultural Reform: Jadidism in Central Asia.* Comparative Studies in Muslim Societies, 27. Berkeley: University of California Press.

2006. "Backwardness and the Quest for Civilization: Early Soviet Central Asia in Comparative Perspective," *Slavic Review,* 65(2): 231–251.

2007. *Islam after Communism: Religion and Politics in Central Asia.* University of California Press.

Khan, Adeel 2002. "Pakistan's Sindhi Nationalism: Migration, Marginalization, and the Threat of 'Indianization'," *Asian Survey,* 42(2): 213–229.

Khan, Akbar 1970. *Raiders in Kashmir.* Karachi: Pak Publishers.

Khan, Rashiduddin 1992. *Federal India: A Design for Change.* New Delhi: Vikas Publishing House.

Kikon, Dolly 2005. "Engaging Naga Nationalism: Can Democracy Function in Militarised Societies?" *Economic and Political Weekly,* 40(26): 2833–2837.

Kim, Jiyul 2006. "Pan-Korean Nationalism, Anti-Great Power-ism and U.S.-South Korean Relations." *Policy Forum Online,* 06–01A [Online] Available at: http://www.nautilus.org/fora/security/0601Kim.html [accessed January 1, 2008].

Kim, Taeho 1997. "Korean Views on Taiwan-PRC Relations and the Japan Factor," in Lilley and Downs (eds.) *Crisis in the Taiwan Strait.* Washington, DC: National Defense University Press, pp. 303–325.

Kirby, William C. 2000. "The Nationalist Regime and the Chinese Party-State," in Goldman and Gordon (eds.) *Historical Perspectives on Contemporary East Asia.* Cambridge, MA: Harvard University Press, pp. 211–237.

2004. "The Chinese Party-State under Democracy and Dictatorship on the Mainland and Taiwan," in Kirby (ed.) *Realms of Freedom in Modern China.* Palo Alto, CA: Stanford University Press, pp. 113–138.

Knaus, John Kenneth 1999. *Orphans of the Cold War: America and the Tibetan Struggle for Survival.* New York: Public Affairs.

Kolas, Ashild 1996. "Tibetan Nationalism: The Politics of Religion," *Journal of Peace Research* 33(1): 51–66.

Kothari, Rajni 1988. "Integration and Exclusion in Indian Politics." *Economic and Political Weekly,* 23(43): 2223–2229.

Kotkin, Stephen 1991. *Steeltown, USSR: Soviet Society in the Gorbachev Era.* Berkeley: University of California Press.

Kramer, Tom 2007. *The United Wa State Party: Narco-Army or Ethnic Nationalist Party?* Policy Studies 38, EWC.

Kukreja, Veena 2003. *Contemporary Pakistan: Political Processes, Conflicts and Crises.* New Delhi: Sage Publications.

Kumar, Anjali 1994. "China's Reform, Internal Trade and Marketing," *The Pacific Review,* 7(3): 323–340.

Kymlicka, Will 1995. *Multicultural Citizenship: A Liberal Theory of Minority Rights.* New York: Oxford University Press.

  2007. *Multicultural Odysseys: Navigating the International Politics of Diversity.* New York: Oxford University Press.

Kymlicka, Will and Baogang He (eds.) 2006. *Multiculturalism in Asia.* Oxford: Oxford University Press.

Lai, Hongyi Harry 2002. "China's Western Development Program: Its Rationale, Implementation, and Prospects." *Modern China,* 28(4): 432–466.

Lai, Tse-han, Myers Ramon, and Wou Wei 1991. *A Tragic Beginning: the Taiwan Uprising of February 28, 1947.* Palo Alto, CA:Stanford University Press.

Laitin, David D. 1998. *Identity in Formation: The Russian-Speaking Populations in the Near Abroad.* Ithaca, NY: Cornell University Press.

Lamb, Alastair 1991. *Kashmir: A Disputed Legacy.* Hertingfordbury: Roxford Books.

Lijphart, Arend 1977. *Democracy in Plural Societies: A Comparative Exploration.* New Haven, CT: Yale University Press.

Lin, Chen-wei 2001. "Taiwan's Democratic National Identity, Lee Teng-hui, and Japan," *Journal of Contemporary China,* 10(26): 173–177.

Linz, Juan and Alfred Stepan 1996. *Problems of Democratic Transition and Consolidation, Southern Europe, South America and Post-Communist Europe.* Baltimore, MD: The John Hopkins University Press.

Linz, Juan J., Alfred Stepan, and Yogendra Yadav 2007. "'Nation State or State Nation?' India in Comparative Perspective," in Bajpai (ed.) *Democracy and Diversity: India and the American Experience.* New Delhi: Oxford University Press.

Liu, Yawei 2000. "Les élections des comités villageois en Chine," *Perspectives Chinoises,* 60: 21–39.

Loganathan, K. 1998. "Indo-Lanka Accord and the Ethnic Question: Lessons and Experiences," in Rupesinghe (ed.) *Negotiating Peace in Sri Lanka: Efforts, Failures, and Lessons Learnt.* Ceylon: Foundation for Co-Existence.

Mackerras, Colin 1994. *China's Minorities: Integration and Modernization in the Twentieth Century.* Hong Kong: Oxford University Press.

  2004. "What is China? Who is Chinese? Han-Minority Relations, Legitimacy, and the State," in Gries and Rosen (eds.) *State and Society in 21st-Century China: Crisis, Contention, and Legitimation.* London: Routledge, pp. 216–234.

Madan, T. N. 1987. "Secularism in Its Place." *Journal of Asian Studies,* 46(4): 747–759.

Magdalena, F. V. 1997. *The Peace Process in Mindanao: Problems and Prospects.* Singapore: Institute for Southeast Asian Studies.

Majul, Cesar Adib 1973. *Muslims in the Philippines.* 2nd edition. Quezon City: Published for the Asian Center by the University of the Philippines Press.

Makley, Charlene 2007. *The Violence of Liberation: Gender and Tibetan Buddhist Revival in Post-Mao China.* Berkeley: University of California Press.

Malia, Martin 1995. *The Soviet Tragedy: A History of Socialism in Russia, 1917–1991.* New York: Free Press.

Malley, Michael 1999. "Regions: Centralization and Resistance," in Emmerson (ed.) *Indonesia Beyond Suharto,* New York: The Asia Society, pp. 71–105.

Mangunwijaya, Y. B. 1998. *Menuju Republik Indonesia Serikat.* Jakarta: Gramedia.

Martin, Terry 2001. *The Affirmative Action Empire: Nations and Nationalism in the Soviet Union, 1923–1939.* Ithaca, NY: Cornell University Press.

May, R. J. 1990. "Ethnic Separatism in Southeast Asia," *Pacific Viewpoint,* 31(2): 28–59.

McAdam, Doug, John D. McCarthy, and Mayer N. Zald (eds.) 1996. *Comparative Perspectives on Social Movements: Political Opportunities, Mobilizing Structures, and Cultural Framings.* New York: Cambridge University Press.

McDonald, Jr., Angus, W. 1976. "Mao Tse-tung and the Hunan Self-Government Movement, 1920: An Introduction and Five Translations," *China Quarterly,* 68: 751–777.

McGlinchey, Eric M. 2007. "Divided Faith: Trapped between State and Islam in Uzbekistan," in Sahadeo and Zanca (eds.) *Everyday Life in Central Asia.* Bloomington: Indiana University Press.

McGrath, Allen 1996. *The Destruction of Pakistan's Democracy.* Karachi: Oxford University Press.

McGregor, Katharine 2007. *History in Uniform: Military Ideology and the Construction of Indonesia's Past.* Singapore: National University of Singapore Press.

McKenna, T. M. 1998. *Muslim Rulers and Rebels: Everyday Politics and Armed Separatism in the Southern Philippines.* Berkeley: University of California Press.

Mearsheimer, John 1990. "Back to the Future: Instability in Europe after the Cold War," *International Security,* 15(1): 5–56.

Megoran, Nick 2007. "On Researching 'Ethnic Conflict': Epistemology, Politics, and a Central Asian Boundary Dispute," *Europe-Asia Studies,* 59(2): 253–277.

Miller, Michelle 2006. "What's Special about Special Autonomy in Aceh?" in Reid (ed.) *Verandah of Violence.* Singapore: Singapore University Press, pp. 292–314.

Misra, Udayon 2003. "Naga Peace Talks: High Hopes and Hard Realities," *Economic and Political Weekly,* 38 (7): 586–592.

Mong, Sai Kham 2007. "The Shan in Myanmar," in Ganesan and Hlaing (eds.) *Myanmar: State, Society and Ethnicity*. Singapore: ISEAS, pp. 272–273.

Morris, E. E. 1983. Islam and Politics in Aceh: A Study of Center-Periphery Relations in Indonesia. *PhD Thesis*. Ithaca, NY: Cornell University.

Mullaney, Thomas M. 2004. "55 + 1 = 1 or the Strange Calculus of Chinese Nationhood," *China Information*, 18(2): 197–205.

Münninghoff, H. F. 1995. *Report of Human Rights Violations Toward Local People in the Area of Timika, District of Fak Fak, Irian Jaya, 1994–1995*. Jayapura.

Myoe, Maung Aung 2002. *Neither Friends nor Foe: Myanmar's Relations with Thailand Since 1988: A View from Yangon*. IDSS Monograpy No. 1, IDSS, Singapore.

Nairn, Tom 1981 [1977]. *The Break-up of Britain: Crisis and Neo-Nationalism*. 2nd edition. London: Verso [London: New Left Books].

Nanayakkara, V. K. 2006. "From Dominion to Republican Status: Dilemmas of Constitution Making in Sri Lanka," *Public Administration and Development*, 26(5): 425–437.

Naquin, Susan 2000. *Peking: Temples and City Life, 1400–1900*. Berkeley: University of California Press.

Narang, A. S. 2003. "India: Ethnicity and Federalism," in B. D. Dua and M. P. Singh (eds.) *Indian Federalism in the New Millennium*. New Delhi: Manohar Books.

Nasr, Vali R. 2000. "International Politics, Domestic Imperatives, and Identity Mobilization: Sectarianism in Pakistan, 1979–1998," *Comparative Politics*, 32(2): 171–190.

Nehru, Jawaharlal 1941. *Toward Freedom: The Autobiography of Jawaharlal Nehru*. New York: John Day.

O'Leary, Brendan 2005. "Debating Consociational Politics: Normative and Explanatory Argument," in Noöl (ed.) *From Power Sharing to Democracy: Post Conflict Institutions in Ethnically Divided Societies*. Montreal and Kingston: McGill-Queen's University Press, pp. 3–43.

O'Shaughnessy, Thomas 1975. "How Many Muslims Has the Philippines?" *Philippine Studies*, 23: 375–382.

Oldenburg, Philip 1985. "A Place Insufficiently Imagined: Language, Belief and the Pakistan Crisis of 1971," *Journal of Asian Studies*, 44(4): 711–733.

Ollapally, Deepa M. 2008. *The Politics of Extremism in South Asia*. Cambridge: Cambridge University Press.

Omar, Ariffin 1993. *Bangsa Melayu: Aspects of Democracy and Community among the Malays*, Kuala Lumpur: Oxford University Press.

Oo, Zaw and Min Win 2007. *Assessing Burma's Ceasefire Accords*. Policy Studies 39, East West Center, Washington DC.

Osborne, R. 1985. *Indonesia's Secret War: The Guerilla Struggle in Irian Jaya*. Sydney: Allen & Unwin.

Perry, Elizabeth J. and Mark Selden (eds.) 2006. *Chinese Society: Change, Conflict and Resistance*. 2nd edition. London: Routledge.

Philips, C. H. and Mary Doreen Wainwright (eds.) 1970. *The Partition of India: Policies and Perspectives: Policies and Perspectives*. Cambridge, MA: The MIT Press.

Pitsuwan, Surin 1985. *Islam and Malay Nationalism: A Case Study of the Malay Muslim of Southern Thailand*. Bangkok: Thai Khadi Research Institute, Thammasat University *Propinsi Sumatera Utara* nd [1953?]. Jakarta: Republik Indonesia Kementerian Penerangan.

Puri, Balraj 1993. *Kashmir Towards Insurgency*. New Delhi: Orient Longman.

Racine, Jean-Luc 2002. "Pakistan and the 'India Syndrome'," in Jaffrelot (ed.) *Pakistan: Nationalism Without a Nation?* New York: Palgrave.

2006. "L'Inde émergente, ou la sortie des temps postcoloniaux," *Hérodote*, 120 (1): 28–47.

Rahman, Tariq 1996. *Language and Politics in Pakistan*. Karachi: Oxford University Press.

Rajah, Ananda 2002. "A 'Nation of Intent' in Burma: Karen Ethno-nationalism, Nation, and Narration of Nation," *The Pacific Review*, 15(4): 517–537.

Ramage, Douglas E. 1995. *Politics in Indonesia: Democracy, Islam, and the Ideology of Tolerance*. London: Routledge.

Raman, G. Venkat 2006. "Decentralization as a Developmental Strategy in China: A Development Model for Developing Countries," *China Report*, 42(4): 369–385.

Ramsey, S. Robert 1987. *The Languages of China*. Princeton: Princeton University Press.

Ramusack, Barbara. 1977. *The Princes of India in the Twilight of Empire*. Columbus: The Ohio State University Press.

Rawski, Eveyln 1998. *The Last Emperors: A Social History of Qing Imperial Institutions*. Berkeley: University of California Press.

Reid, Anthony 1974. *The Indonesian National Revolution*. Melbourne: Longman.

1979. *The Blood of the People: Revolution and the End of Traditional Rule in Northern Sumatra*. Kuala Lumpur: Oxford University Press.

1997. "Endangered Identity: Kadazan or Dusun in Sabah (East Malaysia)," *Journal of Southeast Asian Studies*, 28(1): 120–136.

2004. "War, Peace and the Burden of History in Aceh," *Asian Ethnicity*, 5(3): 301–314.

2005. *An Indonesian Frontier: Acehnese and Other Histories of Sumatra*. Singapore: Singapore University Press.

2007. "Indonesia's Post-revolutionary Aversion to Federalism," in He, Galligan, and Inoguchi (eds.) *Federalism in Asia*. Cheltenham: Edward Elgar, pp. 144–164.

2009. *Imperial Alchemy: Nationalism and Political Identity in Southeast Asia*. Cambridge: Cambridge University Press.

Reid, Anthony and Zheng Yangwen 2009. *Negotiating Asymmetry: China's Place in Asia*. Singapore: NUS Press.

Robb, Peter 1995. *The Concept of Race in South Asia*. New Delhi: Oxford University Press.

Roberts, Sean R. 1998. "Negotiating Locality, Islam and National Culture in a Changing Borderlands: The Revival of the *Mashrap* Ritual among Young Uighur Men in the Ili Valley," *Central Asian Survey*, 17(4): 673–699.

2006. "Dangerous Clan Conflict or Muslim Civil Society?: Towards an Alternative Understanding of Central Asia's Democratic Development," *The Roberts Report* [Online] Available at: http://roberts-report.blogspot. com/2006/12/dangerous-clan-conflict-or-muslim-civil.html [accessed April 4, 2008].

Robinson, Francis 1974. *Separatism Amongst the Indian Muslims: The Politics of the United Provinces, 1860–1923*. Cambridge: Cambridge University Press.

Roeder, Philip 1991. "Soviet Federalism and Ethnic Mobilization," *World Politics*, 43: 196–232.

Rudelson, Justin J. 1997. *Oasis Identities: Uyghur Nationalism Along China's Silk Road*. New York: Columbia University Press.

Ruegg, David Seyfort 1995. *Ordre spirituel et ordre temporel dans la pensée bouddhique de l'Inde et du Tibet*. Publications de l'Institut de Civilisation Indienne. Paris: Collège de France.

Rummel, R. J. 1998. *Statistics of Democide: Genocide and Mass Murder Since 1900*. Rutgers University: Transaction Books.

Sakhong, Lian 2003. *In Search of Chin Identity*. Copenhagen: NIAS Press.

Samad, Yunas 1995. *A Nation in Turmoil: Nationalism and Ethnicity in Pakistan, 1937–1958*. New Delhi: Sage Publications.

Saravanamuttu, P. 2003. "Sri Lanka: The Best and Last Chance for Peace?" *Conflict, Security and Development*, 3(1): 129–138.

Sarvananthan Muthukrishna. 2007. "In Pursuit of a Mythical State of Tamil Eelam: A Rejoinder to Christian Stokke," *Third World Quarterly*, 28(6): 1185–1195.

Sautman, Barry 1997. "Racial Nationalism and China's External Behavior," *World Affairs* [Online] (fall). Available at: http://findarticles.com/p/articles/ mi_m2393/is_n2_v160/ai_20000642/print [accessed August 7, 2007].

2000. "Association, Federation and 'Genuine' Autonomy: The Dalai Lama's Proposals and Tibet Independence," *China Information*, 14(2): 31–91.

Schatz, Edward 2004. *Modern Clan Politics: The Power of "Blood" in Kazakhstan and Beyond*. Seattle and London: University of Washington Press.

2009. "The Soft Authoritarian 'Tool Kit': Agenda-Setting Power in Kazakhstan and Kyrgyzstan," *Comparative Politics*, 41(2).

Schiffrin, Harold Z. 1970. *Sun Yat-Sen and the Origins of the Chinese Revolution*. Berkeley: University of California Press.

Schiller, A. Arthur 1955. *The Formation of Federal Indonesia, 1945–1949*. The Hague: Van Hoeve.

Schoeberlein-Engel, John S. 1994. *Identity in Central Asia: Construction and Contention in the Conceptions of "Ozbek," "Tajik," "Muslim," "Samarqandi" and Other Groups*. Unpublished PhD dissertation, Harvard University.

Schubert, Gunter 2004. "Taiwan's Political Parties and National Identity: The Rise of an Overarching Consensus," *Asian Survey*, 44(4): 534–554.

Schulze, Kirsten 2006. "Insurgency and Counter-Insurgency: Strategy and the Aceh Conflict, October 1976- May 2004," in Reid (ed.) *Verandah of Violence*. Singapore: Singapore University Press, pp. 225–271.

Scott, James C. 1992. *Domination and the Arts of Resistance: Hidden Transcripts.* New Haven, CT: Yale University Press.

1998. *Seeing Like a State: How Certain Schemes to Improve the Human Condition Have Failed.* New Haven, CT: Yale University Press.

Selth, Andrew 1986. "Race and Resistance in Burma, 1942–1945," *Modern Asian Studies,* 20(3): 483–507.

Sen, L. P. 1969. *Slender Was the Thread: Kashmir confrontation, 1947–48.* Bombay: Orient Longsman.

Shastri, A. 2002. "Sri Lanka in 2001: Year of Reversals," *Asian Survey,* 42 (1): 177–182.

2005. "Channelling Ethnicity Through Electoral Reform in Sri Lanka," *Commonwealth and Comparative Politics,* 43(1): 34–60.

Sheng, Michael 1997. *Battling Western Imperialism: Mao, Stalin, and the United States.* Princeton: Princeton University Press.

Shnirelman, Victor A. 1996. *Who Gets the Past?: Competition for Ancestors among Non-Russian Intellectuals in Russia.* Baltimore, MD: Johns Hopkins University Press.

Siddiqa, Ayesha 2007. *Military, Inc.: Inside Pakistan's Military Economy.* London: Pluto Press.

Sidhu, Waheguru Pal Singh and Dong Yuan Jing 2003. *China and India: Cooperation or Conflict?* Boulder, CO: Lynne Rienner Publishers.

Silverstein, Josef 1980. *Burmese Politics: The Dilemma of National Unity.* New Brunswick and New Jersey: Rutgers University Press.

1997. "Fifty Years of Failure in Burma," in Brown and Ganguly (eds.) *Government Policies and Ethnic Relations in Asia and the Pacific.* Cambridge, MA: The MIT Press.

Sisson, Richard and Leo E. Rose 1990. *War and Secession: Pakistan, India and the Creation of Bangladesh.* Berkeley: University of California Press.

Sjamsuddin, Nazaruddin 1985. *The Republican Revolt: A Study of the Acehnese Rebellion.* Singapore: Institute of Southeast Asian Studies.

Slezkine, Yuri 1994. "The USSR as a Communal Apartment, or How a Socialist State Promoted Ethnic Particularism," *Slavic Review,* 53(2): 414–452.

Smith, C. 2007. "The Eelam Endgame?" *International Affairs,* 83(1): 69–86.

Smith, Donald Eugene 1963. *India as a Secular State.* Princeton: Princeton University Press.

Smith, Graham et al. 1998. "The Central Asian States as Nationalising Regimes," in Smith, Law, Wilson, Bohr, and Allworth (eds.) *Nation-Building in the Post-Soviet Borderlands: The Politics of National Identities.* Cambridge: Cambridge University Press, pp. 139–164.

Smith, Martin 1999. *Burma: Insurgency and the Politics of Ethnicity.* Dhaka: University Press; White Lotus: Bangkok; London and New York: Zed books Ltd.

2007. *State of Strife: The Dynamics of Ethnic Conflict in Burma.* Policy studies 36. East West Center: Washington DC.

Smith, Warren W., Jr. 1996. *Tibetan Nation: A History of Tibetan Nationalism and Sino-Tibetan Relations.* Boulder, CO: Westview Press.

Snyder, Jack 2000. *From Voting to Violence: Democratization and Nationalist Conflict*. New York: W. W. Norton.

Solnick, Steven L. 1999. *Stealing the State: Control and Collapse in Soviet Institutions*. Cambridge, MA: Harvard University Press.

Song, Liming 1998. "Reflections on the Seventeen-point Agreement of 1951," *Tibet Through Dissident Chinese Eyes: Essays on Self-Determination*. Armonk, NY: M. E. Sharpe, pp. 55–70.

South, Ashley 2007. "Karen Nationalist Communities: The 'Problem' of Diversity," *Contemporary Southeast Asia*, 29(1): 55–76.

Sperling, Elliot 1994. "Hu Yaobang's Visit to Tibet, May 22–31, 1980," in Barnett, Robert, and Akiner (eds.) *Resistance and Reform in Tibet*. Bloomington: Indiana University Press, pp. 267–284.

Stainton, Michael 1999. "Aboriginal Self-Government: Taiwan's Unfinished Agenda," in Rubinstein (ed.) *Taiwan: A New History*. Armonk, NY: M. E. Sharpe, pp. 419–435.

Stanley, P. W. 1974. *A Nation in the Making: The Philippines and the United States, 1899–1921*. Cambridge, MA: Harvard University Press.

Stepan, Alfred 1999. "Federalism and Democracy: Beyond the US Model," *Journal of Democracy*, 10: 19–34.

2004. "Toward a New Comparative Politics of Federalism: Multinationalism and Democracy," in Gibson (ed.) *Federalism and Democracy in Latin America*. Baltimore, MD: John Hopkins University Press, pp. 29–84.

Stoddard, Heather 1985. *Le mendiant de l'Amdo*, Recherches sur la Haute Asie, No. 9. Paris: Société d'Ethnographie.

Stokke, K. 2006. "Building the Tamil Eelam State: Emerging State Institutions and Forms of governance in LTTE-controlled areas in Sri Lanka," *Third World Quarterly*, 27(6): 1021–1040.

2007. "War by Other Means: The LTTE's Strategy of Institutionalizing Power Sharing in the Context of Transition from War to Peace –a Response to Muttukrishna Saravanantha," *Third World Quarterly*, 28(6): 1197–1201.

Sukarno 1933. *Mentjapai Indonesia Merdeka*. Reprinted Surabaya: Fadjar, n.d. [1970?]

1966. *Sukarno: An Autobiography, as Told to Cindy Adams*. Hong Kong: Gunung Agung.

Sulaiman, M. Isa 2000. *Aceh Merdeka: Ideologi, Kepemimpinan dan Gerakan*. Jakarta: Pustaka al Kausar.

2006. "From Autonomy to Periphery: A Critical Evaluation of the Acehnese Nationalist Movement," in Reid (ed.) *Verandah of Violence*. Singapore: Singapore University Press, pp. 121–148.

Sun, Yat-sen. 1924. "Lecture One," in Sun Yat-sen (ed.) *The Three Principles of the People*. Taipei: The China Publishing Company. 1981.

Sun, Yat-Sen 1929. *San Min Chu I: The Three Principles of the People*. Translated from Mandarin by Frank W. Price, in Chen (ed.). Shanghai: China Committee, Institute of Pacific Relations.

Suny, Ronald Grigor 1993. *The Revenge of the Past: Nationalism, Revolution, and the Collapse of the Soviet Union*. Palo Alto, CA: Stanford University Press.

Swami, Praveen 2006. *India, Pakistan and the Secret Jihad: The Covert War in Kashmir, 1947 – 2004*. London: Routledge.

Tan, Tai Yong 2008. *Creating Greater Malaysia: Decolonisation and the Politics of Merger*. Singapore: Institute of Southeast Asian Studies.

Taylor, J. G. 1991. *Indonesia's Forgotten War: The Hidden History of East Timor*. Atlantic Highlands, NJ: Zed Books.

1999. *East Timor: The Price of Freedom*. New York: Zed Books.

Teiwes, Frederick C. 1990. *Politics at Mao's Court: Gao Gang and Party Factionalism in the Early 1950s*. Armonk, NY: M. E. Sharpe.

Than, Tin Maung Maung 2005. "Dreams and nightmares: state building and ethnic conflict in Myanmar (Burma)," in Snitwongse and Thompson (eds.) *Ethnic Conflicts in Southeast Asia*. Singapore: ISIS and ISEAS, pp. 65–108.

Thawnghmung, Ardeth 2008. *The Karen Revolution in Burma: Divided Voices, Uncertain Ends*. Policy Studies 45, East West Center, Washington DC.

Tian, Qunjian 2004. "Chin Develops Its West: Motivation, Strategy and Prospect," *Journal of Contemporary China*, http://www.informaworld.com/smpp/title%7Econtent=t713429222%7Edb=all%7Etab=issueslist%7Ebranches=13 – v13, 13(41): 611–636.

Tibet Information Network 2000. *China's Great Leap West*. London: Tibet Information Network.

Tiro, Hasan Muhammad 1948. *Perang Atjeh, 1873–1927M*. Stencilled Jogjakarta: n.p.

Tiro, Hasan Muhammad 1982. *The Price of Freedom: The Unfinished Diary of Tengku Hasan di Tiro*, n.p. [Stockholm?]: State of Acheh Sumatra.

Tiro, Hasan Muhammad n. d.[1958]. *Demokrasi Untuk Indonesia*, Atjeh: no publisher given.

Tishkov, Valery 1995. "'Don't Kill Me, I'm a Kyrgyz!': An Anthropological Analysis of Violence in the Osh Ethnic Conflict," *Journal of Peace Research*, 32(2): 133–149.

Tønneson, Stein and Hans Antlov (eds.) 1996. *Asian Forms of the Nation*. Richmond, Surrey: Curzon.

Townsend, James 1992. "Chinese Nationalism." *Australian Journal of Chinese Affairs*, 27: 97–120.

Toynbee, Arnold J. 1931. *A Journey to China or Things Which are Seen*. Constable: London.

Tsai, June 2006 "Analyst Perceives Growth of 'Taiwan Identity'," *Taiwan Journal* [Online] 24 (35). Available at: http://taiwanjournal.nat.gov.tw/site/tj/ct.asp?CtNode=122&xItem=23320 [accessed September 11, 2007].

Tsering, Shakya 1993. "Whither the Tsampa Eaters?" *Himal*, Sept-Oct: 8–11.

1999. *The Dragon in the Land of Snows: A History of Modern Tibet since 1947*. London: Pimlico.

Tuttle, Gray 2005. *Tibetan Buddhists in the Making of Modern China*. New York: Columbia University Press.

Uyangoda, J. 2005a. "Ethnic Conflict, Ethnic Imagination and Democratic Alternatives for Sri Lanka," *Futures*, 37(9): 959–988.

2005b. "Ethnic Conflict, the State and the Tsunami Disaster in Sri Lanka," *Inter-Asia Cultural Studies*, 6(3): 341–352.

Van Evera, Stephen 1994. "Hypothesis on Nationalism and War," *International Security*, 18(4): 5–39.

Varshney, Ashutosh 1998. "India Defies the Odds: Why Democracy Survives," *Journal of Democracy*, 9(3): 36–50.

Von Furer-Haimendorf, Christof 1938. "Through the Unexplored Mountains of the Assam-Burma Border," *The Geographical Journal*, 91(3): 201–216.

Wachman, Alan M . 2007. *Why Taiwan? Geostrategic Rationales for China's Territorial Integrity*. Palo Alto, CA: Stanford University Press.

Waldron, Arthur 1997. "Back to Basics: The U.S. Perspective on Taiwan-PRC Relations," in Lilley and Downs (eds.) *Crisis in the Taiwan Strait*. Washington, DC: National Defense University Press, pp. 327–347.

Wang, Gungwu and Yongnian Zheng 2000. *Reform, Legitimacy and Dilemmas: China's Politics and Society*. Singapore University Press.

Wang, Shaoguang 2004. "Minzhuzhuyi yu Minzhuzhuyi [Nationalism and Democracy]," *Zhongguo Gonggong Xingzheng [China Public Administration Review]*, 1(1): 83–99.

Wang, Yao 1994. "Hu Yaobang's Visit to Tibet, May 22–31, 1980," in Barnett and Akiner (eds.) *Resistance and Reform in Tibet*. Bloomington: Indiana University Press, pp. 285–289.

Waseem, Mohammed 1992. "Pakistan's Lingering Crisis if Dyarchy," *Asian Survey*, 32(7): 617–634.

Weber, Eugen 1976. *Peasants into Frenchmen: The Modernization of Rural France, 1870–1914*. Stanford University Press.

Wedeman, Andrew 2004. "The Intensification of Corruption in China," *China Quarterly*, 180: 895–921.

Weerakoon, B. 1998. "Government of Sri Lanka LTTE Peace Negotiations 1989/90," in Rupesinghe (ed.) *Negotiating Peace in Sri Lanka: Efforts, Failures, and Lessons Learnt*. Ceylon: Foundation for Co-Existence.

Welch, Holmes 1968. *The Buddhist Revival in China*. Harvard East Asian series, 33. Cambridge, MA: Harvard University Press.

Weller, R. Charles 2007. *Rethinking Kazakh and Central Asian Nationhood: A Challenge to Prevailing Western Views*. Los Angeles, CA: Asia Research Associates.

Wen, Bo et al. 2004. "Genetic Evidence Supports Demic Diffusion of Han Culture," *Nature* [Online] 431(16): 302–305. Available at: http://www.nature.com/ nature/journal/ v431/n7006/abs/nature02878.html [accessed August 6, 2007].

Whitehead, Andrew 2007. *A Mission in Kashmir*. New Delhi: Viking Penguin.

Wilson, A. J. 1988. *The Break-up of Sri Lanka: The Sinhalese-Tamil Conflict*. London: C. Hurst & Co.

Windrow, Hayden 2005. "From State to Nation: The Forging of the Han Through Language Policy in the PRC and Taiwan," *NYU Journal of International Law and Politics* [Online] 37: 1. Available at: http://www.law.nyu.edu/journals/ jilp/issues/37/37_2_Windrow.pdf [accessed August 12, 2007].

Womack, Brantly 2006. *China and Vietnam: The Politics of Asymmetry*. Cambridge: Cambridge University Press.

Wong, Joseph. 2003. "Deepening Democracy in Taiwan," *Pacific Affairs,* 76(2): 235–256.

Wong, Ka-ying, Timothy 2001. "From Ethnic Nationalism to Civic Nationalism: The Formation and Changing Nature of Taiwanese Nationalism," *Asian Perspective,* 25(3): 175–206.

Wright, Lawrence 2006. *The Looming Tower: Al-Qaeda and the Road to 9/11.* New York: Alfred A. Knopf.

Wright, Tim 2004. "The Political Economy of Coal Mine Disasters in China: 'Your Rice Bowl or Your Life'," *China Quarterly,* 179: 629–646.

Wurfel, David 1988. *Filipino Politics: Development and Decay.* Ithaca, NY: Cornell University Press.

Xu, Ben 2001. "Chinese Populist Nationalism: Its Intellectual Politics and Moral Dilemma," *Representations,* 76: 120–140.

Yamin, Muhammad (ed.) 1959. *Naskah Persiapan UndangUndang Dasar 1945.* Jakarta: Jajasan Prapantja, 3 vols.

Yang, Ch'ing-K'un. 1994 [1961]. *Religion in Chinese Society: A Study of Contemporary Social Functions of Religion and some of their Historical Factors.* Taipei: SMC Publishing.

Yang, Dali 2006a. *Remaking the Chinese Leviathan: Market Transition and the Politics of Governance in China.* Palo Alto, CA: Stanford University Press.

2006b. "Economic Transformation and Its Political Discontents in China," *Annual Review of Political Science,* 9: 143–164.

Yeh, Emily 2006. "'An Open Lhasa Welcomes You': Disciplining the Researcher in Tibet," in Thøgersen and Heimer (eds.) *Doing Fieldwork in China.* University of Hawaii Press, pp. 96–109.

Zaheer, Hasan 1994. *The Separation of East Pakistan: The Rise and Realization of Bengali Muslim Nationalism.* New York: Oxford University Press.

Zhang, Fa, Zhang Yiwu, and Wang Yichuan 1994. "Cong 'Xiandaixing' Dao 'Zhongghuaxing' [From 'Modernity' to 'Chinese-ness']," *Wenyi Zhengming,* 2: 10–20.

Zhang, Le-Yin 1999. "Chinese Central-Provincial Fiscal Relationships, Budgetary Decline and the Impact of the 1994 Fiscal Reform: An Evaluation," *The China Quarterly,* 157: 115–141.

Zhang, Tianlu 1997. *Population and Development in Tibet and Related Issues.* Translated from Mandarin by Chen Guansheng and Li Peizhu. Beijing: Foreign Languages Press.

Zhang, Xudong 1998. "Nationalism, Mass Culture, and Intellectual Strategies in Post-Tiananmen China," *Social Text,* 55: 109–140.

Zhang, Yisun et al. 1998 (1993). *Bod Rgya tshig mdzod chen mo/ Zang Han da cidian.* Beijing: Mi rigs dpe skrun khang/ Minzu chubanshe.

Zhao, Suisheng 1997. "'Chinese Intellectuals' Quest for National Greatness and Nationalistic Writing in the 1990s," *The China Quarterly,* 152: 725–745.

2004. *A Nation-State by Construction: Dynamics of Modern Chinese Nationalism.* Palo Alto, CA: Stanford University Press.

2005. "Chinese Pragmatic Nationalism: Is It Manageable?" *The Washington Quarterly,* 29(1): 131–144.

Zheng, Shan (ed.) 2001. *A History of Development of Tibet*. Chen Guansheng and Li Peizhu, trans. Beijing: Foreign Languages Press.

Zheng, Yongnian 1994. "Perforated Sovereignty: Provincial Dynamism and China's Foreign Trade," *The Pacific Review,* 7(3): 309–321.

    1999. *Discovering Chinese Nationalism in China: Modernization, Identity and International Relations*. Cambridge: Cambridge University Press.

    2004. *Globalization and State Transformation in China*. Cambridge: Cambridge University Press.

    2007. *De Facto Federalism in China: Reform and Dynamics of Central-Local Relations*. Singapore: World Scientific.

Zhu, Fang 1998. *Gun Barrel Politics: Party-Army Relations in Mao's China*. Boulder, CO: Westview Press.

Index

Macapagal-Arroyo, Maria Gloria,
179, 273
Macau, 204, 207, 215
Madras (Indian state), 66
Maharashtra (Indian state), 65
Majul, Cesar Adib, 169
Malaka, Tan, 33
Malaya, 36, 37, 48
Malaysia
British colonialism in, 35, 48–50
communism in, 48
democracy in, 50
federalism in, 48
identity of, unformed, 279
vs. Indonesia, 26, 31, 48
Malay language of, 33
minorities in, 20
UMNO as nationalist party
of, 48
Malia, Martin, 255
Malolos Republic, 31
Maluku (Indonesian province), 174
Manchuria, 202
Mandarin Chinese language, 23, 201,
205, 213
Manipur (Indian state), 71, 73
Mansfield, Edward D., 217
Mao ZeDong, 35, 202, 210, 232
Marcos, Ferdinand, 177, 178, 276
Martin, Terry, 248
Marxism, 22, 34, 223, 231
Masjumi/Masyumi (Islamic
Indonesian party), 41, 175
McKenna, T. M., 169
Megawati (Indonesian president), 46,
187, 190–191
Megoran, Nick, 250
Melaka (Crown Colony Strait
Settlement), 35, 48
MILF (Moro Islamic Liberation
Front), 178–179, 273
Minahasa (Indonesian ethnic group),
39
Mindanao (Philippines province), 2–6,
166, 173, 177–179, 194, 265,
270
Ming dynasty (China), 207

Minnanhua Chinese language, 205,
213
Minto-Morley Reforms, 86, 267
Misra, Udayon, 74
Misuari, Nur, 177
Mizoram (Indian state), 272
MNLF (Moro National Liberation
Front), 177–179, 194
mobilization
accommodation vs., 26
Central Asian, 244, 247, 250, 252,
255, 261–262
cultural, 244
ethnic, 84, 103, 246–247, 280
political, 66, 84, 87, 148, 162, 246,
253
religious, 58, 86
repression of, 175, 268–269, 276
secessionist, 7, 276
sub-state nationalist, 14, 22, 25,
165, 244, 272, 274, 276–277,
278
Mon (Burmese state/ethnic group)
as anti-British, 139
arms for democracy program, 144
autonomy sought by, 139–140
Burma population percentage, 138
as Burmese state, 136
as ceasefire group, 151–153, 152
ethnicity, 157
inter-tribal warfare, 138
native language, 147
NMSP in, 146, 150, 151, 152, 154,
155, 160
public support for, 159
rebellion in, 144
statehood, 141, 142–143, 145, 148,
153
Mon National Democratic Front
(MNDF), 159
Mongolia, 20, 22, 201, 232
Moro Islamic Liberation Front
(MILF), 178–179, 273
Moro nation (Bangsa Moro)
(Philippines)
Bangsa Moro Development Agency,
179